CRITICAL CARE NURSING

Curriculum and Case Studies

Sandra W. Haak, R.N., M.S., CCRN
Clinical Assistant Professor
College of Nursing
University of Utah
Clinical Specialist, Critical Care
Holy Cross Hospital
Salt Lake City, Utah

Susan Gale Osguthorpe, R.N., M.S., CCRN
Clinical Director, Cardiovascular Nursing
Virginia Mason Hospital
Seattle, Washington

Christine P. Chytraus, R.N., B.S.N., CCRN
Coordinator, P.A.R./Ministay
St. Mark's Hospital
Salt Lake City, Utah

Monica L. Meyer, R.N., M.S., CCRN
Product Specialist/Territory Manager, Critical Care Division
American Hospital Supply Corporation
West Germany

AN ASPEN PUBLICATION®
Aspen Publishers, Inc.   1986

Rockville, Maryland
Royal Tunbridge Wells

Library of Congress Cataloging in Publication Data
Main entry under title:

Critical care nursing.

"An Aspen publication."
Includes bibliographies and index.
1. Intensive care nursing—Study and teaching. 2. Intensive care nursing—Case studies. I.
Haak, Sandra W. [DNLM: 1. Critical Care—case studies. 2. Critical Care—education—
nurses' instruction. 3. Curriculum—nurses' instruction. 4. Education, Nursing. WY 18
C9345] RT120.I5C75   1986   610.73'61   85-28743
ISBN: 0-87189-271-5

Editorial Services: Carolyn Ormes

Library of Congress Catalog Card Number: 85-28743
ISBN: 0-87189-271-5

Printed in the United States of America

1 2 3 4 5

To the critical care nurses
we have practiced with, taught, and supervised

Table of Contents

Preface

This book is written primarily for practicing staff nurses, clinical specialists, nursing supervisors, and inservice educators. It is intended to aid these nursing practitioners and educators in developing organized, comprehensive educational courses for adult critical care nurses. It may also be used by nurses undertaking self-directed study to increase or refresh their knowledge of adult critical care nursing. The curriculum establishes achievable behavioral objectives for nurse students and provides example case studies that allows practical application of the didactic content.

The need for educating critical care nurses beyond their basic nursing preparation was recognized in the 1960s with the development of coronary care nursing courses provided by regional medical programs. In the evolution of critical care nursing during the past two and a half decades, the regional medical program coronary care nursing courses have been phased out and the number of critical care units (CCUs), patients, and nurses have mushroomed. Turnover among critical care nurses has been a consistent problem and has generally been attributed to stress in the workplace. Various methods have been used to reduce "burnout" and other aspects of stress related to the nature of critical care nursing.

We believe that some of the stress is related to inadequate knowledge resulting in inability to anticipate and meet rapid changes in patient needs. We propose that stress and turnover of this nature can be reduced by formally educating nurses about pathophysiology, principles of critical care practice, and technical and psychosocial skills related to patient care. Nurses who expect and recognize complications are not surprised; therefore, they respond quickly and appropriately.

Formal classes provide a mechanism to ensure that specific content is presented systematically. The advantages of formal classes are enhanced if nurses from more than one hospital attend class together. The per student cost of teaching is reduced if more students attend a class. In addition, class members have an opportunity to share experiences outside of the work setting. Sharing experiences allows students to learn about aspects of critical care practice that are common among nurses and settings.

This book is the result of our efforts over the past ten years to provide comprehensive critical care nursing education for staff nurses practicing in the adult critical care setting. Initially, a respiratory care course was developed in Spring 1975 to meet the educational needs of the nurses practicing in the intensive and coronary care unit (ICU/CCU) at Holy Cross Hospital in Salt Lake City, Utah. This was followed by a coronary care course in Fall 1975. An intensive care course was developed and offered in Spring 1976. We soon recognized that the need for such courses was ongoing because of turnover at Holy Cross Hospital as well as in critical care units of other hospitals. Nurses and personnel outside the critical care unit also expressed interest and enrolled in these classes.

In 1978 one of us left Holy Cross Hospital to become the nursing coordinator of the ICU/CCU at St. Mark's Hospital. She noted that the educational needs among the nurses at St. Mark's Hospital were similar to those at Holy Cross Hospital. At the time, each hospital in Salt Lake City attempted to provide its employees with critical care education specific to the perceived needs of the individual hospital. This was costly in terms of time spent by the nurse students and nurse teachers in repetitious learning and teaching. In addition, available structured classes were offered infrequently and enrollment was limited so that newly hired nurses often waited several months to a year for these educational opportunities. We observed that some of the turnover among critical care nurses in our city was essentially an exchange of nurses between hospitals. Dissatisfied nurses often seemed to seek employment in another critical care unit without evaluating whether the undesirable factors were unique to the setting or common to critical care nursing practice. They hoped and believed that the "new" critical care unit would be different and therefore better.

The authors shared a common goal of achieving

among staff nurses a standard level of basic knowledge about adult critical care nursing. We also shared the belief that structured education could provide transferable knowledge useful in any critical care setting. We hoped that by developing and presenting a standard course available to the nurses of Holy Cross and Saint Mark's Hospitals that we could (1) improve the quality of patient care, (2) reduce the cost and rate of turnover, and (3) make the nurse teacher time more cost effective.

We developed two courses that contained content needed by the nurses at both hospitals. Each hospital agreed to teach the courses once a year on a staggered schedule using the same content outlines and texts. In this way, staff nurses employed at both institutions had two opportunities a year to enroll in the structured educational program. Any nurse who later went to work at the other hospital did not have to repeat the courses. Subsequently, in response to specific needs, we developed an advanced cardiac care course and a neurological care course. The entire package was re-

viewed and restructured in 1980 because of budgetary constraints. At that time it assumed the present form of three sequential courses.

In the process of developing the neurological course we discovered and incorporated the expertise of the clinical specialists at the Veterans Administration Medical Center in Salt Lake City. These professionals also shared our goal of standardized, comprehensive critical care education for staff nurses and the belief that this could be accomplished through shared resources. The group of cooperating hospitals has since expanded to a total of five.

The cooperative effort has been successful in that there is sufficient demand to offer the total curriculum annually. Two of the three courses are repeated once or twice a year. The continued interest of nurses outside the cooperating hospitals indicates that the courses are valued by others. We continue to feel that there are distinct advantages to the cooperative venture and encourage others to organize and cooperate in a similar manner.

Acknowledgments

First, we thank our families and friends for their encouragement and faith. We gratefully acknowledge expertise and assistance given by the following clinical specialists:

Sherry Brown, R.N., M.S.
Clinical Specialist for Surgical Intensive Care
VA Hospital Medical Center, Salt Lake City, Utah

Pamela Cipriano, R.N., M.S.
Assistant Director of Nursing
University of Utah Medical Center, Salt Lake City, Utah

Susan Kralick-Goldberg, R.N., M.S.
Thoracic Patients' Clinical Specialist
VA Hospital Medical Center, Salt Lake City, Utah

Patricia S. Hartley, R.N., M.S.
Assistant Director of Nursing
St. Mark's Hospital, Salt Lake City, Utah

Jolene Heath, R.N., M.S.
Neurology Clinical Specialist
VA Hospital Medical Center, Salt Lake City, Utah

Susan J. Quaal, R.N., C.V.S., M.S., CCRN
Cardiovascular Clinical Specialist
VA Hospital Medical Center, Salt Lake City, Utah

We also appreciate the support and technical assistance provided by:

Administration and Staff
Holy Cross Hospital, Salt Lake City, Utah
St. Mark's Hospital, Salt Lake City, Utah
Veterans Administration Medical Center, Salt Lake City, Utah

Bobbi and Jim Maire
Maire Graphics, Salt Lake City, Utah

Aspen Systems Corporation

Part I

Overview and Use of the Curriculum

Chapter 1

Curriculum Overview

This book presents a 165-hour adult critical care nursing education curriculum originally developed for Holy Cross Hospital and St. Mark's Hospital in Salt Lake City, Utah. It has since been revised to be useful to a universal audience of adult critical care nurses and educators. The curricular philosophy, purpose, objectives, and conceptual framework are described in this chapter. In addition, course outlines with objectives for each of the three courses, unit objectives, and content outlines are presented in subsequent chapters. Case studies and vignettes are included to develop application skills and to aid in transfer of these skills to the practice setting.

PHILOSOPHY

We believe that the essence of critical care nursing is continuous specific observation combined with accurate interpretation and judicious intervention. We further believe that critical care nurses require education beyond their basic nursing preparation to develop and maintain the advanced body of knowledge as well as the decision-making and technical skills required by the rapidly changing specialty of critical care nursing.

This philosophy is congruent with the philosophy and Scope of Practice of the American Association of Critical-Care Nurses (AACN). The AACN Scope of Practice states:

> Critical care nursing practice is a dynamic process the scope of which is defined in terms of the critically ill patient, the critical care nurse, and the environment in which critical care nursing is delivered; all three components are essential elements for the practice of critical care nursing.

The critically ill patient

The critically ill patient is characterized by the presence of real or potential life-threaten-ing health problems and by the requirement for continuous observation and intervention to prevent complications and restore health. The concept of the critically ill patient includes the patient's family and/or significant others.

The critical care nurse

The critical care nurse is a registered professional nurse committed to ensuring that all critically ill patients receive optimal care. This nurse's practice is based on the following:

a) individual professional accountability
b) thorough knowledge of the interrelatedness of body systems and the dynamic nature of the life process
c) recognition and appreciation of the individual's wholeness, uniqueness, and significant social and environmental relationships
d) appreciation of the collaborative role of all members of the health care team.

To continually refine the practice, the critical care nurse participates in ongoing educational activities. In addition to basic preparation, the critical care nurse acquires an advanced knowledge of psychosocial, physiological, and therapeutic components specific to the care of the critically ill. Clinical competency and the ability to effectively interact with patients, families and other members of the health care team are developed. Additionally, an awareness of the responsibility for a therapeutic environment is cultivated.

The critical care nurse utilizes the nursing process as a framework for practice. In caring for the critically ill, the nurse will collect data, identify and determine the priority of the patient's problems/needs, formulate an appropriate plan of nursing care, implement the plan of nursing care according to the priority of the identified problems/needs, and evaluate the process and outcome of nursing care.

The critical care environment

A critical care unit is any geographically designated area which is designed to facilitate the care of the critically ill patient by critical care nurses. It is an area where safety, organizational, and ethical standards are maintained for patient welfare. Although critical care nursing usually occurs in a critical care unit, it can occur in any setting that meets the environmental and nursing standards, such as an area which has a psychologically supportive environment for the patients and significant others, adequately functioning equipment and supplies, readily available emergency equipment, facilities to meet staff needs, and ready access to support departments.

Source: Reprinted from *AACN Position Statement: Scope of Critical Care Nursing Practice* with permission of American Association of Critical-Care Nurses, © 1980.

PURPOSE

The purpose of the adult critical care nursing education curriculum is to provide a formal framework that will assist critical care nurses and educators in learning and teaching required knowledge and skills for professional practice of adult critical care nursing. This formal educational program is designed to meet part of the standards of the Joint Commission on Accreditation of Hospitals, as well as the educational and practice goals of the American Association of Critical-Care Nurses.

CURRICULUM OBJECTIVES

On completion of the entire critical care nursing education curriculum, the nurse student is prepared to:

1. assess critically ill adults using inspection, palpation, percussion, and auscultation, as well as electronic equipment
2. make nursing diagnoses of critically ill adults based on information gained in patient assessment

3. plan appropriate nursing care for critically ill adults
4. implement nursing care for critically ill adults
5. evaluate nursing care of critically ill adults
6. demonstrate understanding of proper use of simple and sophisticated patient care equipment
7. successfully complete the CCRN certification examination administered by the American Association of Critical-Care Nurses Certification Corporation.

CONCEPTUAL FRAMEWORK

The conceptual framework was developed from a deductive analysis of adult patients requiring critical care nursing. A diagram of the conceptual framework is presented in Figure 1–1. Common to all adult patients requiring critical care nursing are needs for observation and maintenance of cardiopulmonary, renal, and nervous system function as well as fluid, electrolyte, and acid-base balance. In addition, patients experience alterations of activity, stimulation, and sensation imposed by disease, therapy, and environment. The physiological effects of critical system dysfunction combined with the physical and psychological effects of placement in the critical care unit (CCU) require an integrated approach to the physiological and psychosocial aspects of patient care.

The program of study begins with an overview of adult critical care nursing, which reviews the goals and

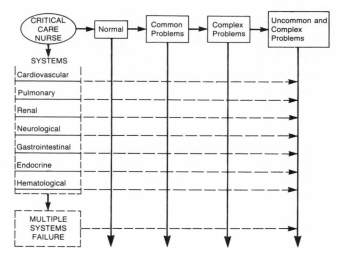

Figure 1–1 Conceptual Framework for Critical Care Nursing Education Curriculum

purposes of critical care units (CCUs) as well as the responsibilities of each nurse working in such settings. Study of patient care problems follows in a sequence that is designed to move from common through complex to uncommon and complex problems seen in the general adult critical care patient population. For this reason, cardiovascular and pulmonary problems are presented early in the curriculum and cardiomyopathies and multiple systems failure are presented near the end. The study of patient problems is designed so that normal system anatomy, physiology, and assessment are reviewed before system dysfunctions are studied. Complications are considered with primary problems and psychosocial aspects are integrated throughout.

CURRICULAR DIVISIONS

The total critical care nursing education curriculum is divided into three courses of equal length: Course I, "Basic Critical Care Nursing"; Course II, "Intermediate Critical Care Nursing"; and Course III, "Advanced Critical Care Nursing." Each course is further divided into 24 or 25 units. Outlines and behavioral objectives are provided for each division.

Placement of specific topics or units into the basic, intermediate, or advanced course was determined by evaluating critical care nursing practice. Patient census, admitting diagnoses, and length of stay were considered as well as nursing judgment errors. Observations were made regarding the strengths and weaknesses of undergraduate nursing programs. Finally, other critical care nursing courses were examined.

Most patients, regardless of their admitting diagnosis or surgical procedure, are placed in the critical care unit because they have or might develop life-threatening dysfunction of the cardiopulmonary system. This cardiopulmonary dysfunction is either the primary problem or a secondary result of a primary problem in another body system. Thus, it was decided that foundations in cardiopulmonary system dysfunction as well as fluid, electrolyte, and acid-base imbalances were important and these topics were placed in the basic course.

A fairly heavy emphasis is placed on neurological content in the intermediate and advanced courses. Although neurological and neurosurgical patients are few in number compared to cardiopulmonary patients, they represent a significant number of patient days because their length of stay is often prolonged, for example, two to four months with botulism toxicity or Guillain-Barré syndrome. In addition, the quality of the patient outcome is directly related to the quality of nurse's judgment, intervention, and independent nursing care.

Most of the patient problems studied in the advanced course are rarely seen in comparison to those of the earlier courses. However, when such patients are hospitalized, their stays are usually lengthy; their management is complicated and controversial; and their outcome is uncertain but related to the quality of independent nursing care. Consequently, they consume much nursing time and energy. Including study of these problems in the curriculum can facilitate constructive dialogue between nurses and physicians caring for these difficult and challenging patients.

LENGTH AND SEQUENCE OF COURSES

Each of the three courses is arranged to provide 55 contact hours of instruction. The suggested schedule fits the academic year with each course being 11 weeks in length and having two class periods per week. Each class period is two and one-half clock hours which allows 125 minutes for instruction and 25 minutes for breaks when based on a 50-minute teaching hour.

The behavioral objectives and content are planned so that each unit builds on the one before and then each course builds on the preceding one. Thus, the nurse student is expected to progress in sequence from basic to advanced, beginning with "Critical Care Nursing" in Course I and continuing through "Multiple Systems Failure" in Course III. Students progressing in a different order are expected to gain prerequisite knowledge by independently and concurrently reviewing content from previous courses.

SUMMARY

The critical care nursing education curriculum represents a pragmatic compromise between the ideals and theory of nursing education in the academic setting and the realities and limits of hospital-based inservice education. It is not presented as the best or as the only way to teach critical care nursing. The intent is to provide a framework for nurses to learn and teach the advanced body of knowledge as well as the decision-making and technical skills required for nursing practice in the rapidly changing area of adult critical care.

Chapter 2

User's Guide

The information presented in this chapter describes the structure, content, and appropriate use of the critical care nursing education curriculum. Specific suggestions for nurse educators and students are also included. For general information on teaching and learning critical care knowledge and skills in the hospital inservice setting, we recommend *The Educational Process in Critical Care Nursing* by JoAnn "Grif" Alspach (St. Louis: Mosby, 1982). This book is written specifically for hospital-based critical care nurse educators and addresses problems encountered in that setting.

DEVELOPMENT CRITERIA

The following is a list of the specific criteria that the critical care nursing education curriculum has been developed to meet.

1. The content is suitable for critical care nurses throughout the United States.
2. The content is grouped by body systems and includes patient problems seen in general adult critical care nursing practice.
3. The sequence of study is from normal to abnormal, simple to complex, and common to uncommon. Thus, normal anatomy and physiology of a system is reviewed before the pathophysiology is studied. Also, common and simple patient problems are presented before uncommon and complex problems are studied.
4. The format is such that courses can be presented by an individual educator or by multiple lecturers who may be coordinated by someone with little background in teaching.

STUDENT PREREQUISITES

Nurses beginning study in the critical care nursing education curriculum with the basic course are assumed to have the following prerequisites:

1. A.A. or B.S. degree or diploma in nursing
2. registered nurse license
3. a minimum of one year of general duty nursing experience
4. a foundation in the nursing process and nursing diagnosis
5. current employment in an adult critical care nursing unit as defined by the AACN Scope of Practice
6. certification as a Basic Life Support Provider by the American Heart Association
7. previous exposure to physical assessment and cardiac dysrhythmia recognition either in undergraduate study or inservice education
8. access to a clinical specialist or other Master's-prepared nurse for assistance in learning, transfer, and application of information presented in the curriculum to clinical practice

Nurses studying in the intermediate course are assumed to have all of the prerequisites listed previously as well as:

1. a minimum of three months of adult critical care nursing experience
2. demonstrated mastery of the content presented in the basic course. This can be established by a certificate of attendance and satisfactory completion of the basic or an equivalent course and/or passing a challenge examination of the basic course.

Nurses studying in the advanced course are assumed to have all of the prerequisites listed previously as well as:

1. a minimum of one year of adult critical care nursing experience
2. demonstrated mastery of the content presented in the intermediate course. This can be established by a certificate of attendance and satisfactory completion of the intermediate or an

equivalent course and/or passing a challenge examination of the intermediate courses.

3. certification as an Advanced Cardiac Life Support Provider by the American Heart Association

BEHAVIORAL OBJECTIVES AND UNIT OUTLINES

Behavioral objectives are presented with the course outlines and with the unit content outlines to aid in standardizing course content. Nurse managers who review the curriculum are always interested in specifics about course content. This information will help them make decisions about adopting the curriculum as well as waiving other educational requirements for nurses who complete the curriculum.

Lecturers frequently need guidelines to what they should or should not include. The outlines are particularly helpful in reducing repetition and/or omission in courses with multiple lecturers. At times in the past we provided very detailed outlines to guest lecturers. This led to criticisms that the lecturer was not allowed enough academic freedom. Subsequently, the outlines were made more general so that they would define the subject area without dictating the contents. Lecturers are given a copy of the unit objectives and content outline as well as the appropriate case study. They are encouraged to follow the general format of the outline because it is helpful to the students who also have a copy of the outline. Lecturers who complain that they do not like the outline are reminded that the most important effect of their lecture is that the student can achieve the objectives. We try to convey the notion that they may depart from the curricular content outline as long as the student behavioral objectives are met.

CASE STUDIES AND STUDY QUESTIONS

The case studies and study questions were developed to facilitate transfer and application of information from the classroom to clinical practice. The nurse students frequently comment that after the case study is reviewed in class they have a much better grasp of the lecture material than when this is omitted.

The unit numbers given after the title of each case study correspond to the course and unit to which the case study relates. Most case studies are appropriate for use with more than one unit. Therefore, more than one unit number may follow the case study title. The first unit number given is related to the primary patient problem. The additional unit numbers are related to secondary patient problems or information. Thus, the title "Case Study in Head Injury" is followed by the notation "Units II-10 and II-8, II-13, III-5, III-22," which indicates that the case study is appropriate for use with Unit 10, "Head Trauma and Surgery" of Course II, "Intermediate Critical Care Nursing." In addition, it may be used with Unit 8, "Alterations of Consciousness" and Unit 13, "Psychosocial Aspects of Critical Care" of Course II and Unit 5, "Crisis Intervention and Ethics in Critical Care" and Unit 22, "Perinatal Complications" of Course III.

INTEGRATION OF MEDICAL AND NURSING PRACTICE MODELS

The medical and nursing disciplines are each generally guided by a model that is a set of beliefs about illness and health. Medical practice is guided by a biomedical model that views disease as being caused by malfunction of specific molecules or organs. As a result, medicine is involved with pathology, diagnosis, and cure of disease. Nursing practice is guided by a holistic model that views the interrelationships and interconnections of a person's mind, body, and environment as a dynamic network. As a result, nursing is involved with identifying and modifying physiological and psychological states and related responses.

Medical and nursing practitioners determine patient problems through a reasoning process that includes diagnosis as an act of gathering information about what is causing difficulty, interfering with normal functioning, or needing correction. Physicians' conclusions are labelled medical diagnoses and nurses' conclusions are labelled nursing diagnoses. The content of medical and nursing diagnoses are different because nursing and medical practice are guided by different models and because the practitioners are educated and licensed to practice differently.

Medical diagnoses are used for patient problems that are treated with methods legally defined as medical practice such as prescription drugs, surgery, or radiation. Medical treatment is prescribed by physicians but can be performed by physicians or nurses. Nursing diagnoses are used for patient problems that can be treated by nurses independent of physicians with modalities such as biofeedback, relaxation, imagery, meditation, music therapy, and therapeutic touch. The independent aspects of nursing practice are sometimes pushed out of view because many tasks that nurses perform in CCUs are delegated medical responsibilities.

Patient needs are best met when physicians and nurses collaborate and work interdependently in

CCUs. Nurses are required to know and understand both models and diagnoses because:

1. The nurse's usual introduction to a patient is the medical admitting diagnosis heard on the telephone prior to the patient's arrival in the unit. Being able to create an instant mental image of anticipated needs allows the nurse to quickly assemble needed equipment prior to the patient's arrival. In addition, required changes in patient assignments can be predicted.
2. One of the underlying goals of the critical care nursing education curriculum is to promote respect, professionalism, and teamwork among nursing, medical, and support personnel. We believe that this is helped when physicians and support staff participate in presenting the curriculum. The medical model is an approach that physicians, respiratory therapists, cardiology technicians, and others know and understand.
3. The role collaboration and rapid teamwork required of nurses in critical care are facilitated by using language familiar to all members of the health care team, i.e. by using both medical diagnosis and nursing diagnosis. A productive emphasis on the differences between medicine and nursing can be made during discussion of the approaches and techniques of patient care management.

We believe that nurses who understand medical diagnoses from the biomedical model as well as nursing diagnoses from the holistic model and can perform medical interventions as well as nursing interventions are better practitioners.

TEACHING METHODS

Most of the units are designed to be taught by lectures and discussions augmented with use of the chalkboard, overhead transparencies, and/or slides. This format is not meant to eliminate the use of slide/tape programs, films, or self-study approaches. In general the lecture/discussion method is the most familiar to inservice educators and requires little capital expense to implement. The class size and available equipment will determine the best way to structure the few workshops and demonstrations that require equipment.

Occasionally, nurses have completed part of the curriculum by self-paced study. The nurse student is expected to use the behavioral objectives and case study questions as guides for learning. Study materials are the text reading assignments as well as audiovisual

programs available within the hospital or nearby health science libraries. A nurse educator meets with the individual on a regular basis to answer questions and evaluate learning. This method has worked best with intermediate and advanced practitioners and is usually unsatisfactory with new or beginning practitioners. For the method to be successful, the learner must be highly motivated and self-directed and the educator must set and maintain deadlines. Learning contracts can be utilized to help set and meet goals and objectives.

RECOMMENDED TEXTBOOKS

In addition to this book, each nurse student is expected to use a general critical care nursing reference as a companion text. Depending on how the course and testing are conducted, it may not be essential that all students use the same text. The textbooks listed below have been used successfully. Corresponding reading assignments are given in Table 2–1.

Alspach, J., and Williams, S. *Core Curriculum for Critical Care Nursing,* 3rd ed. Philadelphia, PA: W.B. Saunders Company, 1985.
Holloway, N. *Nursing the Critically Ill Adult: Applying Nursing Diagnosis,* 2nd ed. Menlo Park, CA: Addison-Wesley, 1984.
Hudak, C., Lohr, T., and Gallo, B. *Critical Care Nursing,* 4th ed. Philadelphia, PA: Lippincott, 1986.
Johanson, B., Dungca, C., Hoffmeister, D., and Wells, S. *Standards for Critical Care,* 2nd ed. St. Louis: Mosby, 1985.
Kenner, C., Guzzetta, C., and Dossey, B. *Critical Care Nursing: Body–Mind–Spirit,* 2nd ed. Boston: Little, Brown, 1985.

SELECTING LECTURERS

In selecting lecturers, both the students and the principles of teaching should be remembered. It is important to present the curriculum and its courses as a staircase with each unit forming a step leading to the top. The courses should not be presented as a series of inservice lectures with the result that learning is horizontal and without growth. The nurse students may perceive that they are not learning anything new and that the courses are not valuable. Learner motivation will decline and the cost-benefit ratio will suffer. Lecturers should be advanced practitioners who are knowledgable about teaching and learning, are familiar with the total curriculum, and are capable of motivating learners.

Table 2–1 Reading Assignments

Unit	Alspach and Williams	Holloway	Hudak et al.	Johanson et al.	Kenner et al.
COURSE I: BASIC CRITICAL CARE NURSING					
I-1 Critical Care Nursing	pp. 627–651, 673–674	Ch. 1, 2, pp. 601–603	Ch. 1–6, 38	Std. 59, 60	Ch. 1–3
I-2 Cardiovascular Anatomy, Physiology, and Assessment	pp. 101–133	Ch. 3	Ch. 7, 8	–	Ch. 14
I-3 Introduction to Electrocardiography and Monitoring	pp. 135–138	pp. 123–146	–	–	pp. 384–403
I-4 Angina and Myocardial Infarction (MI)	pp. 153–174	pp. 190–211	Ch. 11	Std. 11, 12	Ch. 16
I-5 Basic Cardiac Dysrhythmias	pp. 140–145	pp. 146–188	Ch. 9	Std. 21	pp. 403–421
I-6 Cardiac Failure and Pulmonary Edema	pp. 178–182	pp. 212–220, 400–402	Ch. 10	Std. 1, 15, 16	Ch. 15
I-7 Electrical Management of Cardiac Dysrhythmias	pp. 174–178	pp. 257–264	Ch. 9	Std. 23	–
I-8 Cardiac Catheterization and Cardiovascular Angiography	pp. 147–150	pp. 100–105	–	Std. 26	–
I-9 Cardiac Surgery	pp. 161, 173–207	–	Std. 27, 28	–	Ch. 18
I-10 Vascular Disease	pp. 80–83	pp. 410–414	–	Std. 29, 30, 31	Ch. 12
I-11 Pulmonary Anatomy, Physiology, and Assessment	pp. 2–35	pp. 374–393	Ch. 13, 14	–	Ch. 9
I-12 Supporting Respiration	pp. 40–71, 92–94	pp. 424–453	Ch. 15	Std. 5, 6, 7, 8	Ch. 9
I-13 Chest Trauma and Surgery	pp. 83–86	pp. 421–423, 453–459	Ch. 16	Std. 3, 9, 10	Ch. 11
I-14 Acute Respiratory Failure	pp. 71–76, 86–97	pp. 403–410, 414–416	Ch. 16, 17	Std. 2	Ch. 10, 13
I-15 Obstructive Pulmonary Disease	pp. 76–80	pp. 416–421	Ch. 16	Std. 73, 74	Ch. 13
I-16 Invasive Hemodynamic Monitoring	pp. 151–153	pp. 105–120	Ch. 8	Std. 25	Ch. 4
I-17 Renal Anatomy, Physiology, and Assessment	pp. 348–370	pp. 277–288	Ch. 18, 19	–	–
I-18 Fluid and Electrolyte Imbalance	pp. 426–449	pp. 308–330	Ch. 19	–	–
I-19 Acid-Base Imbalance	pp. 378–379	pp. 330–348	–	–	–
I-20 Acute Renal Failure and Dialysis	pp. 370–420	pp. 288–304	Ch. 20, 21, 22	Std. 52, 53, 54, 55	Ch. 26
I-21 Urological Trauma and Surgery	pp. 420–426	–	–	–	Ch. 34
I-22 Electrical Safety	–	–	–	–	pp. 108–113
I-23 Legal Aspects of Critical Care Nursing	–	pp. 597–600	Ch. 38, 39	–	Ch. 6
I-24 Infection Control and Management	–	–	–	Std. 61	–
					–
COURSE II: INTERMEDIATE CRITICAL CARE NURSING					
II-1 Advanced Cardiac Dysrhythmias	pp. 135–147	Ch. 8	–	–	pp. 403–421
II-2 Introduction to Twelve-Lead Electrocardiograms (ECGs)	pp. 138–147	–	–	–	pp. 415–416
II-3 Cardiac Drugs	pp. 155–156, 161–164	Appendix 2	–	Appendix F	–
II-4 Hypertension and Hypertensive Crisis	pp. 185–189	–	–	Std. 20	–
II-5 Nervous System Anatomy and Physiology	pp. 220–251	–	Ch. 23	–	–
II-6 Nervous System Assessment	pp. 251–258	pp. 535–562	Ch. 24	–	Ch. 20
II-7 Neurological Diagnostic Studies	pp. 258–261	pp. 562–569	Ch. 24	–	–
II-8 Alterations in Consciousness	pp. 261–284	pp. 571–588	Ch. 25	Std. 32	–
II-9 Seizure Disorders	pp. 302–310	pp. 588–591	Ch. 28	Std. 41	–
II-10 Head Trauma and Craniotomy	pp. 284–295	–	Ch. 27	Std. 33, 36, 37	Ch. 23
II-11 Cerebrovascular Disease	pp. 291–295, 310–317	–	Ch. 28	Std. 34, 35, 39	Ch. 24
II-12 Drug Toxicity and Poisoning	pp. 327–340	–	Ch. 36	Std. 66, 67	–
II-13 Psychosocial Aspects of Critical Care	pp. 652–674	Ch. 13	Ch. 2–6	Std. 59, 60	Ch. 5, 7
II-14 Gastrointestinal System Anatomy, Physiology, and Assessment	pp. 564–586	pp. 464–469	Ch. 29, 30	–	Ch. 25
II-15 Nutrition Assessment and Therapy	pp. 586–592	pp. 475–488	Ch. 31	Std. 57, 58	Ch. 29
II-16 Gastrointestinal Bleeding	pp. 592–596	pp. 469–474	Ch. 32	Std. 49	–
II-17 Gastrointestinal Surgery	pp. 612–621	–	–	Std. 45, 50, 51	Ch. 34
II-18 Hepatic Failure	pp. 600–612	–	Ch. 33	Std. 46	–
II-19 Acute Pancreatitis	pp. 596–600	–	–	Std. 47, 48	–
II-20 Endocrine System Anatomy, Physiology, and Assessment	pp. 452–466	–	Ch. 34	–	Ch. 28
II-21 Metabolic Crises of Diabetes Mellitus	pp. 466–468, 483–493	–	Ch. 35	Std. 56	Ch. 30, 31

Table 2–1 continued

Unit	Alspach and Williams	Holloway	Hudak et al.	Johanson et al.	Kenner et al.
II-22 Diabetes Insipidus and Syndrome of Inappropriate Antidiuretic Hormone (ADH) Secretion	pp. 468–474	–	Ch. 28	–	–
II-23 Adrenal Dysfunction	pp. 480–483	–	–	–	–
II-24 Thyroid Dysfunction	pp. 474–480	–	–	–	Ch. 32
II-25 Shock	pp. 207–217	pp. 223–238	–	Std. 16, 17	–
COURSE III: ADVANCED CRITICAL CARE NURSING					
III-1 Near Drowning	pp. 91–92	–	–	Std. 4	–
III-2 Hematological System Anatomy and Physiology	pp. 496–519	–	–	–	–
III-3 Acquired Coagulopathy	pp. 519–530, 554–558	pp. 238–242	–	Std. 65	–
III-4 Acute Immunological Disorders	pp. 540	–	–	Std. 62	–
III-5 Crisis Intervention and Ethics in Critical Care	pp. 652–654, 667–674	–	Ch. 5	–	Ch. 6, 7, 8
III-6 Cardiopulmonary Interrelationships	pp. 41–71, 153–158	–	–	–	–
III-7 Pulmonary Diagnostic Studies	pp. 35–40	pp. 393–398	–	–	pp. 225–227
III-8 Assessment of Abnormal Heart Sounds	pp. 126–133	–	–	–	pp. 374–380
III-9 Cardiovascular Diagnostic and Therapeutic Studies	pp. 133–153	Ch. 4	–	Std. 13, 22	pp. 381–384
III-10 Twelve-Lead Electrocardiogram (ECG) Interpretation	pp. 138–147	–	–	–	–
III-11 Acute Pericarditis and Endocarditis	pp. 182–185, 189–190	pp. 221–223	–	Std. 18, 19	Ch. 17, 19
III-12 Cardiomyopathies	pp. 190–193	–	–	Std. 14	–
III-13 Mechanical Cardiac Assist	–	pp. 264–271	–	Std. 24	–
III-14 Brain Tumors	–	–	–	Std. 36, 37, 40	–
III-15 Central Nervous System (CNS) Infection	pp. 317–320	–	–	Std. 42	–
III-16 Multiple Sclerosis	–	–	–	–	–
III-17 Parkinson's Disease	–	–	–	–	–
III-18 Spinal Cord Trauma	pp. 295–302	–	–	–	–
III-19 Guillain-Barré Syndrome	pp. 320–323	–	–	Std. 44	Ch. 22
III-20 Botulism Toxicity	–	–	–	–	–
III-21 Myasthenia Gravis	pp. 323–327	–	–	Std. 43	Ch. 21
III-22 Perinatal Complications	–	–	–	–	–
III-23 Musculoskeletal Injury in Multiple Trauma	–	–	–	Std. 63	Ch. 33, 35
III-24 Burn Injury	–	pp. 356–372	Ch. 37	Std. 64	Ch. 36
III-25 Multiple Systems Failure	–	–	–	–	Ch. 37

It is usually necessary to present the curriculum using more than one instructor in hospital-based education. Learners can benefit from exposure to different teachers, and the learning time lost while teachers and learners adjust to each other can be minimized with attention to key details. Nurse students are usually concerned about the relationship between lecture content and future test questions. Their anxiety will be lessened and learning enhanced if this is clarified and discrepancies do not occur. If blocks of content are taught by one lecturer or are team taught, unnecessary repetition and omission can be avoided. For example, the oxyhemoglobin curve is not listed specifically in any unit outline. It could be discussed as part of gas transport in Unit I-11, "Pulmonary Anatomy, Physiology, and Assessment," or with oxygen therapy in Unit I-12, "Supporting Respiration." If it is included in both, there is danger of boring repetition. If it is omitted, learners are left with a gap. Omission is especially bothersome when two presenters assure a class that they will not cover a topic because it will be or has been covered elsewhere!

In keeping with the goal of promoting respect, professionalism, and teamwork, lecturers should be selected carefully. Good teachers are found in all professional groups. Lecturers who are unaware of specifics of the holistic nursing practice model and nursing diagnosis can teach with a nurse educator who can tie the information to nursing practice. Teacher qualities that are particularly desirable are:

- knowledge of the subject matter that is more advanced than that of the students
- interest in teaching as well as concern and respect for students
- demonstrated ability to teach characterized by: (a) spontaneous delivery; (b) organized presentation; (c) adaptation to learner level; and (d) use of appropriate audiovisual materials
- attitude that supports the objectives and intent of the curriculum
- respect for all members of the critical care team without sexist or elitist attitudes

SCHEDULING CLASSES

Since hospitals are primarily in the business of caring for patients, rather than educating nurses, meeting patient care needs will take precedence over meeting nurses' educational needs. Thus, the classes should be scheduled at a time when meeting patient needs is least likely to interfere with class attendance for nurse educators and students.

Class attendance and quality may also be affected if the usual surgical schedule creates consistent increases in the number of patients who require 1:1 staffing ratios on certain days. For example, if a large proportion of cardiac surgery is done on Wednesdays and this produces real or perceived understaffing, it may not be wise to schedule classes for Wednesdays. The nurse students, nurse educators, and physician lecturers may be too fatigued, busy, and/or distracted to be attentive in class.

Few critical care nursing units can write their work schedule to allow large groups of nurses to have the same time off to attend class. Because class attendance cannot be guaranteed, a mechanism for makeup must be provided to nurses who miss class because of their work schedule. This can be done by encouraging nurse students to ask a classmate to tape the lecture and obtain any handouts. Nurse managers may be able to arrange release time for nurse students by asking other staff members to work partial shifts during the course.

In order to facilitate student progression and ease the burden of teaching, two or more institutions can teach different courses simultaneously. This requires fewer nurses to be off duty at one time but may affect class and work schedules. If the institutions cooperate

in scheduling classes on different days, the effects on staffing can be minimized.

A shared teaching schedule might be as follows:

Fall:	Course I at hospital A
	Course III at hospital B
Winter:	Course II at hospital A
	Course I at hospital B
Spring:	Course III at hospital A
	Course II at hospital B

Classes at hospital A might be held on Mondays and Wednesdays from 4:00 to 6:30 p.m. while those at hospital B might be on Tuesdays and Thursdays from 7:00 to 9:30 p.m. In any event, the time and place the classes are held should be as consistent as possible. In addition, the best classroom environment available should be used.

Rescheduling: A Cautionary Note

Occasionally, a lecturer will ask to reschedule a presentation. Before granting the request, the effect on the nurse students should be considered. Rescheduling one presentation is usually accomplished by trading time slots with another class. Thus, two or more units are scheduled out of sequence, which is disruptive to the knowledge building process. Frequent or unannounced changes in the topic schedule will discourage nurse students from reading before class. Generally, lecturer and student needs are best accommodated by changing lecturers rather than topics.

ADAPTING THE CURRICULUM

The suggested time for each unit is generally considered too short by specialists in the subject. Each topic could easily be expanded to two or three times the suggested amount. The goal of presenting a general, broad-based critical care course must be kept in mind. It is not expected that everything about a topic will be explored in class. The nurse students should expect to spend time outside of the classroom reading and studying, as well as viewing and listening to audiovisual materials. Interested nurse students should be guided to further study. If the time is to be adjusted, careful thought must be given to eliminating or expanding sections of the content outlines.

Some of the units or content outlines may include subjects that are unnecessary for nurses in some CCUs. For example, if the hospital does not have facilities for a diagnostic or surgical procedure, class time spent on such topics may be inappropriate. The units may be eliminated completely or abbreviated. Sometimes, the topic is not inappropriate but the objectives or the time allotted require adjustment. For instance, at hospitals that transfer most neurological and neurosurgical patients, the course content pertaining to procedures done only at the tertiary care center may be eliminated but the units related to assessing and stabilizing the patient before transfer would be retained. Aspects of neurological care related to convalescence should be included in the course if patients are returned to the hospital for recovery. If patients are routinely sent to another agency for diagnostic testing, it is helpful to nurses, patients, and families if preparation and recovery for these procedures is included.

In making adjustments, it is important to maintain the logical sequence of units so that movement from normal to abnormal and simple to complex remains intact. Maximal learning will be achieved with careful attention to proper groundwork and foundation. In other words, units should not be substituted so that a complex topic is taught early in a system sequence, e.g., placing "Mechanical Cardiac Assist" before "Cardiac Failure." Similarly, a unit from a different system should not appear before the review of anatomy, physiology, or assessment, e.g., replacement of "Cardiac Surgery" with "Brain Tumors." In the same sense, before eliminating a unit completely, it is important to review the outline to make sure that support for a later unit is not left out.

Once the curriculum is established it is important to avoid making changes in the content in an effort to address a current problem in one hospital or one intensive care unit. One must approach curriculum changes with a certain amount of caution and long-term vision. Each change must be considered carefully. Some questions that must be asked and answered before making changes are:

- Why is this change thought to be needed?
- Are the factors indicating a need for change internal or external to the curriculum?
- Do these factors affect all of the nurses who will be taking the courses?
- How long will the factors be present?
- Can these factors be altered satisfactorily without changing the curriculum?

INTEGRATING CLINICAL PRACTICE

The curriculum does not include a formal clinical practice component with instructor supervision be-cause the majority of nurse students and educators participating in the curriculum are expected to be practicing in the same setting. In this situation, critical care clinical specialists teach the curriculum content and consult with nurse students in their actual practice. Thus, bedside instruction in clinical practice happens informally and spontaneously.

One of the compelling reasons for an ongoing schedule of standardized, hospital-based courses is the inevitability of turnover and the desire to have new nurses integrated in the shortest time possible. The skill and competence of the nursing staff of a CCU must be viewed as a whole because essentially any nurse may be required for any patient assignment at any time. Thus, a unit's staff is as well-educated, safe, and competent as its weakest member.

With proper leadership, nurses who have not completed the critical care nursing education curriculum can provide safe, competent care within their limitations. Many hospitals have a "float" or temporary reassignment policy in effect that periodically moves nurses from noncritical care nursing units into CCUs. These nurses are then responsible for the care of critical care patients. The new critical care nurse who is enrolled in the critical care nursing education curriculum and studying while practicing is similar to the "float" nurse.

The CCU's senior nurses who have learned in the same curriculum can be expected to be aware of the sequence of study. The entire nursing staff should be expected to assist new nurses as they would "floats." It is very helpful if a specific staff member is identified as a resource for the new nurse when patient assignments are made at the beginning of the shift. All critical care nurses should be provided with the following guidelines:

1. Know your limitations.
2. If you are not familiar with a patient problem or piece of equipment, ask for assistance before proceeding.
3. Request a bedside, joint assessment in which you and the reporting nurse review the patient's present condition. This will prevent misinterpreting a report and missing changes in the patient's condition between shifts.
4. It is not enough to simply follow the physician's orders. Patient conditions change often and completely so that the physician's previous order may not be appropriate to the patient's current condition. If you question a physician's order on this basis, review the situation with the physician.

EVALUATION

The purpose and nature of evaluation is somewhat different in hospital-based education than in academia. Typically hospital inservice class members are graded using a pass/fail system rather than letter grades. Certificates of satisfactory completion are given to those who pass. Certificates of attendance may be given to those who do not meet the criteria for passing. Student performance is not entirely a private matter between student and instructor. The results of nurse student evaluation are used by members of the hospital management team in job performance evaluations of nurse students and nurse educators. Merit increases and other salary adjustments may depend on classroom performance. Information about evaluation of nurse student performance is required as documentation for the Joint Commission on Accreditation of Hospitals. The effect of classroom learning on job performance can be evaluated through chart audit and critical incident techniques. Thus, some aspects of the evaluation process will be determined by the hospital's documentation requirements.

The concept of using evaluation as a learning experience for students and teachers should not be overlooked. In general, evaluation methods should be consistent with the behavioral objectives, reflect the realities of practice, and require application and/or analysis. The situations and problems encountered in practice are generally more exacting tests of nurses' knowledge and skills than tests made by instructors. Information or skills that demand identification in practice, e.g., cardiac dysrhythmia patterns, should be tested by simulating the practice situation. Information that the nurse would be expected to be able to locate but not recite, e.g., a nursing care plan for an obscure restrictive cardiomyopathy, can be evaluated by methods that allow use of notes and reading material. Teamwork among nurses is required in practice and can be enhanced with assignments that encourage collaboration.

Evaluating the efficiency of the curriculum is facilitated by using pretests and post-tests. Students can be informed about their progress through quizzes, study questions, and nursing care plans. Because of the salary implications of failing a student, evaluation methods should be as objective as possible. Test questions and answer keys should withstand appeal to managers not involved in teaching.

Specific time for testing and evaluation is not written into the curriculum. If quizzes or other evaluation are done in class, the time must be scheduled in addition or in place of content presentation. Because of the improbability of having all class members present for an exam and the difficulties inherent in scheduling those who miss for an alternate time, take-home exams may be the most successful.

For the most part, the evaluation method and frequency can be left to the discretion of the "lead" teacher who will probably be held accountable for the overall program. Part of determining the evaluation method is considering the requirements as to resources, time, and skills of the responsible nurse educator. Evaluation methods and tools require development, administration, grading, and interpretation. A rule of thumb is that an assignment that requires teacher grading should not be made if it cannot be graded and returned to students in time to enhance learning. Assignments that can be self-graded or graded in class can be used if educator time is at a premium and cannot be used for grading activities.

Nurse students who are judged by their resume or performance to have mastered some of the curriculum content can be given the opportunity to challenge all or parts of the curriculum. This can be done by asking them to complete the final exam or other pertinent evaluation material, such as a nursing care plan for one of the case studies.

The evaluation process should include student evaluation of the instruction and lecturers. Information about the evaluation should be shared with the lecturers so that they may have an opportunity to improve their performance. This can be done by asking the nurse students to complete evaluation forms for each lecturer. The ratings for each lecturer can then be compiled and tabulated. The information can then be sent to the lecturer as the second paragraph of the letter thanking them for their presentation. This information can also be given to the lecturer's superior and thus be part of the lecturer's performance evaluation.

The questions on the lecturer evaluation form should be clear and ask for pertinent information from the nurse students. The students should be directed by the questions to focus most on the learning process and less on the performance aspects of teaching. Questions, such as, Was the presentation given in an organized manner?, and Were the handouts used to illustrate and clarify points in the lecture? are better than, How would you rate the style of the presentation?, and Was the handout useful? If a copy of the evaluation form is also given to the lecturer before the presentation, the lecturer evaluation process will have the effect of teaching students and lecturers about teaching.

SUMMARY

Users who are using the critical care nursing education curriculum for their first venture into presenting formal instruction are encouraged to utilize our suggestions and to present at least the basic course as written. After evaluation of this first course, needed changes can be made based on experience rather than projection. Users with prior experience in presenting similar programs are encouraged to combine their experience, knowledge of their employing hospital, and our suggestions to adapt the curriculum for successful use.

Part II

Course Outlines

Chapter 3

Course I: Basic Critical Care Nursing

Course I is designed to prepare registered nurses with a minimum of one year of general duty nursing experience for beginning practice in adult critical care. On completion of the course, the nurse should be able to provide competent nursing care to adult critical care patients who have commonly occurring problems.

We suggest that the course be given in 55 contact hours of instruction arranged as two sessions per week for 11 weeks. Each session is two and a half clock hours and provides 2.5 contact hours. The final examination is suggested to be an additional 2.5 contact hours. The schedule of classes is shown in Table 3–1.

COURSE OBJECTIVES

At the end of the course, the nurse student is prepared to:

1. assess adult patients with common critical illnesses using inspection, palpation, percussion, and auscultation, as well as electronic equipment
2. make nursing diagnoses of adults with common critical illnesses based on assessment data
3. plan appropriate nursing care for adult patients with common critical illnesses
4. implement nursing care for adult patients with common critical illnesses
5. evaluate nursing care of adults with common critical illnesses
6. demonstrate understanding of proper use of patient care equipment commonly found in critical care units (CCUs)

EVALUATION

The nurse students' knowledge will be evaluated at the discretion of the primary instructor before, during, and at completion of the course through:

1. pretest
2. quizzes
3. homework assignments

Table 3–1 Schedule of Classes for Course I: Basic Critical Care Nursing

Class	Unit	Topic	Time (hr)
1	I-0	Introduction	0.5
	I-1	Critical Care Nursing	2
2	I-2	Cardiovascular Anatomy, Physiology, and Assessment	2.5
3	I-3	Introduction to Electrocardiography and Monitoring	2.5
4	I-4	Angina and Myocardial Infarction	2.5
5, 6	I-5	Basic Cardiac Dysrhythmias	5
7	I-6	Cardiac Failure and Pulmonary Edema	2.5
8	I-7	Electrical Management of Cardiac Dysrhythmias	2.5
9	I-8	Cardiac Catheterization and Cardiovascular Angiography	1
	I-9	Cardiac Surgery	1.5
10	I-10	Vascular Disease	2.5
11	I-11	Pulmonary Anatomy, Physiology, and Assessment	2.5
12	I-12	Supporting Respiration	2.5
13	I-13	Chest Trauma and Surgery	2.5
14	I-14	Acute Respiratory Failure	2.5
15	I-15	Obstructive Pulmonary Disease	2.5
16	I-16	Invasive Hemodynamic Monitoring	2.5
17	I-17	Renal Anatomy, Physiology, and Assessment	2.5
18	I-18	Fluid and Electrolyte Imbalance	2.5
19	I-19	Acid-Base Imbalance	2.5
20	I-20	Acute Renal Failure and Dialysis	1.5
	I-21	Urological Trauma and Surgery	1
21	I-22	Electrical Safety	1
	I-23	Legal Aspects of Critical Care Nursing	1.5
22	I-24	Infection Control and Management	2.5
23	Exam	Final Examination	2.5

4. makeup assignments utilizing student behavioral objectives from missed units in conjunction with readings and case studies
5. final examination

UNIT OUTLINES

Unit I-0: Introduction to Basic Critical Care Nursing

Time: 0.5 hour

Student Behavioral Objectives

1. State the plan of study.
2. Identify and locate reference materials available for student use.

Content:

I. Course overview
II. Reference materials
III. Evaluation and grading
IV. Pretest

Unit I-1: Critical Care Nursing

Time: 2 hours

Student Behavioral Objectives

1. Discuss the unique features of critical care nursing practice.
2. Devise a personal plan directed at avoiding "burnout."
3. Discuss critical care nursing practice standards set by the Joint Commission on Accreditation of Hospitals and the American Association of Critical-Care Nurses.
4. Describe the impact of the critical care unit (CCU) environment on patients, families, and personnel.

Content

I. Critical Care Units (CCUs)
   A. History
   B. Current philosophy, purpose, and objectives
   C. Pertinent standards
      1. Joint Commission on Accreditation of Hospitals
      2. American Association of Critical-Care Nurses
   D. Physical design

E. Administrative organization
II. Critical care nursing
   A. Critical care nursing practice
      1. Characteristics of critical care nurses
      2. Nurse and physician interdependence
      3. Nurse's role and responsibilities
   B. American Association of Critical-Care Nurses
      1. Purpose and philosophy
      2. Standards of care
      3. CCRN examination
III. Critical care unit environment
   A. Sources of stress for patients, families, and personnel
   B. Manifestations of environmental stress
   C. Management of environmental stress
      1. Patients and families
      2. Co-workers and self

Unit I-2: Cardiovascular Anatomy, Physiology, and Assessment

Time: 2.5 hours

Student Behavioral Objectives

1. Describe the normal anatomy of the cardiovascular system and its respective physiological functions.
2. Discuss the conduction system of the heart with reference to inherent characteristics, normal sequence of activation, and relationship to mechanical activity.
3. Outline a systematic approach to cardiovascular assessment.

Content

I. Heart and vascular system
   A. Heart
      1. Chambers
      2. Valves
      3. Blood supply
   B. Great vessels
   C. Arterial, venous, and capillary beds
   D. Differences in pulmonary and systemic circulations
II. Electrical conduction system of the heart

III. Cardiovascular regulation

IV. Assessment
   A. History
   B. Physical examination
      1. Inspection
      2. Palpation
      3. Percussion
      4. Auscultation
   C. Documentation of findings

Unit I-3: Introduction to Electrocardiography and Monitoring

Time: 2.5 hours

Student Behavioral Objectives

1. Describe the components and function of the continuous bedside electrocardiography (ECG) monitoring system.
2. Describe the proper use of an ECG monitoring system.
3. Identify and measure the individual elements of ECG waveforms correctly.
4. Outline a systematic approach to accurate interpretation of ECG waveform patterns.

Content

I. Continuous ECG monitoring systems
   A. Bedside units
   B. Central stations
   C. Arrhythmia computers
   D. Telemetry set-ups
   E. Monitoring procedures
      1. Application of leads
      2. Setting alarms
      3. Recording waveforms
   F. Equipment malfunction
      1. Determining the problem
      2. Appropriate actions

II. Introduction to electrocardiography
   A. Electrophysiology of the cardiac cell membrane
   B. The electrocardiogram
      1. Leads
      2. Waveforms
   C. Systematic approach to accurate interpretation

Unit I-4: Angina and Myocardial Infarction

Time: 2.5 hours

Student Behavioral Objectives

1. Compare and contrast the pertinent pathophysiology of angina and myocardial infarction (MI).
2. Identify the risk factors associated with atherosclerotic coronary artery disease.
3. Describe the clinical manifestations of angina and MI.
4. Explain the medical and nursing management required by patients with angina and MI.

Content

I. Atherosclerosis
   A. Risk factors
   B. Pathogenesis

II. Coronary artery disease (CAD)
   A. Major presentations
   B. Angina and variant angina
      1. Clinical presentation and assessment
      2. Management and nursing care
   C. Myocardial infarction (MI)
      1. Clinical presentation and assessment
      2. Management and nursing care
      3. ECG changes
      4. Enzyme changes
   D. Complications and prognosis

III. Case studies
   A. Angina pectoris
   B. Acute myocardial infarction
   C. Acute anterolateral myocardial infarction

Unit I-5: Basic Cardiac Dysrhythmias

Time: 5 hours

Student Behavioral Objectives

1. Identify the basic cardiac dysrhythmias accurately.
2. Describe the usual management of the identified dysrhythmias.
3. Discuss the pharmacology of selected antidysrhythmic agents.

Content

　I. Sinus rhythms

　II. Atrial rhythms

　III. Junctional rhythms

　IV. Ventricular rhythms

　V. Conduction defects

　　A. Atrioventricular block

　　B. Intraventricular block

　VI. Antidysrhythmic pharmacology

Unit I-6: Cardiac Failure and Pulmonary Edema

Time: 2.5 hours

Student Behavioral Objectives

　1. Compare and contrast management of acute and chronic cardiac failure.

　2. Describe the clinical manifestations and emergency management of pulmonary edema.

　3. Identify and discuss the relationships between pathophysiology, clinical manifestations, and treatment measures with respect to cardiac failure.

　4. Describe the pharmacological and clinical effects of drugs used in management of cardiac failure.

Content

　I. Cardiac failure

　　A. Pathogenesis and pathophysiology

　　　1. Acute

　　　2. Chronic

　　B. Clinical presentation and assessment

　　　1. Acute

　　　2. Chronic

　　C. Management and nursing care

　　　1. Acute

　　　2. Chronic

　II. Acute pulmonary edema

　　A. Pathogenesis and pathophysiology

　　　1. Cardiac

　　　2. Noncardiac

　　B. Clinical presentation and assessment

　　C. Management and nursing care

　　　1. Immediate nursing actions

　　　2. Additional emergency measures

　　　3. Continued care

　III. Case study in cardiac failure and pulmonary edema

Unit I-7: Electrical Management of Cardiac Dysrhythmias

Time: 2.5 hours

Student Behavioral Objectives

　1. Describe the nurse's role and responsibilities in caring for patients requiring artificial cardiac pacing, cardioversion, and defibrillation.

　2. Demonstrate recognition of signs and symptoms indicating need for artificial cardiac pacing, cardioversion, and defibrillation.

　3. Describe the prevention, identification, and management of complications associated with artificial cardiac pacing, cardioversion, and defibrillation.

　4. Demonstrate correct technique of cardioversion and defibrillation in a controlled setting.

Content

　I. Artificial cardiac pacemakers

　　A. Indications for use

　　B. Types and modes of cardiac pacing

　　C. Complications

　　D. Interpretation of ECG waveforms in cardiac pacing

　　E. Nursing care

　II. Cardioversion and defibrillation

　　A. Differentiation of cardioversion and defibrillation

　　B. Clinical indications for procedure

　　C. Preparation of the patient

　　D. Procedure

　　E. Complications

　　F. Nursing care

　III. Demonstration and workshop

　　A. Cardiac pacemakers

　　B. Cardioversion

　　C. Defibrillation

　IV. Case studies

　　A. Artificial cardiac pacemaker

　　B. Cardiac dysrhythmia

Unit I-8: Cardiac Catheterization and Cardiovascular Angiography

Time: 1 hour

Student Behavioral Objectives

1. State the clinical indications for cardiac catheterization and cardiovascular angiography.
2. Describe appropriate patient teaching relative to cardiac catheterization and cardiovascular angiography.
3. Discuss preparatory and postprocedural nursing care for cardiac catheterization and cardiovascular angiography.

Content

I. Cardiac catheterization
   A. Indications and technique for procedure
   B. Nursing care
      1. Patient teaching
      2. Patient preparation
      3. Postprocedural care
      4. Prevention and intervention for complications

II. Cardiovascular angiography
   A. Indications and technique for procedure
   B. Nursing care
      1. Patient teaching
      2. Patient preparation
      3. Postprocedural care
      4. Prevention and intervention for complications

Unit I-9: Cardiac Surgery

Time: 1.5 hours

Student Behavioral Objectives

1. Describe the surgical techniques employed in intervention for coronary artery and cardiac valve disease.
2. Explain the nursing care required by postoperative cardiovascular surgical patients.
3. Demonstrate understanding of nursing care directed at prevention, recognition, and intervention of cardiac surgery complications.

Content

I. Surgical techniques and procedures
   A. Anesthesia
   B. Myocardial revascularization
      1. Indications for procedure
      2. Technique
   C. Cardiac valve repair and replacement
      1. Indications for procedure
      2. Technique

II. Postoperative nursing
   A. Routine care protocols
   B. Complications

III. Case studies
   A. Coronary artery bypass surgery
   B. Aortic stenosis with valve replacement

Unit I-10: Vascular Disease

Time: 2.5 hours

Student Behavioral Objectives

1. Describe the pathophysiology pertinent to acute venous and arterial vascular disease.
2. Outline a systematic approach to assessing patients with acute venous and arterial vascular disease.
3. Discuss the methods used in management of patients with acute venous and arterial vascular disease.
4. Explain the nursing care required by patients with acute venous and arterial vascular disease.

Content

I. Acute venous thromboembolic disease
   A. Thrombophlebitis
      1. Pathogenesis
      2. Clinical presentation and assessment
      3. Management and nursing care
   B. Pulmonary embolus
      1. Pathogenesis and prophylaxis
      2. Clinical presentation and assessment
      3. Management and nursing care

II. Acute arterial thromboembolic disease
   A. Acute arterial occlusion
      1. Pathogenesis
      2. Clinical presentation and assessment

3. Management and nursing care
B. Dissecting aortic aneurysm
  1. Pathogenesis
  2. Clinical presentation and assessment
  3. Management and nursing care
III. Case study in dissecting aortic aneurysm

Unit I-11: Pulmonary Anatomy, Physiology, and Assessment

Time: 2.5 hours

Student Behavioral Objectives

1. Describe the functional anatomy of the pulmonary system.
2. Explain oxygenation in terms of external and internal respiration, as well as gas transport.
3. Discuss the regulating mechanisms by which alveolar ventilation is matched to metabolic demand.
4. Outline a systematic approach to pulmonary assessment.

Content

I. Functional pulmonary anatomy
  A. Respiratory tract
    1. Conducting airways
    2. Gas exchange units
  B. Pulmonary circulation
  C. Thoracic cage and muscles of respiration
II. Oxygenation
  A. External respiration
  B. Gas transport
  C. Internal respiration
III. Pulmonary regulation
IV. Assessment
  A. History
  B. Physical examination
    1. Inspection
    2. Palpation
    3. Percussion
    4. Auscultation
  C. Documentation of findings

Unit I-12: Supporting Respiration

Time: 2.5 hours

Student Behavioral Objectives

1. Describe appropriate nursing intervention to establish and maintain optimal airway patency while minimizing the complications of airway intubation procedures in critically ill patients.
2. Describe the physiological and psychological consequences of ventilator therapy in terms of cause, effect, and preventive measures.
3. Outline a nursing care plan for the patient on continuous ventilatory support, including the weaning phase.

Content

I. Establishing and maintaining a patent airway
  A. Signs and symptoms of inadequate airway
  B. Methods
    1. Positioning of head and mandible
    2. Suctioning the airways
    3. Oropharyngeal and nasopharyngeal airways
    4. Endotracheal and tracheostomy tubes
  C. Complications of artificial airway procedures
II. Oxygen therapy
  A. Indications for oxygen therapy
  B. Hazards of oxygen therapy
  C. Methods of oxygen administration
III. Ventilatory support
  A. Indications for artificial ventilation
  B. Temporary
    1. Mouth-to-mouth resuscitation
    2. Resuscitation bag
IV. Continuous mechanical ventilation
  A. Types of ventilators
    1. Pressure cycled
    2. Volume cycled
    3. Other types
  B. Specific modes used with volume cycled ventilators
    1. Assist/control (A/C)
    2. Intermittent mandatory ventilation (IMV)
    3. Positive end expiratory pressure (PEEP)
    4. Continuous positive airway pressure (CPAP)
  C. Initiating mechanical ventilation
    1. Settings

2. Assessment
3. Adjustment
D. Maintaining mechanical ventilation
E. Weaning mechanical ventilation

V. Case study in supporting respiration

Unit I-13: Chest Trauma and Surgery

Time: 2.5 hours

Student Behavioral Objectives

1. Describe the pathophysiology pertinent to chest trauma and surgery.
2. Outline a systematic approach to assessing patients with chest trauma and surgery.
3. Discuss the methods used in managing patients with chest trauma and surgery.
4. Explain the nursing care required by patients with chest trauma and surgery.

Content

I. Chest trauma
   A. Precipitating factors and pathophysiology
      1. Closed chest
      2. Open chest
   B. Clinical presentation and assessment
      1. Without disruption of the pleural space
      2. With disruption of the pleural space

II. Chest Surgery
   A. Pleural abrasion
   B. Partial pulmonary resection
   C. Pneumonectomy
   D. Repair of cardiovascular structures

III. Closed chest drainage

IV. Postoperative nursing
   A. Routine protocols
   B. Complications

V. Case study in chest trauma requiring surgery

Unit I-14: Acute Respiratory Failure

Time: 2.5 hours

Student Behavioral Objectives

1. Describe the pathophysiology pertinent to acute respiratory failure and adult respiratory distress syndrome (ARDS).
2. Outline a systematic approach to assessing patients with acute respiratory failure and ARDS.
3. Discuss the methods used in managing patients with acute respiratory failure and ARDS.
4. Explain the nursing care required by patients with acute respiratory failure and ARDS.

Content

I. Acute respiratory failure
   A. Precipitating factors and pathophysiology
   B. Clinical presentation and assessment

II. Adult respiratory distress syndrome (ARDS)
   A. Precipitating factors and pathophysiology
   B. Clinical presentation and assessment
   C. Differentiation from acute respiratory failure

III. Patient management and nursing care
   A. Routine protocols
   B. Complications

IV. Case studies
   A. Acute respiratory failure
   B. ARDS

Unit I-15: Obstructive Pulmonary Disease

Time: 2.5 hours

Student Behavioral Objectives

1. Describe the pathophysiology pertinent to acute episodes of selected obstructive pulmonary diseases.
2. Outline a systematic approach to assessing patients with acute episodes of selected obstructive pulmonary diseases.
3. Discuss the methods used in managing patients with acute episodes of selected obstructive pulmonary diseases.
4. Explain the nursing care required by patients with acute episodes of selected obstructive pulmonary diseases.

Content

I. Acute respiratory failure in chronic bronchitis
   A. Precipitating factors and pathophysiology
   B. Clinical presentation and assessment

II. Acute respiratory failure in emphysema
   A. Precipitating factors and pathophysiology

B. Clinical presentation and assessment

C. Differentiation from chronic bronchitis

III. Asthma and status asthmaticus

A. Precipitating factors and pathophysiology

B. Clinical presentation and assessment

IV. Patient management and nursing care

A. Routine protocols

B. Complications

V. Case studies

A. Emphysema

B. Asthma

Unit I-16: Invasive Hemodynamic Monitoring

Time: 2.5 hours

Student Behavioral Objectives

1. Describe the proper assembly and operation of a continuous flush system used with invasive hemodynamic monitoring devices.
2. Describe the location and placement procedure for invasive hemodynamic monitoring devices.
3. Describe the proper assembly and operation of a thermodilution cardiac output measurement system.
4. Interpret and discuss the information obtained from each of the invasive hemodynamic monitoring devices.
5. Describe appropriate identification and correction of common problems encountered in invasive hemodynamic monitoring.

Content

I. Cardiovascular pressure monitoring

A. Continuous flush system

1. Principles of assembly

2. Principles of use

B. Catheter location and placement

1. Arterial

2. Right atrial

3. Pulmonary artery and capillary

4. Left atrial

C. Troubleshooting common problems

1. Recognition

2. Correction

II. Thermodilution cardiac output

A. Principles of system assembly

B. Principles of use

C. Troubleshooting common problems

1. Recognition

2. Correction

III. Interpretation of data

IV. Workshop

Unit I-17: Renal Anatomy, Physiology, and Assessment

Time: 2.5 hours

Student Behavioral Objectives

1. Describe the physiology of renal regulation of fluid and electrolyte balance.
2. Relate alterations in renal circulation to glomerular filtration rate.
3. Explain the mechanisms that regulate plasma osmolality.
4. Identify and interpret selected sources of data used in renal assessment.

Content

I. Physiology of the renal system

A. Formation of urine

B. Body water regulation

C. Electrolyte regulation

D. Excretion of metabolic waste products

E. Role of the kidney in blood pressure regulation

II. Assessment

A. History

B. Physical examination

C. Laboratory studies

D. Documentation of findings

III. Interpretation of assessment data

A. Signs and symptoms

B. Laboratory studies

C. Documentation of findings

Unit I-18: Fluid and Electrolyte Imbalance

Time: 2.5 hours

Student Behavioral Objectives

1. Outline the precipitating factors for common fluid and electrolyte imbalances.

2. Describe major clinical manifestations of common fluid and electrolyte imbalances.
3. Explain the methods used in correcting common fluid and electrolyte imbalances.
4. Discuss the nursing care required by patients with common fluid and electrolyte imbalances.

Content

I. Fluid imbalance
   A. Dehydration
   B. Overhydration

II. Electrolyte imbalance
   A. Sodium
   B. Potassium
   C. Calcium
   D. Phosphate
   E. Magnesium

III. Management and nursing care

IV. Vignettes of fluid and electrolyte imbalance

Unit I-19: Acid-Base Imbalance

Time: 2.5 hours

Student Behavioral Objectives

1. Describe pulmonary and renal regulation of acid-base balance.
2. Outline the precipitating factors and major clinical manifestations of common acid-base imbalances.
3. Explain the methods used in correcting common acid-base imbalances.
4. Discuss the nursing care required by patients with common acid-base imbalances.

Content

I. Terminology

II. Physiological function of buffer systems
   A. Pulmonary
   B. Renal
   C. Blood

III. Clinical states of acid-base imbalance
   A. Acidosis
      1. Respiratory
      2. Metabolic
   B. Alkalosis
      1. Respiratory

      2. Metabolic
   C. Compensated

IV. Management and nursing care

V. Vignettes of acid-base imbalance

Unit I-20: Acute Renal Failure and Dialysis

Time: 1.5 hours

Student Behavioral Objectives

1. Describe and contrast the pathophysiology pertinent to acute renal failure with respect to prerenal, renal, and postrenal failure.
2. Outline the systemic effects of acute renal failure.
3. Discuss the methods used, including dialysis, in managing patients with acute renal failure.
4. Explain the nursing care required by patients with acute renal failure and dialysis therapy.

Content

I. Acute renal failure
   A. Precipitating factors and pathophysiology
   B. Clinical presentation and assessment
   C. Patient management and nursing care
      1. Routine protocols
      2. Complications

II. Dialysis
   A. Hemodialysis
   B. Peritoneal dialysis
   C. Nursing responsibilities

III. Case study in acute renal failure requiring dialysis

Unit I-21: Urological Trauma and Surgery

Time: 1 hour

Student Behavioral Objectives

1. Describe selected urological surgical procedures.
2. Outline methods used in draining the upper and lower urinary tract.
3. Explain the nursing care required by patients with urological trauma and surgery.

Content

I. Urological trauma
   A. Precipitating factors and pathophysiology

1. Fracture of the kidney
2. Rupture of the bladder
B. Clinical presentation and assessment
II. Urological surgical procedures
A. Repair of the kidney
B. Repair of the bladder
III. Urinary drainage
A. Upper urinary tract
B. Lower urinary tract
IV. Postoperative nursing care
A. Routine protocols
B. Complications
V. Case study in urological trauma requiring surgery

Unit I-22: Electrical Safety

Time: 1 hour

Student Behavioral Objectives

1. Identify fundamental physical properties and physiological effects of electrical current.
2. State principles of electrical safety pertinent to critical care.
3. Recognize and describe appropriate intervention in clinical situations with increased risk of electrical accidents.

Content

I. Electrical current
A. Physical properties
B. Physiological effects
II. Principles of electrical safety in critical care
III. Recognizing and avoiding electrical hazards
A. Nurse's role
B. Patients at risk
C. Equipment at risk
D. Safe use of equipment in patient care
IV. Vignettes of electrical mishaps

Unit I-23: Legal Aspects of Critical Care Nursing

Time: 1.5 hours

Student Behavioral Objectives

1. Define malpractice as it applies to critical care nursing practice.

2. Discuss critical care situations with legal implications.
3. Describe appropriate ways of minimizing legal risks in critical care nursing practice.

Content

I. Definitions of pertinent legal terms and concepts
A. Malpractice
B. Commission
C. Negligence
D. Omission
E. Death
II. Critical care situations with legal implications
A. Equipment malfunction
B. Improper equipment use
C. Inappropriate practice by health team members
D. Withdrawing life support
E. Not resuscitating patients
III. Minimizing legal risks
A. Education
B. Practice
C. Documentation

Unit I-24: Infection Control and Management

Time: 2.5 hours

Student Behavioral Objectives

1. Describe proper isolation procedures for critical care patients.
2. Demonstrate understanding of proper care of equipment used with isolated critical care patients.
3. Discuss nursing management of draining wounds in terms of dressing techniques and dressing changes.
4. Outline the nursing implications of intravenous administration of selected antibiotics.

Content

I. Infection control in critical care
A. Surveillance
B. Environmental risk factors
C. Protection of personnel
D. Protection of patients and families

II. Isolation procedures in critical care units

    A. Illnesses requiring isolation

    B. Maintaining observation of the patient

    C. Care of equipment taken into the isolation room

    D. Transporting the patient for diagnostic procedures

    E. Cardiac arrest in isolated patients

    F. Caring for the isolated patient after death

    G. Discontinuing isolation

III. Nursing care in management of infection

    A. Draining wounds

        1. Dressing changes

        2. Special techniques

    B. Intravenous administration of antibiotics

    C. Complications

IV. Case studies

    A. Subacute bacterial endocarditis

    B. Esophageal perforation

    C. Meningitis

Chapter 4

Course II: Intermediate Critical Care Nursing

Course II is designed to continue the preparation of registered nurses for practice in adult critical care. It is expected that nurses enrolled in this course are currently practicing in a critical care setting and have a minimum of three months' experience in adult critical care nursing. After completing the course, the nurse should be able to provide competent nursing care to adult critical care patients with complex problems.

We suggest that the course be given in 55 contact hours of instruction arranged as two sessions per week for 11 weeks. Each session is two and a half clock hours and provides 2.5 contact hours. The final examination is suggested to be an additional 2.5 contact hours. Table 4–1 lists the units and time allotment for each unit topic.

COURSE OBJECTIVES

At the end of the course, the nurse student is prepared to:

1. assess adult patients with complex critical illnesses using inspection, palpation, percussion, and auscultation, as well as electronic equipment
2. make nursing diagnoses of adults with complex critical illnesses based on assessment data
3. plan appropriate nursing care for adult patients with complex critical illnesses
4. implement nursing care for adult patients with complex critical illnesses
5. evaluate nursing care of adults with complex critical illnesses
6. demonstrate understanding of proper use of sophisticated patient care equipment found in critical care units

EVALUATION

The nurse students' knowledge will be evaluated at the discretion of the primary instructor before, during, and at completion of the course through:

1. pretest
2. quizzes
3. homework assignments

Table 4–1 Schedule of Classes for Course II: Intermediate Critical Care Nursing

Class	Unit	Topic	Time (hr)
1	II-0	Introduction	0.5
1 and 2	II-1	Advanced Cardiac Dysrhythmias	4.5
3	II-2	Introduction to Twelve-Lead Electrocardiograms (ECGs)	2.5
4	II-3	Cardiac Drugs	2.5
5	II-4	Hypertension and Hypertensive Crisis	2.5
6	II-5	Nervous System Anatomy and Physiology	2.5
7	II-6	Nervous System Assessment	1.5
	II-7	Neurological Diagnostic Studies	1
8	II-8	Alterations in Consciousness	2.5
9	II-9	Seizure Disorders	2.5
10	II-10	Head Trauma and Craniotomy	2.5
11	II-11	Cerebrovascular Disease	2.5
12	II-12	Drug Toxicity and Poisoning	2.5
13	II-13	Psychosocial Aspects of Critical Care	2.5
14	II-14	Gastrointestinal System Anatomy, Physiology, and Assessment	2.5
15	II-15	Nutrition Assessment and Therapy	2.5
16	II-16	Gastrointestinal Bleeding	1.5
	II-17	Gastrointestinal Surgery	1
17	II-18	Hepatic Failure	1.5
	II-19	Acute Pancreatitis	1
18	II-20	Endocrine System Anatomy, Physiology, and Assessment	2.5
19	II-21	Metabolic Crises of Diabetes Mellitus	2.5
20	II-22	Diabetes Insipidus and Syndrome of Inappropriate Antidiuretic Hormone Secretion	2.5
21	II-23	Adrenal Dysfunction	1.5
	II-24	Thyroid Dysfunction	1.0
22	II-25	Shock	2.5
23	Exam	Final Examination	2.5

4. makeup assignments utilizing student behavioral objectives from missed units in conjunction with readings and case studies
5. final examination

UNIT OUTLINES

Unit II-0: Introduction to Intermediate Critical Care Nursing

Time: 0.5 hour

Student Behavioral Objectives

1. State the plan of study.
2. Identify and locate reference materials available for student use.

Content

    I. Course overview
    II. Reference materials
    III. Evaluation and grading
    IV. Pretest

Unit II-1: Advanced Cardiac Dysrhythmias

Time: 4.5 hours

Student Behavioral Objectives

1. Describe the electrophysiological mechanisms and effects of cardiac dysrhythmias.
2. Distinguish between atrioventricular (AV) dissociation and AV block.
3. Distinguish between ventricular aberrancy and ectopy.
4. Differentiate selected intraventricular blocks.
5. Recognize preexcitation syndrome.
6. Discuss management and nursing intervention for selected cardiac dysrhythmias.

Content

    I. Review of basic cardiac dysrhythmias
    II. Mechanisms and effects of cardiac dysrhythmias
        A. Electrophysiological mechanisms that produce dysrhythmias
        B. Local and systemic circulatory effects of cardiac dysrhythmias
    III. AV junctional dysrhythmias
        A. Distinguishing AV dissociation and AV block

        B. Preexcitation syndromes
    IV. Ventricular dysrhythmias
        A. Intraventricular blocks
        B. Distinguishing ventricular aberrancy and ectopy

Unit II-2: Introduction to Twelve-Lead Electrocardiograms

Time: 2.5 hours

Student Behavioral Objectives

1. Explain the procedure for obtaining a standard twelve lead (12-lead) ECG.
2. Explain the value of the 12-lead ECG to nursing care of critically ill patients.
3. Describe a systematic approach to accurate nursing interpretation of a 12-lead ECG.
4. Distinguish between ventricular aberrancy and ectopy using the 12-lead ECG.
5. Describe the location and evolution of myocardial ischemia and infarction through interpretation of selected 12-lead ECGs.

Content

    I. Procedure for obtaining a standard ECG
        A. Preparation of patient
        B. Recording the ECG
    II. Nursing interpretation of 12-lead ECG
        A. Systematic approach
        B. Characteristics of normal 12-lead ECG
        C. Determining axis
    III. Use of ECG interpretation in nursing care
        A. Selecting monitoring lead
        B. Distinguishing dysrhythmias
            1. Ventricular ectopy and aberrancy
            2. Malfunctioning cardiac pacemaker
        C. Predicting and confirming complications
            1. Patterns of myocardial damage
            2. Pattern of extension of myocardial damage
            3. Change in axis
    IV. Interpretation of 12-lead ECGs from cardiovascular case studies

Unit II-3: Cardiac Drugs

Time: 2.5 hours

Student Behavioral Objectives

1. Classify selected cardiac drugs.
2. Discuss the pharmacodynamics of selected cardiac drugs.
3. Explain the nursing implications of administering selected cardiac drugs.

Content

    I. Nurse's role in administering cardiac drugs
      A. Intervention in dysrhythmias
      B. Titration in manipulation of cardiac output

    II. Maximizing cardiac cell environment
      A. Correction of hypoxia
      B. Correction of acid-base disturbance
      C. Correction of electrolyte imbalance

    III. Antidysrhythmics
      A. Class I
      B. Class II
      C. Class III
      D. Class IV

    IV. Chronotropic drugs
      A. Positive
      B. Negative

    V. Inotropic drugs

    VI. Vasoactive drugs
      A. Vasopressors
      B. Vasodilators

    VII. Other drugs
      A. Analgesics and sedatives
      B. Diuretics

Unit II-4: Hypertension and Hypertensive Crisis

Time: 2.5 hours

Student Behavioral Objectives

1. Describe the pathophysiology pertinent to hypertension and hypertensive crisis.
2. Outline a systematic approach to assessing patients with hypertension and hypertensive crisis.
3. Discuss the rationale for methods used in management of patients with hypertension and hypertensive crisis.
4. Explain the nursing care required by patients with hypertension and hypertensive crisis.

Content

    I. Hypertension
      A. Classification
      B. Theories of pathophysiology
      C. Complications and prognosis
      D. Management and rationale
        1. Lifestyle
        2. Stepped approach
        3. Aiding patient compliance

    II. Hypertensive crisis
      A. Clinical presentation and assessment
      B. Complications
      C. Management and rationale
        1. Nursing
        2. Medical

    III. Case study in hypertension with hypertensive crisis

Unit II-5: Nervous System Anatomy and Physiology

Time: 2.5 hours

Student Behavioral Objectives

1. Identify and describe the structures and functions included in each division of the central nervous system (CNS).
2. Diagram the cerebral circulation defining the structures served by each major artery.
3. Describe the important features of cerebral autoregulation and the effect of disrupted autoregulation on cerebral function.
4. Identify and describe the functional relationships that exist between the divisions of the nervous system.

Content

    I. Functional anatomy of the nervous system
      A. Definitions
      B. Central nervous system (CNS)
        1. Structures
        2. Vascular supply
      C. Peripheral nervous system
        1. Structures
        2. Vascular supply

    II. Physiology of the nervous system
      A. Cerebral autoregulation and metabolism
      B. Synaptic transmission

C. Sensory transmission
D. Neuromuscular transmission
E. Reflex arcs

III. Functional relationships
A. Reticular activating system
B. Blood-brain barrier

Unit II-6: Nervous System Assessment

Time: 1.5 hours

Student Behavioral Objectives

1. Outline a systematic approach to nervous system assessment.
2. Explain the use and value of the Glasgow Coma Scale.
3. Describe and interpret nervous system assessment of each of the following: structures of the head, face, and neck; general cerebral function; cranial nerve function; motor and sensory function; and verbal response.

Content

I. Assessment of the nervous system
A. Approach
B. Glasgow Coma Scale

II. Assessment and interpretation
A. Structures of the head, face, and neck
B. General cerebral function
C. Cranial nerve function
D. Motor and sensory function
E. Verbal response

III. Documentation of assessment findings

Unit II-7: Neurological Diagnostic Studies

Time: 1 hour

Student Behavioral Objectives

1. Describe the purpose of selected neurological diagnostic studies.
2. Identify and describe appropriate nursing care for each of the selected neurological diagnostic studies.

Content

I. Laboratory studies

II. Radiological studies
A. Skull series
B. Computerized tomography (CT) scan
C. Angiography

III. Special procedures
A. Electroencephalography (EEG)
B. Electromyography
C. Lumbar puncture
D. Radioisotope scan

Unit II-8: Alterations in Consciousness

Time: 2.5 hours

Student Behavioral Objectives

1. Describe the pathogenesis and pathophysiology pertinent to alterations in level of consciousness.
2. Explain the physiological dysfunction underlying the symptoms of increased intracranial pressure (ICP).
3. Outline a systematic approach to assessment of patients with altered level of consciousness and/or increased ICP.
4. Describe and differentiate methods used to manage patients with increased ICP.
5. Plan specific nursing care required by patients with altered level of consciousness, including monitoring ICP.

Content

I. Clinical presentation and assessment
A. Signs and symptoms of altered consciousness
B. Pathogenesis and pathophysiology underlying signs and symptoms of altered consciousness
1. Increased intracranial pressure
2. Central nervous system causes
3. Endogenous causes
4. Exogenous causes
C. Monitoring
1. Intracranial pressure
2. Cerebral function
D. Complications of altered consciousness

II. Management
A. Supportive care with maintenance of vital functions

B. Definitive treatment of underlying causes of altered consciousness
C. Controlling intracranial pressure
D. Controlling cerebral function
E. Determining brain death and withdrawing life support

III. Case studies
    A. Altered level of consciousness
    B. Head injury
    C. Increased intracranial pressure and induced barbiturate coma

Unit II-9: Seizure Disorders

Time: 2.5 hours

Student Behavioral Objectives

1. Explain the physiological dysfunction underlying the symptoms of seizure disorders and status epilepticus.
2. Outline a systematic approach to assessing patients with seizure disorders and status epilepticus including precipitating factors and clinical presentation.
3. Describe and differentiate methods used to manage patients with seizure disorders and status epilepticus.
4. Explain the specific nursing care required by patients with seizure disorders and status epilepticus.

Content

I. Seizure disorders
    A. Classification and terminology
    B. Signs and symptoms of seizure disorders
    C. Pathogenesis and pathophysiology underlying signs and symptoms of seizure disorders
    D. Management and nursing care
        1. Observations
        2. Medications
        3. Prevention of complications

II. Status epilepticus
    A. Clinical presentation and assessment
    B. Immediate intervention
    C. Pathogenesis and pathophysiology underlying signs and symptoms of status epilepticus
    D. Management and nursing care

        1. Supportive care with maintenance of vital functions
        2. Controlling seizure activity
        3. Definitive treatment of underlying causes of status epilepticus
        4. Prevention of complications

III. Case study in seizures

Unit II-10: Head Trauma and Craniotomy

Time: 2.5 hours

Student Behavioral Objectives

1. Describe the precipitating factors and pathophysiology of dysfunction related to head trauma and craniotomy.
2. Outline a systematic approach to assessing patients with head trauma and craniotomy.
3. Explain interpretation of assessment findings pertinent to head trauma and craniotomy.
4. Discuss the rationale for methods used in managing patients following head trauma and craniotomy.
5. Explain and plan nursing care required by patients following head trauma and craniotomy.

Content

I. Head trauma
    A. Classification and terminology
        1. Open and closed head injury
        2. Coup and contrecoup head injury
        3. Blunt and penetrating trauma
    B. Assessment of head trauma
        1. Physical signs
        2. History of loss of consciousness
        3. Symptoms
    C. Pathophysiology underlying signs and symptoms of head trauma
    D. Immediate intervention
    E. Complications and prognosis

II. Craniotomy
    A. Preoperative care
    B. Intraoperative factors
        1. Surgical approaches
        2. Patient positioning
        3. Anesthesia
    C. Complications

III. Management following head trauma and/or cra-
niotomy
   A. Observations
   B. Supportive care
   C. Prevention of complications

IV. Case studies
   A. Craniotomy following head trauma
   B. Brain tumor

Unit II-11: Cerebrovascular Disease

Time: 2.5 hours

Student Behavioral Objectives

1. Describe the precipitating factors and pathophysiology of dysfunction related to cerebrovascular
   disease.
2. Outline a systematic approach to assessing patients with cerebrovascular disease.
3. Explain interpretation of assessment findings
   pertinent to cerebrovascular disease.
4. Compare and contrast methods used in managing
   patients with cerebrovascular disease.
5. Explain and plan nursing care required by patients with cerebrovascular disease.

Content

I. Cerebrovascular disease
   A. Classification and terminology
      1. Cerebrovascular accident
      2. Ischemia and infarction
      3. Thrombosis and hemorrhage
   B. Assessment of cerebrovascular disease
      1. History
      2. Physical signs and symptoms

II. Cerebrovascular accident or arterial occlusion
   A. Pathophysiology underlying signs and
      symptoms
      1. Intracranial
      2. Extracranial
   B. Immediate intervention
   C. Complications and prognosis

III. Intracranial aneurysms
   A. Pathophysiology underlying signs and
      symptoms
      1. Before rupture
      2. After rupture

B. Immediate intervention
C. Complications and prognosis

IV. Intracranial hematomas
   A. Pathophysiology underlying signs and
      symptoms
   B. Immediate intervention
   C. Complications and prognosis

V. Case studies
   A. Cerebrovascular accident
   B. Subarachnoid hemorrhage

Unit II-12: Drug Toxicity and Poisoning

Time: 2.5 hours

Student Behavioral Objectives

1. Describe the precipitating factors and pathophysiology of dysfunction related to drug toxicity and
   poisoning with selected substances.
2. Outline a systematic approach to interpreting assessment of drug toxic and poisoned patients.
3. Discuss methods used in managing patients with
   drug toxicity and poisoning.
5. Explain and plan nursing care required by drug
   toxic and poisoned patients.

Content

I. General management of drug toxicity and poi-
   soning
   A. Clinical manifestations and assessment
   B. Supportive care
   C. Initial intervention to limit toxic effects of
      the agent
   D. Psychosocial intervention for patient and
      family
   E. Complications

II. Specific intervention for selected toxic agents
   A. Sedatives, hypnotics, and analgesics
   B. Tricyclic antidepressants
   C. Petroleum products

III. Case studies
   A. Acetaminophen ingestion
   B. Tricyclic antidepressant ingestion

Unit II-13: Psychosocial Aspects of Critical Care

Time: 2.5 hours

Student Behavioral Objectives

1. Define and discuss psychosocial concepts that affect patients, families, and personnel in the critical care setting.
2. Outline assessment of psychosocial phenomena in patients, families, and personnel.
3. Discuss nursing intervention to reduce impact of negative psychosocial phenomena.
4. Discuss nursing intervention for patients and families in psychosocial crisis.

Content

I. Psychosocial concepts
  A. Self-concept
  B. Self-esteem
  C. Stress
  D. Body image
  E. Pain

II. Assessment and intervention for psychosocial phenomena
  A. Fear and anxiety
  B. Loneliness
  C. Powerlessness
  D. Sensory overload and deprivation
  E. Suicide
  F. Death and grief
  G. Crisis

III. Crisis intervention
  A. Recognition
  B. Goals
  C. Nursing intervention

Unit II-14: Gastrointestinal System Anatomy, Physiology, and Assessment

Time: 2.5 hours

Student Behavioral Objectives

1. Identify and describe the major physiological functions of the divisions of the gastrointestinal (GI) system and the accessory organs of digestion.
2. Outline a systematic approach to assessing the abdomen, the GI system, and the accessory organs.

Content:

I. Physiological function
  A. Gastrointestinal system
  B. Accessory organs of digestion

II. Assessment
  A. Approach
    1. History
    2. Physical examination
    3. Diagnostic studies
  B. Interpretation
    1. Abdomen
    2. Gastrointestinal system
    3. Accessory organs
  C. Documentation of findings

Unit II-15: Nutrition Assessment and Therapy

Time: 2.5 hours

Student Behavioral Objectives

1. Describe assessment and interpretation of nutritional status.
2. Compare and contrast enteral and parenteral nutritional therapy.
3. Explain the nursing care required by patients with therapeutic nutritional needs.

Content

I. Assessment of nutritional status
  A. Patients needing assessment
  B. Technique of assessment
  C. Interpretation of assessment results

II. Nutritional therapy
  A. Modified diets
    1. Restrictions
    2. Altered consistency
  B. Enteral nutrition
  C. Parenteral nutrition

III. Nursing responsibilities
  A. Related to nutrition in general
  B. Specific to modified diets
  C. Specific to enteral nutrition
  D. Specific to parenteral nutrition

IV. Vignette of nutritional support

Unit II-16: Gastrointestinal Bleeding

Time: 1.5 hours

Student Behavioral Objectives

1. Describe the pathophysiology pertinent to GI bleeding.
2. Outline a systematic approach to assessing patients with GI bleeding.
3. Discuss methods of managing patients with GI bleeding.
4. Plan and explain nursing care required by patients with GI bleeding.

Content

   I. Ulcers of the GI tract
     A. Precipitating factors
     B. Clinical presentation and assessment
     C. Complications
     D. Management
       1. Nursing care
       2. Medical therapy
       3. Surgical therapy
  II. Varices of the GI tract
     A. Precipitating factors
     B. Clinical presentation and assessment
     C. Complications
     D. Management
       1. Nursing care
       2. Medical therapy
       3. Surgical therapy
 III. Case study in gastrointestinal bleeding

Unit II-17: Gastrointestinal Surgery

Time: 1 hour

Student Behavioral Objectives

1. Describe the pathophysiology pertinent to GI surgery.
2. Outline a systematic approach to assessing patients following GI surgery.
3. Discuss prevention and management of complications following GI surgery.
4. Plan and explain nursing care required by patients following GI surgery

Content

   I. Gastrointestinal surgery
     A. Procedures
     B. Postoperative management and nursing care
  II. Complications of gastrointestinal surgery
     A. Prevention
     B. Management
       1. Infection
       2. Obstruction
       3. Paralytic ileus
       4. Electrolyte and fluid imbalance
       5. Jaundice
       6. Perforation
 III. Case study in esophageal perforation

Unit II-18: Hepatic Failure

Time: 1.5 hours

Student Behavioral Objectives

1. Describe the pathophysiology pertinent to hepatic failure.
2. Outline a systematic approach to assessing patients with hepatic failures.
3. Discuss techniques used in managing patients with hepatic failure.
4. Plan and explain nursing care required by patients with hepatic failure.

Content

   I. Assessment
     A. Clinical presentation
     B. Monitoring progress
  II. Pathophysiology
     A. Specific to liver
     B. Systemic effects of hepatic dysfunction
 III. Medical management and nursing care
     A. Routine protocols
     B. Complications
       1. Prevention
       2. Management
 IV. Case study in fulminating hepatitis

Unit II-19: Acute Pancreatitis

Time: 1 hour

Student Behavioral Objectives

1. Describe the pathophysiology pertinent to acute pancreatitis.
2. Outline a systematic approach to assessing patients with acute pancreatitis.
3. Discuss management of patients with acute pancreatitis.
4. Plan and explain nursing care required by patients with acute pancreatitis.

Content

I. Assessment
   A. Clinical presentation
   B. Monitoring progress

II. Pathophysiology
   A. Specific to pancreatitis
   B. Systemic effects of pancreatic dysfunction

III. Medical management and nursing care
   A. Routine protocols
   B. Complications
      1. Prevention
      2. Management

IV. Case study in acute pancreatitis

Unit II-20: Endocrine System Anatomy, Physiology, and Assessment

Time: 2.5 hours

Student Behavioral Objectives

1. Describe the anatomic locations and glands of the endocrine system.
2. List the hormones produced by each endocrine gland and the regulation of their production.
3. Describe the effects of each hormone on its respective target cells.
4. Outline a systematic process of assessing endocrine function.

Content

I. Functional anatomy of the endocrine system
   A. Pituitary gland
   B. Thyroid gland
   C. Parathyroid gland
   D. Adrenal glands
   E. Pancreas

II. Hormone production in the endocrine system
   A. Pituitary gland
   B. Thyroid gland
   C. Parathyroid gland
   D. Adrenal glands
   E. Pancreas

III. Assessment
   A. Approach
   B. History
   C. Physical examination
   D. Diagnostic studies
   E. Documentation of findings

Unit II-21: Metabolic Crises of Diabetes Mellitus

Time: 2.5 hours

Student Behavioral Objectives

1. Describe the pathophysiology pertinent to metabolic crises associated with diabetes mellitus, i.e., diabetic ketoacidosis, hyperglycemic hyperosmolar nonketotic coma, and hypoglycemic reaction.
2. Outline a systematic approach to assessing the diabetic in a metabolic crisis.
3. Compare and contrast management methods used in diabetes and its metabolic crises.
4. Explain the nursing care required by diabetics and those with associated metabolic crises.

Content

I. Pathophysiology
   A. Diabetes mellitus
   B. Diabetic ketoacidosis
   C. Hyperglycemic hyperosmolar nonketotic coma
   D. Hypoglycemic reaction

II. Clinical presentation and assessment
   A. Precipitating factors
   B. History
   C. Physical examination
   D. Laboratory studies

III. Management
   A. Goals
   B. Medical therapy
   C. Nursing care

IV. Case study in diabetes mellitus

Unit II-22: Diabetes Insipidus and Syndrome of Inappropriate Antidiuretic Hormone Secretion

Time: 2.5 hours

Student Behavioral Objectives

1. Describe the pathophysiology pertinent to diabetes insipidus and syndrome of inappropriate ADH (SIADH) secretion.
2. Outline a systematic approach to assessing patients with diabetes insipidus or SIADH secretion.
3. Compare and contrast management methods used in patients with diabetes insipidus or SIADH secretion.
4. Explain the nursing care required by patients with diabetes insipidus or SIADH secretion.

Content

   I. Pathophysiology
      A. Diabetes insipidus
      B. Syndrome of inappropriate antidiuretic hormone (ADH) secretion

  II. Clinical presentation and assessment
      A. Precipitating factors
      B. History
      C. Physical examination
      D. Laboratory studies

 III. Management
      A. Goals
      B. Medical therapy
      C. Nursing care

  IV. Case studies
      A. Diabetes insipidus
      B. Syndrome of inappropriate ADH secretion

Unit II-23: Adrenal Dysfunction

Time: 2.5 hours

Student Behavioral Objectives

1. Describe pertinent etiology and precipitating factors relative to adrenal dysfunction.
2. Outline the clinical presentation and assessment of patients with adrenal dysfunction.
3. Discuss management methods used in patients with adrenal dysfunction.
4. Explain the nursing care required by patients with adrenal dysfunction.

Content

   I. Etiology and precipitating factors
      A. Hypersecretion
      B. Hyposecretion

  II. Clinical presentation and assessment
      A. Hyposecretion and Addisonian crisis
      B. Hypersecretion and pheochromocytoma

 III. Management
      A. Goals
      B. Medical therapy
      C. Nursing care

  IV. Case study in acute adrenal insufficiency

Unit II-24: Thyroid Dysfunction

Time: 2.5 hours

Student Behavioral Objectives

1. Describe pertinent etiology and precipitating factors relative to thyroid dysfunction.
2. Outline the clinical presentation and assessment of patients with thyroid dysfunction.
3. Discuss management methods used in patients with thyroid dysfunction.
4. Explain the nursing care required by patients with thyroid dysfunction.

Content

   I. Etiology and precipitating factors
      A. Hypersecretion
      B. Hyposecretion

  II. Clinical presentation and assessment
      A. Hyposecretion and myxedema coma
      B. Hypersecretion and thyroid crisis

 III. Management
      A. Goals
      B. Medical therapy
      C. Nursing care

  IV. Case study in acute hyperthyroid crisis

Unit II-25: Shock

Time: 2.5 hours

Student Behavioral Objectives

1. Compare and contrast the initiating and precipitating factors relative to shock.

2. Discuss the pathophysiology of shock as a phenomenon of tissue deprived of usual metabolic substrates and waste removal.
3. Outline the clinical presentation and assessment of patients in shock.
4. Explain management and nursing care required by patients in shock.

Content

I. Classification and terminology

II. Initiating and precipitating factors
   A. Hypovolemic and hemorrhagic
   B. Cardiogenic
   C. Septic

III. Pathophysiology
   A. Cell dysfunction
   B. Organ dysfunction

IV. Clinical presentation and assessment
   A. Early
   B. Progression
   C. Late

III. Management
   A. Goals
   B. Medical therapy
   C. Nursing care

IV. Prevention

V. Case studies
   A. Multiple trauma with shock
   B. Multiple systems failure
   C. Intraaortic balloon pump counterpulsation
   D. Left ventricular bypass

Chapter 5

Course III: Advanced Critical Care Nursing

Course III is designed to complete the preparation of registered nurses for practice in adult critical care. It is expected that nurses enrolled in this course are currently practicing in a critical care setting and have a minimum of one year's experience in adult critical care nursing. On completion of the course, the nurse should be able to provide competent nursing care to all adult critical care patients, as well as successfully write the CCRN examination sponsored by the American Association of Critical-Care Nurses.

We suggest that the course be given in 55 contact hours of instruction arranged as two sessions per week for 11 weeks. Each session is two and a half clock hours and provides 2.5 contact hours. The final examination is suggested to be an additional 2.5 contact hours. The schedule of classes is shown in Table 5-1.

COURSE OBJECTIVES

At the end of the course, the nurse student is prepared to:

1. assess adult patients with uncommon and complex critical illnesses using inspection, palpation, percussion, and auscultation, as well as electronic equipment
2. make nursing diagnoses of adults with uncommon and complex critical illnesses based on assessment data
3. plan appropriate nursing care for adult patients with uncommon and complex critical illnesses
4. implement nursing care for adult patients with uncommon and complex critical illnesses
5. evaluate nursing care of adults with uncommon and complex critical illnesses
6. demonstrate understanding of proper simultaneous use of numerous pieces of sophisticated

patient care equipment found in critical care units.

Table 5-1 Schedule of Classes for Course III: Advanced Critical Care Nursing

Class	Unit	Topic	Time (hr)
1	III-0	Introduction	0.5
	III-1	Near Drowning	2
2	III-2	Hematological System Anatomy and Physiology	1
	III-3	Acquired Coagulopathy	1.5
3	III-4	Acute Immunological Disorders	2.5
4	III-5	Crisis Intervention and Ethics in Critical Care	2.5
5	III-6	Cardiopulmonary Interrelationships	2.5
6	III-7	Pulmonary Diagnostic Studies	2.5
7	III-8	Assessment of Abnormal Heart Sounds	2.5
8	III-9	Cardiovascular Diagnostic and Therapeutic Studies	2.5
9	III-10	Twelve-Lead Electrocardiogram (ECG) Interpretation	2.5
10	III-11	Acute Pericarditis and Endocarditis	2.5
11	III-12	Cardiomyopathies	2.5
12	III-13	Mechanical Cardiac Assist	2.5
13	III-14	Brain Tumors	2.5
14	III-15	Central Nervous System (CNS) Infection	2.5
15	III-16	Multiple Sclerosis	1.5
	III-17	Parkinson's Disease	1
16	III-18	Spinal Cord Trauma	2.5
17	III-19	Guillain-Barré Syndrome	1.5
	III-20	Botulism Toxicity	1
18	III-21	Myasthenia Gravis	2.5
19	III-22	Perinatal Complications	2.5
20	III-23	Musculoskeletal Injury in Multiple Trauma	2.5
21	III-24	Burn Injury	2.5
22	III-25	Multiple Systems Failure	2.5
23	Exam	Final Examination	2.5

EVALUATION

The nurse students' knowledge will be evaluated at the discretion of the primary instructor before, during, and at completion of the course through:

1. pretest
2. quizzes
3. homework assignments
4. makeup assignments utilizing student behavioral objectives from missed units in conjunction with readings and case studies
5. final examination

UNIT OUTLINES

Unit III-0: Introduction to Advanced Critical Care Nursing

Time: 0.5 hour

Student Behavioral Objectives

1. State the plan of study.
2. Identify and locate reference materials available for student use.

Content

   I. Course overview
  II. Reference materials
 III. Evaluation and grading
  IV. Pretest

Unit III-1: Near Drowning

Time: 2 hours

Student Behavioral Objectives

1. Compare the pathophysiology of freshwater near drowning with that of saltwater.
2. Outline a systematic approach to assessing victims of near drowning.
3. Discuss management of near drowning victims including prevention of complications.
4. Explain the standard nursing care plan for victims of near drowning.

Content

   I. Pathophysiology of near drowning
      A. Freshwater
      B. Saltwater

  II. Clinical presentation and assessment
      A. History
      B. Physical signs and symptoms
      C. Laboratory data

 III. Management
      A. Routine protocols
         1. Medical
         2. Nursing
      B. Complications
         1. Prevention
         2. Intervention

  IV. Case study in near drowning

Unit III-2: Hematological System Anatomy and Physiology

Time: 1 hour

Student Behavioral Objectives

1. Discuss the hematological functions of the spleen, liver, bone marrow, thymus, and lymph system.
2. Describe the physiological mechanisms involved in hemostasis and fibrinolysis.
3. Explain assessment of hemostasis and fibrinolysis.

Content

   I. Functional anatomy of hematological system
      A. Spleen
      B. Liver
      C. Bone marrow
      D. Thymus
      E. Lymph system

  II. Physiological mechanisms
      A. Erythrocyte production and destruction
      B. Hemostasis
      C. Fibrinolysis

 III. Assessment
      A. Hemostasis
      B. Fibrinolysis

Unit III-3: Acquired Coagulopathy

Time: 1.5 hours

Student Behavioral Objectives

1. Describe precipitating factors and pathophysiology pertinent to selected acquired coagulopathies.
2. Compare clinical presentations of patients with acquired coagulopathies.
3. Discuss methods and rationale used in managing patients with selected acquired coagulopathies.
4. Plan and explain nursing care required by patients with selected acquired coagulopathies.

Content

I. Precipitating factors and pathophysiology
   A. Platelet deficiency
   B. Vitamin K deficiency
   C. Dilution of clotting factors by transfusion
   D. Excessive anticoagulation
      1. Warfarin
      2. Heparin
   E. Disseminated intravascular coagulopathy (DIC)
II. Clinical presentation
III. Management and nursing care
   A. General support protocols
   B. Specific to coagulopathy
IV. Case study in DIC

Unit III-4: Acute Immunological Disorders

Time: 2.5 hours

Student Behavioral Objectives

1. Describe the normal physiological function of the immune system.
2. Discuss the pathophysiology pertinent to selected dysfunctions of the immune system.
3. Plan and explain nursing care required by patients with immune system dysfunction.

Content

I. Physiology of the immune system
   A. Immune response
   B. Inflammatory response
II. Dysfunction of the immune system
   A. Hyperimmune responses
   B. Hypoimmune responses

III. Nursing care in immune system dysfunction
   A. Hyperimmunity
   B. Hypoimmunity
IV. Case study in acquired immune deficiency syndrome (AIDS)

Unit III-5: Crisis Intervention and Ethics in Critical Care

Time: 2.5 hours

Student Behavioral Objectives

1. Describe the behavioral manifestations and assessment of patients and families in crisis.
2. Plan and explain nursing intervention for patients and families in crisis.
3. Discuss selected ethical issues in critical care.
4. Consider different beliefs about selected ethical issues in critical care.

Content

I. Crisis intervention
   A. Definitions of crisis and crisis intervention
   B. Precipitating factors of crisis
   C. Behavioral manifestations of crisis and assessment
   D. Nursing intervention in crisis
II. Ethical issues
   A. Concepts used in ethics
   B. Withholding treatment
   C. Withdrawing life support
   D. Euthanasia

Unit III-6: Cardiopulmonary Interrelationships

Time: 2.5 hours

Student Behavioral Objectives

1. Describe the interrelationships of the cardiac and pulmonary systems.
2. Analyze and interpret patient data in assessing alterations and compensation in cardiopulmonary functions.
3. Explain the nursing care required by patients with both cardiac and pulmonary dysfunction.

Content

I. Interrelationships of the cardiac and pulmonary systems

A. Anatomic placement
B. Effect of respiration on cardiac performance
C. Effect of cardiac function on pulmonary performance
D. Shunting

II. Analysis and interpretation of cardiopulmonary patient data
   A. Measured data
   B. Calculated data

III. Nursing care

IV. Vignettes of cardiopulmonary dysfunction

Unit III-7: Pulmonary Diagnostic Studies

Time: 2.5 hours

Student Behavioral Objectives

1. Describe the purposes, procedures, and nursing interpretation of pulmonary function tests.
2. Explain the nursing care required before, during, and after pulmonary function tests.
3. Distinguish normal from abnormal positions of endotracheal tubes and balloon-tipped pulmonary artery catheters as seen on chest x-rays.
4. Recognize and describe the appearance on chest x-rays of selected abnormalities that require immediate intervention.

Content

I. Pulmonary function tests
   A. Purposes
   B. Procedures
   C. Nursing interpretation
   D. Nursing care

II. Chest x-rays
   A. X-ray technique
      1. Density
      2. Contrast
      3. Dimension
      4. Direction
      5. Angle
   B. Normal chest x-rays
      1. Approach to interpretation
      2. Cardiac silhouette
      3. Lung fields

C. Abnormal chest x-ray interpretation
   1. Endotracheal tube position
   2. Pulmonary artery catheter position
   3. Pneumothorax
   4. Mediastinal shift
   5. Pulmonary edema
   6. Fractures
   7. Cardiomegaly

Unit III-8: Assessment of Abnormal Heart Sounds

Time: 2.5 hours

Student Behavioral Objectives

1. Describe the altered anatomy and physiology that causes selected abnormal heart sounds.
2. Demonstrate competence in assessing abnormal heart sounds.
3. Interpret assessment findings and indicate the implicated cardiovascular abnormalities.

Content

I. Causes of abnormal heart sounds
   A. Altered chamber compliance
   B. Restricted flow
   C. Regurgitant flow

II. Assessing abnormal heart sounds
   A. Auscultation technique
   B. Specific sounds
      1. Gallops
      2. Murmurs
      3. Rubs
      4. Clicks and snaps
   C. Documentation

III. Implications of abnormal sounds
   A. Gallops
   B. Systolic sounds
   C. Diastolic sounds
   D. Rubs

Unit III-9: Cardiovascular Diagnostic and Therapeutic Studies

Time: 2.5 hours

Student Behavioral Objectives

1. Discuss the purposes of selected cardiovascular diagnostic and therapeutic studies.

2. Describe the procedures used in selected diagnostic and therapeutic studies.
3. Explain the nursing care required before, during, and after selected cardiovascular diagnostic studies.

Content

I. Stress testing
   A. Purpose
   B. Method
   C. Complications
   D. Related nursing care
      1. Before procedure
      2. During procedure
      3. After procedure

II. Echocardiography
   A. Purpose
   B. Method
   C. Complications
   D. Related nursing care
      1. Before procedure
      2. During procedure
      3. After procedure

III. Radionuclide imaging
   A. Purpose
   B. Method
   C. Complications
   D. Related nursing care
      1. Before procedure
      2. During procedure
      3. After procedure

IV. Cardiac catheterization and angiography
   A. Purpose
   B. Method
   C. Complications
   D. Related nursing care
      1. Before procedure
      2. During procedure
      3. After procedure

V. Cardiac dysrhythmia mapping
   A. Purpose
   B. Method
   C. Complications
   D. Related nursing care
      1. Before procedure

2. During procedure
3. After procedure

VI. Percutaneous transluminal angioplasty
   A. Purpose
   B. Method
   C. Complications
   D. Related nursing care
      1. Before procedure
      2. During procedure
      3. After procedure

Unit III-10: Twelve-Lead Electrocardiogram Interpretation

Time: 2.5 hours

Student Behavioral Objectives

1. Identify changes in axis on selected ECG recordings.
2. Identify and explain intraventricular block and hemiblock on selected ECG recordings.
3. Distinguish ventricular aberrancy and ectopy on selected ECG recordings.
4. Compare and contrast evolving and extending myocardial infarctions on selected ECG recordings.

Content

I. Axis
   A. Determination
   B. Significance of change

II. Intraventricular block
   A. Complete
   B. Hemiblock

III. Aberrancy and ectopy
   A. Useful clues
   B. Significance

IV. Myocardial infarction
   A. Evolution
   B. Extension

V. Practice analyzing ECG recordings

Unit III-11: Acute Pericarditis and Endocarditis

Time: 2.5 hours

Student Behavioral Objectives

1. Describe the pathophysiology pertinent to acute pericarditis, pericardial tamponade, and endocarditis.
2. Outline a systematic approach to assessment of patients with acute pericarditis, pericardial tamponade, and endocarditis.
3. Discuss methods and rationale for managing patients with acute pericarditis, pericardial tamponade, and endocarditis.
4. Plan and explain nursing care required by patients with acute pericarditis, pericardial tamponade, and endocarditis.

Content

  I. Acute pericarditis
     A. Pathophysiology
     B. Clinical presentation and assessment
     C. Complications
     D. Medical management and nursing care
 II. Pericardial tamponade
     A. Precipitating factors and pathophysiology
     B. Clinical presentation and assessment
     C. Complications
     D. Medical management and nursing care
III. Endocarditis
     A. Precipitating factors and pathophysiology
     B. Clinical presentation and assessment
     C. Complications
     D. Medical management and nursing care
 IV. Case studies
     A. Acute pericarditis
     B. Subacute bacterial endocarditis

Unit III-12: Cardiomyopathies

Time: 2.5 hours

Student Behavioral Objectives

1. Describe the pathophysiology pertinent to selected cardiomyopathies.
2. Outline a systematic approach to assessment of patients with selected cardiomyopathies.
3. Discuss methods and rationale for managing patients with selected cardiomyopathies.
4. Plan and explain nursing care required by patients with selected cardiomyopathies.

Content

  I. Myocardial disease
 II. Cardiomyopathies
     A. Classification
     B. Pathophysiology and precipitating factors
     C. Clinical presentation and assessment
     D. Complications
     E. Medical management and nursing care
III. Case study in idiopathic hypertrophic subaortic stenosis

Unit III-13: Mechanical Cardiac Assist

Time: 2.5 hours

Student Behavioral Objectives

1. Discuss the physiological effects of mechanical cardiac assist devices.
2. Outline a systematic approach to assessment of patients utilizing mechanical cardiac assist devices.
3. Describe the procedures for insertion, operation, and removal of mechanical cardiac assist devices.
4. Plan and explain nursing care required by patients utilizing mechanical cardiac assist devices.

Content

  I. Rotating tourniquets
     A. Indications
     B. Physiological effects
     C. Procedures
        1. Application
        2. Operation
        3. Removal
     D. Nursing care
        1. Routine protocols
        2. Complications
 II. Intraaortic balloon pump (IABP)
     A. Indications
     B. Physiological effects
     C. Procedures
        1. Insertion
        2. Operation
        3. Removal
     D. Nursing care

1. Routine protocols
2. Complications

III. Left ventricular assist
   A. Indications
   B. Physiological effects
   C. Procedures
      1. Insertion
      2. Operation
      3. Removal
   D. Nursing care
      1. Routine protocols
      2. Complications

IV. Artificial heart
   A. Indications
   B. Physiological effects
   C. Procedures
      1. Insertion
      2. Operation
      3. Removal
   D. Nursing care
      1. Routine protocols
      2. Complications

V. Case studies
   A. Intraaortic balloon pump counterpulsation
   B. Left ventricular bypass

Unit III-14: Brain Tumors

Time: 2.5 hours

Student Behavioral Objectives

1. Describe the pathophysiology pertinent to selected brain tumors.
2. Outline a systematic approach to assessing patients with brain tumors.
3. Discuss the methods and rationale used in managing patients with selected brain tumors.
4. Plan and explain nursing care required by patients with selected brain tumors.

Content

I. Classification and terminology of brain tumors

II. Pathophysiology of brain tumors
   A. Gliomas
   B. Meningiomas
   C. Acoustic neuromas
   D. Metastatic tumors

E. Pituitary tumors

III. Clinical manifestations and assessment

IV. Medical management and nursing care
   A. Routine protocols
   B. Complications
      1. Prevention
      2. Intervention

V. Case study in brain tumor

Unit III-15: Central Nervous System Infection

Time: 2.5 hours

Student Behavioral Objectives

1. Describe the precipitating factors and pathophysiology pertinent to selected central nervous system (CNS) infections.
2. Outline a systematic approach to assessing patients with CNS infections.
3. Discuss the methods and rationale used in managing patients with CNS infections.
4. Plan and explain nursing care required by patients with CNS infections.

Content

I. Precipitating factors for CNS infection
   A. Bacterial
   B. Viral

II. Pathophysiology
   A. Meningitis
   B. Encephalitis
   C. Brain abscess

III. Clinical manifestations and assessment

IV. Medical management and nursing care
   A. Routine protocols
   B. Complications
      1. Prevention
      2. Intervention

V. Case study in meningitis

Unit III-16: Multiple Sclerosis

Time: 1.5 hours

Student Behavioral Objectives

1. Describe the precipitating factors and pathophysiology pertinent to multiple sclerosis.

2. Outline a systematic approach to assessing patients with multiple sclerosis.
3. Discuss the methods and rationale used in managing patients with multiple sclerosis.
4. Plan and explain nursing care required by patients with multiple sclerosis.

Content

I. Precipitating Factors

II. Pathophysiology

III. Clinical manifestations and assessment

IV. Medical management and nursing care
   A. Routine protocols
   B. Complications
      1. Prevention
      2. Intervention

V. Case study in multiple sclerosis

Unit III-17: Parkinson's Disease

Time: 1 hour

Student Behavioral Objectives

1. Describe the precipitating factors and pathophysiology pertinent to Parkinson's disease.
2. Outline a systematic approach to assessing patients with Parkinson's disease.
3. Discuss the methods and rationale used in managing patients with Parkinson's disease.
4. Plan and explain nursing care required by patients with Parkinson's disease.

Content

I. Precipitating factors

II. Pathophysiology

III. Clinical manifestations and assessment

IV. Medical management and nursing care
   A. Routine protocols
   B. Complications
      1. Prevention
      2. Intervention

V. Case study in Parkinson's disease

Unit III-18: Spinal Cord Trauma

Time: 2.5 hours

Student Behavioral Objectives

1. Describe the precipitating factors and pathophysiology pertinent to spinal cord trauma and related complications.
2. Outline a systematic approach to assessing patients with spinal cord trauma and related complications.
3. Discuss the methods and rationale used in acute care of patients with spinal cord trauma.
4. Plan and explain acute nursing care required by patients with spinal cord trauma and related complications.

Content

I. Precipitating factors and pathophysiology

II. Complications
   A. Spinal shock
   B. Autonomic dysreflexia

III. Clinical manifestations and assessment

IV. Acute medical management and nursing care
   A. Routine protocols
   B. Complications
      1. Prevention
      2. Intervention

V. Case study in spinal cord trauma

Unit III-19: Guillain-Barré Syndrome

Time: 1.5 hours

Student Behavioral Objectives

1. Describe the precipitating factors and pathophysiology pertinent to Guillain-Barré syndrome.
2. Outline a systematic approach to assessing patients with Guillain-Barré syndrome.
3. Discuss the methods and rationale used in acute care of patients with Guillain-Barré syndrome.
4. Plan and explain acute nursing care required by patients with Guillain-Barré syndrome.

Content

I. Precipitating factors and pathophysiology

II. Clinical manifestations and assessment

III. Acute medical management and nursing care
   A. Routine protocols
   B. Complications

1. Prevention
2. Intervention

IV. Case study in Guillain-Barré syndrome

Unit III-20: Botulism Toxicity

Time: 1 hour

Student Behavioral Objectives

1. Describe the precipitating factors and pathophysiology pertinent to botulism toxicity.
2. Outline a systematic approach to assessing patients with botulism toxicity.
3. Discuss the methods and rationale used in acute care of patients with botulism toxicity.
4. Plan and explain acute nursing care required by patients with botulism toxicity.

Content

I. Precipitating factors and pathophysiology

II. Clinical manifestations and assessment

III. Acute medical management and nursing care
   A. Routine protocol
   B. Complications
      1. Prevention
      2. Intervention

IV. Case study in botulism toxicity

Unit III-21: Myasthenia Gravis

Time: 2.5 hours

Student Behavioral Objectives

1. Describe the precipitating factors and pathophysiology pertinent to myasthenia gravis.
2. Outline a systematic approach to assessing patients with myasthenia gravis.
3. Discuss the methods and rationale used in acute care of patients with myasthenia gravis.
4. Plan and explain acute nursing care required by patients with myasthenia gravis.

Content

I. Precipitating factors and pathophysiology

II. Clinical manifestations and assessment

III. Acute medical management and nursing care
   A. Routine protocols

B. Complications
   1. Prevention
   2. Intervention

IV. Case study in myasthenia gravis

Unit III-22: Perinatal Complications

Time: 2.5 hours

Student Behavioral Objectives

1. Describe the pertinent precipitating factors or pathophysiology for selected complications of childbearing.
2. Explain assessment of a childbearing woman and her fetus as appropriate to selected perinatal complications.
3. Discuss methods of managing selected perinatal complications.
4. Outline nursing care specific to the childbearing woman and her fetus in selected perinatal complications.

Content

I. The pregnant critical care patient
   A. Effect of critical illness on pregnancy
      1. Trauma
      2. Preexisting disease
   B. Assessing the mother
      1. Prenatal
      2. Onset and progress of labor
      3. Postpartum
   C. Assessing the fetus
      1. Fetal heart tones
      2. Fetal movement
      3. Fetal position
   D. Coordinating with obstetrical services
      1. Prenatal
      2. Peripartum
      3. Postpartum

II. Hemorrhage
   A. Precipitating factors
      1. Ectopic pregnancy
      2. Abortion
      3. Placenta previa
      4. Abruptio placenta
      5. Postpartum hemorrhage

III. Pregnancy induced hypertension
  A. Pathophysiology
  B. Clinical manifestations
  C. Medical management and nursing care
    1. Routine protocols
    2. Complications

IV. Case studies
  A. Head injury
  B. Chest trauma requiring surgery
  C. Placenta previa
  D. Abruptio placenta

Unit III-23: Musculoskeletal Injury in Multiple Trauma

Time: 2.5 hours

Student Behavioral Objectives

1. Explain priorities of managing musculoskeletal injury in patients with multiple trauma.
2. Describe the pertinent pathophysiology for musculoskeletal injury and muscle compartment syndrome.
3. Explain assessment of musculoskeletal injury and muscle compartment syndrome.
4. Discuss methods used in managing victims of musculoskeletal injury and muscle compartment syndrome.
5. Outline and explain nursing care required by victims of musculoskeletal injury including those with casts, traction, and muscle compartment syndrome.

Content

I. Pathophysiology
  A. Fracture
  B. Muscle injury and compartment syndrome

II. Clinical manifestations and assessment
  A. Fracture
  B. Muscle injury and compartment syndrome

III. Medical management and nursing care
  A. Priorities of management in multiple trauma
  B. Fracture
    1. Casts
    2. Traction
  C. Muscle injury and compartment syndrome

IV. Case studies

A. Musculoskeletal trauma
B. Multiple trauma with shock

Unit III-24: Burn Injury

Time: 2.5 hours

Student Behavioral Objectives

1. Describe the pathophysiology pertinent to burn injuries.
2. Outline a systematic approach to assessing burn victims.
3. Discuss methods used in resuscitating and managing burn victims.
4. Plan and explain the nursing care required by burn victims.

Content

I. Precipitating factors and clinical manifestations
  A. Thermal burns
  B. Electrical burns
  C. Inhalation injury

II. Immediate care
  A. Assessment
    1. Extent and depth of burn
    2. Associated injuries
  B. Resuscitation
    1. Calculating fluid requirements
    2. Care of the burn injuries
    3. Care of inhalation injury
    4. Care of associated injuries
  C. Triage

III. Pathophysiology
  A. Thermal burns
  B. Electrical burns
  C. Inhalation injury

IV. Medical management and nursing care
  A. Routine protocols
  B. Complications
    1. Prevention
    2. Intervention

V. Case study in burn injury

Unit III-25: Multiple Systems Failure

Time: 2.5 hours

Student Behavioral Objectives

1. Describe the precipitating factors and pathophysiological interrelationships pertinent to multiple systems failure.
2. Outline a systematic approach to assessing clinical manifestations, analyzing data, and establishing significance of findings in patients with multiple systems failure.
3. Discuss prevention and management of multiple systems failure.
4. Explain nursing care required by patients with multiple systems failure.

Content

I. Precipitating factors and pathophysiological interrelationships
   A. Pulmonary dysfunction
   B. Cardiovascular dysfunction
   C. Renal dysfunction
   D. Hepatic dysfunction
   E. Neurological dysfunction

II. Medical management
   A. Prevention
   B. Goals in intervention
   C. Therapy for one system without compromising another
   D. Complications and prognosis

III. Nursing care
   A. Assessing and monitoring
      1. Clinical manifestations
      2. Gathering and analyzing data
      3. Establishing significance of findings
   B. Interventions
      1. Establishing priorities
      2. Coordinating efforts
   C. Psychological care of patient and family

IV. Case study in multiple systems failure

PART III

Case Studies and Vignettes

The patients and situations presented in the following case studies and vignettes have been developed as composites of patients we have seen and cared for during our nursing and teaching careers. Names and facts have been altered so that none of the patients or situations depicts real persons or actual happenings. Any resemblances to real persons or events are coincidental.

The unit numbers given after the title of each case study correspond to the course and unit for which they are appropriate. The first unit given is related to the primary patient problem. The additional units are related to secondary patient problems or information. For example, the three case studies: "Acute Anterolateral MI," "Acute MI," and "Angina Pectoris" each include the notation "Units I-4 and II-2, III-10." This indicates that they can be used in Unit 4, "Angina and Myocardial Infarction" of Course I. The case studies could also be used with Unit 2, "Introduction to Twelve-Lead Electrocardiograms" of Course II, and Unit 10, "Twelve-Lead Electrocardiogram Interpretation" of Course III, because ECGs are included.

Reference laboratory values and an abbreviation key for use with the case studies may be found in Appendixes C and D, respectively. All blood gases are from 4500 feet above sea level and reference values for that altitude are provided in Appendix C. ECGs presented in the case studies are provided courtesy of the Cardiology Department of St. Mark's Hospital in Salt Lake City, Utah.

NOTICE

Nursing and medicine are constantly changing sciences. The authors and publisher have made every effort to ensure that drug and therapy selections and dosages set forth in the text are in accord with current recommendations and practice at the time of publication. In view of continuing research and changes in government regulations, as well as the constant flow of information regarding clinical practice, drug therapy, and dosages, the reader is responsible for checking package inserts and current literature for changes in therapeutic indications, methods, dosage, precautions, and contraindications. This is especially important when the recommended therapeutic agent is a new and/or infrequently used drug, or a drug being used in a new application.

Chapter 6

Cardiovascular Case Studies

ACUTE ANTEROLATERAL MYOCARDIAL INFARCTION

Units I-4 and II-2, III-10

Present Illness

Timothy Milton, a 60-year-old single, white, cab driver, was seen in the emergency department (ED) on April 13 because of a "cramping ache" in his chest. He was admitted to the hospital with a medical diagnosis of acute anterolateral myocardial infarction (MI).

While driving home after work on April 12, Mr. Milton developed aching in his chest and slight, regular palpitations. The ache was still present when he went to bed, when he woke up several times during the night, and when he got up in the morning, seven hours after retiring. He drank some soda water but when the aching did not improve, he came to the ED. In the ED, he complained of chest pain which was accompanied by diaphoresis, slight shortness of breath, and nausea. Relief of pain was obtained with intravenous morphine sulfate. When Mr. Milton was admitted to the Critical Care Unit (CCU), his symptoms were generally unremarkable except for recurrent pain.

Past Medical History

Mr. Milton experienced the usual childhood illnesses without rheumatic fever. As an adult, he had a history of hypertension (documented on discharge from the army at age 45 and when hospitalized two years ago) which had not been treated. Past surgery included a tonsillectomy and adenoidectomy as a child. A cataract was removed from his right eye (OD) two years ago.

His father had died of an MI at age 55. His mother was alive and well although the patient did not know her age. Two brothers, aged 65 and 58, were alive and well. The patient lived alone and worked approxi-mately 72 hours per week as a cab driver. He had been married and divorced twice, the last divorce was three or four years ago. He had no children.

Physical Exam on Admission to the CCU

General: White male in no acute distress. Appeared his stated age. Vital signs were: blood pressure (BP), 140/95 millimeters of mercury (mm Hg), temperature (T), 98.6 °F (37 °C), heart rate (HR), 55 beats per minute, respiratory rate (RR), 18 breaths per minute.

Head, Ears, Eyes, Nose, and Throat (HEENT): Left pupil briskly reactive to light, right pupil had phagotomy scar. Optic fundi: sharp disks with narrow arteries, no hemorrhages or exudates. Ears: left tympanic membrane had diffuse light shadow, right tympanic membrane within normal limits. Oropharynx: edentulous.

Neck: Supple, without masses or thyromegaly.

Chest: Clear to auscultation and percussion.

Cardiovascular system (CV): Point of maximal impulse (PMI) sixth intercostal space (ICS) in the midclavicular line (MCL) of normal intensity and duration, without heaves or thrills. Split S_1, normal S_2; S_4 present but no S_3. Grade 2/6 systolic ejection murmur heard at the base. Jugular venous pulse (JVP) not visualized. Peripheral pulses full, equal, and without bruits.

Abdomen: Without masses, tenderness, or splenomegaly. Liver palpated at rib border. Bowel sounds normal.

Genitourinary system (GU): Circumcised male, testes down.

Musculoskeletal system: Within normal limits.

Neurological status (Neuro): Oriented to person, place, and time. Cranial nerves II–XII grossly intact. Deep tendon reflexes (DTRs) 2+ with symmetrical flexor plantar responses. Motor and sensory grossly normal.

Laboratory Studies

Serum cardiac enzyme levels: Creatine kinase (CK), 164 IU/L; lactic dehydrogenase (LDH), 219 IU/L; serum glutamic-oxaloacetic transaminase (SGOT), 31 IU/L.

Complete blood cell count (CBC), electrolytes, and urinalysis: results within normal limits.

ECG: ST elevation in leads I, aV$_L$, and V$_{1-6}$ (see Figure 6–1.)

Medical Diagnoses

1. Acute anterolateral MI: generally uncomplicated.
2. Organic Heart Disease (OHD): etiology atherosclerotic cardiovascular disease (ASCVD).
3. Hypertension (HTN): untreated for 15 years. Probably essential HTN given age of onset and absence of indication of pheochromocytoma, Cushing's syndrome, hyperaldosteronism, renal bruit, or azotemia.

Management

Vital signs were stable for the remainder of April 13 with a sinus bradycardia of 56/min. Early in the morning of April 14, the patient awoke with nausea and diaphoresis, BP decreased to 90/60 mm Hg with sinus bradycardia of 40/min. Premature ventricular beats (PVBs) were present. The patient was treated with 0.5 milligrams (mg) atropine sulfate intravenously (IV) twice with resolution of signs and symptoms. Heart rate increased to 70/min and BP increased to 130/68 mm Hg. Unifocal PVBs were then treated with a 1 mg/kg bolus of lidocaine (Xylocaine) hydrochloride IV followed by a lidocaine drip at 2 mg/min. Assessment later in the day showed BP, 130/90 mm Hg; T, 98.4 °F (36.9 °C); HR, 60/min; and RR, 18/min. Mr. Milton did not complain of further chest pain. However, he did say that his nausea persisted after meals.

On April 15, the LDH value rose to 310 IU/L; other enzymes remained essentially at the same level as the admission values. The ECG showed ST elevation which was diminishing from previous levels. The lido-

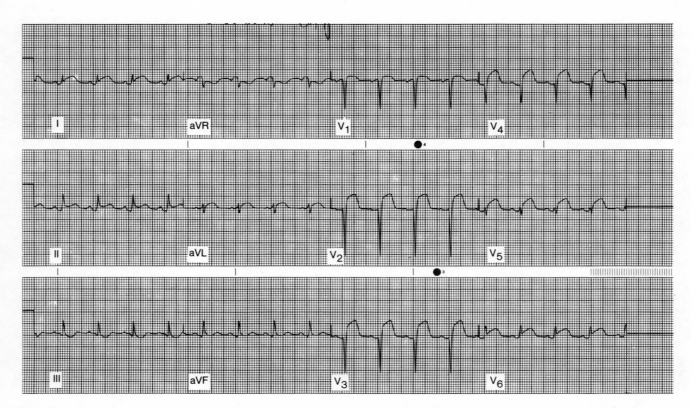

Figure 6–1 Acute Anterolateral Myocardial Infarction. *Source:* Cardiology Department of St. Mark's Hospital, Salt Lake City, Utah.

caine was discontinued without return of the PVBs. Mr. Milton's vital signs remained stable, no further arrhythmias were noted, and his nausea resolved. On April 16 he was moved out of the CCU and started on a cardiac rehabilitation program.

On April 17 a treadmill test was done at 50% effort with negative results. Mr. Milton was discharged on April 27. The medical plan was to continue treatment of his hypertension with propranolol (Inderal). Mr. Milton planned to return to driving his cab but for fewer hours per week.

Study Questions

1. Identify actual and potential nursing problems or nursing diagnoses for Mr. Milton.
2. Complete a nursing care plan for the first 24 hours of hospitalization for an MI patient with dysrhythmias.
3. Outline the patient teaching Mr. Milton should receive his first day in the CCU.
4. What information should be included in a cardiac teaching program?
5. Mr. Milton planned to drive his cab for fewer hours per week. Should he make any other lifestyle changes? Could you explore these with him while he was in the CCU?

ACUTE MYOCARDIAL INFARCTION

Units I-4 and II-2, III-10

Present Illness

Millicent Ingersoll, aged 81 years, was seen in her physician's office for a complaint of pain in the left side of her chest. She stated that the pain seemed to start on the side of her left breast, then spread across and up her chest. The pain had a pressurelike quality and was very intense. After involving her entire chest, the pain began to radiate into her neck giving her a choking sensation. After taking Ms. Ingersoll's history and performing a physical examination and 12-lead ECG, the physician requested that Ms. Ingersoll be admitted to the CCU with an admitting diagnosis of possible acute MI.

Past Medical History

Ms. Ingersoll's past history was relatively benign. In her early 40s she had a cholecystectomy and Billroth II surgery performed. She apparently recovered uneventfully and had no sequellae. When she was exam-

ined a year prior to this admission, her ECG showed frequent PVBs and her systolic BP was 180 mm Hg. Propranolol (Inderal) therapy, 20 mg twice daily (bid), resulted in return of a regular rhythm and systolic BP of 130–140 mm Hg. She did not smoke or use alcohol. Both parents had died of heart disease in old age, her father at 81 and her mother at 72 years of age.

Physical Exam on Admission to the CCU

General: The patient was alert and oriented; appeared pale and uncomfortable; and stated that she did not feel well because of chest discomfort. Vital signs were within normal limits.
HEENT: Unremarkable.
Neck: Without abnormalities.
Chest: Symmetrical excursion. Lungs clear to auscultation and percussion.
CV: Good central and peripheral pulses present. No bruits heard over major arteries. Precordium was quiet and heart sounds were regular and normal without murmur or gallop.
Abdomen: Flat. Midline epigastric scar. Active bowel sounds heard in all four quadrants. Soft, nontender, and without masses or organomegaly.
Pelvic: Exam deferred.
Extremities: Normal without deformity, cyanosis, clubbing or edema.
Neuro: Grossly intact.

Laboratory Studies

CBC and urinalysis: results within normal limits.
Cardiac enzyme levels: results pending.
Chest x-ray: read as normal.
ECG: ST elevation in the inferior leads consistent with acute inferior wall MI (see Figure 6–2.)

Medical Diagnosis

Acute inferior wall MI.

Management

On the second hospital day, Ms. Ingersoll's total serum CK level rose to 546 IU/L with an elevated MB fraction of 35%. Her ECG remained consistent with acute inferior MI and demonstrated the typical evolutionary changes over three days.

Ms. Ingersoll's BP, HR, and cardiac rhythm were stable throughout her hospital stay and she experienced no complications. She was moved from the CCU to progressive care on the third hospital day. She was allowed to sit in a chair on the second hospital day.

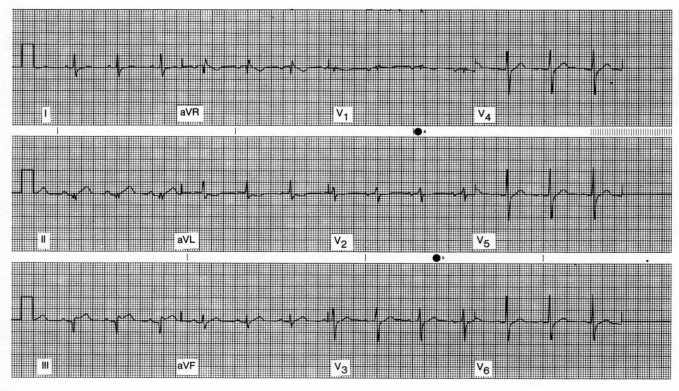

Figure 6–2 Acute Inferior Myocardial Infarction. *Source:* Cardiology Department of St. Mark's Hospital, Salt Lake City, Utah.

She ambulated on the fourth day and continued to increase her activity without difficulty. She was discharged at the end of a nine-day hospital stay. Her medical regimen at discharge included a no-added-salt diet, graded exercise program, and propranolol, 20 mg bid.

Study Questions

1. What findings on the ECG indicate myocardial injury, myocardia ischemia, and myocardial infarction? What ECG change usually persists after the patient has recovered from an MI?
2. Which coronary arteries supply the inferior wall of the heart? Lateral wall? Anterior wall? Posterior wall?
3. What serum enzymes are included in a cardiac enzyme profile?
4. What actual and potential nursing diagnoses or nursing problems should be listed on Ms. Ingersoll's nursing care plan?
5. Complete a nursing care plan for the first 24 hours of hospitalization for a patient with an uncomplicated MI.

ACUTE PERICARDITIS

Units III-11 and III-10

Present Illness

Ivan Pugh, a used-car salesman, aged 35 years, was admitted to the hospital after two days of severe retrosternal distress. Four weeks prior to admission, the patient had had a mild upper respiratory tract infection (URI) which included a nonproductive cough, low-grade fever, and myalgia. He gradually got better over a 14-day period, but continued to feel weak and anorexic, with an intermittent grabbing pain in the retrosternal region. The pain was worse with deep respiration but was unaffected by exertion. One week ago his nonproductive cough worsened, and three days ago he noted an oppressive sensation over the left side of his chest that was partially relieved by sitting upright and leaning forward while resting his elbows on a table. During the past two days, the oppressive sensation prevented him from sleeping or working and was accompanied by dyspnea and orthopnea. He denied hiccups, dysphagia, and hoarseness.

Past Medical History

He had the usual childhood illnesses without sequellae. He had no previous heart disease or other serious illness. His family history was negative for heart disease or other serious illnesses. He smoked one-half pack of cigarettes per day for ten years, drank alcohol occasionally, exercised regularly, and had never been overweight.

Physical Exam on Admission to the CCU

General: Patient was well-developed, sat up with legs dangling, and leaned forward with arms resting on bedside table. He was pale, anxious, and in moderate distress. Vital signs were: BP, 108/86 mm Hg (decreased by 16–18 mm Hg with inspiration); T, 97.9 °F (36.6 °C); HR, 90/min with regular rhythm; RR, 22/min.
Skin: Cool and dry.
HEENT: Without abnormalities.
Neck: Supple. Hepatojugular reflux present while supine. No jugular venous distention (JVD) while sitting upright. No thyroid enlargement.
Chest: Symmetrical excursion. Lungs dull to percussion in the left base. Bronchial breath sounds heard at left lung base and radiated upward to the inferior margin of the left scapula.
CV: Peripheral pulses present, equal, and weak. No bruits heard over major arteries. Precordium quiet with PMI barely palpated at fifth ICS of left MCL. Heart sounds barely audible. Pericardial friction rub heard at left sternal border.
Abdomen: Flat with diminished bowel sounds heard in all quadrants. Soft, nontender, and without masses. Inferior liver border palpated one finger breadth below the costal margin.
GU: Normal male.
Neuro: Within normal limits.

Laboratory Studies

Blood chemistry levels: serum sodium (Na), 143 mEq/L; serum potassium (K), 4.2 mEq/L; serum chloride (Cl), 104 mEq/L; carbon dioxide (CO_2), 28 mmol/L; blood glucose, 85 mg/dL; blood urea nitrogen (BUN), 18 mg/dL; uric acid, 7.8 mg/dL; serum cholesterol, 155 mg/dL; serum triglyceride, 88 mg/dL; SGOT, 108 IU/L, serum glutamic-pyruvic transaminase (SGPT), 65 IU/L; LDH, 380 IU/L.
Hematology: hemoglobin (Hgb), 14.4 g/dL; hematocrit (Hct), 43%; white blood cell count (WBC), 4.8 × 10^9/L with normal differential; prothrombin time

(PT), within normal limits. Erythrocyte sedimentation rate (ESR), 44 mm/hr (Westergren method).
ECG: normal sinus rhythm with ST-T wave changes indicative of acute pericarditis. (See Figure 6–3.)

Medical Diagnosis

Idiopathic pericarditis.

Management

Mr. Pugh was admitted to the CCU for bed rest and cardiac monitoring. The physician prescribed nonsteroidal antiinflammatory medication. Mr. Pugh's pulsus paradoxus and his pain gradually diminished. His cardiac rhythm showed a few PVBs during the first 24 hours. After several days, he was transferred out of the CCU. He was discharged seven days after admission without medication or restriction.

Study Questions

1. Describe the technique of determining pulsus paradoxus. What is the importance of pulsus paradoxus?
2. How does one differentiate a pericardial friction rub from a pleural friction rub?
3. How does pericardial effusion alter cardiac hemodynamics?
4. Why are nonsteroidal antiinflammatory medications included in the medical management for pericarditis?
5. Plan nursing care for Mr. Pugh. Include actual and potential nursing problems or nursing diagnoses, outcomes, and actions in the plan.

ANGINA PECTORIS

Units I-4 and II-2, III-10

Present Illness

Adam Peterson was a newspaper editor aged 42 years who came to the ED complaining of chest pain radiating into both arms, accompanied by diaphoresis and shortness of breath. Mr. Peterson had been having episodes of transient substernal and shoulder pain over the past week. He was admitted to the CCU with a medical diagnosis of chest pain, rule out MI.

Past Medical History

Mr. Peterson was being treated for hypertension and was currently taking metoprolol tartrate (Lopressor),

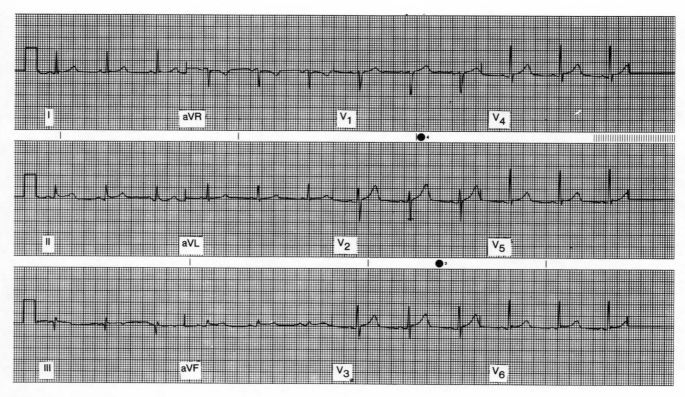

Figure 6–3 Acute Pericarditis. *Source:* Cardiology Department of St. Mark's Hospital, Salt Lake City, Utah.

100 mg bid. He did not exercise, was overweight, had smoked a pack of cigarettes daily for 20 years, and was under considerable job stress.

Physical Exam on Admission to the CCU

General: Well-developed, overweight, anxious, diaphoretic, white male. Complaining of pain in both arms. Vital signs were: BP, 180/100 mm Hg; T, 98.6 °F (37 °C); HR, 95/min; RR, 20/min.

HEENT: Normocephalic. Pupils: equal, round, reactive to light and accommodation (PERRLA). Extraocular movements (EOMs) intact.

Neck: Midline trachea. Thyroid not palpable.

Chest: Symmetrical. Lungs clear to auscultation and percussion.

Back: Straight, no CVA tenderness.

CV: Sinus rhythm; no rubs, murmurs, or gallops.

Abdomen: Protuberant. Active bowel sounds. Soft, nontender, without masses or organ enlargement.

GU: Normal male. Rectal exam deferred.

Extremities: Peripheral pulses present, equal, and strong. Full range of motion (ROM).

Neuro: Grossly intact.

Laboratory Studies

CBC and urinalysis: results within normal limits.

Cardiac isoenzyme levels: at upper limits of normal range.

ECG: ST segment depression and T wave inversion consistent with subendocardial ischemia in the inferior and anterior leads. An incomplete left bundle branch block was also noted. (See Figure 6–4.)

Medical Diagnoses

1. Angina pectoris.
2. Subendocardial ischemia.

Management

Mr. Peterson stayed in the CCU for three days. His serum cardiac enzyme levels and ECGs confirmed a diagnosis of subendocardial ischemia rather than myocardial infarction.

Coronary artery angiography was done to clarify his coronary artery anatomy. Angiography findings indicated 35–40% occlusion of the left anterior descending

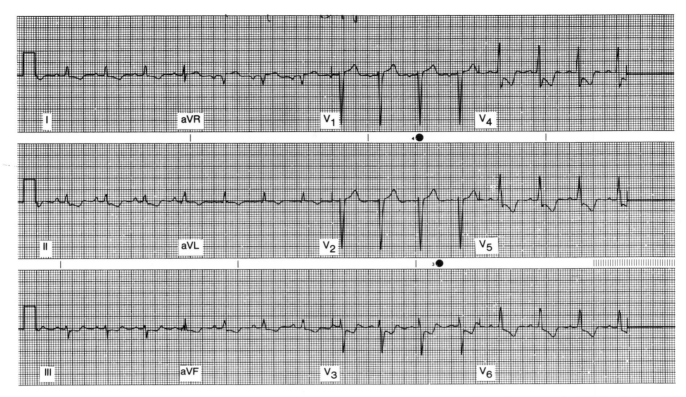

Figure 6–4 Subendocardial Ischemia, Incomplete Left Bundle Branch Block. *Source:* Cardiology Department of St. Mark's Hospital, Salt Lake City, Utah.

artery. The possibility of coronary artery vasospasm was not excluded because no ergonovine trial was done. Repeat evaluation for coronary artery bypass surgery was planned for the future with conservative medical treatment in the interim.

Mr. Peterson's discharge medications included: digoxin (Lanoxin), 0.25 mg daily; controlled release nitroglycerin (Nitro-Bid), 6.5 mg every 12 hours; nifedipine (Procardia), 10 mg three times daily (tid); and sublingual nitroglycerin (Nitrostat), 0.4 mg as needed for chest pain.

Study Questions

1. What mechanism is thought to explain the typical distribution of cardiac chest pain?
2. Describe the signs and symptoms of digoxin toxicity. What nursing intervention is indicated if the patient develops these symptoms?
3. What is meant by "conservative medical treatment" for angina pectoris?
4. What information should be included in patient

teaching about medications while the patient is in the CCU? Before discharge?
5. During his stay in the CCU, Mr. Peterson asked if he should change his lifestyle since he really did not have a "heart attack." How would you respond?
6. What information should be reported to the progressive care unit staff when a patient with angina pectoris is transferred from the CCU?

AORTIC STENOSIS WITH VALVE REPLACEMENT

Units I-9 and II-2, III-10

Present Illness

Vincent Roberts, aged 42 years, was admitted to the hospital on June 23 for cardiac surgery. Surgical replacement of his aortic valve was planned for June 25.

Early in the year, in January, he had begun to feel ill much of the time. Symptoms that led him to consult his physician in February were leg swelling, dyspnea when walking briskly or up stairs, and orthopnea. He was hospitalized in February for 11 days during which his congestive heart failure (CHF) improved with diuretics and digitalis. Mr. Roberts hoped he would feel better soon and so refused referral to a cardiologist.

At home, Mr. Roberts continued to be symptomatic. After four weeks he agreed to see a cardiologist who admitted him to the hospital in March for cardiac catheterization. Following the cardiac catheterization, cardiac surgery with valve replacement was recommended and Mr. Roberts agreed to the procedure. However, the surgery had to be delayed because Mr. Roberts became ill with an upper respiratory infection. After a lengthy convalescence, Mr. Roberts' health was judged well enough to proceed with the surgery.

At the time of admission his medications were digoxin, 0.5 mg daily, and chlorthalidone (Hygroton), 50 mg daily. He tried to follow a 1500-mg salt-restricted diet.

Past Medical History

Mr. Roberts was noted to have a systolic cardiac murmur during a physical examination in late adolescence. Because he had no symptoms, he was inducted into the army and served during World War II as a supply clerk. Following the war he had a tonsillectomy and removal of impacted wisdom teeth, complicated by osteomyelitis of the jaw. He also had a bilateral inguinal herniorrhaphy. Mr. Roberts denied having rheumatic fever or remembering having to stay in bed for a long period of time during his childhood.

Mr. Roberts did not know much about his family medical history. He was able to report that his parents died in old age. He stated that he had one brother, age 55, with "heart trouble" and a sister, age 52, with "lung trouble."

Mr. Roberts was employed in a downtown highrise apartment building as a night janitor. He lived with his wife, aged 54 years, and son, aged 14 years, in the apartment building. He had missed very few days of work during the past 15 years.

Mr. Roberts had smoked about two packs of cigarettes per day for the past 34 years. When he became ill with the upper respiratory infection he began to fear that he would develop emphysema. With encouragement from his wife and physician he stopped smoking in April. Since then, his coughing and expectoration decreased greatly.

Physical Exam on Admission for Cardiac Surgery

General: Middle-aged man in no acute distress but appearing chronically ill. Ht, 5 ft, 7 in; wt, 90 kg (decreased from 102.7 kg on previous admission). Vital signs were BP, 140/85 mm Hg; T, 98.6 °F (37 °C); HR, 80/min and irregular; RR, 18/min.

HEENT: Normocephalic. PERRLA. EOMs intact.

Neck: Midline trachea. Thyroid not palpable. JVD to 10 cm while sitting up 30 degrees.

Chest: Increased anteroposterior diameter. Symmetrical excursion with decreased movement of diaphragm. Breath sounds distant with scattered rhonchi.

CV: Atrial fibrillation with moderate ventricular response. Grade 4/6 systolic ejection murmur heard at the second right intercostal space with radiation to the right carotid area. Also, a grade 2/6 holosystolic murmur heard at the apex which radiated to the lower left sternal border and left axilla.

Back: Slight kyphosis, no costovertebral angle (CVA) tenderness.

Abdomen: Rounded. Active bowel sounds in all quadrants. Soft, nontender, without masses or splenomegaly. Liver enlarged to 2 cm below the right costal margin.

GU: Normal male. Rectal exam deferred.

Extremities: Peripheral pulses present, equal, and strong. Full ROM.

Neuro: Grossly intact.

Laboratory Studies

CBC, serum electrolytes, blood glucose, BUN, and urinalysis: results within normal limits.

Serum triglycerides level: 110 mg/dL.

Serum cholesterol level: 276 mg/dL.

Liver function tests: results were at upper limits of normal range.

Chest x-ray: consistent with aortic valve disease.

ECG: atrial fibrillation with left ventricular hypertrophy and secondary ST segment and T wave changes. (See Figure 6–5.)

Cardiac catheterization results showed the following *resting* data:

Cardiac output	4.4 L/min
Cardiac index	2.2 L/min/m²
Right atrial pressure (RAP)	10 mm Hg
Right ventricular pressure (RVP)	38/8 mm Hg
Pulmonary artery pressure (PAP)	35/20 mm Hg
Pulmonary capillary wedge pressure (PCWP)	15 mm Hg
Left ventricular pressure (LVP)	195/10–15 mm Hg
Aortic pressure (AP)	125/70 mm Hg
Peak systolic gradient	70 mm Hg

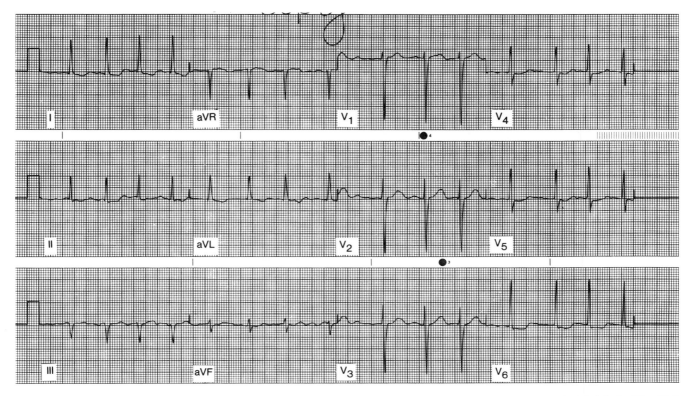

Figure 6–5 Left Ventricular Hypertrophy. Atrial Fibrillation. *Source:* Cardiology Department of St. Mark's Hospital, Salt Lake City, Utah.

Mean aortic valve gradient	35 mm Hg
Calculated aortic valve area	0.67 cm²

The results of the cardiac catheterization were interpreted as significant aortic stenosis without CAD.

Medical Diagnoses

1. Atrial fibrillation.
2. Probable inactive rheumatic heart disease.
3. Aortic stenosis.
4. Congestive heart failure.

Management

Mr. Roberts did very well following his cardiac valve replacement surgery. He was returned to the critical care unit (CCU) from surgery with an endotracheal tube and on a continuous mechanical ventilator. He was successfully weaned from the ventilator and extubated in the evening on the day of surgery. The nurses were careful to medicate him adequately for pain. Mr. Roberts was very cooperative when the nurses helped him to cough and deep breathe. His chest tube drainage and urine output were within the expected ranges. His vital signs also remained stable and within the expected ranges through the first postoperative night.

In the morning, the nurse noted that Mr. Roberts was in a normal sinus rhythm; his sternal dressing was intact, clean, and dry. The chest tubes were secure, patent, and draining well. Two nurses helped him to sit up in bed and dangle his legs over the side. Mr. Roberts experienced a moment of dizziness but his heart rate and blood pressure changed only 10 points. Within two minutes Mr. Roberts reported that he was again clear headed and ready to eat breakfast.

Mr. Roberts' recovery continued to be uneventful and was discharged ten days after admission. He was able to return full time to his duties at the apartment building by the end of the summer.

Study Questions

1. What hemodynamic changes does aortic stenosis cause?
2. Draw a set of cardiac chamber pressure curves that illustrate the pressure gradient across the aortic valve.

3. Why do patients with aortic stenosis sometimes develop angina pectoris although their coronary arteries are not narrowed by plaque formation?
4. What is meant by "fixed cardiac output" in reference to aortic stenosis? What implications would this have to a patient who engages in strenuous physical activity?
5. Outline the preoperative and postoperative nursing care required by patients undergoing cardiac valve replacement.

ARTIFICIAL CARDIAC PACEMAKER

Units I-7 and II-2, III-10

Present Illness

Gertie O'Brien, aged 79 years, was seen in the ED for a syncopal episode. Ms. O'Brien had been in relatively good health until she experienced a syncopal episode around 1600 hours. There was appropriate recovery, and she was able to eat the evening meal. After dinner she had another syncopal attack which lasted longer than the first. Her neighbor called a cab, which delivered her to the ED. Following evaluation in the ED, Ms. O'Brien was admitted to the CCU for observation.

Past Medical History

Ms. O'Brien was evaluated two months previous to this admission for a disorder of cardiac rhythm. At that time, she was noted to have episodes of ventricular tachycardia. She was treated with disopyramide phosphate (Norpace), 100 mg every 8 hours (q8h), and digoxin (Lanoxin), 0.125 mg daily. Ms. O'Brien was to return to the clinic one month after beginning the regimen; however, she did not keep her clinic appointment.

Physical Exam on Admission

General: Slightly built with weight proportional to height. Vital signs were: BP, 104/56 mm Hg; T, 98.6 °F (37 °C); HR, 50/min, regular; RR 16/min.
HEENT: Unremarkable.
Neck: Normal on examination. Jugular veins slightly distended in the supine position.
Chest: Lungs and heart clear to inspection, percussion, palpation, and auscultation.
Abdomen: Scaphoid. Active bowel sounds in all quadrants. No tenderness, organomegaly, or masses.

Extremities: Peripheral pulses present, equal, and moderate. No deformities, edema, or varices noted.
Skin: Warty excrescences (growths) on face and back.
Neuro: Oriented to person, time, and place. Cranial nerves II–XII grossly intact. DTRs symmetrical, 1+ in upper extremities, 2+ in lower extremities.

Laboratory Studies

CBC and urinalysis: results within normal limits.
Serum electrolyte levels: K, 6.0 mEq/L; all others in normal range.
Serum digoxin level: results pending.
Chest x-ray: showed scattered califications in the lung fields but was unchanged from previous films.
ECG: sinus bradycardia with rate of 57 and complete right bundle branch block. (See Figure 6–6.)

Medical Diagnosis

Cardiac rhythm disturbance.

Management

During the night, Ms. O'Brien had short episodes of ventricular tachycardia with return to sinus bradycardia. In the early morning, one PVB did produce the R-on-T phenomenon and the patient developed coarse ventricular fibrillation. The nursing staff quickly defibrillated her. Sinus bradycardia returned at a rate of 38/min. Atropine sulfate, 0.5 mg, was given twice with no increase in the cardiac rate.

Subsequently, her BP and level of consciousness began to decrease. The physician elected to insert a temporary transvenous pacemaker. Following establishment of cardiac pacing, Ms. O'Brien's blood pressure returned to previous levels and she became alert and oriented once again. Her ECG showed 100% ventricular paced rhythm with a rate of 72/min. (See Figure 6–7.)

Study Questions

1. How does a cardiac pacemaker work?
2. With regard to cardiac pacing, what is the difference between unipolar and bipolar; capturing and sensing; temporary and permanent; ventricular and atrial pacing?
3. How does an AV sequential pacemaker work? What is the advantage of this pacing mode over ventricular pacing?
4. In assessing the pacemaker function, what obser-

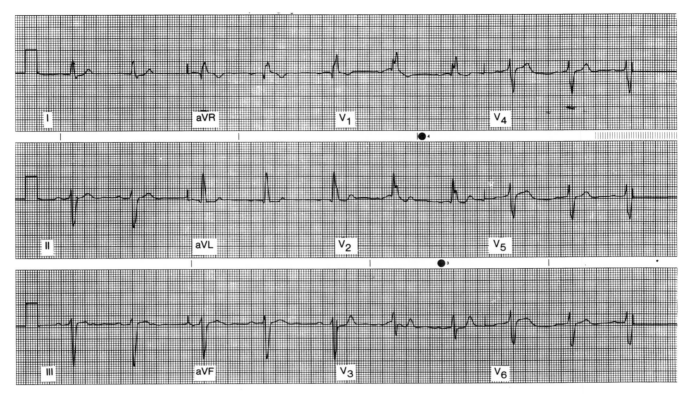

Figure 6–6 Sinus Bradycardia with Complete Right Bundle Branch Block. *Source:* Cardiology Department of St. Mark's Hospital, Salt Lake City, Utah.

vations indicate correct sensing? Incorrect sensing? Correct capture? Lack of capture?

5. Why is it important to have the patient change positions while assessing the pacemaker function?

CARDIAC DYSRHYTHMIA
Units I-7 and II-2, III-10

Present Illness

Francis Zanetti, aged 73 years, was admitted to the CCU following two hours of crushing chest pain and evaluation in the ED.

Past Medical History

Mr. Zanetti had angina for 30 years which he managed with two to five sublingual nitroglycerin (Nitrostat) tablets per day. He had two previous MIs, one six years ago at age 67, and one fifteen years ago at age 58. He was diagnosed as having adult onset diabetes melli-

tus (AODM) at age 55 which he has managed by dietary restriction of carbohydrates.

Family history was positive for CAD, CHF, diabetes, MI, and tuberculosis; negative for alcoholism and renal disease.

Mr. Zanetti had been living alone in a downtown hotel for the past three years following his wife's death. He saw his children and grandchildren once a year at Christmas. Mr. Zanetti spent most of his time watching out of his tenth floor window.

Physical Exam on Admission

General: Pleasant elderly man with dyspnea and in moderate distress. Vital signs were: BP, 100/50 mm Hg; T, 97 °F (36.1 °C); HR, 110/min; RR, 28/min. Estimated wt, 70 kg.
HEENT: Within normal limits.
Neck: Jugular venous distention while sitting up 30 degrees.
Chest: Symmetrical excursion. Lungs had fine rales in bases.

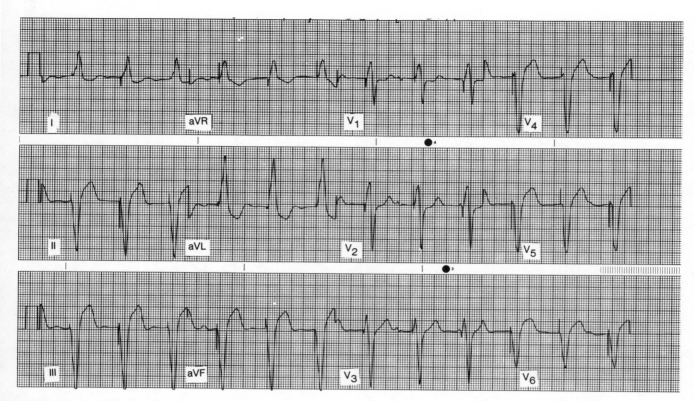

Figure 6–7 Artificially Paced Ventricular Rhythm. *Source:* Cardiology Department of St. Mark's Hospital, Salt Lake City, Utah.

CV: Sinus tachycardia with frequent multifocal PVBs. Irregular rhythm to heart sounds which included a summation gallop but no rub or murmur.

Extremities: 1+ nonpitting edema. Pulses present, weak, and thready.

Neuro: Oriented to person, place, and time, but responded slowly to questions. Cranial nerves II–XII grossly intact. DTRs 1+ and symmetrical.

Laboratory Studies

Arterial blood gases (ABGs) on oxygen (O_2) at 4 L/min per nasal cannula: carbon monoxide saturation (CO sat), 2.5%; oxygen saturation (O_2 sat), 85.6%; partial pressure of oxygen (Po_2), 52 torr; partial pressure of carbon dioxide (Pco_2), 30 torr; bicarbonate (HCO_3), 19.8 mEq/L; pH 7.42; base excess −2.6; O_2 content 19.8%; Hgb 16.8 g/dL.

Blood chemistry levels: Na, 140 mEq/L; K, 5 mEq/L; Cl, 105 mEq/L; CO_2, 24 mmol/L; glucose, 183 mg/dL; BUN, 17 mg/dL; total CK, 18 IU/L; LDH, 226 IU/L; SGOT, 48 IU/L.

Hematology: WBC, 11.2×10^9/L; red blood cell (RBC) count, 5.1×10^{12}/L; Hgb, 17.0 g/dL; Hct, 51.7%.

Coagulation: PT, 11.5 sec; partial thromboplastin time (PTT), 33.1 sec.

ECG: Normal sinus rhythm with frequent multifocal PVBs. ST segment elevation and T wave inversion in leads II, III, aV_F that had developed since the previous tracing. Q waves in leads I and aV_L and poor R wave progression in leads V_{1-4} were also present in the previous tracing.

Medical Diagnoses

1. CAD.
2. Previous high lateral and anterior MIs.
3. Possible acute inferior MI.

Management

Shortly after he arrived in the CCU, Mr. Zanetti developed ventricular tachycardia. His BP was 100/50

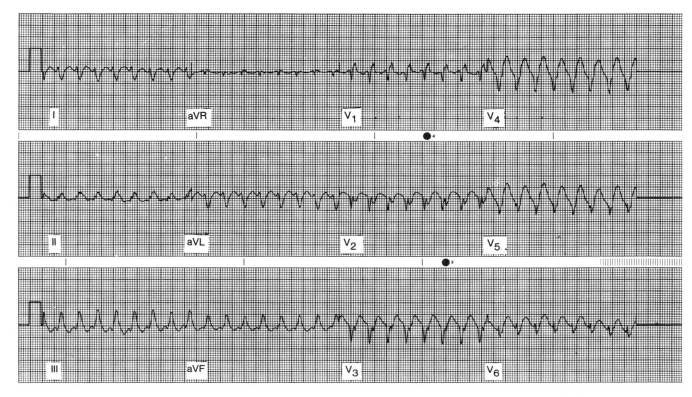

Figure 6-8 Ventricular Tachycardia. *Source:* Cardiology Department of St. Mark's Hospital, Salt Lake City, Utah.

mm Hg and he remained conscious. A 70-mg bolus of lidocaine (Xylocaine) hydrochloride was given IV followed by a continuous infusion of 4 mg/min. The continuous infusion was prepared with 2 g lidocaine in 500 mL of 5% dextrose in water (D5W). After 30 minutes the ventricular tachycardia was still present. (See Figure 6-8.)

Mr. Zanetti's blood pressure and level of consciousness began to decrease. Successful synchronized cardioversion was carried out after 10 mg diazepam (Valium) was administered IV. Subsequent PVBs were suppressed with procainamide (Pronestyl) hydrochloride as a continuous infusion at 3 mg/min. Topical sustained release nitroglycerin (Nitrol) ointment was added to the drug regimen.

Serial cardiac enzymes showed no elevations indicating MI. Serial ECGs demonstrated resolution of the ST-T wave changes in the inferior leads without development of Q waves. On the third hospital day, the patient was started on oral procainamide and the infusion rate was gradually decreased.

The patient was transferred out of the CCU on the fifth hospital day and discharged on the seventh hospital day. Discharge medications were procainamide and cutaneous sustained release nitroglycerin (Transderm-Nitro). Instructions included a graded exercise program.

Study Questions

1. What assessment findings did the nurse consider in deciding whether to administer lidocaine hydrochloride or carry out cardioversion at the onset of Mr. Zanetti's ventricular tachycardia?
2. What changes in Mr. Zanetti's condition indicated the need for cardioversion?
3. What is the difference between synchronized cardioversion and defibrillation? When is each used?
4. The continuous lidocaine infusion was prepared with 2 g lidocaine in 500 mL of D5W. How many milliliters per hour should the patient receive in order to achieve the 3 mg/min dose?
5. What nursing outcomes must be achieved in the CCU before the patient can be transferred to the

progressive care unit? What nursing activities will aid in meeting the outcome criteria?

CARDIAC FAILURE AND PULMONARY EDEMA

Units I-6 and II-2, III-10, III-13

Present Illness

Ralph Adams, aged 44 years, was brought to the ED by ambulance after collapsing at the airport prior to departing on a business trip. He had eaten a large business lunch before going to the airport. During the assessment and initiation of treatment in the ED, he stated that he needed to be on the airplane to attend to his business. After several short bursts of ventricular tachycardia which caused him to become nauseated and short of breath, he agreed to be admitted to the CCU only until he felt better. Three hours after arrival in the ED he was transferred to the CCU. This was his first hospital admission.

Past Medical History

About three years ago, the patient noted chest discomfort unrelated to exertion which he dismissed with various rationalizations. He tried without success to relieve the chest discomfort with various over-the-counter antacids. Two years ago, an ECG done during a routine physical exam required by his employer was interpreted as normal with low voltage T waves in the precordial leads.

Family history was positive for early CAD among the men and adult onset diabetes mellitus among the women. There were no family members with renal disease, tuberculosis, or cancer.

The patient was a vice-president for a large advertising agency. His job involved frequent travel and entertainment of clients. He drank alcohol as part of "doing business." This usually consisted of a martini at lunch and two whiskey sours before dinner. He smoked occasionally, especially while working on important business deals. He engaged in no regular exercise program but did play racquetball occasionally as part of his business-related social life. Mr. Adams and his wife owned their own home in an affluent neighborhood. Their three teenaged children attended private schools. Their lifestyle included entertaining at home and at their country club.

Physical Exam on Admission to the CCU

General: Pale, gray, diaphoretic, dyspneic man. Ht, 5 ft, 10 in; wt, 86 kg (14 kg overweight for his height). Vital signs were: BP, 98/62 mm Hg; T, 98.6 °F (37 °C); HR, 90/min, with regular irregular rhythm; RR, 24/min.
Skin: Moist, cool, dusky.
HEENT: Normal findings.
Neck: Supple. Nodes and thyroid not palpable. JVD to angle of jaw while supine.
Chest: Symmetrical excursion. Moist rales and rhonchi scattered throughout both lung fields. Heart sounds distant with summation gallop and without rubs or murmurs. Normal sinus rhythm with frequent PVBs.
Abdomen: Obese. Bowel sounds present in all quadrants. Not tender to palpation. No masses or organomegaly appreciated.
GU: Normal male. Rectal deferred.
Extremities: Pulses present and equally moderate in upper extremities and femoral arteries. Faint in lower extremities below the groin.
Neuro: Oriented to person, place, and time. Cranial nerves II–XII grossly intact. DTRs symmetrical and 2+ with plantar flexion.

Laboratory Studies

Blood chemistry levels: Na, 140 mEq/L; K, 4.3 mEq/L; Cl, 109 mEq/L; CO_2, 23 mmol/L; glucose, 112 mg/dL; BUN, 17 mg/dL; creatinine, 1.2 mg/dL; uric acid, 6.1 mg/dL; LDH, 237 IU/L; SGOT, 25 IU/L; total CK, 685 IU/dL; CK from skeletal and cardiac muscle (CK-MM), 529 IU/L; CK from cardiac muscle (CK-MB), 126 IU/L; CK from brain and kidney (CK-BB), 0 IU/L; total bilirubin, 0.5 mg/dL; cholesterol, 220 mg/dL.

A second set of serum enzymes showed the following values: LDH, 298 IU/L; SGOT, 192 IU/L; gamma glutamyl transpeptidase (GGTP), 26 IU/L.

Urinalysis: straw-colored; specific gravity, 1.009; pH 6; rare WBC per high power field (hpf).

Hematology: RBC, 4.84×10^{12}/L; Hgb, 16.4 g/dL; Hct, 47.2%; mean corpuscle volume (MCV), 97.5 μmg^3; mean cell hemoglobin (MCH), 34.0 pg; mean cell hemoglobin concentration (MCHC), 34.8%; WBC, 5.1×10^9/L.

WBC differential: band neutrophils (bands), 2%; segmented neutrophils (segs), 62%; lymphocytes (lymphs), 28%; monocytes (monos), 6%; eosinophils (eos), 2%; and adequate platelets.

ABGs	On room air	On O_2, 4 L/min by cannula
pH	7.45	7.43
pCO_2 (torr)	32	34
pO_2 (torr)	63	95
O_2 sat (%)	85.4	90.3
Base excess (mEq/L)	−0.1	−0.2
HCO_3 (mEq/L)	22.3	22.7
CO sat (%)	9.9	7.7
Hbg (g/dL)	15.2	15.3
O_2 content (vol %)	17.8	19.0

ECG: sinus tachycardia with frequent PVBs. Atrial and ventricular rate, 114/min; PR interval, 0.18 sec; QRS duration, 0.08 sec; normal axis. R waves absent in leads V_{1-4}. ST segment elevation in leads V_{1-4}, II, III, and aV_F. ST segment depression in aV_L. (See Figure 6–9.) Interpretation: acute anterior and inferior wall MI.

Medical Diagnosis

Acute anterior and inferior MI with early cardiogenic shock.

Management

Oxygen at 4 L/min was administered via a nasal cannula in the ED. Mr. Adams was given lidocaine (Xylocaine) hydrochloride, 100 mg, as a bolus IV, in the ED and a lidocaine infusion was started at 2 mg/min. On arrival in the CCU, he was noted to have frequent PVBs as well as one salvo of five ectopic ventricular beats. A 0.5 mg/kg bolus of lidocaine was given IV and the infusion rate was increased to 4 mg/min. The nurses instructed the patient to notify them if he developed numbness or tingling, chest pain, light headedness, or other discomfort. A portable chest x-ray was done shortly after Mr. Adams arrived in the CCU which showed pulmonary vascular congestion. Furosemide (Lasix), 20 mg, was administered IV and an indwelling urinary catheter was inserted and connected to a urinemeter.

One hour after arrival in the CCU, Mr. Adams' BP was noted to be barely audible at 60/35 mm Hg. An arterial line was placed in the left radial artery. A pulmonary artery thermodilution catheter was placed via

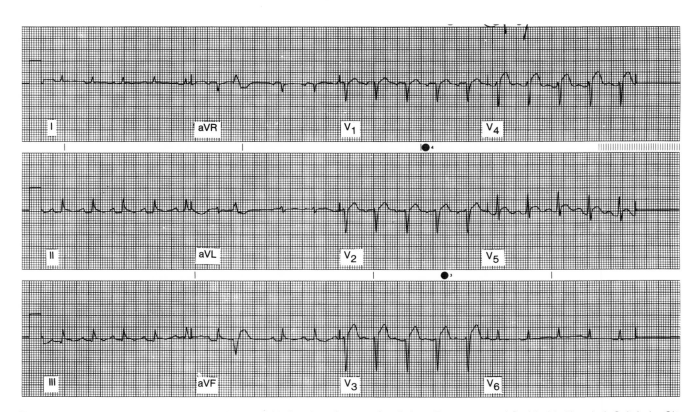

Figure 6–9 Acute Anterior and Inferior Myocardial Infarction. *Source:* Cardiology Department of St. Mark's Hospital, Salt Lake City, Utah.

the left subclavian artery through an introducer with a side port for infusion.

Initial readings from the pulmonary artery catheter were:

Arterial pressure	80/60 mm Hg, mean 73 mm Hg
RAP	mean 15 mm Hg
Right ventricle (RV) pressure	35/10 mm Hg
PAP	35/18 mm Hg, mean 29 mm Hg
Pulmonary capillary wedge pressure (PCWP)	mean 25 mm Hg
Cardiac output (Qt)	2.8 L/min

An infusion of dopamine hydrochloride (Intropin), 400 mg in 500 mL D5W, was begun at 5 μg/kg/min. Morphine sulfate was titrated intravenously to reduce the patient's pain, anxiety, and dyspnea. Mr. Adams continued to have 10–15 PVBs per minute although the lidocaine infusion continued at 4 mg/min. The oxygen was changed to 15 L/min by mask. Sodium nitroprusside (Nipride) was cautiously administered as an IV infusion of 50 mg in 250 mL D5W at 0.5 μg/kg/min. The patient's BP and cardiac output began to improve.

Study Questions

1. Identify and list Mr. Adams' risk factors for developing atherosclerosis.
2. What signs and symptoms of cardiac failure would be expected to accompany Mr. Adams' low BP?
3. Explain the rationale and method for administering dopamine hydrochloride and sodium nitroprusside simultaneously.
4. What nursing outcomes would be desirable for this patient's nursing diagnoses?
   a. Cardiac output, alterations in: decreased
   b. Gas exchange, impaired
   c. Comfort, alterations in: pain
   d. Anxiety
5. What interventions are needed to accomplish the outcomes identified above?
6. What interventions would be appropriate if Mr. Adams continues to state that he wishes to leave the hospital?

CORONARY ARTERY BYPASS SURGERY

Units I-9 and II-2, III-10

Present Illness

Claudia West, aged 63 years, had a history of severe CAD and was admitted with a chief complaint of increasing difficulty with angina pectoris that was not controlled with her current medications.

Past Medical History

Six years ago Ms. West had a coronary artery bypass procedure done. In the past two years she was admitted several times with unstable angina. Angiograms were done five and three years ago.

Coronary angiography one month ago demonstrated complete occlusion of the left coronary artery mainstem with previous grafts to the left anterior descending and circumflex branches; partial occlusion of the left anterior descending graft; complete occlusion of the circumflex graft; total occlusion of the obtuse marginal branch; and partial occlusion of the right coronary artery. The total occlusion of the obtuse marginal branch and partial occlusion of the right coronary artery had developed since the previous angiograms.

Ms. West experienced a significant hypotensive episode following the angiogram which was successfully treated with dopamine hydrochloride (Intropin) infusion, verapamil (Calan), and nitroglycerin (Nitrol) ointment.

Ms. West's father died at age 70 years of CAD, her mother died at age 91 years of hypertension and a stroke, and one brother died at age 60 of heart disease and diabetes. Another brother was living, aged 70 years, and had peripheral vascular disease that required lower extremity vascular bypass surgery. Two siblings were healthy. Ms. West did not smoke and drank very little alcohol.

Physical Exam on Admission

General: Pale, gray-haired, somewhat sour-faced but otherwise pleasant and alert elderly woman lying in bed with a nasal oxygen cannula in place. Ht, 5 ft 3 in; wt, 146 lb. Vital signs were: BP, 140/70 mm Hg; T, 98.6 °F (37 °C); HR, 76/min, with regular rhythm; RR, 20/min.

HEENT: Normocephalic. Ears unremarkable. PEERLA. Corneas clear and sclera white. EOMs intact.

Neck: Supple. Nodes and thyroid not palpable. JVD to angle of jaw while supine. Carotid pulses equal and without bruits.

Chest: Symmetrical excursion. Lungs clear to auscultation and percussion. Heart sounds normal without gallops, rubs, or murmurs. Normal sinus rhythm without ectopic activity.

Abdomen: Flat with well-healed right upper quadrant (RUQ) scar. Bowel sounds present in all quadrants. No bruits heard. No tenderness, masses, or organomegaly found on palpation.

GU: Normal female. Rectal deferred.

Extremities: No clubbing, cyanosis, or edema. Pulses present and equally moderate in upper and lower extremities.

Neuro: Oriented to person, place, and time. Cranial nerves II–XII grossly intact. DTRs symmetrical and 2+ in upper extremities. Ankle and knee jerk absent in right lower extremity. Plantar flexion present in both feet.

Laboratory Studies

CBC, chemistries, and urinalysis: results and levels within normal limits.

ECG: changes consistent with old anteroseptal and inferior infarcts as well as lateral ischemia. (See Figure 6–10.)

Medical Diagnoses

1. Unstable angina pectoris.
2. Known severe CAD. Status post MI.
3. Status post coronary artery bypass graft (CABG) surgery; with one graft clotted.

Management

The day of admission, Ms. West's physician ordered a propranolol regimen in an effort to control her angina pain with medication. This was unsuccessful and after several days Ms. West's physician recommended CABG surgery. Mr. and Ms. West discussed the proposed surgery and agreed that this was worth a try. Ms. West was scheduled for CABG surgery the second week of her hospital stay.

During the surgical procedure the cardiovascular surgeon placed grafts from the aorta to the obtuse marginal and circumflex branches of the left coronary artery as well as to the right coronary artery. Following surgery, Ms. West had an uncomplicated recovery.

She was returned to the critical care unit (CCU) with

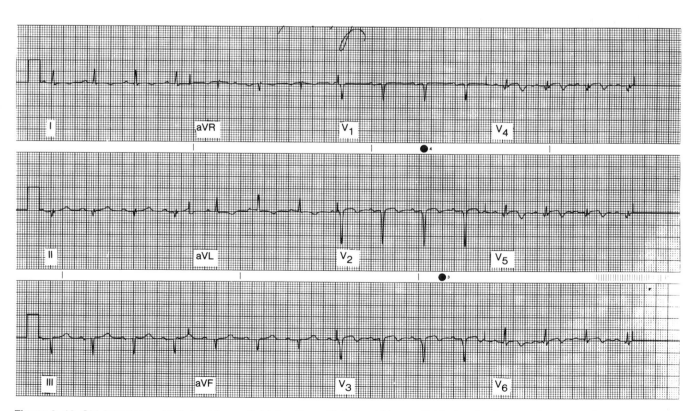

Figure 6–10 Old Anterior and Inferior Myocardial Infarction with Lateral Myocardial Ischemia. *Source:* Cardiology Department of St. Mark's Hospital, Salt Lake City, Utah.

an endotracheal tube and on a continuous mechanical ventilator. She was weaned from the ventilator slowly and extubated the morning of the first postoperative day. Ms. West was reluctant to turn, deep breathe, or cough. The nurses tried to provide adequate pain relief before carrying out these postoperative routines. The nurses also provided encouragement and allowed Mr. West to help his wife because they noted that she coughed better with his help.

Ms. West recovered steadily but due to her debilitation prior to surgery, her progress was slow. She was transferred out of the CCU on the fifth postoperative day.

Study Questions

1. What ECG changes would indicate myocardial ischemia?
2. Explain the surgical technique for CABG.
3. What are possible complications of CABG surgery?
4. Outline a nursing care plan for Ms. West's first two postoperative days.
5. What information should the patient and family receive prior to surgery?

DISSECTING AORTIC ANEURYSM

Units I-10 and II-2, III-10

Present Illness

David Aamodt, aged 65 years, was seen by his physician for a sharp stabbing pain which developed suddenly in his right lower abdomen and back. Mr. Aamodt had been sweeping the floor in his woodworking shop when he experienced a very sharp stabbing pain in the right lower quadrant (RLQ) of his abdomen. He lay down on the couch in his office. The pain spread to his back and he began to suspect that something very serious was wrong. When the pain did not subside in an hour, he called his wife who took him to the family physician's office. The physician found a large pulsating mass in Mr. Aamodt's abdominal RLQ. Mr. Aamodt's BP was 160/88 mm Hg which was higher than his usual BP of 140/80 mm Hg. Mr. Aamodt was admitted to a nearby medical center with a diagnosis of dissecting abdominal aortic aneurysm of six hours' duration.

Past Medical History

Mr. Aamodt had no previous history of vascular disease. He denied having leg claudication or night cramping. He stated that he had not had any serious illness or surgery in the past and this was his first hospitalization.

Mr. Aamodt knew nothing about his blood relatives' medical history because he never knew his parents or family. He had lived in an orphanage until he was apprenticed to a carpenter at age 16. When the carpenter died he willed his property to Mr. Aamodt. Mr. and Ms. Aamodt were pleased to receive this inheritance which included a modest home and a large shed which housed an efficient woodworking shop.

Mr. Aamodt had smoked two packs of Camel cigarettes per day for 50 years.

Physical Exam on Admission

General: A large white man with an apprehensive manner and pale face. Vital signs were: BP, 160/84 mm Hg; HR, 90/min; RR, 16/min.
HEENT: Within normal limits except that fundoscopic exam revealed grade 2 arteriosclerotic changes of both fundi.
Neck: No lymphadenopathy or palpable thyroid.
Chest: Increased anterior-posterior (AP) diameter. Breath sounds were diminished, no abnormal sounds were heard. Heart sounds were distant, no abnormal sounds were heard.
Abdomen: Flat. Faint bowel sounds, bruit heard in RLQ. Large pulsatile mass in RLQ.
Extremities: Peripheral pulses equal and strong in upper extremities; weak in lower extremities; more diminished on right than left side. Color and warmth equal in upper extremities; feet pale and cool, slight bluish cast to right leg.
Neuro: Grossly intact.

Laboratory Studies

CBC, PT, PTT, serum electrolytes, and urinalysis: results and levels within normal limits.
BUN: 20 mg/dL; serum creatinine: 1.5 mg/dL.
Mr. Aamodt's blood was typed and cross-matched with ten units of blood.
Abdominal x-ray: showed calcification of the abdominal aorta and common iliac arteries as well as a dissecting aneurysm distal to the renal arteries.
ECG: normal sinus rhythm. Nonspecific ST-T wave changes. (See Figure 6–11.)

Medical Diagnosis

Dissecting abdominal aortic aneurysm.

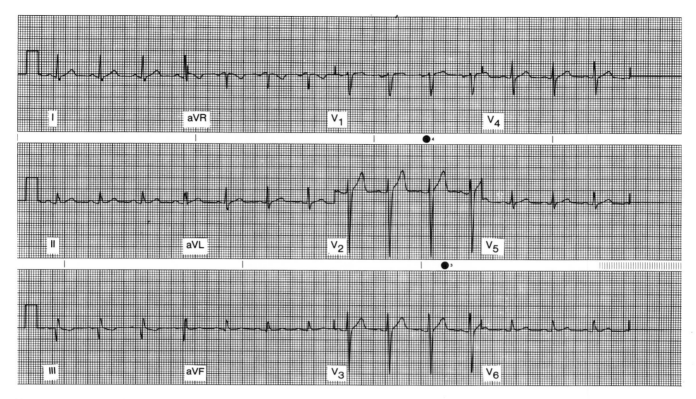

Figure 6–11 Normal Sinus Rhythm with Nonspecific ST-T Wave Changes. *Source:* Cardiology Department of St. Mark's Hospital, Salt Lake City, Utah.

Management

Emergency surgical resection and repair of the abdominal aortic aneurysm was carried out in an effort to avoid rupture of the aneurysm. The nurses did as much preoperative teaching as the time allowed. Included in this preoperative instruction were:

- turning, deep breathing, and coughing
- requesting pain medication
- presence of intravenous fluids and equipment
- presence of indwelling catheter and nasogastric tube
- routines of the critical care unit (CCU)

Despite the preoperative instruction, Mr. Aamodt was very apprehensive when he was taken to surgery.

The operative procedure consisted of clamping the aorta and iliac arteries proximal and distal to the aneurysm for an extended period of time. The aneurysm was dissected and the atherosclerotic plaque was removed. A Dacron prosthesis was sewn in proximally and distally. Then the remaining aorta was approximated and sewn around the graft. Two units of blood were given in the operating room to replace most of the estimated blood loss.

Mr. Aamodt was taken to the CCU while still intubated and placed on a continuous mechanical ventilator. His condition was satisfactory. The physician's postoperative orders were:

1. Check vital signs with femoral, popliteal, posterior tibial, and dorsalis pedis pulses every 15 minutes for one hour or until stable, then every 30 minutes for two hours, then every hour
2. Morphine sulfate as an intravenous titrate. May receive total of 15 mg every four hours (q4h) as needed (prn) to relieve pain.
3. Give patient trimethobenzamide (Tigan), 200 mg intramuscularly (IM), q4h for nausea
4. Notify physician of arterial systolic pressure greater than 160 mm Hg or arterial diastolic pressure greater than 90 mm Hg
5. Double lumen nasogastric tube connected to low constant suction
6. Record hourly intake and output

7. Give patient nothing by mouth (NPO)
8. Maintain patient on continuous mechanical ventilator with settings: fraction of inspired oxygen (FIO_2), 0.40; synchronized intermittent mandatory ventilation (SIMV), 15/min; and tidal volume (VT), 800 cc.
9. Cephalothin (Keflin) sodium, 1 g IV q6h.
10. Intravenous fluid lactated Ringer's solution, IV at 20 mL/hr plus amount equal to urine output and nasogastric drainage of the preceding hour.

Mr. Aamodt was alert on arrival in the CCU and occasionally assisted the ventilator. His wife visited with him for a few minutes and then went home to rest.

Mr. Aamodt's vital signs stabilized during the first hour he was in the CCU. His urine output dropped from 50 mL the first hour to 25 mL the second hour and then steadily increased over the next few hours to 50 mL/hr. Skin warmth, pulses, movement, and sensation remained intact in both lower extremities. He was extubated in the afternoon of the first postoperative day. The nasogastric tube was removed the third postoperative day because active bowel sounds were present. He was transferred out of the CCU on the fifth postoperative day.

Study Questions

1. What are the differences and similarities in vascular dynamics and pathophysiology of venous and arterial peripheral vascular disease?
2. Mr. Aamodt had a dissecting aneurysm. Name and describe two other types of aortic aneurysms including the signs and symptoms they produce.
3. Although Mr. Aamodt had emergency surgery, several laboratory tests were performed. How would a deviation from normal in the hematology, coagulation, or serum chemistry results have altered the scheduling of surgery? How would such deviations have predicted postoperative complications?
4. Why is it important for the nurse to include observation of lower extremity pulses, color, skin temperature, sensation, and movement in vital sign measurements?
5. Outline a nursing care plan for Mr. Aamodt that clearly identifies potential complications and appropriate prevention and intervention.

HYPERTENSION WITH HYPERTENSIVE CRISIS

Units II-4 and II-8

Present Illness

Lloyd Langdon, aged 63 years, was seen by his physician and admitted to the CCU on May 15 with complaints of palpitations and chest pain. For approximately two weeks prior to this admission, Mr. Langdon had experienced headaches, flashing lights in his vision, nausea, vomiting, and dry mouth. He was on a methyldopa (Aldomet) regimen for treatment of hypertension. Mr. Langdon stopped taking the methyldopa two days prior to admission because of the nausea and vomiting he was experiencing. He did not report this to his physician.

Past Medical History

Mr. Langdon had a past history of hypertension managed with methyldopa for 10 years. He stated he had not had chest pain, fever, chills, sweats, diarrhea, shortness of breath, or edema. He denied being told by a physician that he had heart disease or diabetes mellitus. He did have a history of smoking, alcoholism, and left inguinal hernia repair. Family history was negative for diabetes, heart disease, renal disease, and hypertension.

Physical Exam on Admission to the CCU

General: Patient was of average build and in moderate distress. Vitals signs were: BP, 210/130 mm Hg; T, 98.6 °F (37 °C); HR, 80/min and irregular; RR 18/min.
HEENT: EOMs full. PERRLA. Fundi with 2:6 arteriovenous "nicking"; optic disks blurred with decreased venous pulsations; several recent flame hemorrhages. Tympanic membranes were not visible due to bilaterally impacted cerumen.
Neck: Supple without lymphadenopathy or palpable thyroid. No JVD or bruits.
Lungs: Clear to auscultation and percussion although breath sounds were diminished throughout.
CV: Normal sinus rhythm with frequent PVBs. PMI at fifth ICS/MCL. Normal S_1 and S_2, S_3 also present. Grade 2/6 systolic ejection murmur heard at left sternal border of third ICS.
Abdomen: Flat. Active bowel sounds in all quadrants. Soft, nontender, without organomegaly or masses.
GU: Normal male genitalia and prostate. Guaiac negative stool.
Extremities: All peripheral pulses palpable and equally moderate.

Neuro: Cranial nerves II–XII grossly intact. DTRs symmetrical and 2+. Plantar flexion response present.

Laboratory Studies

Hematology: CBC and WBC differential within normal limits.

Serum electrolyte and chemistry levels: Na, 130 mEq/L; K, 2.7 mEq/L; Cl, 87 mEq/L; CO_2, 36 mmol/L; BUN, 21 mg/dL; and creatinine, 1.4 mg/dL.

Urinalysis: 4+ protein reaction and 15 RBCs per high power field.

Medical Diagnoses

1. Hypertension.
2. Acute hypertensive crisis.

Management

When Mr. Langdon was admitted to the CCU the nurses made him comfortable in bed and then began the ordered medication regimen. An infusion of sodium nitroprusside was begun at 6.5 μg/kg/min. An intravenous bolus of lidocaine, 1 mg/kg, was given and an infusion was begun at 2 mg/min. Furosemide, 20 mg daily, and potassium chloride, 30 mEq three times daily (tid), were also started.

On May 16 at 1900 hours, Mr. Langdon received droperidol (Inapsine) IV to relieve his complaints of nausea. He suddenly became unresponsive to verbal stimuli. His BP had been controlled by the sodium nitroprusside and ranged 145–150/80–85 mm Hg. At the time of this reaction, Mr. Langdon's BP was acutely elevated to 250/120 mm Hg. Fundoscopic examination at the time showed blurred optic disks without evidence of retinal hemorrhage. A nasogastric tube was inserted and the aspirate was positive for blood when tested with guaiac reagent. A medical diagnosis of possible acute reaction to droperidol was made.

On May 17 there were no residual effects from the acute episode of the previous day. Oral antihypertensive therapy was begun with hydralazine (Apresoline) and clonidine hydrochloride (Catapres). The oral medications were not expected to take immediate effect, so the nitroprusside was continued at 3.3 μg/kg/min. Stools tested positive for blood. Blood chemistry that day showed: Na, 118 mEq/L; K, 3.6 mEq/L; Cl, 87 mEq/L; CO_2, 27 mmol/L; BUN, 20 mg/dL; and creatinine, 1.2 mg/dL. Urinalysis results included 4+ protein reaction and rare RBCs per high power field.

On May 19 the sodium nitroprusside infusion was discontinued and Mr. Langdon's BP was adequately controlled with oral agents. A 24-hour urine collection was analyzed on May 20. Important results were: creatinine, 50.6 mg/dL, and protein, 162 mg. A renal specialist was consulted. An intravenous pyelogram (IVP) on May 21 showed a small, nonfunctioning right kidney. The physicians concluded that Mr. Langdon had suffered a renal infarct due to occlusion of the right renal artery.

Study Questions

1. What pathophysiological mechanism is thought to explain hypertensive crisis and its manifestations?
2. What observations of the neurological system are important in assessing the status of patients in hypertensive crisis?
3. Why was the patient's serum sodium 130 mEq/L on admission and 118 mEq/L on May 17?
4. How did the droperidol cause the alteration in Mr. Langdon's level of consciousness?
5. Identify and list three actual nursing diagnoses or nursing problems with the desired outcomes for Mr. Langdon? What nursing interventions will achieve the desired outcomes?

IDIOPATHIC HYPERTROPHIC SUBAORTIC STENOSIS

Units III-12 and II-2, III-9, III-10

Present Illness

Christopher Tolman, aged 50 years, was admitted to the CCU by a cardiologist because of complaints of recurrent light-headedness and precordial pain. Several weeks ago, he ran about 300 feet to take cover from a thunderstorm. After reaching shelter he became extremely faint, short of breath, and light-headed and he experienced chest pain. After sitting for about ten minutes, his symptoms resolved and he was able to go about his business. During the past week he had essentially a continual feeling of light-headedness without syncope. Mild exertion precipitated severe chest pain. These symptoms prompted him to see his family physician who referred him to the cardiologist.

Past Medical History

Mr. Tolman was first told he had a cardiac murmur at 19 years of age while involved in college athletics. Although he was examined at regular intervals, a murmur was not mentioned again until age 32. Since that time, a murmur was reported at every physical examination.

While in his early 30s, he experienced mild exertional dyspnea unrelated to the level of exertion. In his late 40s, moderate exertion consistently produced dyspnea. About a year and a half ago, the exertional dyspnea increased and was associated with precordial chest pain. He had also had episodes of extreme fatigue during the past four years.

Over the years, various labels were attached to his murmur and dyspnea. Some of the terms used were: aortic stenosis, mitral regurgitation, and flow murmur. Different regimens were prescribed accordingly, including digitalis, nitrates, and diuretics. Mr. Tolman often discontinued the prescribed medications after a couple of weeks because his symptoms worsened or did not improve. He never explained his lack of compliance to the prescribing physician but instead sought another physician. Mr. Tolman reported that his father died at age 52 and had similar complaints in the two years preceding his death.

Physical Exam on Admission to the CCU

General: Pleasant demeanor, not in acute distress. Average weight for height. Vital signs were: BP, 168/74 mm Hg in both arms; T, 98.6 °F (37 °C); HR, 80/min; RR, 16/min.
Skin: Pink, warm, and dry.
HEENT: Normal findings on examination.
Neck: Supple. No cervical lymphadenopathy. No JVD at 45 degree elevation. Prominent jugular venous a wave when supine. No hepatojugular reflux. Bisferious carotid pulses present.
Chest: Symmetrical excursion. Lungs clear to percussion and auscultation.
CV: Double apical pulse palpable at fifth ICS, 3 cm left of MCL. Thrill present at lower left sternal border. Grade 4/6 systolic ejection murmur heard best at Erb's point with radiation across entire chest. Wide splitting of S_2. S_4 gallop heard over left ventricle.
Abdomen: Flat. Active bowel sounds all quadrants. Soft, nontender, without organomegaly or masses.
Extremities: No clubbing or cyanosis. Pulses present, equal, and of moderate intensity.
Neuro: Normal findings on exam.

Laboratory Studies

CBC and serum chemistry levels: within normal limits.
ECG: normal sinus rhythm with first degree atrio-

ventricular block. Left ventricular hypertrophy and intraventricular conduction delay. (See Figure 6–12.)

Medical Diagnosis

Obstructive cardiomyopathy.

Management

Echocardiography was done the afternoon of Mr. Tolman's admission to the hospital. Asymmetric septal hypertrophy was observed. Cardiac catheterization was carried out the following morning. Data obtained included:

Bisferious contour to brachial pulse	
RAP, mean	7 mm Hg
RVP	50/10 and 35/5 mm Hg
Peak systolic gradient, right ventricular outflow tract	15 mm Hg
PAP	20/10 mm Hg
PCWP	15 mm Hg
Left ventricular pressure (LVP)	208/15 and 140/10 mm Hg
Peak systolic gradient, left ventricular outflow tract	68 mm Hg
Cardiac index at rest	3.0 L/min/m²

Left ventriculogram showed a small chamber with marked inward bulge of inferior wall segment during systole and moderate reflux into left atrium. Coronary arteriography did not show significant stenosis of the coronary arteries. Medical diagnosis of idiopathic hypertrophic subaortic stenosis (IHSS) was made.

Medications tried during the cardiac catheterization indicated that beta adrenergic blockade would be a useful approach to improving Mr. Tolman's health. Propranolol, (Inderal), 40 mg qid, was instituted. Six months later, Mr. Tolman was continuing to take the propranolol and reported that he had experienced minimal symptoms.

Study Questions

1. How does IHSS cause obstruction to ventricular outflow?

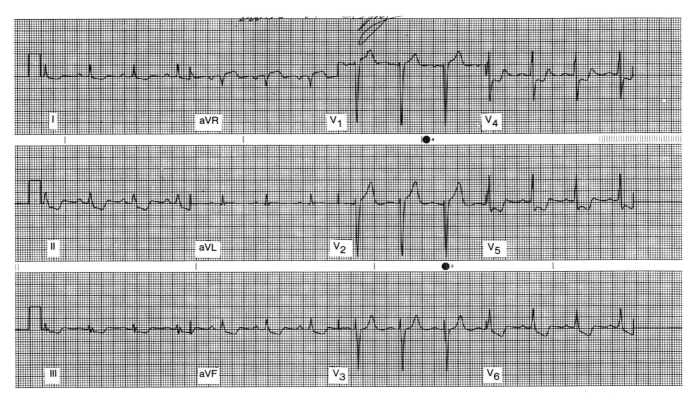

Figure 6–12 Normal Sinus Rhythm with 1 Degree Atrioventricular Block, Left Ventricular Hypertrophy, and Intraventricular Conduction Delay. *Source:* Cardiology Department of St. Mark's Hospital, Salt Lake City, Utah.

2. What is the most likely reason Mr. Tolman discontinued the prescribed medications? How might this have been avoided?
3. Why is propranolol used in management of IHSS? What other medications might be used?
4. Ms. Tolman would like to know what her husband's future health might be like. Of what complications of IHSS should she be made aware that Mr. Tolman might experience in the future?
5. Outline the essential nursing care for Mr. Tolman during his stay in the CCU.

INTRAAORTIC BALLOON PUMP COUNTERPULSATION

Units III-13 and I-6, II-2, III-10

Present Illness

Milton Shaw, a 57-year-old tool- and die-maker, was admitted to the CCU because of severe, crushing retrosternal pain. The patient was in his usual state of good health until early the morning of admission when he became aware of a sensation of epigastric bloating and fullness during his morning calisthenics. He was concerned but continued his morning routine and ate breakfast. Before he left for work, the discomfort progressed to severe, crushing retrosternal pain and was accompanied by numbness and tingling of his left arm as well as nausea, vomiting, and diaphoresis. His wife called their family physician who instructed her to call an ambulance and meet him in the ED.

Past Medical History

Mr. Shaw suffered similar pain while at a toolmakers' convention 18 months before. He was hospitalized in a distant hospital for a week. Mr. Shaw reported that when he was discharged, he was told that he had not had a heart attack but that he did have high blood pressure and heart trouble. When he returned from the convention, Mr. Shaw saw his family physician who documented the hypertension and prescribed 50 mg hydrochlorothiazide (Hydro-Diuril) daily. The physician also recommended that Mr. Shaw restrict his salt intake, lose weight, and begin a regular exercise program.

Mr. Shaw reported that neither he nor a family member had a history of diabetes, kidney disease, rheumatic fever, or gout. Mr. Shaw's father and grandfather had died at age 60 of heart disease. His mother was alive and 80 years of age but bedridden with severe arthritis and hypertension.

Mr. Shaw had been smoking a pack of cigarettes per day for 40 years. He usually drank six beers per day. He lived with his second wife and their three young children. Four children from Mr. Shaw's previous marriage were grown and maintained contact with Mr. and Ms. Shaw.

Physical Exam on Admission

General: An overweight man who appeared to be his stated age and was in acute distress. Vital signs were: BP, 108/92 mm Hg; T, 99 °F (37.2 °C); HR, 98/min and irregular; RR, 22/min and labored.

Skin: Pale, cool, moist.

HEENT: PERRLA. Optic fundi showed atrioventricular nicking but no exudates. Ears, nose, and mouth unremarkable.

Neck: Supple. Thyroid smooth and not enlarged. JVD to 7 cm but no hepatojugular reflux while sitting up 45 degrees.

Chest: Increased AP diameter. Excursion symmetrical. Moist rales heard at both lung bases. Broad, sustained PMI palpated at fifth ICS, 2 cm left of MCL. Heart sounds faint, normal S_1, paradoxical S_2, S_4 present and loudest at mitral area. Grade 3/6 holosystolic murmur present at mitral area.

Abdomen: Obese with faint bowel sounds in all quadrants. Soft and nontender to light and deep palpation. No organomegaly or masses appreciated.

Extremities: No deformities, clubbing, or peripheral edema noted. Peripheral pulses present, faint, and equal.

Neuro: Cranial nerves II–XII grossly intact. DTRs 1+ and symmetrical. Flexor plantar response present.

Laboratory Studies

Admission CBC, blood chemistry levels, and urinalysis: results were within normal limits.

Blood for cardiac enzymes was drawn in the ED.

Admission chest x-ray: cardiomegaly. Prominent hilar vessels and pulmonary vascular congestion. No pleural effusion.

ECG: sinus rhythm at 98/min. PR interval 0.14 sec. QRS duration 0.10 sec. ST segment elevation in leads I, II, aV_L, aV_F, and V_{1-6}. ST segment depression in leads III and aV_R. Very poor R wave progression in the precordial leads (V_{1-6}). Interpreted as indicating an acute anterolateral myocardial infarction. (See Figure 6–13.)

Medical Diagnoses

1. Acute anterolateral MI.
2. Left ventricular dysfunction.

Management

While Mr. Shaw was in the ED, he began to have frequent multifocal PVBs. His weight was estimated as 100 kg and he was given 100 mg lidocaine as an IV bolus. While a lidocaine infusion was being prepared, he developed ventricular tachycardia and lost consciousness. The ventricular tachycardia was converted to a sinus rhythm with a single direct current synchronized countershock of 250 joules. The lidocaine infusion of 2 g in 500 mL D5W was begun at 4 mg/min. Mr. Shaw regained consciousness quickly with the return of sinus rhythm. Oxygen was administered at 2 L/min via nasal cannula and ABGs were ordered.

On arrival in the CCU, Mr. Shaw was alert, restless, and complaining of severe chest pain in addition to the inconvenience of being hospitalized. He was given 2 mg morphine sulfate IV for his pain. Because the pain was only partially relieved, the dose was repeated five minutes later. The oxygen was continued as the ABG results were satisfactory. Although his pain was not completely relieved, Mr. Shaw began to rest better after the second dose of morphine and after hearing that his wife had notified his assistant at work of his hospitalization.

A flow-directed pulmonary artery catheter and a radial arterial line were inserted by the physician on duty in the CCU. The following measurements were made: arterial pressure, 90–100/60 mm Hg with mean 70 mm Hg; pulmonary capillary wedge pressure, mean 18–20 mm Hg. The indwelling urinary catheter drained an average of 10 mL urine per hour. The cardiac rhythm was sinus tachycardia (104/min) with four to ten PVBs per minute. The heart sounds continued to be poor in quality and moist rales increased throughout both lungs. His skin remained cool and clammy with a graying color. Mr. Shaw's mental status became somewhat cloudy although he continued to complain of chest pain.

The physician elected to augment Mr. Shaw's cardiac function with intraaortic balloon pumping because of the patient's unstable clinical state, which consisted of persistent chest pain unrelieved by morphine sulfate; relative arterial hypotension; oliguria;

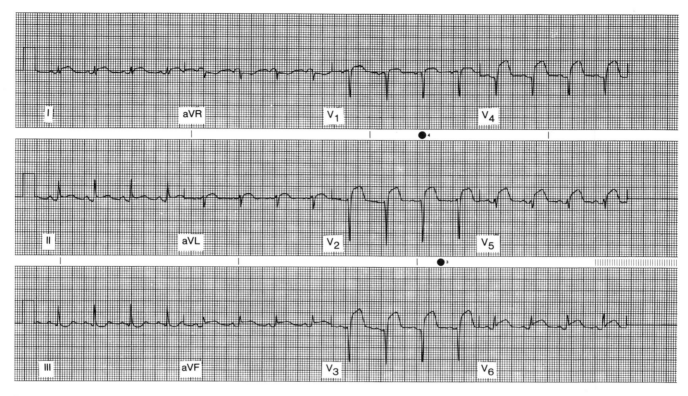

Figure 6–13 Acute Anterolateral Myocardial Infarction. *Source:* Cardiology Department of St. Mark's Hospital, Salt Lake City, Utah.

and ventricular ectopy. With the assistance of the nurses, the physician inserted a 40-cc intraaortic balloon percutaneously. Counterpulsation was begun at a 1:1 ratio with full volume in the balloon. Good diastolic augmentation was achieved with pressures of 90/115/60 mm Hg and mean 80 mm Hg. Mr. Shaw experienced almost immediate relief of his chest pain. Over the next hour, Mr. Shaw's ventricular ectopy decreased to zero to two PVBs per minute and his urine output increased to 35 mL/hr. He became more alert and stated that he was no longer nauseated and wanted a snack. A nitroglycerin (Nitrol) ointment regimen of 1 inch q4h was instituted.

Ms. Shaw visited and reassured her husband that she and the children were ''fine'' and he should ''hurry and get well.''

Study Questions

1. What measures can be used to relieve the severe pain of myocardial ischemia, in addition to narcotic medication?
2. Why was Mr. Shaw's urine output only 10 mL/hr when his arterial systolic pressure was 90–100 mm Hg? Should that pressure have provided adequate renal perfusion?
3. How does the IABP improve myocardial oxygenation?
4. How would you respond to questions from Ms. Shaw as to how long Mr. Shaw would be using the IABP?
5. Identify and describe the actual and potential nursing diagnoses or nursing problems and outcomes that are unique to patients using the IABP?
6. What nursing interventions are essential to achieving the desired outcomes for patients with IABP counterpulsation?

LEFT VENTRICULAR BYPASS

Units III-13 and I-9, III-5, III-25

Present Illness

Albert Goodwin, aged 43 years, was a white, married, stage director who was admitted to the critical care unit (CCU) on May 3 following cardiac surgery.

The patient had been in good health until the previous January at which time he suffered an anterior wall MI. Subsequent arteriography revealed complete occlusion of the anterior descending branch of the left coronary artery. There were no significant lesions in the circumflex branch. Mr. Goodwin had symptoms of unstable angina, so that the coronary arteriography was repeated in April. The results indicated that CAD had progressed to include a significant lesion in the circumflex branch of the left coronary artery and a left ventricular aneurysm.

Past Medical History

In addition to the hospital admissions previously mentioned, Mr. Goodwin had been hospitalized for ulcers 15 years ago. He had no medical history of diabetes, hypertension, or renal disease. He smoked one pack of cigarettes per day and drank alcohol very rarely (usually only at Christmas). Family history was unremarkable except that his mother, age 62, had an "abdominal tumor."

Physical Exam on Admission

General: Patient appeared to be his stated age and was not in distress. Vital signs were: BP, 120/82 mm Hg; T, 98 °F (36.7 °C); HR, 72/min and regular; RR, 14/min.
Skin: Warm, pink, and dry.
HEENT: PERRLA. Optic fundi, ears, nose, and mouth unremarkable.
Neck: Supple. Thyroid smooth and not enlarged. No JVD or hepatojugular reflux.
Chest: Increased AP diameter. Excursion symmetrical. Lungs clear to auscultation and percussion. Broad, sustained PMI palpated at fifth ICS, 2 cm left of MCL. Heart sounds: normal S_1 and S_2, S_4 present and loudest at mitral area. No rubs or murmurs heard.
Abdomen: Flat with active bowel sounds in all quadrants. Soft and nontender to palpation. No organomegaly or masses noted.
Extremities: No deformities, clubbing, or peripheral edema noted. Peripheral pulses present and equal.
Neuro: Cranial nerves II–XII grossly intact. DTRs 1+ and symmetrical. Flexor plantar response present.

Laboratory Studies

Admission hematology, coagulation, serum chemistries, and urinalysis: findings within normal limits.

Medical Diagnoses

1. CAD.
2. Unstable angina.
3. History of MI.

Management

Mr. Goodwin had cardiac surgery on May 3 when two CABGs were placed from his aorta to the branches of the left coronary artery. In addition, plication of a left ventricular aneurysm was performed.

The immediate postoperative course was complicated by left ventricular failure and a "pump lung" syndrome. The patient was treated with vasopressor infusions including norepinephrine (Levophed) bitartrate in an effort to wean him from the cardiopulmonary bypass machine. This was not successful, so a trial with the IABP was conducted without improvement and accompanied by anuria.

Transapical left ventricular bypass was considered and instituted. A venous uptake cannula was placed through the apex of the left ventricle and an arterial perfusion catheter was placed in the right femoral artery. The left ventricle was thus bypassed with an extracorporeal roller pump mechanism. Mr. Goodwin was then transferred to the CCU. His medical problems were identified as: left ventricular failure and dysfunction; adult respiratory distress syndrome (ARDS); and renal failure.

A nephrologist was consulted in regard to Mr. Goodwin's renal failure and daily hemodialysis was begun. Mr. Goodwin's left ventricular failure and dysfunction were managed by complete unloading of the left ventricle such that left atrial pressures were maintained at 4–5 mm Hg.

After 12 hours of full mechanical support of the left ventricle, decompensation and failure of the right ventricle became evident. Mr. Goodwin began to have high central venous and right atrial pressures. The output of the left ventricular bypass was then limited by the right ventricular output. The patient was digitalized cautiously because of his renal failure. Mr. Goodwin also received dopamine hydrochloride and sodium nitroprusside (Nipride) infusions in an effort to increase his cardiac output.

Mr. Goodwin's pulmonary insufficiency was managed with continuous ventilator support with positive end expiratory pressure (PEEP). Mr. Goodwin's pulmonary status gradually improved as a result of this regimen.

On May 8, massive elevations of serum liver enzyme levels were noted, although the etiology remained unclear. The enzyme levels gradually decreased over the next several days.

Transapical left ventricular bypass was discontinued on May 13, ten days after insertion. Mr. Goodwin was managed for two more days with dopamine hydrochloride and sodium nitroprusside support to maintain an adequate cardiac output and reduced atrial pressures.

Attempts were made to maintain Mr. Goodwin's nutritional status with an enteral diet and parenteral hyperalimentation. Fourteen days after admission, Mr. Goodwin began to have fever spikes with temperatures to 102.2 °F (39 °C); results of numerous blood cultures were negative. Smears and cultures of his sputum showed gram-negative *Pseudomonas aeruginosa*. The WBC count elevated to 26.0×10^9/L with presence of toxic granulations. There was no clear source of infection although the pulmonary system was suspected.

On May 25, bilateral palmar erythema and thoracic spider angiomata were noted in addition to hepatomegaly. The following day, May 26, the patient developed clinical manifestations of septic shock with hypotension, acidosis, and fever. Attempts were made to identify the source of the sepsis. The patient was scheduled for a liver scan and IV cholangiogram. Tobramycin sulfate (Nebcin) and chloramphenicol (Chloromycetin) were added to the regimen. A large dose (2 g) of methylprednisolone sodium succinate (Solu-Medrol) was administered. Mr. Goodwin's status began to deteriorate so cardiovascular support with dopamine hydrochloride was reinstituted.

Physical examination at that time located a very tender abdomen with increasing abdominal distention. All surgical wounds were examined for evidence of infection but none was found. Radiographic examination of the abdomen demonstrated air in the biliary tree. Following this examination, Mr. Goodwin suffered a cardiac arrest and was successfully resuscitated. Surgical consultation followed and the patient was taken to the operating room for an exploratory laparotomy. Ischemic necrosis of nearly the entire small bowel was found.

Mr. Goodwin was supported through the night with antibiotics, controlled continuous mechanical ventilation, dopamine hydrochloride, and intermittent doses of sodium bicarbonate. His BP gradually decreased despite maximum infusion rates of dopamine. The concomitant acidemia led to severe hypotension, bradycardia, and ultimately asystole. Mr. Goodwin was pronounced dead in the early morning of May 27.

Study Questions

1. What signs and symptoms would indicate right ventricular failure in a patient with a left ventricular bypass device?

2. What psychoemotional support should be offered to the patient and family?
3. Outline the essential nursing diagnoses or nursing problems, outcomes, and activities for May 5.
4. If two nurses were assigned to care for this patient, how might they organize and share the nursing activities and responsibilities?
5. LV bypass technique is one of several experimental approaches to cardiopulmonary failure. How can nurses prepare themselves to care unexpectedly for patients being managed by unusual or experimental methods?

SUBACUTE BACTERIAL ENDOCARDITIS

Units III-11 and I-24, II-2, III-10, III-18

Present Illness

Gregory Johnson, a quadriplegic man aged 25 years, was admitted to the CCU in acute distress from an intermittent infectious process. Mr. Johnson had intermittent fever, chills, and cough for three months prior to admission. Additional complaints were: anorexia (20-lb weight loss over 3 months), vague left upper quadrant (LUQ) abdominal fullness, and a urinary tract infection unresponsive to antibiotics.

Past Medical History

He had been healthy until 18 months ago when he sustained a C5-C6 spinal fracture in a motor vehicle accident. Ten months ago, mitral valve leaflet prolapse was determined to be the cause of a systolic murmur present since adolescence. Five months ago, he had a tooth extracted. There was no other significant patient or family medical history.

Physical Exam on Admission

General: Lean, pale, malnourished man lying in bed with oxygen cannula in place and worried manner. Vital signs were: BP, 90/60 mm Hg; T, 102.2 °F (39 °C); HR, 114/min; RR, 24/min and labored.
HEENT: Exam findings were within normal limits except for poor dental hygiene.
Chest: Pectus carinatum. Lungs clear to percussion and auscultation.
CV: PMI at fifth ICS/MCL. Grade 4/6 systolic murmur at apex radiating to left axilla. Loud friction rub heard over left chest.
Abdomen: Distended. Active bowel sounds in lower quadrants, faint in upper quadrants. Soft with spleen palpated at 10 cm below the left costal margin.

Extremities: Pulses present and equally weak. No clubbing, cyanosis, or edema. Withering in lower extremities. Some atrophy in upper extremity muscles.

Neuro: Cranial nerves II–XII grossly intact. Sensory and motor deficit consistent with C5-C6 spinal cord lesion.

Laboratory Studies

Hematology: Hct, 25.4%; WBC, 0.9×10^9/L; lymphs, 66%; segs, 20%; bands, 8%; monos, 4%; metamyelocytes (metas), 2%; platelets, 93.0×10^9/L; ESR, 55 mm/hr.

Serum chemistry levels: BUN, 17 mg/dL; creatinine, 1.2 mg/dL; albumin, 2.9 mg/dL; globulin, 5 mg/dL.

Urinalysis: occult blood and 4+ bacteria.

X-rays: chest showed mild cardiomegaly. Abdomen showed massive, enlarged spleen.

ECG: sinus tachycardia. (See Figure 6–14.)

Medical Diagnoses

1. Subacute bacterial endocarditis (SBE).
2. Mitral valve leaflet prolapse.
3. Spinal lesion at C5-C6.

Management

Shortly after Mr. Johnson was admitted, an echocardiogram was done which showed pansystolic prolapse of mitral valve leaflets with vegetations and posterior pericardial effusion. The echocardiogram was followed by a pericardiocentesis which yielded 300 mL of straw-colored transudate.

Specimens were obtained and sent for cultures with the following results: blood grew microaerophilic alpha hemolytic *Streptococcus* organisms and Group D *Enterobacter* organisms. Urine grew multiple organisms. Pericardial effluent grew no organisms. After the cultures were obtained, IV antibiotic therapy was instituted with 3.5 million units penicillin, q4h, and 80 mg gentamicin (Garamycin), q8h.

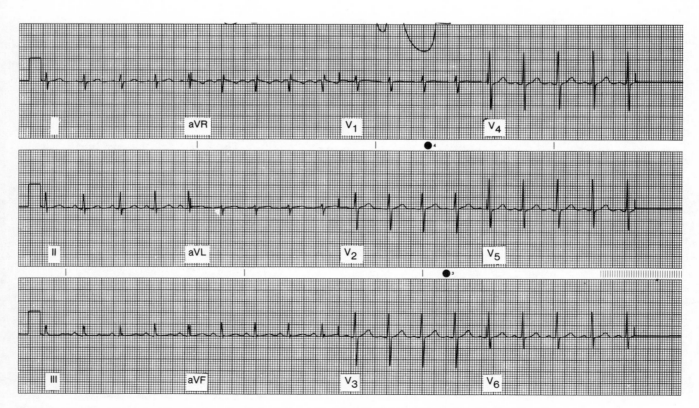

Figure 6–14 Sinus Tachycardia. *Source:* Cardiology Department of St. Mark's Hospital, Salt Lake City, Utah.

Splenectomy was carried out on the 12th hospital day. Two days after surgery, the WBC count rose to 7.8×10^9/L, Hct to 28.7%, and platelets to 189.0×10^9/L. Histological examination of the spleen showed a large splenic infarct with a periinfarction abscess. Culture specimens grew alpha hemolytic *Streptococcus* organisms.

Mr. Johnson had three jacksonian seizures on the 19th hospital day. A brain scan with flow study and a CT scan of the head were read as within normal limits. An electroencephalogram (EEG) showed a focal slow-wave abnormality over the right frontotemporal region. The seizures were thought to be caused by microemboli. Administration of phenytoin (Dilantin), 100 mg tid, was begun.

On the 26th hospital day, the patient became afebrile and seizure-free. Subsequent blood cultures did not show any bacterial growth. A repeat EEG was read as being within normal limits. An echocardiogram showed decreased size of mitral valve leaflet vegetations.

The penicillin and gentamicin were discontinued after six weeks of therapy. The patient was discharged from the hospital at the end of the seventh week with instructions about antibiotic prophylaxis for dental and diagnostic procedures.

Study Questions

1. How does endocarditis develop?
2. Why do quadriplegics and paraplegics frequently have difficulty with urinary tract infections?
3. What is pectus carinatum? How is it significant?
4. Identify three actual nursing problems Mr. Johnson had at the time of admission and the appropriate outcomes for discharge from the CCU.
5. List and explain the nursing interventions required to achieve each outcome.

Chapter 7

Pulmonary Case Studies

ACUTE RESPIRATORY FAILURE

Units I-14 and I-12, II-2, II-8, III-10

Present Illness

Anton Bates, a 52-year-old white shepherd was admitted to the CCU of a tertiary hospital following respiratory arrest and management at a small hospital in a rural area. Mr. Bates had come to the ED of the small hospital on the morning of June 20 complaining of severe shortness of breath, chills, and cough. Mr. Bates had been seen in the hospital's clinic one week previously for pleuritic chest pain. An ECG done at that time showed nonspecific ST segment depression. The patient was sent back to his ranch with instructions to return if further symptoms developed.

Personnel at the small hospital reported that, shortly after checking in to the ED, Mr. Bates collapsed in a respiratory arrest. He was ventilated with a resuscitation bag and oxygen. Mr. Bates regained consciousness with spontaneous breathing. ABG results were: Po_2, 71 torr: Pco_2, 58 torr; and pH 7.0. His neck veins were distended. He was given 80 mg furosemide (Lasix) and 200 mEq sodium bicarbonate. Oxygen at 2 L/min was administered by nasal cannula.

The transfer report explained that Mr. Bates was transferred from the ED to the monitored bed unit where he had another respiratory arrest. He was intubated with an endotracheal tube and continuous mechanical ventilation was begun. During the intubation procedure, Mr. Bates vomited and aspirated. He next had a grand mal seizure which was controlled with IV diazepam (Valium). Subsequently, he became difficult to ventilate. His pulmonary compliance had increased dramatically and he had signs and symptoms of expiratory obstruction. A loading dose of 500 mg aminophylline (Aminophyllin) was administered IV.

According to the referral, Mr. Bates' cardiac rhythm was unstable in that he had atrial fibrillation with variable ventricular response rates. When the ventricular response rate reached 160–170/min, the atrial fibrillation was accompanied by systolic arterial hypotension palpated at 70–80 mm Hg. Attempts to cardiovert were unsuccessful.

Mr. Bates was referred to the tertiary hospital 40 miles away for further management. An air transport team consisting of a physician and a nurse went to the small hospital to transfer Mr. Bates. Before departure, the air transport team placed an arterial line in the left radial artery and a flow-directed pulmonary artery thermodilution catheter via the right subclavian vein. Initial hemodynamic data were: arterial pressure, 110/70 mm Hg, mean 80 mm Hg; right atrial pressure (RAP), 12 mm Hg; right ventricular pressure (RVP), 32/12 mm Hg; pulmonary artery pressure (PAP), 32/19 mm Hg, mean, 27 mm Hg; and pulmonary capillary wedge pressure (PCWP), 17 mm Hg. Mr. Bates arrived at the tertiary hospital six hours after entering the health care system.

Past Medical History

The referring physician reported that Mr. Bates had a history of peptic ulcer disease and gastrointestinal (GI) bleeding. There was no known history of hypertension, diabetes, alcohol abuse, or seizures. Apparently, Mr. Bates had smoked one to two packs of cigarettes per day since he was 12 years old. No family history was available.

Physical Exam on Admission to the Tertiary Hospital

General: Small, wiry man, appeared older than his stated age. Not alert or oriented, became combative and thrashing with noxious stimuli. Vital signs were: BP, 110/70, mean 80 mm Hg; T, 101.6 °F (38.6 °C); HR 160/min and irregularly irregular; RR 75/min on continuous mechanical ventilator (patient was "double breathing").

Skin: Warm and dry with gray cast. Poor hygiene.

Head, Eyes, Ears, Nose, and Throat (HEENT): PERRL. Fundoscopic exam unremarkable. Doll's eyes present. Mucous membranes moist and pink. Poor oral hygiene. Teeth in poor condition.

Neck: JVD at jaw angle with head of bed up 30 degrees.

Chest: Increased AP diameter. Bilateral diffuse rhonchi and expiratory wheezes.

Cardiovascular system (CV): Atrial fibrillation with ventricular response rate 150–160/min and occasional ventricular ectopy. Varied intensity of S_1 and S_2. No gallops, rubs, or murmurs heard. Hemodynamic data: RAP, 13 mm Hg; PAP, 35/20 mm Hg, mean 28 mm Hg; PCWP, 20 mm Hg.

Abdomen: Scaphoid. Faint bowel sounds heard in all quadrants. Soft and without masses or organomegaly.

Extremities: Without deformity, clubbing, or cyanosis. Pulses present, equal, and faint.

Neurological status (Neuro): No response to verbal stimuli. Thrashed and moved all extremities with equal strength with painful stimuli. Patient made no verbal responses and did not open his eyes. DTRs 1+ and symmetrical. Plantar flexor response intact.

Laboratory Studies

Blood gas results on FIO_2 1.0: Pao_2, 124 torr; $Paco_2$, 42 torr; pH 7.49; P_vO_2, 34 torr; $C(a-v)o_2$, 6%.

Chest x-ray: Endotracheal tube and pulmonary artery catheter in place. Bilateral upper lobe infiltrates with dense infiltrate in right upper lobe and some evidence of volume loss suggested by elevated minor fissure. Diffuse patchy infiltrate in left upper lobe. Faint right basilar infiltrate.

ECG: Atrial fibrillation with rapid ventricular response. ST segment depression and T wave inversion suggest lateral and inferior myocardial ischemia. (See Figure 7–1.)

Medical Diagnoses

1. Acute respiratory failure, infectious origin. Possibilities are bacteria, mycoplasma, Legionnaire's disease, or virus.

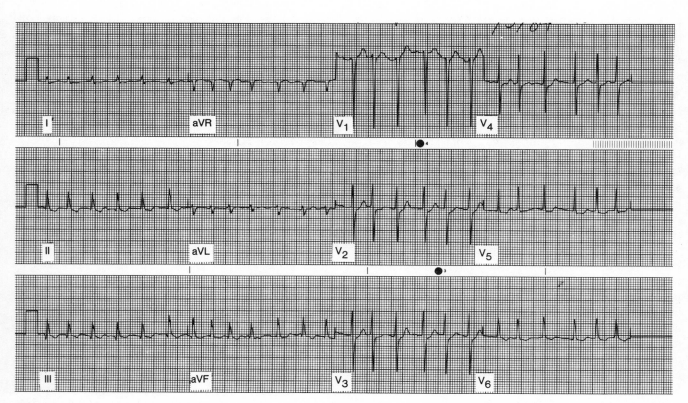

Figure 7–1 Atrial Fibrillation with Rapid Ventricular Response. Lateral and Inferior Myocardial Ischemia. *Source:* Cardiology Department of St. Mark's Hospital, Salt Lake City, Utah.

2. Possible adult respiratory distress syndrome (ARDS).
3. Pulmonary aspiration of gastric contents.
4. Atrial fibrillation, secondary to hypoxia and/or metabolic disturbance.
5. Possible pulmonary embolus secondary to atrial fibrillation.
6. History of seizure, secondary to hypoxia and/or metabolic disturbance.
7. History of peptic ulcer disease.

Management

Medical management of Mr. Bates' respiratory failure was initiated with mechanical ventilation including positive end expiratory pressure (PEEP) increased in 2.5-cm H_2O increments while monitoring ABGs and $C(a-v)O_2$. The physician hoped to obtain adequate oxygenation with an FIO_2 of 0.50 or less. In order to achieve the goal, the FIO_2 was initially decreased to 0.60. Bronchodilators in the form of IV aminophylline infusion and aerosolized isoetharine hydrochloride (Bronkosol) were used to reduce bronchospasm and expiratory obstruction. Hydrocortisone sodium succinate (Solu-Cortef) was administered IV as 500 mg q6h for 48 hours.

The infectious process was managed by obtaining blood and sputum samples for culture, as well as cold agglutinin and complement fixation titers. Gentamicin, (Garamycin), 80 mg IV q6h, and ampicillin (Omnipen) were the initial antibiotics ordered. The physician planned to add erythromycin (Ilotycin) to the regimen if laboratory tests indicated that mycoplasma was the infecting organism.

The physician ordered digitalizing doses of digoxin (Lanoxin) as an approach to controlling Mr. Bates' ventricular response to the atrial fibrillation.

Two hours after admission to the tertiary CCU, the patient was awake and following commands although he was confused. His BP remained stable at 110/70 mm Hg. His temperature was 101.8 °F (38.8 °C). The atrial fibrillation was still present with a ventricular response rate of 140/min although 0.5 mg of digoxin had been administered. His respiratory rate was 40/min. Mr. Bates' static pulmonary compliance was measured as 36–37 cc/cm H_2O. Mechanical ventilation with FIO_2 0.60 and 5 cm H_2O PEEP was continued. ABG results on these settings were: PaO_2, 67 torr, and $PaCO_2$, 37 torr.

Study Questions

1. What is the most likely etiology of Mr. Bates' respiratory arrest?

2. What observations are important when PEEP is being increased in addition to ABG results? What is meant by "best PEEP"?
3. Why is it desirable to obtain adequate oxygenation with an FIO_2 of 0.50 or less?
4. How does measurement of static pulmonary compliance aid in managing patients on continuous mechanical ventilation?
5. Outline the essential nursing interventions related to achieving adequate oxygenation with spontaneous ventilation.

ADULT RESPIRATORY DISTRESS SYNDROME

Units I-14 and I-12

Present Illness

Henry Smith was a 40-year-old white farmer who had a farming accident in which he fell into a manure bin. While he was in the bin, he aspirated fillage and inhaled carbon dioxide, methane, hydrogen sulfide, and ammonia gases. There were witnesses to the accident; however, Mr. Smith was in the bin for an unknown period of time. When he was rescued he was not breathing, although a faint carotid pulse was detected. Paramedics intubated him at the scene and transported him to the ED. Enroute, Mr. Smith became very combative and required sedation with diazepam (Valium) and pancuronium bromide (Pavulon). Mr. Smith's BP was 80/40 mm Hg on arrival in the ED. A dopamine hydrochloride (Intropin) infusion was begun and resulted in a satisfactory rise in BP. A chest x-ray which showed bilateral diffuse pulmonary infiltrates was obtained in the ED. ABG results while on continuous ventilation with an FIO_2 of 1.0 were: pH, 7.25; PaO_2, 40 torr; and $PaCO_2$, 40 torr. Mr. Smith was taken to the critical care unit (CCU) one hour after admission to the ED.

Past Medical History

Mr. Smith's family reported that he had no history of surgery in the past or chronic illness. He was not taking any medication routinely. He complained of arthritis but had not seen a physician for this complaint. Mr. Smith was married and had three children aged 11, 13, and 15 years. He did not use tobacco or alcohol.

Physical Exam on Admission to the CCU

General: Heavily sedated, dark-skinned man, covered with manure. Unresponsive to stimuli initially but became more responsive during examination. Patient requested to be "put out." Vital signs were: BP, 108/90 mm Hg with 5 μg/kg/min dopamine hydrochloride; T, 101.4 °F (38.5 °C); HR, 155/min and regular; RR 20/min on continuous ventilation in assist/control (A/C) mode.

Respiratory: Endotracheal tube down right naris. Large amounts of frothy, bloody secretions bubbling from endotracheal tube. Bilateral rales greater in the bases. No wheezing. Volume cycled ventilator in control mode with tidal volume (V_T), 800 cc; FIO_2, 1.0; RR, 20/min; PEEP, 10 cm H_2O.

CV: No JVD. Sinus tachycardia. Heart sounds clear and without rub, murmur, or gallop sounds. Peripheral pulses present, equal, and strong in all extremities. Skin dry, torso warm, extremities cool. Arterial line in right femoral artery and balloon-tipped thermodilution catheter in pulmonary artery via right subclavian vein.

GI: Double lumen nasogastric tube down left naris draining large amounts of thick brown, foul-smelling liquid. The guaiac test on the gastric aspirate was positive. No burns seen in mouth. Teeth in good repair. Abdomen flat and without bowel sounds in any quadrant. Soft and nontender to palpation. No organomegaly or masses felt. The guaiac test on feces was positive.

GU: Indwelling urinary catheter draining clear, light yellow urine. Normal genitalia.

Neuro: PERRL. When pancuronium bromide wore off, DTRs and plantar flexor responses were decreased but symmetrical. Sensory and motor responses were grossly intact.

Musculoskeletal system: Large, raised, firm ecchymosis on right arm extending from shoulder to middle of forearm.

Laboratory Studies

Blood for CBC and serum chemistries were obtained on admission. The pertinent results are shown with "Management and Clinical Data." Admission ECG showed sinus tachycardia and ST segment elevation in all leads.

Medical Diagnosis

Acute respiratory failure with adult respiratory distress syndrome (ARDS) secondary to manure aspiration.

Management and Clinical Data

Selected hematology and serum chemistry results were used to monitor Mr. Smith's progress. Some of the results were:

Time (hr)	WBC × 10⁹/L	Hgb (g/L)	Hct (%)	Lactic acid (mEq/L)	Serum K (mEq/L)
0 (admission)	2.5	19.1	52.9	8.2	2.4
12 hr	6.5	14.8	41.7	6.9	3.7
36 hr	10.9	12.3	37.2	3.2	3.8
72 hr	13.1	14.8	42.4	1.6	3.7

Hemodynamic data were also used to evaluate progress and the effect of therapy. Some of the results were:

Time (hr)	Dopamine, (μg/kg/min)	RA (mm Hg)	MPA (mm Hg)	PCW (mm Hg)
4	10	5	21	4
10	15	9	25	10
17	9	11	30	8
24	—	8	30	10
48	—	8	22	12
72	—	9	28	13

Time (hr)	Qt (L/min)	SVR (RU)	PVR (RU)	C(a-v)o₂ (%)	Qo₂ (cc/min)
4	4.3	19	3.9	8.0	346
10	6.5	14	2.3	6.0	388
17	6.0	11	3.7	6.8	407
24	8.5	10	2.4	4.7	402
48	7.5	9	1.3	5.3	393
72	8.6	9	1.8	4.9	416

The invasive hemodynamic monitoring was continued until the fifth hospital day.

Ventilation was monitored with blood gas results as reflected below:

	Ventilation status			Blood gas values			
Time	F_{IO_2}	PEEP (cm H_2O)	breaths/min	pH	Pa_{CO_2} (torr)	Pa_{O_2} (torr)	Pv_{O_2} (torr)
Admission	1.00	10	20	7.31	34.2	73	—
4 hr	1.00	12	20	7.29	32.5	128	41
5 hr	0.80	12	20	7.28	28.3	105	42
7 hr	0.60	14	20	7.30	31.9	134	49
10 hr	0.45	15	20	7.34	27.7	78	35
17 hr	0.40	15	12	7.38	33.3	124	37
24 hr	0.40	5	12	7.42	33.6	104	39
48 hr	—	—	Extubated	—	—	—	—
49 hr	0.50	Spontaneous	—	7.46	36.3	87	32
50 hr	0.54	Spontaneous	—	7.44	36.8	71	31
61 hr	0.60	Spontaneous	—	7.45	37.9	45	30
61 hr	—	—	Reintubated	—	—	—	—
5 days	—	—	Extubated	—	—	—	—

Mr. Smith's pulmonary shunt was: 20% on admission, 13% at the end of the first day, and 8% just before discharge.

After Mr. Smith was extubated the second time (day 5), he complained of severe headache and nasal congestion. Sinus x-rays showed right maxillary and ethmoid sinusitis. Sinus irrigation was done and a large amount of pus was obtained. Antibiotics were prescribed and Mr. Smith was transferred out of the CCU nine days after admission.

Study Questions

1. What features distinguish ARDS from acute respiratory failure?
2. What is the significance of Mr. Smith's 20% pulmonary shunt on admission?
3. What observations are used to monitor and predict the outcome of weaning from mechanical ventilation?
4. Define and explain the following techniques related to mechanical ventilation: assist/control (A/C); synchronized intermittent mandatory ventilation (SIMV); positive end expiratory pressure (PEEP); and continuous positive airway pressure (CPAP).
5. Compare and contrast the essential nursing care for Mr. Smith with that of Mr. Bates in the case study in acute respiratory failure.

ASTHMA

Units I-15 and II-2, III-4, III-10

Present Illness

Mary Callister was a 42-year-old white woman admitted to the critical care unit (CCU) for an acute asthmatic attack. For three weeks prior to admission, Ms. Callister had increasing difficulty with cough; thick, white sputum; shortness of breath; syncopal episodes associated with wheezing; and intermittent fevers with temperatures of 100–101 °F (37.8–38.8 °C).

Past Medical History

Ms. Callister's medication allergies were erythromycin and penicillin. Her illnesses included: asthma precipitated by dust, pollens, fumes, and air pollution requiring multiple ED visits and hospital admissions over the past ten years; hypertussive syncope accompanied by seizurelike activity for one year; remote thrombophlebitis.

Surgical procedures included: left brachial artery embolectomy postarterial line four years ago; right knee repair ten years ago; remote hemorrhoidectomy; remote tonsillectomy and adenoidectomy.

Current medications were: sustained release theophylline (Theodur), prednisone, phenytoin (Dilantin), warfarin sodium (Coumadin), terbutaline sulfate (Brethine), and metaproterenol sulfate (Alupent) inhaler.

Ms. Callister was married and had two children in college. Although she had never smoked she was forced to retire from her job four years ago because of her chronic obstructive lung disease.

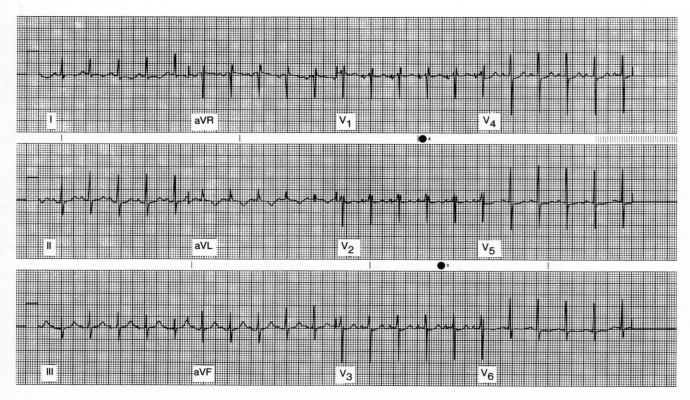

Figure 7–2 Sinus Tachycardia with Incomplete Right Bundle Branch Block. *Source:* Cardiology Department of St. Mark's Hospital, Salt Lake City, Utah.

Physical Exam on Admission to the CCU

General: Heavy-set, agitated, diaphoretic woman breathing with pursed lips. Vital signs were: BP, 100/60 mm Hg; T, 101 °F (38.3 °C).

HEENT: Normocephalic. PERRLA. Tympanic membranes intact and clear.

Chest: Dyspneic with rib retraction. Unable to complete a sentence without taking a breath. Fair inspiratory effort. A few diffuse inspiratory wheezes, marked expiratory wheezing.

CV: JVD to 7 cm while sitting up 45 degrees. PMI not palpable. Heart sounds very difficult to hear. Peripheral pulses present and thready; left radial pulse barely palpable.

Abdomen: Rounded with active bowel sounds. Soft and nontender to palpation.

Neuro: Oriented to person, place, and time. Cranial nerves II–XII intact. Sensory and motor function intact.

Laboratory Studies

Hematology: WBC, 9.5×10^9/L; Hgb, 18.2 g/dL; Hct, 52.3%.

Chest x-ray: diffuse infiltrates, air trapping.

ECG: sinus tachycardia with incomplete right bundle branch block. (See Figure 7-2.)

Medical Diagnosis

Acute asthmatic attack.

Management and Clinical Data

Ms. Callister's ventilation and oxygenation were managed and monitored by ABG results. Some of them were:

	Ventilation status			Blood gas values		
Time	F$_{IO_2}$	Mode	breaths/min	pH	Paco$_2$ (torr)	Pao$_2$ (torr)
Admission	2 L/min	Cannula	Spontaneous	7.44	45.2	65
6 hr	4 L/min	Cannula	Spontaneous	7.18	94.4	57
6 hr	—	—	Intubated	—	—	—
6 hr	0.40	SIMV	10	7.19	88.0	56
7 hr	0.40		15	7.35	60.8	79
11 hr	0.35		12	7.40	48.8	91
18 hr	0.40		15	7.20	86	91
24 hr	0.40	A/C	15	7.47	47.1	74
72 hr	—		Extubated	—	—	—
3 days	0.40	Mask	Spontaneous	7.41	53	68
6 days	0.21		Spontaneous	7.47	33.7	61

Ms. Callister was transferred out of the CCU on the fourth day and discharged on the seventh day. Pulmonary spirogram studies were also used to evaluate her progress. The results were:

Day	FVC/% predicted	F$_E$V1/FVC	F$_E$F 25–75%/FVC
3	2.48 L/52%	.75 L/30%	0.35 L/14%
6	3.50 L/73%	1.70 L/48%	0.75 L/21%

There was marked improvement with a bronchodilator.

Study Questions

1. Why is asthma considered an obstructive pulmonary disease?
2. What is hypertussive syncope?
3. What trends in ABG results indicate increasing decompensation in patients with acute asthma attacks?
4. What adjustments can be made in continuous mechanical ventilation to ease a patient's sensation of not getting enough air?
5. What nursing interventions will help calm hypoxic, agitated patients?

CHEST TRAUMA REQUIRING SURGERY

Units I-13 and II-13, III-5, III-22

Present Illness

Cathy Stillman, aged 16 years, sustained a gunshot wound in her lower chest and upper abdomen during a domestic quarrel. She was eight weeks pregnant and was shot by a former girlfriend of the father of her baby. It was unclear what her current relationship was with the baby's father. The patient was seen in the ED at 0330 and was taken to the operating room (OR) for repair of thoracic and abdominal injuries shortly afterward.

After surgery, Cathy was brought to the critical care unit (CCU) to recover. At the time of her arrival there the assailant had not been arrested but had telephoned the patient's mother with threats of further injury. The nursing staff was instructed to release information to Cathy's mother (Ms. Stillman) only. No police officers were stationed in the hospital.

Past Medical History

Cathy was unable to give her past medical history at the time of admission. When Ms. Stillman, her mother, gave telephone permission for surgical repair of Cathy's wounds, she stated that Cathy had never been "real sick" but had "been in a lot of trouble." Apparently, Cathy lived with her mother and several older and younger siblings.

Physical Exam on First Postoperative Day

General: A black adolescent of average height for weight, who appeared considerably older than her stated age and complained loudly of severe pain. Vital signs were: BP, 110/70 mm Hg; T, 99 °F (37.2 °C); HR, 90/min; RR, 20/min.

HEENT: Normocephalic and atraumatic. PERRLA. Normal fundoscopic exam. EOMs intact. Nasal oxygen cannula in place with oxygen running at 4 L/min. Double lumen nasogastric (NG) tube connected to low constant suction draining "coffee ground" material. Septum midline. Turbinates pale and boggy. Pharynx clear and without exudate. Teeth in good repair.

Neck: Supple. No palpable cervical lymph nodes. Thyroid palpable as smooth but not enlarged. No JVD.

Chest: Symmetrical excursion. Chest tube in left posterior thorax draining sanguinous fluid. No air leak observed. No crepitus or subcutaneous emphysema noted.

Lungs: Scattered rales and rhonchi. Diminished breath sounds in the bases. Poor cough effort productive of white sputum. Guarding and splinting with deep breaths.

CV: Normal sinus rhythm without ectopy. Normal heart sounds without rubs, murmurs, or gallops.

Abdomen: Slightly rounded and distended. Midline dressing intact and dry. Colostomy in left upper quadrant; mucosa pink and moist; no drainage in bag. No skin breakdown. Bowel sounds very faint and occasional. Soft and very tender. Inadequate palpation due to guarding.

Extremities: Pulses present, equal, and moderate. No lacerations or other evidence of trauma.

Neuro: Alert and oriented to person, place, and time. Cranial nerves II–XII grossly intact. DTRs symmetrical 1+ and 2+, flexor plantar response present.

Laboratory Studies

Admission urinalysis: within normal limits

Admission ABGs on oxygen at 10 L/min: CO sat, 1.5%; O_2 sat, 98%; Po_2, 219 torr; Pco_2, 30.0 torr; HCO_3, 18.5 mEq/L; base excess −4.7; pH 7.40; Hgb, 10.0 g/dL; and Cao_2, 13.5 vol%.

Admission WBC differential: segmented neutrophils (segs), 53%; lymphocytes (lymphs), 44%; monocytes (monos), 3%; platelets, adequate.

Admission coagulation: PT, 11.1 sec; PTT, 25.2 sec.

Serum chemistry:

Component	Value Admission	Value Postoperative
Na (mEq/L)	139	133
K (mEq/L)	3.9	3.1
Cl (mEq/L)	116	105
CO₂ (mmol/L)	20	21
Glucose (mg/dL)	108	120
BUN (mg/dL)	9	5

Hematology:

Component	Value Admission	Value Postoperative
WBC (× 10⁹/L)	8.7	13.0
RBC (× 10¹²/L)	3.40	4.24
Hgb (g/dL)	10.4	12.7
Hct (%)	30.9	38.5
MCV (cubic micrometers)	90.7	90.8
MCH (pg)	30.6	30.0
MCHC (%)	33.7	33.0

Medical Diagnosis

Status post gunshot wound and repair of left lung and colon.

Management

Postoperative medications were cefoxitin (Mefoxin), 1 g IV q6h, and meperidine (Demerol), 50–100 mg IM q4h prn pain. The IV fluids ordered by the surgeon were 5% dextrose in 0.2% normal saline with 20 mEq/L potassium chloride infused at 125 mL/hr as maintenance and 5% dextrose in 0.45% normal saline with 40 mEq/L potassium infused as replacement for nasogastric drainage.

Each time the nurses approached Cathy for turning, coughing, and deep breathing Cathy whined and cried and complained of severe pain. The nurses were careful to administer pain medication before carrying out the routine but Cathy continued to complain and coughed very poorly. As a result of her poor cough effort, Cathy's breath sounds diminished in the bases and became more and more moist in the middle and upper lobes.

Study Questions

1. What potential complications is Cathy at risk to develop considering the nature of her injury?
2. What implications do the circumstances surrounding Cathy's injury have for nursing?
3. Plan nursing care and outcomes for Cathy based on the following nursing diagnoses:

   > Anxiety
   > Bowel elimination, alterations in: Incontinence
   > Breathing patterns, ineffective
   > Mobility, impaired physical
   > Nutrition, alterations in: Less than body requirements
   > Self-concept, disturbance in
   > Skin integrity, impairment of: Actual

4. What nursing interventions are required to monitor Cathy's pregnancy?
5. What nursing interventions might improve Cathy's cooperation during coughing?

EMPHYSEMA

Units I-15 and I-12, I-14, II-2, II-13, III-5, III-10

Present Illness

Alfred Frost, aged 63 years, with advanced chronic obstructive pulmonary disease (COPD) was admitted to the CCU for progressive respiratory distress. His respiratory status began deteriorating three months prior to admission following an upper respiratory tract infection. Since then he had used oxygen at home, intermittently produced large amounts of purulent nonbloody sputum, and lost 10 lb.

Past Medical History

Mr. Frost was allergic to penicillin. His past medical illnesses included: spring hayfever and rare asthma since puberty; progressive emphysema with a reversible component for 18 years; and adenocarcinoma of the lung for 2 years.

Surgeries were: right inguinal herniorrhaphy 12 years ago; Billroth II gastrojejunostomy followed by right upper lobe atelectasis requiring tracheostomy 10 years ago; right upper lobectomy for benign organized pneumonitic process 10 years ago; appendectomy and repair of perforated sigmoid diverticulitis with peritonitis 9 years ago.

Mr. Frost's religion was Greek Orthodox. He was the owner of a movie theater. He had been a heavy cigarette smoker and exposed to toxic chemicals during his working life.

Physical Exam on Admission to CCU

General: Thin, wasted, tired looking man in acute respiratory distress. Vital signs were: BP, 140/100 mm Hg; rectal T, 97.8 °F (36.5 °C); HR, 134 /min; RR, 40/min.
HEENT: PERRLA. Foul odor to breath.
Chest: Increased AP diameter. Decreased breath sounds in the right lower lobe posteriorly and anteriorly with scattered loud wheezes, rhonchi, and rales. Prolonged expiratory time and rib retractions with dyspnea and tachypnea noted.
CV: Sinus tachycardia. Heart sounds difficult to hear. Normal S_1 and S_2 with summation gallop. Skin warm and moist. Peripheral pulses present, equal, and strong. Pitting edema (2+) noted on lower extremities and sacrum.
Abdomen: Scaphoid. Several mature scars. Bowel sounds active in all quadrants. Soft, nontender without masses. Lower liver edge palpable 2 cm below right costal margin.
GU: Normal adult male.
Neuro: Grossly intact although patient fatigued quickly.

Laboratory Studies

Hematology on admission: WBC, 13.0×10^9/L; Hgb, 17.2 g/dL; Hct, 50.8%.
Chest x-ray: extensive, severe alveolar disease with possible pneumonia in lower two-thirds of right lung. Mass 8 × 5 cm extending outward from right side of superior mediastinum. Severe emphysema.
ECG: sinus rhythm with occasional ventricular ec-

topic beats. Pulmonary disease pattern. Old septal infarct. (See Figure 7–3.)

Medical Diagnoses

1. Acute respiratory failure.
2. Chronic obstructive pulmonary disease.
3. Adenocarcinoma of the lung.

Management and Clinical Data

Mr. Frost required aerosolized bronchodilators every one to two hours initially. An aminophylline (Aminophyllin) infusion was administered as well. The frequency of the aerosol treatments was gradually reduced to every four hours. Supplemental oxygen was administered by nasal cannula. Mr. Frost's progress was followed by the ABG results which were:

Time (hr)	O_2 (L/min)	pH	$Paco_2$ (torr)	Pao_2 (torr)	Cao_2 (%)
0 (admission)	2	7.06	92.8	30	8.8
2	4	7.18	66.2	62	20.0
4	6	7.21	72.3	69	21.4
6	4	7.28	60.8	55	19.9
9	4	7.35	52.8	48	19.6
24	4	7.37	52.2	62	21.7
Discharge	2	7.40	57.8	66	21.3

Measurements of pulmonary mechanics were used to evaluate Mr. Frost:

Day	FVC / % predicted	FEV1 / % FVC	FEF 25–75% / % FVC
Admission	1.56 L / 45%	0.54 L / 34%	0.25 L / 6%
1	1.94 L / 53%	0.70 L / 21%	0.30 L / 8%
2	2.27 L / 54	0.51 L / 23%	0.24 L / 11%
Discharge	1.47 L / 34	0.53 L / 36%	0.18 L / 12%

The nurses worked with the dietitian to provide small, frequent, high-calorie and high-protein meals. This approach, adapted to his anorexia, dyspnea, and previous gastric surgery, improved Mr. Frost's nutritional status. Mr. Frost was transferred out of the CCU on the second hospital day and discharged five days after admission.

One month after discharge Mr. Frost was readmitted in acute respiratory failure. He and his family decided no resuscitation should be performed and he died two days after readmission.

Study Questions

1. Describe the pathophysiology of Mr. Frost's chronic respiratory failure. What changes occur when acute respiratory failure is superimposed?

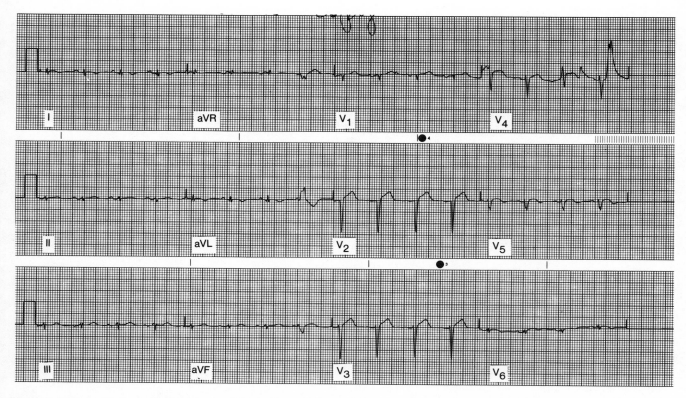

Figure 7–3 Sinus Rhythm with Ventricular Ectopic Beats, Pulmonary Disease Pattern, and Old Septal Myocardial Infarction. *Source:* Cardiology Department of St. Mark's Hospital, Salt Lake City, Utah.

2. According to the spirogram results, was Mr. Frost improved at discharge?
3. Why did Mr. Frost's $Paco_2$ increase when he was receiving 6 L/min of oxygen?
4. If it is not possible to achieve normal ABG levels in a patient with respiratory failure, what ABG levels are considered to be acceptable?
5. Identify Mr. Frost's nursing problems. What outcomes are appropriate for him in view of his end-stage respiratory failure?

NEAR DROWNING

Unit III-1

Present Illness

Vera Jones, aged 25 years, was admitted to the CCU following a canoeing accident. Ms. Jones was canoeing with friends in a freshwater lake during a windstorm when the canoe overturned. She was not wearing a lifejacket when she entered the very cold water and quickly became hypothermic. No one in the party was an experienced swimmer or canoeist and none of them noticed Ms. Jones struggling for her life. Fortunately, some amateur scuba drivers were practicing nearby and came to their aid. One of the divers located Ms. Jones about two feet under the water's surface. When she was brought to the surface, Ms. Jones was not breathing but did have a slow pulse. The diver began mouth-to-mouth resuscitation in the water. By this time, the lake patrol arrived and moved Ms. Jones onto its boat. Resuscitation was continued while the patrol arranged for transportation from the lake to the nearest emergency facility which was 40 miles away.

Past Medical History

Her past medical history was unknown.

Physical Exam on Admission to the ED

General: A spontaneously breathing, semiconscious young woman in moderate respiratory distress. Vital signs were: BP, 100/60 mm Hg; rectal T, 94 °F (34.4 °C), HR, 130/min; RR, 12/min and labored.

HEENT: Normocephalic. Small ecchymosis above right eye. Pupils round and reactive to light. Right pupil 3 mm, left pupil 4 mm. Fundoscopic exam findings were normal. EOMs grossly intact although patient was not fully cooperative. Tympanic membranes intact. Nasal septum midline, mucosa reddened. Teeth in good repair. Pharynx slightly injected.

Neck: ROM not tested. Thyroid and lymph nodes not palpable.

Chest: Normal AP diameter. Excursion symmetrical. Breath sounds include rales and rhonchi throughout all lung fields. Heart sounds normal and without rubs, murmurs, or gallops.

Abdomen: Flat with bowel sounds in all quadrants. Soft, nontender, and without masses or organomegaly.

Extremities: No deformities or signs of injury. Peripheral pulses present, moderate, and equal.

Neuro: Semiconscious. Responds to deep pain and voice. Attempts to follow commands but does not answer questions. Moves all four extremities with equal strength. DTRs symmetrical at 2+ with plantar flexion response present.

Laboratory Studies

ABGs on oxygen at 10 L/min by mask: Pao_2, 57 torr; $Paco_2$, 43.3 torr; pH 7.13; base excess, -13.5; and HCO_3, 14.7 mEq/L.
CBC and serum electrolytes: results were pending.

Medical Diagnoses

1. Freshwater near-drowning.
2. Possible head and/or spinal cord injury.

Management

In the ED, Ms. Jones was intubated with a 7F endotracheal tube. Her lungs were suctioned and a sample was sent to the laboratory for culture. She was temporarily placed on a pressure cycled ventilator and ventilated with an FIO_2 of 0.50. A double lumen nasogastric tube was inserted and connected to low constant suction. Lake water began to drain from Ms. Jones' stomach. An IV was started and 5% dextrose in lactated Ringer's solution was infused at a slow rate. An indwelling urinary catheter was inserted to facilitate monitoring renal function and urine output. Skull, cervical, and chest x-rays as well as an ECG were done. A second set of ABGs indicated improved ventilation and acid-base status.

Ms. Jones was transferred to the CCU where she was placed on a volume cycled ventilator. The ventilator settings were: V_T, 600 mL; FIO_2, 0.50; and SIMV, 15/min. ABGs drawn 30 minutes later showed slight improvement in Pao_2 and $Paco_2$ values. Five-cm H_2O PEEP was added and subsequent ABGs showed satisfactory oxygenation and more normal acid-base status.

During the next 24 hours, Ms. Jones was kept on bed rest and observed closely for signs and symptoms of complications of near drowning. She steadily improved and had no complications so the nurses began to wean her from the ventilator. Ms. Jones was extubated 48 hours after admission and transferred out of the CCU on the third hospital day.

Study Questions

1. What is the etiology of the pulmonary edema seen in freshwater drowning? How does it compare with that of saltwater drowning?
2. Describe the pathophysiology related to the potential complications of near drowning.
3. Why was the range of motion in Ms. Jones' neck not tested when she was examined in the ED?
4. Outline and explain a nursing care plan for Ms. Jones.
5. If Ms. Jones asks about the other people in the boating party, how can information be obtained?

PULMONARY FIBROSIS

Units I-15 and I-16, I-23, II-13, III-5, III-6

Present Illness

Valerie Hall, aged 47 years, was admitted to the hospital for diagnosis and management of severe, diffuse, infiltrative pulmonary disease. Ms. Hall's pulmonary disease had a gradual and insidious onset. She believed that her problems began when she became short of breath and had severe dyspnea on exertion on a camping trip four years ago. However, she actually had already begun to decrease her activity due to shortness of breath seven years prior to this admission. Two years ago she began having transient episodes of dyspnea when she walked up the seven steps in front of her home. Her shortness of breath had since progressed from dyspnea on exertion to dyspnea at rest. Six months ago she developed a persistent productive cough. For two weeks prior to admission she had a low-grade fever accompanied by chills which was treated with combined trimethoprim and sulfamethoxazole (Bactrim). She felt increasingly fatigued and also complained of pain and stiffness in her large joints which was worse in the morning.

Past Medical History

Ms. Hall had croup and asthma when she was a child. She did not know of any allergies. She denied serious illness, surgery, and trauma. She was married and a housewife with five grown children who lived near her in a small community. She and her husband were active members of the Church of Jesus Christ of Latter-Day Saints (Mormon) and did not smoke or drink. Her husband was frequently unemployed so they did not "have much money for doctors."

Physical Exam on Admission

General: Thin, pleasant person who became dyspneic while resting in bed and talking. Vital signs were: BP, 110/74 mm Hg; T, 103.2 °F (39.5 °C); HR, 92/min; RR, 34/min.
HEENT: Unremarkable.
Chest: Normal configuration with decreased expansion despite normal diaphragmatic movement. Harsh breath sounds without crackles or wheezes. Pleural rub in right base.
CV: Normal sinus rhythm without gallops, rubs, or murmurs.
GI: Flat with active bowel sounds in all quadrants. Soft and without tenderness, masses or organomegaly.
Neuro: Grossly intact.

Laboratory Studies

Admission ABGs on oxygen at 4 L/min by nasal cannula: pH 7.43; $Paco_2$, 38 torr; Pao_2, 46 torr; pulmonary shunt (Qs/Qt), 20%.
Chest x-ray: extensive bilateral pulmonary infiltrates.

Medical Diagnosis

Pulmonary fibrosis of unknown etiology.

Management and Clinical Data

During the first few days Ms. Hall received broad-spectrum antibiotics and supplemental oxygen. Diagnostic tests were done to identify the underlying cause of her respiratory failure. On day four, the etiology of Ms. Hall's pulmonary disease was still unclear so she was taken to the operating room for an open lung biopsy. The pathology report of the lung biopsy indi-

cated an "acute and organizing interstitial pneumonitis of unknown etiology." Following the biopsy her worsening pulmonary status required that she be admitted to the CCU.

When Ms. Hall was admitted to the CCU, the physicians and nurses inserted hemodynamic monitoring catheters and gathered baseline data. Mechanical ventilation was instituted on day four. Initially Ms. Hall did well with the mechanical ventilation but then she began to deteriorate and was unable to be weaned from the ventilator.

During the period of mechanical ventilation several chest tubes had to be inserted because of pneumothoraxes. When very high PEEP levels were required, special valves had to be inserted in the tubing to the waterseal drainage units to prevent the ventilator tidal volume from blowing out of the lungs through the chest tubes. Blood gas results were used to monitor the effectiveness of the mechanical ventilation. Some of the blood gas results were:

		Ventilator status				Blood gas values			
Day	FIo₂	PEEP (cm H₂O)	Mode	Breaths/min	pH	Paco₂ (torr)	Pao₂ (torr)	Pvo₂ (torr)	Qs/Qt (%)
4	0.60	5	IMV	12	7.36	47.1	51	35	49
7	1.00	10	IMV	20	7.45	55.0	92	44	36
13	.65	30	IMV	20	7.41	45.9	49	35	51
16	1.00	40	A/C	20	7.45	37.8	59	37	39
17	1.00	15	A/C	12	7.42	41.8	47	33	53
18	1.00	20	A/C	22	7.43	48.7	47	33	52
19	1.00	49	A/C	22	7.31	61.7	56	36	44
20	1.00	15	IMV	16	7.10	78.0	35	29	81
21	1.00	15	A/C	15	7.01	85.7	24	15	83

Some of the hemodynamic data obtained during this period was:

Day	RAP (mm Hg)	MPA (mm Hg)	PCWP (mm Hg)	Qt (L/min)	SVR (RU)	PVR (RU)	C(a-v)o₂ (%)	Qo₂ (cc/min)
4	10	40	18	12.4	8	1.8	3.75	465
7	10	26	7	9.2	10	2.1	3.50	320
13	8	32	10	5.3	15	4.2	4.84	256
16	20	36	12	5.7	20	4.2	5.26	300
18	16	38	16	6.8	12	3.2	3.91	251
19	24	52	29	5.4	13	4.3	5.60	302
21	13	46	14	10.6	6	3.0	3.27	347

On day 21, the hypoxemia, acidosis, and increasing shunt were thought to indicate irreversible pulmonary damage. Ventilator support was withdrawn with the family's knowledge and consent.

Study Questions

1. Describe the pathophysiological process responsible for pneumothorax during ventilation with PEEP.

2. What are the legal and ethical implications of discontinuing the ventilator?
3. What was the purpose of the special valves inserted in the waterseal tubing during ventilation with high levels of PEEP?
4. Identify Ms. Hall's actual nursing diagnoses or nursing problems and appropriate outcomes as well as the nursing interventions required to achieve the outcomes.
5. Explain how the nursing actions will assist in resolving the problems and accomplishing the goals.

SUPPORTING RESPIRATION

Unit I-12

Present Illness

Caroline Young, aged 70 years, was admitted with complaints of weakness, anorexia, and constipation alternating with diarrhea with occasional blood-streaked stools. Diagnostic studies showed a neoplastic lesion in her sigmoid colon. She was scheduled for exploratory laparotomy and probable colectomy.

Past Medical History

Ms. Young had mild hypertension diagnosed when she was 45 years old. The hypertension had been controlled with diet except during periods of stress which required thiazide diuretics. She had a mild cough during the winter months which she had not described to her family doctor. Ms. Young had been a schoolteacher, lived alone, and had never married.

Physical Exam on Admission

General: Thin, pleasant elderly woman who seemed very fit for her age. Ht, 5 ft, 4 in; wt, 110 lb. Vital signs were: BP, 160/92 mm Hg; T, 98 °F (36.7 °C); HR, 84/min; RR, 16/min.
HEENT: Unremarkable.
Chest: Symmetrical excursion. Lungs clear to percussion and auscultation. Heart sounds normal with grade 2/6 systolic murmur at aortic area. No rubs or gallops.
Abdomen: Scaphoid. Bowel sounds hyperactive in all quadrants. Soft with mild tenderness. No palpable masses or organomegaly.
Extremities: Pulses present and equal. ROM limited at knees and hips. No edema noted.

Neuro: Alert and oriented to person, place, and time. Cranial nerves II–XII grossly intact.

Laboratory Studies

Coagulation, CBC, serum electrolytes, serum chemistries, and urinalysis: within normal limits.
ABG and pulmonary function: tests were not done.

Medical Diagnosis

Neoplastic lesion of the colon.

Management

Ms. Young received a customary bowel preparation regimen prior to surgery. An exploratory laparotomy, colon resection, and colostomy were performed with general anesthesia consisting of halothane (Fluothane), nitrous oxide, and tubocurarine chloride. The patient's vital signs remained stable throughout the eight-hour procedure and there was no evidence of intraoperative or anesthetic complications. Six units of blood were transfused which equaled the estimated blood loss. At the end of the procedure, Ms. Young's respirations were inadequate and required support. The endotracheal tube was left in place and she was transferred to the CCU for mechanical ventilation with a volume ventilator.

Initial settings on the ventilator were: V_T, 750 cc; F_{IO_2}, 0.40; and SIMV, 10/min. ABGs were obtained after 30 minutes. The ABG results were: pH 7.47; P_{CO_2}, 32 torr; P_{O_2}, 63 torr; O_2 sat, 92.8%; base excess 1.1; HCO_3, 23.2 mEq/L; Hgb, 13.6 g/dL; Ca_{O_2}, 17.3%; and CO sat, 2.4%.

Study Questions

1. Explain the aspects of surgical procedures and anesthesia that contribute to hypoventilation in the early postoperative period.
2. Distinguish between various types of ventilators: pressure cycled, volume cycled, and time cycled.
3. What observations are important in assessing the effect of the mechanical ventilator on the patient?
4. What means of communication can be used by alert patients who are mechanically ventilated?
5. What are the appropriate outcomes for Ms. Young if the following nursing diagnoses are used?

   Bowel elimination, alterations in: Incontinence

Breathing patterns, ineffective
Comfort, alterations in: Pain
Fluid volume deficit, potential
Self-concept, disturbance in

Skin integrity, impairment of: Potential

6. Arrange the preceding nursing diagnoses in order of priority from most important to least important.

Chapter 8

Renal Case Studies

ACUTE RENAL FAILURE REQUIRING DIALYSIS

Units I-20 and I-24

Present Illness

Claude Nissen, aged 66 years, was a retired high school teacher who was admitted to the hospital for cholecystectomy. He tolerated the surgery well and was recovering on the surgical nursing unit. On the first postoperative morning his vital signs were: BP, 116/66 mm Hg; T, 100 °F (37.8 °C); HR, 86 and regular; RR, 16 and unlabored. In the afternoon, his vital signs were: BP, 124/72 mm Hg; T, 104 °F (40 °C); HR, 96/min and regular; RR, 20/min and unlabored. He had voided 200 mL urine during the last eight hours. A tepid sponge bath decreased his temperature. Blood, urine, sputum, and wound drainage specimens were collected and sent for culture. Mr. Nissen was transferred to the critical care unit (CCU) for management of probable sepsis and acute renal failure.

Past Medical History

The patient had suffered repeated attacks of cholecystitis over the past five years. He had never been hospitalized and had no other significant medical history.

Physical Exam on Admission to the CCU

General: An elderly patient who appeared older than his stated age. Obviously uncomfortable. Vital signs were: BP, 120/82 mm Hg; T, 101 °F (38.5 °C); HR, 112/min and regular; RR, 24/min and deep. His skin was warm and dry.
Head, Ears, Eyes, Nose, and Throat (HEENT): Unremarkable.

Chest: Lungs and heart were within normal limits when inspected, palpated, percussed, and auscultated.
Abdomen: Distended. Large bulky dressing over incision was intact and dry. A Penrose drain in the right upper quadrant drained serosanguinous fluid without odor onto separate dressing.
Extremities: No deformities. Peripheral pulses were present and bounding.
Neurological Status (Neuro): Grossly intact.

Laboratory Studies

CBC and serum chemistry: results were within normal limits except WBC, 29.0×10^9/L; K, 5.0 mEq/L; and BUN, 92 mg/dL.

Medical Diagnoses

1. Status post cholecystectomy.
2. Possible sepsis.
3. Possible renal failure.

Management

Mr. Nissen continued to have an elevated temperature of 101 °F (38.5 °C) with spikes to 103 °F (39.4 °C) despite antibiotic therapy. The initial cultures showed no growth after 48 hours. The Penrose drain began to drain purulent, bile-stained fluid and the surgeon identified an intraabdominal abscess. Mr. Nissen was taken to the operating room and the abscess was incised and drained. The drainage was cultured and grew multiple organisms. A blood culture grew similar organisms. The antibiotics were changed to a combination which the culture sensitivity indicated would be effective. Because his urine output and renal function had not improved, an external arteriovenous (AV) shunt was placed in his left arm. Hemodialysis was instituted and continued for five hours every other day for 14 days. The sepsis gradually resolved following drainage of the abscess and institution of appropriate antibiotic therapy. Mr. Nissen was transferred out of the CCU on the 21st hospital day and was discharged on the 30th day with near normal renal function.

Study Questions

1. Describe the pathophysiological mechanisms responsible for Mr. Nissen's sepsis and renal failure.
2. Describe appropriate assessment of AV shunts and AV fistulas.
3. Why was incision and drainage of the abscess required? Would the antibiotics have been effective alone?
4. What were the potential complications of Mr. Nissen's cholecystectomy, sepsis, and acute renal failure?
5. What nursing interventions are important for prevention of the complications you described in question 4?

UROLOGICAL TRAUMA REQUIRING SURGERY

Unit I-21

Present Illness

William Trapp, a cowboy aged 55 years, was thrown from a bucking horse during a roundup. A large bull trod on his abdomen while he was on the ground before fellow riders turned the herd. He was noted to be in acute distress and was evacuated by helicopter for treatment at the hospital. During assessment in the ED, bloody fluid returned from an abdominal tap. An indwelling urinary catheter was placed and drained bloody urine. Skull, cervical, chest, and pelvic x-rays did not show any fractures.

Mr. Trapp was taken to the OR for exploratory laparotomy. His spleen was fractured and his left kidney was lacerated. The surgeons removed his spleen and repaired his kidney. No other major internal injuries were found. Mr. Trapp tolerated the surgery well and was admitted to the critical care unit (CCU) in stable condition.

Past Medical History

Mr. Trapp had always been in good health. He had been thrown from horses on two previous occasions and received minor injuries which had healed well.

Physical Exam on Admission to the CCU

General: Well-tanned wiry man who appeared older than his stated age. Ht, 5 ft, 6 in; wt, 150 lb. Vital signs were: BP, 120/80 mm Hg; T, 97 °F (36.1 °C); HR, 88/min; RR, 20/min.
HEENT: Normocephalic. No external evidence of trauma. PERRL at 3 mm. Tympanic membranes intact. Edentulous. Small lesion on right lower gum. Tonsils surgically absent. Double lumen nasogastric tube in right naris connected to low constant suction returning minimal amount of bile-colored gastric drainage.
Neck: No evidence of trauma. No palpable lymph nodes or thyroid enlargement.
Chest: Symmetrical and equal excursion. No evidence of trauma. Breath sounds diminished in the bases and with scattered rhonchi in large airways. Productive cough. Cardiac rhythm was normal sinus rhythm with occasional ventricular ectopy. PMI in sixth ICS in left MCL. Normal S_1 and physiologically split S_2. An S_4 gallop but no rub or murmur was heard.
Abdomen: Flat. Dressings midline and left flank were dry and intact. No bowel sounds heard in any quadrant. Soft and tender.
GU: Indwelling catheter draining pink tinged urine at 30 mL/hr.
Neuro: Grossly intact.
Extremities: Swarthy with equal peripheral pulses. Tobacco stains on second and third fingers of right hand. IV fluids of 5% dextrose in normal saline (D5NS) and 5% dextrose in 0.2% normal saline (D5/.2NS) infusing through 16-gauge angiocatheter in right forearm at 50 mL/hr and 100 mL/hr, respectively. Whole blood infusing through 16-gauge angiocatheter in left forearm at 150 mL/hr.

Laboratory Studies

Preoperative CBC, coagulation, and serum chemistry values: findings were within normal limits.
Urinalysis: confirmed the presence of hematuria.

Medical Diagnosis

Status post nephrectomy secondary to trauma.

Management

Mr. Trapp remained in the CCU for several days. During this time, nurses observed him for further injuries and complications. They helped Mr. Trapp perform preventive actions such as deep breathing, incentive spirometry, and coughing. Mr. Trapp required frequent dressing changes because of the surgical drains that had been placed. At first the dressings quickly became saturated with serosanguinous fluid and urine and required frequent changes. As the healing process proceeded, the drainage became mostly serous as more urine was drained through the indwelling urinary catheter. As this happened, the nurses were able to decrease the frequency of the dressing changes.

While the dressings were off, the nurses observed ecchymosis where the bull had stepped and in the surrounding area. The nurses marked the extent of the ecchymosis and observed its color in order to monitor the amount of postoperative bleeding. The ecchymosis slowly increased in size during the first 24 hours. After that it remained the same size and subsequently developed the characteristic color changes of the healing process. The rest of Mr. Trapp's recovery was uneventful and he was transferred out of the CCU on the fifth day.

Study Questions

1. What effect is the splenectomy likely to have on Mr. Trapp's future health and lifestyle? The lacerated kidney?

2. Outline the procedure of the "abdominal tap" done in the ED.

3. Considering the nature and circumstances of his accident, what additional injuries might be associated with Mr. Trapp's fractured spleen and lacerated kidney? Explain the observations the nurses should make to detect such complications and the signs and symptoms that would alert them to the development of each complication.

4. Describe the dressings and drains Mr. Trapp could be expected to have postoperatively.

5. Write a nursing care plan for Mr. Trapp's immediate postoperative period.

Chapter 9

Neurological Case Studies

ACETAMINOPHEN INGESTION

Unit II-12

Present Illness

Mary Ellen Green, aged 18 years, ingested approximately 25 (500 mg each) acetaminophen (Tylenol) tablets during an argument with her husband. About four hours later at 0400 hours, she realized that she did not intend to kill herself and went to the ED. When questioned, she denied recent exposure to other drugs, alcohol, or poisons. She claimed to have taken only her oral contraceptive pill on the day of the ingestion. This anxious patient denied discomfort, nausea, vomiting, or abdominal pain.

Past Medical History

Her past medical history was judged unremarkable.

Physical Exam on Admission to the ED

General: An anxious, well-developed, well-nourished young woman in no apparent distress. Wt, 100 lb. Vital signs were: BP, 124/50 mm Hg; T, 98.6 °F (37 °C); HR, 112/min and regular; RR, 14/min.
Head, Ears, Eyes, Nose, and Throat (HEENT): Normal examination. No scleral icterus was present.
Chest: The lungs were clear and the heart was not enlarged. No rubs, murmurs, or gallops were auscultated.
Abdomen: Flat. Normal bowel sounds in all quadrants. Liver spanned 8 cm, was not enlarged, and was mildly tender to palpation.
Genitourinary system (GU): Normal examination.
Extremities: Normal in appearance without petechiae or purpura.

Neurological status (Neuro): Normal cerebral and cerebellar function. Cranial nerves II–XII were grossly intact and no abnormal reflexes were elicited.

Laboratory Studies

CBC; serum electrolytes and chemistries; urinalysis; chest x-ray; and ECG (Figure 9–1) were all within normal limits on admission.

Medical Diagnosis

Acetaminophen ingestion.

Management

In the ED, Ms. Green was given ipecac syrup with copious amounts of fluids to evacuate her stomach. She was also given acetylcysteine (Mucomyst), 140 mg/kg orally in grapefruit juice. Ms. Green was admitted to the CCU for cardiac and respiratory monitoring. Twelve hours after admission, she began to complain of nausea and vomited several times. By morning, she was feeling better and seemed improved. The serum chemistries drawn that morning showed elevated hepatic enzyme values. Ms. Green continued to receive acetylcysteine 70 mg/kg orally (p.o.) q4h and remained in the CCU until her elevated hepatic enzyme values peaked and began to decline.

Study Questions

1. What are the manifestations and mechanisms of acetaminophen toxicity?
2. How can the potential severity be assessed and complications avoided?
3. What drugs or other treatment methods can be used to alter the toxicity of acetaminophen?

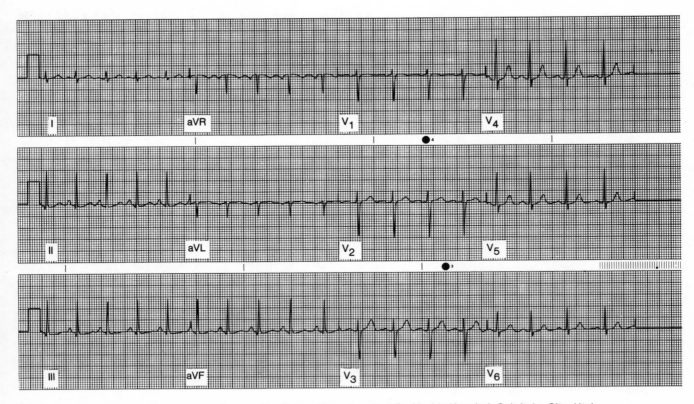

Figure 9–1 Normal Electrocardiogram. *Source:* Cardiology Department of St. Mark's Hospital, Salt Lake City, Utah.

4. What constitutes appropriate management of acetaminophen toxicity?
5. Outline a nursing care plan for Ms. Green. Include aspects that are specific to the acetaminophen ingestion as well as psychosocial considerations.

ALTERED LEVEL OF CONSCIOUSNESS

Units II-8 and II-10, III-23

Present Illness

Charles Wentworth, aged 77 years, was admitted to a tertiary facility with a chief complaint of deteriorating level of consciousness (LOC) following an automobile accident in which he sustained multiple facial fractures and head injury. An acute subdural hematoma was to be ruled out.

The patient was a resident of a very small town and was involved in a high-speed, head-on collision early in the morning. He was taken to the ED of the nearest hospital which was in a larger town 70 miles away where he was stabilized and admitted at 0800 hours. Mr. Wentworth had no neurological deficits until 1500 hours when he suddenly became somnolent. He was transferred by ambulance (300 miles) and admitted to the tertiary hospital at midnight. The referring physician reported that he was blind in the right eye prior to the accident.

Past Medical History

No past medical history was available.

Physical Exam on Admission to the Tertiary CCU

General: Unshaven man, appeared well-nourished and his stated age. Semiconscious and in moderate distress. Vital signs were: BP, 180/90 mm Hg; T, 101 °F (38.3 °C); HR, 92/min; spontaneous RR, 12/min with regular variations in rate and depth.
Head: Multiple facial bruises, asymmetry to mouth. Penrose drain protruding from skin behind right ear.
Eyes: Lids bruised and swollen, conjunctival and scleral hemorrhages, PERRL, 2 mm. Fundi could not be examined.

Ears: Bruising and laceration of right external ear. Tympanic membranes intact.

Nose: Bruised. Septum midline. No apparent deformity. Oxygen at 4 L/min by nasal cannula in place.

Mouth: Teeth missing with bleeding evident from gums. Mandible unstable. Tongue swollen and crusted with bloody mucus. Moist secretions in pharynx. No swallowing observed.

Chest: Abdominal breathing, no movement of rib cage with respirations. Faint bruising of anterior chest. Lungs clear in the upper lobes, rhonchi in the lower lobes. Cardiac rhythm was normal sinus rhythm with occasional PVB. Heart sounds consisted of normal S_1 and S_2 as well as an S_4 gallop. No rubs or murmurs were heard.

Abdomen: Flat with faint bowel sounds in all quadrants. No evidence of trauma. Soft, nontender, and without masses or organomegaly.

GU: Indwelling catheter in place draining 30 mL/hr of yellow, cloudy, foul-smelling urine.

Extremities: No deformities or evidence of trauma. Peripheral pulses all present and equal. IV fluid of D5/.45NS infusing at 125 mL/hr through 19-gauge stainless steel needle in right hand.

Neuro: Opened eyes to name, deep pain, and spontaneously. Speech was not understandable although the patient seemed to make appropriate efforts. Followed commands to move arms and legs some of the time. Right arm and leg strength were less than left.

Laboratory Studies

A CT scan was done immediately after Mr. Wentworth arrived at the tertiary center. Diffuse cerebral edema was present but subdural hematoma was not evident. No other laboratory studies were done at the tertiary center prior to admission to the CCU.

CBC results obtained at 0200: WBC, 9.2×10^9/L; RBC, 5.12×10^{12}/L; Hgb, 14.3 g/dL; and Hct, 44.5%.

Serum electrolytes and chemistries at 0200: Na, 135 mEq/L; K, 4.0 mEq/L; Cl, 105 mEq/L; CO_2, 28 mmol/L; glucose, 131 mg/dL; and BUN, 11 mg/dL.

Medical Diagnoses

1. Head injury.
2. Facial trauma with fractures.

Management

Mr. Wentworth was taken to the critical care unit (CCU) for observation. He received supplemental oxygen and ABGs were monitored. The results were:

Time after admission at midnight*	Oxygen flow (L/min)	Mode	ABGs			
			pH	Paco$_2$ (torr)	Pao$_2$ (torr)	Sao$_2$ (%)
0045 hrs	4	Cannula	7.47	40	58	83.3
0200 hrs	7	Mask	7.43	37	62	88.3
0600 hrs	7	Mask	7.39	37	74	91.3

At 0400 hrs wrist restraints were added to help keep mask in place.

A dexamethasone (Decadron) regimen had been started at the referring hospital and was continued at the tertiary center. Mr. Wentworth's neurological status was checked every hour and was noted to improve gradually. His movements became more purposeful as he tried to remove his oxygen mask and other irritating stimuli. His eyelids swelled during the night and by 0400 hours it was no longer possible to view his pupils. By 0600 hours his speech was understandable and he followed all commands. The right extremities were still weaker than the left in motor strength.

Mr. Wentworth's son and daughter-in-law arrived by car at the tertiary hospital at 0700 hours. Mr. Wentworth recognized them and was obviously very glad to see them. Mr. Wentworth's son confirmed the history of blindness in the right eye. He also stated that the right-sided motor weakness had existed since he had had a "stroke" two years prior to the accident.

Study Questions

1. Compute a Glasgow Coma Score for Mr. Wentworth based on the findings of the admission physical exam. How did you arrive at this score?
2. In what way was Mr. Wentworth's head injury life-threatening at the time of admission to the tertiary hospital?
3. What is the purpose of "neuro checks"? How can they be used to predict complications?
4. What precautions were needed since Mr. Wentworth's facial fractures were not stabilized?
5. Arrange Mr. Wentworth's nursing diagnoses in the order of their priority from most important to least important at the time of admission to the CCU:

    Breathing patterns, ineffective
    Mobility, impaired physical
    Sensory perceptual alterations
    Skin integrity, impairment of: Actual
    Urinary elimination, alterations in patterns

6. Complete a nursing care plan for Mr. Wentworth using the nursing diagnoses above and adding appropriate outcomes and interventions for the first 24 hours.

BOTULISM TOXICITY

Unit III-20

Present Illness

Sylvia Archuleta, aged 36 years, was evaluated in an ambulatory emergency clinic for complaints of sore throat and difficulty swallowing. The physician and nurse noted that she was afebrile and her pharynx was not inflamed. A throat culture for streptococcal screening was done. Ms. Archuleta was discharged with instructions to call the next day for the results of the streptococcal screen and to return if any further symptoms developed.

The following day, Ms. Archuleta returned with the same complaints. In addition, she stated that while watching television during the previous evening, she had noticed problems with blurred and double vision. Her husband volunteered that he thought she wasn't opening her eyes as far as usual and that was why she was having trouble seeing. Ms. Archuleta said she felt she was having trouble breathing and could not breathe deeply because of muscle weakness. When questioned further, Ms. Archuleta related that she had eaten some canned chili sauce the day before at lunch. No one else in the family had eaten any and the remainder was in a jar in the refrigerator at home. Because the physician suspected food botulism toxicity, it was suggested that Ms. Archuleta be admitted to the hospital for observation. Mr. Archuleta was asked to bring the remaining chili sauce in for testing.

Past Medical History

The patient had never had a similar episode in the past and had been in her usual state of good health until these symptoms developed. She denied history of recent viral illness, drug abuse, or eating other foods that the rest of the family had not eaten. All the members of her family were in good health. There was no family history of myasthenia gravis or multiple sclerosis.

Physical Exam on Admission

General: An alert and oriented, pleasant, neatly groomed woman in no apparent distress who began to have difficulty forming words and speaking clearly during the exam. Vital signs were: BP, 110/60 mm Hg; T, 98.2 °F (36.8 °C); HR, 70/min; RR, 16/min, regular and shallow.

HEENT: Normocephalic. Atraumatic. Pupils equal and round with sluggish reaction to light. EOMs not full with disconjugate gaze in most quadrants. External ear canals clear; tympanic membranes intact. Nasal septum midline with normal mucosa. Tongue did not protrude in the midline and gag reflex not present.

Neck: Supple. No thyroid enlargement or lymphadenopathy.

Chest: Normal AP diameter. Minimal, symmetrical excursion. Clear, vesicular breath sounds over all lobes. Patient unable to deep breathe. Heart sounds normal and without rubs, murmurs, or gallops.

Abdomen: Flat with very active bowel sounds in all quadrants. Soft, mildly tender to palpation with no masses or organ enlargement.

Extremities: No deformities. Limb strength equal bilaterally with legs stronger than arms. Peripheral pulses present, equal, and moderate.

Neuro: Normal mental status. Cranial nerve dysfunction symmetrical and most prominent in the EOMs. DTRs symmetrical and 1+ in the upper extremities and 2+ in the lower extremities. No sensory deficits.

Laboratory Studies

CBC and differential; serum electrolytes and chemistry levels; and urinalysis: results were within normal limits.

Cerebral spinal fluid (CSF) from atraumatic spinal tap: clear with normal pressure. Sample sent for culture.

Serum: sent to state lab for botulism toxin level.

Sample of chili sauce sent for culture and botulism toxin level.

Medical Diagnosis

Possible food botulism toxicity.

Management

Although Ms. Archuleta was suspected to be a victim of botulism toxicity, the physicians planned to evaluate her for Guillain-Barré syndrome, chemical toxicity, myasthenia gravis, and/or other food poisoning.

Ms. Archuleta's vital capacity and spontaneous tidal volume were evaluated to determine the adequacy of her pulmonary function. She was unable to perform a satisfactory vital capacity maneuver and her tidal volume was less than 5 cc/kg. Because her pulmonary function seemed inadequate, she was transferred to the CCU, intubated, and mechanically ventilated. Ms.

Archuleta's motor function was rapidly decreasing and she appeared to be unresponsive. However, her sensory function was not impaired, and the nurse explained all procedures to her. The nurse made sure that lidocaine (Xylocaine) spray was available for the intubation. The nurse also explained to Mr. Archuleta that his wife was very alert, but could no longer speak. They worked together to communicate with Ms. Archuleta.

A nasogastric tube was inserted and the physician's orders for purging Ms. Archuleta's GI tract were carried out because bowel sounds were still present. The nurses sent samples of gastric contents and stool to the laboratory. They also observed and documented Ms. Archuleta's neurological and respiratory status. Her primary nurse developed and implemented a nursing care plan for the beginning of Ms. Archuleta's stay in the CCU, which was expected to be lengthy. The local health department was notified of Ms. Archuleta's suspected diagnosis and botulism antitoxin was requested.

Study Questions

1. How does botulism toxin cause motor paralysis?
2. How might the clinical presentation of a patient with wound botulism differ from that of one with food botulism?
3. Why is it important to monitor bowel sounds while giving treatments to purge the GI tract?
4. What is the purpose of botulism antitoxin? How is it administered?
5. What is the usual course of botulism toxicity? How long could Ms. Archuleta require care in the CCU?
6. Outline the nursing care plan that the primary nurse probably wrote at the beginning of Ms. Archuleta's CCU stay. Include short-term and long-term goals for the CCU.

BRAIN TUMOR

Units III-14 and II-8, II-10

Present Illness

Cynthia Mendel, aged 54 years, was admitted with a chief complaint of headaches and loss of balance. Ms. Mendel gave a history of onset of loss of hearing, left facial numbness and tingling, severe intermittent headaches, and balance problems which began 15 months prior to admission. The symptoms were somewhat fluctuant and intermittent but basically were slowly progressive. When she saw her internist seven months prior to admission, the internist found no specific neurological abnormalities but did note mild hypertension for which he prescribed diuretics. Ms. Mendel's BP declined and good control was achieved with combined amiloride hydrochloride and hydrochlorothiazide (Moduretic). Ms. Mendel took the medication sporadically at best. Ms. Mendel reported that her headaches seemed to subside spontaneously. She thought her left facial numbness and tingling as well as hearing improved although she still had difficulty hearing with the left ear.

Her family noted that her gait and balance remained poor and progressively worsened. They also noted irrational behavior which led them to conclude she was not competent to handle her own affairs. Her husband began making more and more decisions for her. The family brought these symptoms to the internist's attention but the patient seemed rational in the office so the internist was unable to evaluate the complaint.

Two weeks prior to admission, the internist did note progressive gait disorder, as well as facial and sixth nerve palsy on the left side. Because this strongly suggested a posterior fossa mass, Ms. Mendel was asked to go to radiology for a CT scan. The patient did not want to go and sought a second opinion from another internist who also recommended CT scan. Ms. Mendel refused but her husband forced her to go.

The CT scan showed a large (5-cm wide) left cerebellar pontine angle tumor which enhanced considerably and caused marked left-to-right shift of the midline structures in the posterior fossa. The brain stem was obviously indipped and mild obstructive hydrocephalus was present. The tumor seemed to arise from the left tentorial region of the foramen magnum. It appeared to be centered over the left internal auditory meatus which was mildly enlarged. Evidence of her irrational behavior was seen in that she attempted to hit the CT scan technician.

Ms. Mendel was immediately referred to the neurosurgeon who saw her the next day. During this exam, Ms. Mendel was extremely agitated and had poor emotional control. She was very talkative and paced about the room frequently. She discussed things rationally at times then suddenly became excited and did not speak coherently. She stated to the neurosurgeon that her headaches and balance problems were still present although not as bad as they once were. She also said that she knew something very bad was wrong with her but she was very scared and did not want to pursue treatment.

Ms. Mendel's family prevailed and Ms. Mendel proceeded with further diagnostic and therapeutic procedures. She was admitted later in the day for angiography to be followed by surgical excision of the tumor.

Past Medical History

Current medications were the amiloride hydrochloride and hydrochlorothiazide. She had taken aspirin in the past for her headaches. She had no known allergies or serious medical illnesses or prior surgery. She was married to a retired police officer. They had several grown children.

Physical Exam on Admission

General: A pleasant, agitated, alert, middle-aged woman. Vital signs were: BP, 130/90 mm Hg; T, 98 °F (36.7 °C); HR, 80/min; RR, 16/min.
HEENT: No external lesions. Sutures closed. Pupils equal, round, and reactive to light. No papilledema on fundoscopic exam. Sensory neural hearing loss on the left. Tympanic membranes intact bilaterally. Nose, mouth, and pharynx normal.
Neck: Supple. Without bruits, thyroid enlargement or lymphadenopathy.
Chest: Lungs and heart clear to auscultation and percussion. Cardiac rhythm was regular sinus.
Abdomen: Scaphoid. Active bowel sounds in all quadrants. Soft and without tenderness, masses, or organ enlargement.
Extremities: Without deformity, clubbing, or edema. Skin warm and moist. Peripheral pulses present, equal, and moderate. Excellent motor strength. No paralysis in extremities.
Neuro: Alert, oriented to person, place and time. Patient reasoned well at times but also had irrational ideas and came to frightened, unreal conclusions. Cranial nerve exam showed: mild but definite, left sixth nerve palsy; mild to moderate left peripheral facial palsy; mild left trigeminal palsy in all three divisions to pinwheel; mildly diminished left corneal reflex; equal, round, reactive pupils; coarse lateral nystagmus with lateral gaze to either side and vertical nystagmus with upgaze; normal gag reflex, swallowing, palate elevation, and tongue protrusion. The patient was very unsteady during the Romberg test and her gait was broad-based and ataxic. She could not perform tandem gait without falling to either side. Slight run ataxia on finger-nose-finger testing. No arm drift or tremor. No peripheral paralysis. Peripheral sensation appeared normal. DTRs normally active and symmetrical in upper and lower extremities except for mildly increased left knee reflex compared to right. Flexor plantar responses present bilaterally.

Laboratory Studies

CBC with differential; serum electrolytes and chemistry levels; urinalysis; and chest x-ray: results were all within normal limits.

Medical Diagnoses

1. Left cerebellar pontine angle tumor, acoustic neuroma versus meningioma.
2. Mild obstructive hydrocephalus.
3. Dementia secondary to posterior fossa mass.

Management

Angiography showed a large posterior mass with a vertebrobasilar system vascular supply. The angiography was to be followed by surgical posterior fossa exploration, decompression, and/or excision of the mass. It was thought that extensive decompression, two-stage removal, and placement of permanent ventriculo-peritoneal shunt would be required. Placement of a ventricular catheter for drainage of cerebrospinal fluid was planned for the first surgery.

The neurosurgeon discussed the planned procedures with Ms. Mendel and her husband in moderate detail and then privately with Mr. Mendel in complete detail because Ms. Mendel was so agitated. Mr. and Mrs. Mendel both understood that the surgery could be life-threatening and more than one operation would probably be required. Mr. Mendel clearly understood the need for two-stage removal as well as the ventricular shunt and that the tumor was life-threatening with or without surgical intervention. He understood that there could be no guarantees as to the success, relative satisfaction, or preservation of neurologic function including cranial nerves, mental abilities, or motor or sensory function postoperatively. Nevertheless, Mr. Mendel requested that the surgery be done. Both Mr. and Ms. Mendel signed the operative consent form.

The first surgery was carried out and consisted of a left posterior fossa craniotomy and stage I subtotal microsurgical excision of an acoustic schwannoma with laser technique. A ventricular catheter was inserted through a left occipital burr hole. The patient was anesthetized from 0730 to 0035 hours; the operation began at 0820 and ended at 0030 hours. Ms. Mendel tolerated the procedure fairly well with little fluctuation in her vital signs. Postoperatively she was transferred to the CCU with an endotracheal tube in place and mechanical ventilation was begun. The neurosurgeon's postoperative orders were:

- do routine CCU cardiac monitoring
- check vital signs and neuro status every hour
- ventilate with VT 750 cc, FIO$_2$, 0.40, SIMV 10/min
- give nothing by mouth
- administer IV fluids: continuous D5/.45NS with KCl 20 mEq/L at 125 mL/hr
- maintain indwelling urinary catheter
- record intake and output (I & O) q1h
- elevate head of bed to 40 degrees
- turn patient q2h, keeping left side predominantly turned downward
- administer following medications:
  dexamethasone (Decadron), 6 mg IV q6h
  cimetidine (Tagamet), 300 mg IV q6h
  morphine sulfate titrate, 2–4 mg IV as needed to keep respiratory rate at 20/min while ventilated
  diazepam (Valium), 5 mg IV or IM q6h as needed for agitation while ventilated
  codeine phosphate, 32 mg IM q4h as needed for pain
  sodium nitroprusside (Nipride) infusion of 50 mg in 250 mL of D5W IV titrate as needed to maintain systolic arterial pressure below 130 mm Hg

Ms. Mendel recovered well from the anesthesia and required minimal sedation while on the ventilator. The neuro checks indicated that she sustained no neurological injury while in surgery. She was extubated on the first postoperative day. After she was extubated, the positioning and activity order was changed to: deep breathe and turn q2h.

Study Questions

1. Why was angiography done prior to surgery?
2. What neuro status observations should be documented prior to administering analgesics and/or sedatives?
3. Why did the surgeon order the patient to be turned ''predominantly left side down'' during the immediate postoperative period?
4. After extubation the physician ordered "Deep breathe and turn q2h." Was the omission of coughing deliberate or an oversight? Why?
5. What are the priorities in postoperative nursing care of patients with brain tumor excision?

CEREBROVASCULAR ACCIDENT

Units II-11 and II-13

Present Illness

Mr. Brown, aged 85 years, accompanied by his elderly wife, was brought to the ED by ambulance. When he had awakened in the morning, his whole right side was paralyzed and he had no sensation in his arm or leg. He tried to get up with help from his wife but could not. Ms. Brown called their physician and described the situation. The physician told her to have her husband taken to the hospital by ambulance where he would meet them. Mr. Brown protested and said he would be better after taking a nap but cooperated with the ambulance crew when they arrived. Mr. Brown seemed very relieved to be cared for by the competent ambulance and ED personnel. He was quickly evaluated in the ED and then admitted to the CCU.

Past Medical History

Ms. Brown served as the historian for her husband. Mr. Brown had not had any significant illness until 24 months ago when he began to develop bilateral senile cataracts. He consumed larger amounts of alcoholic beverages as the encroaching cataracts impaired his ability to pursue his hobby of building ship models. Six months ago the cataracts were successfully removed and lenses implanted. The two eyes were operated on individually one month apart. Since then Mr. Brown's alcohol consumption decreased and he was able to work on his models again.

Ms. Brown said they had never been told that Mr. Brown had high blood pressure, heart disease, lung disease, kidney disease, cancer, or any other serious medical illness. He had not had any surgery or serious injuries during their 65 years of marriage.

Mr. and Ms. Brown lived in their own home in a lower middle class neighborhood. They had four sons who were all living in different parts of the country. Mr. Brown had been a house painter all his life. He began helping his father at age nine and was still active until his cataracts prevented him from continuing.

Physical Exam on Admission to the CCU

General: Semiconscious and aphasic. Made no attept to respond verbally to questions. Vital signs were: PB, 200/110 mm Hg; rectal T, 100 °F (37.8 °C); HR, 86/min and regular; RR, 22/min and stertorous.

HEENT: Face flushed. PERRL, 7 mm. Corneal reflexes present. Unable to test EOMs. Tympanic membranes intact, no history of impaired hearing. Nasal passages clear with septum deviated to the left. Edentulous, full dentures not in place, gums without lesions. Tongue deviated to the left when protruded spontaneously. Facial drooping on left. Oxygen mask in place with flow at 8 L/min.

Chest: Symmetrical excursion while lying in bed. Lungs clear to auscultation and percussion. Breath sounds diminished in the bases. Heart sounds consisted of normal S_1 and S_2 as well as an S_3. Soft systolic ejection murmur heard at second ICS to right of sternum.

Abdomen: Flat. Bowel sounds present all quadrants. Soft and without masses or organomegaly on palpation.

GU: Normal adult male with smooth, enlarged prostate gland.

Extremities: Peripheral pulses present and equal. DTRs in arms and femorals, 2+; popliteals, posterior tibials, and dorsalis pedis, 1+.

Neuro: Spontaneous respirations with regular variation in depth and rate. Flaccid right arm and leg. Spontaneous movements of left arm and leg. Active response to pain with left extremities. Grimace but no movement with pain in right extremities.

Laboratory Studies

CBC with differential and serum electrolyte levels: results were within normal limits.

Serum glucose: mildly elevated.

Medical Diagnoses

1. Cerebrovascular accident (CVA).
   a. Thrombosis or aneurysm of left middle cerebral artery.
   b. Right hemiparalysis and hemiparesis.
   c. Questionable aphasia.
2. Benign prostatic hypertrophy.

Management

On receiving Mr. and Ms. Brown in the CCU, the nurse quickly scanned the physician's orders. Then the nurse oriented the Browns to the physical layout and pertinent policies of the CCU. The nurse completed an initial physical assessment of Mr. Brown while carrying out the medical and nursing orders for supportive management. Nursing actions included:

- continuing oxygen by mask at 8 L/min and obtaining arterial blood gas sample
- taking vital signs q15min until stable; then q30min four times; then q1h; then q4h
- doing neuro checks q1h

- inserting IV device and administering D5W IV at 100 mL/hr
- inserting 16F indwelling urinary catheter connected to a urinemeter
- monitoring and recording intake and output every hour
- suctioning oropharynx to stimulate coughing and remove secretions
- doing frequent mouth care and following Mr. Brown's usual denture care routine
- repositioning Mr. Brown q2h with his body in functional alignment
- doing skin care and some passive range of motion (ROM) with each turning so that all of Mr. Brown's joints were exercised q8h
- administering ordered medications:
  acetylsalicylic acid (aspirin), 650 mg per rectum q6h
  sodium nitroprusside (Nipride) infusion as needed to maintain systolic arterial pressure between 170 and 180 mm Hg

Twelve hours after admission, the nurse assessing Mr. Brown noted that: his eyes were half open; there was ptosis of the right eyelid; and eye movements occurred when the nurse or his wife spoke his name. Mr. Brown's right cheek was more flaccid than the left. His right arm and leg were limp and had no muscle tone. There was some grasp strength in his left hand although he did not grasp on command. He moved his left leg about restlessly. Mr. Brown responded with grunts to painful stimuli. He did not attempt to speak, follow commands, or answer questions.

Study Questions

1. Describe a complete neuro status assessment.
2. How did the physician conclude that Mr. Brown's cerebrovascular accident involved the left middle cerebral artery?
3. What signs and symptoms would alert the nursing staff to occlusion of the left anterior cerebral artery? The left posterior cerebral artery?
4. Why did the physician order the sodium nitroprusside to keep Mr. Brown's systolic arterial pressure between 170 and 180 mm Hg? Should the range be somewhat lower?
5. What nursing diagnoses or nursing problems and outcomes assume priority in the acute care period of a cerebrovascular accident?
6. What other disciplines would be expected to assist in rehabilitation of a patient with a cerebro-

vascular accident? When should disciplines such as physical and occupational therapy be expected to begin working with the patient?

CRANIOTOMY FOLLOWING HEAD TRAUMA

Units II-10 and I-23, II-8, II-13, III-5

Present Illness

Genevieve Hornet, 40 years old, hypertensive, and a mother of four, was admitted to the critical care unit (CCU) four days following head trauma. Her chief complaint was persistent headaches, dizziness, nausea, and vomiting. She had not sought medical help earlier because, as she said, "You only needed to see a doctor if you stayed unconscious." She was seen and admitted now because she came to the clinic for a routine visit concerning her hypertension. When questioned about headaches related to her hypertension, Ms. Hornet explained that she was having headaches but that they were related to being struck on the head.

Four days prior to admission, Ms. Hornet was assaulted in front of her tenement building as she was returning from work at midnight on a Friday. She received blows to the left side of her head and lost consciousness. When she regained consciousness, she was lying on the sidewalk. Ms. Hornet went inside and went to bed. She did not know how many assailants there were, what weapon was used, whether there were any witnesses, or how long she was unconscious. She denied mental changes and seizures.

The nurse practitioner in the clinic asked the physician on duty to see Ms. Hornet. Following the physician's exam, Ms. Hornet was taken to have x-rays taken of her skull and cervical spine and was subsequently admitted to the critical care unit (CCU).

Past Medical History

Ms. Hornet's hypertension was well controlled with methyldopa (Aldomet), 500 mg bid, and chlorothiazide (Diuril), 50 mg daily. She was followed by the nurse practitioner in the medical clinic. She had no other medical problems and denied knowing any of her family's medical history since she did not maintain contact with them.

Ms. Hornet had been hospitalized briefly for the births of her four out-of-wedlock children. Apparently all of the children were full-term infants and their births were not complicated.

Physical Exam on Admission to the CCU

General: Oriented to person, place, and time. Complaining of severe left headache and nausea. Vital signs were: BP, 144/100 mm Hg in the right arm and 150/90 mm Hg in the left arm; T, 97 °F (36.1 °C); HR, 58/min; RR, 12/min.
HEENT: Firm, raised ecchymosis over left temporal area 7 cm in diameter. Pupils round, reactive to light, and slightly unequal (right 3 mm, left 4 mm). EOMs full. Ears, nose, and throat were unremarkable.
Chest and abdomen: Normal findings on exam.
Neuro: Cranial nerves II–XII intact. Sensory function, reflexes, as well as motor function and strength were normal.

Laboratory Studies

CBC, serum electrolyte and chemistry levels, and urinalysis: results were within normal limits.
Skull x-rays: showed a depressed left temporal parietal skull fracture. Cervical spine films showed no fractures or deformities.
CT scan: showed depressed skull fracture and hematoma without a shift in the midline structures.

Medical Diagnoses

1. Head trauma.
2. Depressed left temporal parietal skull fracture.
3. Hypertension.

Management

Ms. Hornet was taken to surgery for an emergency left temporal parietal craniotomy. The 4-cm depressed fracture was elevated and the epidural hematoma was evacuated. Ms. Hornet was returned to the CCU still under the effects of anesthesia with an endotracheal tube in place. She was mechanically ventilated with: VT, 15 cc/kg body weight; FIO$_2$, 0.40; and synchronized intermittent mandatory ventilation (SIMV), 12/min. ABGs were to be drawn in 30 minutes and results called to the neurosurgeon. Vital signs and neuro checks were ordered every 15 minutes until stable, then every 30 minutes four times, followed by hourly measurements. Medications were dexamethasone, (Decadron), 10 mg IV now, then 4 mg IV q6h; and cephalothin (Keflin) sodium, 2 g IV q6h.

Study Questions

1. What additional orders should the nurse obtain from the surgeon?
2. What changes in the neurological exam should be reported to the neurosurgeon immediately?
3. Why were dexamethasone and cephalothin sodium prescribed?
4. Should a member of the health care team notify the police of the circumstances of Ms. Hornet's injury? Who should assume this responsibility?
5. Outline the usual nursing care required by patients post craniotomy. Explain the purpose of each action.
6. What complications is Ms. Hornet at risk to develop?

GUILLAIN-BARRÉ SYNDROME

Unit III-19

Present Illness

Karen Olson, aged 25 years, became ill with an upper respiratory infection which included a severe sore throat and a cough. She saw her physician who did a throat culture and prescribed penicillin V potassium (Pen-Vee K), 250 mg qid. Five days after her first symptoms, Ms. Olson began complaining of severe headaches at midday. In the evening, she told her roommate that her fingers and toes were numb. At bedtime, she was having difficulty walking due to extreme weakness. She assumed she would be better after a night's rest and went to bed. In the morning, her roommate had to help her out of bed and to the bathroom. Ms. Olson's roommate drove her to the hospital where she was evaluated in the ED and admitted to a medical nursing unit.

Twelve hours after admission, respiratory distress became apparent and she was transferred to the CCU.

Past Medical History

Her past medical history was unremarkable.

Physical Exam on Admission to the CCU

Findings were unremarkable except for her neurological status. Ms. Olson had pronounced muscle weakness of the extremities and respiratory muscles. Reflexes were absent.

Laboratory Studies

CBC with differential, serum chemistries, and urinalysis were obtained in the ED. The differential showed evidence of recent viral illness and the other values were within normal limits.

Cerebrospinal fluid (CSF) from lumbar puncture done in the ED was clear with normal pressure, glucose, and chloride levels. The total protein was 45 mg/dL and the cell count showed RBCs, $3-4 \times 10^6$/L and no WBCs.

When Ms. Olson was admitted to the CCU her spontaneous tidal volume was 200 cc and decreasing. She was receiving 100% oxygen by mask and her Pao_2 was 50 mm Hg.

Medical Diagnosis

Acute respiratory failure secondary to Guillain-Barré syndrome.

Management

Ms. Olson required respiratory support in the CCU for several months. During the first four weeks her respiratory status was very unstable and her course was very stormy. Her respiratory status then stabilized and remained unchanged for about four weeks. During the third and fourth months, she was weaned from the ventilator. She was then transferred out of the CCU. Ms. Olson was transferred to a rehabilitation center five months after admission.

Study Questions

1. Describe the pathophysiology pertinent to the acute loss of motor function seen in the Guillain-Barré syndrome.
2. Describe the patterns of developing neurological deficit seen in Guillain-Barré syndrome.
3. What is the expected course and outcome of Guillain-Barré syndrome? How will the quality of nursing care influence the patient outcome?
4. Ms. Olson's roommate telephoned and asked how she could avoid "catching" the Guillain-Barré syndrome from Ms. Olson. How should the nurse respond?
5. Outline and explain the nursing diagnoses or nursing problems, outcomes, and actions that should be included on the nursing care plan during Ms. Olson's second month in the CCU.

HEAD INJURY

Units II-10 and II-8, II-13 III-5, III-22

Present Illness

Mary Peabody, aged 20 years, was involved in an automobile accident in which the small car she was driving was hit broadside on the driver's side by a large truck. The paramedics found her in full respiratory arrest at the scene and victim of a massive head injury. The paramedics began to resuscitate her at the scene and transported her to the nearest full-service ED. Resuscitation was continued in the ED where her spontaneous respirations were judged inadequate. Ms. Peabody was intubated and mechanical ventilation was begun with a pressure cycled ventilator.

Neurological status was evaluated and a Glasgow Coma Scale score of 3 was calculated. Pupils were round and unequal with the right being small and reactive, the left dilated and fixed. Because her wounds and neurological status indicated massive head trauma, a ventricular catheter was placed to monitor her intracranial pressure (ICP). The initial ICP reading was 30 mm Hg. Indirect arterial pressure was 90/60 mm Hg with a calculated mean of 70 mm Hg. Cerebral perfusion pressure was calculated to be 40 mm Hg.

Ms. Peabody was moved to the x-ray department for a skull series, cervical spine films, and CT scan. A basilar skull fracture was visible on the skull x-rays. No fractures were seen on the cervical spine films. No clearly operable lesion or midline shift was seen on the CT scan, so the patient was moved to the critical care unit (CCU) for care and observation. The pressure cycled ventilator was changed to a volume cycled one and an arterial line was inserted in her right radial artery.

Past Medical History

The patient's husband was notified of the accident by the ED staff. Her husband stated that the patient had been in good health and he knew of no serious medical illness in the past. He also stated that she was about two and a half months pregnant. He did not know her family medical history.

The patient and her husband had married about one month ago. They had no relatives in the city or state. Ms. Peabody's mother and siblings resided 2000 miles away. Her father and mother were divorced and her father was living in Europe. Ms. Peabody and her father maintained contact by letter; however, although her father had recently heard of her marriage, he was unaware of her pregnancy. Ms. Peabody's mother and

one sister had attended the wedding and knew of the pregnancy.

Physical Exam on Admission to the CCU

General: A well-proportioned, comatose, young woman. Vital signs were: BP, 90/60 mm Hg with mean 68 mm Hg; T, 99 °F (37.2 °C); HR, 112/min; RR, 12/min, fully controlled by mechanical ventilator; ICP, 40 mm Hg.

HEENT: Spongy area at left temporal region of skull. Ecchymosis behind both ears. External ear canals clear. Tympanic membranes intact. Pupils round and unequal, right 3 mm and reactive, left 6 mm and nonreactive. No eye movements in response to any stimuli. Nose draining clear fluid tinged with blood and positive for glucose. Endotracheal tube protruding from mouth and taped in place.

Chest: Equal excursion with respirations. Scattered rhonchi throughout both lung fields. Diminished breath sounds in left base. Cardiac rhythm sinus tachycardia without ectopics. Heart sounds regular, loud S_1 and S_2. No rubs, murmurs, or gallops.

Abdomen: Flat and without bowel sounds in any quadrant. Soft and without organomegaly or masses on palpation.

GU: Normal female. No vaginal bleeding. Indwelling catheter draining clear yellow urine in scant amounts. Pelvic exam deferred.

Extremities: Pulses present, equal and brisk. DTRs not elicited on the right; 1+ on the left.

Skin: 5-cm abrasions on right shoulder, left shin, and right knee.

Neuro: Eyes as above. No motor response to pain. Verbalization not testable.

Laboratory Studies

ABG results on ventilator with settings of V_T, 800 cc; F_{IO_2}, 0.70, assist/control (A/C) mode, 12/min; PEEP, 5 cm H_2O: $Paco_2$, 28 torr; Pao_2, 72 torr; Sao_2, 94.8%; Cao_2, 18.5%; HCO_3, 25.6 mEq/L; CO sat, 1.6%; pH 7.56; base excess 5.7; Hgb 15.1 g/dL.

Hematology results: WBC, 15.1 × 10^9/L; RBC, 4.61 × 10^{12}/L; Hgb, 14.5 g/dL; and Hct, 42.8%.

Serum electrolyte and chemistry levels: Na, 142 mEq/L; K, 3.6 mEq/L; Cl, 102 mEq/L; CO_2, 29 mmol/L; glucose, 169 mg/dL; and BUN, 17 mg/dL.

Medical Diagnosis

Severe head injury secondary to motor vehicle accident.

Management

Ms. Peabody stayed in the CCU for several months. During this time, her pregnancy spontaneously terminated. Her ICP declined to normal levels and monitoring was discontinued. Her respiratory status improved after several setbacks and she was eventually weaned from the ventilator in the fourth month. Her neurological status did not improve other than regaining adequate spontaneous respiration. She was transferred to progressive care and subsequently to a nursing home.

Study Questions

1. Compute a Glasgow Coma Scale score based: (a) on the admission exam, and (b) on the final management information.
2. How does controlled artificial hyperventilation assist in lowering ICP?
3. What implications did the calculated cerebral perfusion pressure of 40 mm Hg have?
4. What signs and symptoms would have alerted the nurse of the onset of Ms. Peabody's spontaneous abortion? What actions would have been appropriate?
5. Plan nursing care including actions and outcomes for the third month of Ms. Peabody's stay in the CCU using the following nursing diagnoses:
    Breathing patterns, ineffective
    Family process, alterations in
    Mobility, impaired physical
    Sensory perceptual alterations
    Tissue perfusion, alterations in

INCREASED INTRACRANIAL PRESSURE (ICP) AND INDUCED BARBITURATE COMA

Units II-8 and I-12, I-24, II-10, III-15

Present Illness

Sally Cunningham, aged 24 years, was a waitress and part-time model who was seen in the ED on June 1 after falling down a flight of stairs at home. Her mother reported that she was motionless for approximately 15 minutes and occasionally seemed to not be breathing during that time. When the paramedics arrived she was able to speak but was very lethargic. Exam in the ED found her lethargic, cooperative, easily agitated, verbally responsive, and in a very confused state. Ms. Cunningham was taken to the radiology department for a skull series, cervical spine films, and a CT scan.

When the procedures in the radiology department were completed, Ms. Cunningham was admitted to the CCU.

Past Medical History

Ms. Cunningham had no previous history of head trauma or seizures. She did not smoke, used alcohol rarely, and did not use "street drugs." Her family history was unremarkable.

Physical Exam on Admission to the CCU

General: A confused but cooperative young woman in moderate distress. Vital signs were: BP, 116/74 mm Hg; T, 98.2 °F (36.8 °C); HR, 92/min; RR, 12/min.

HEENT: No tenderness to palpation. Ecchymosis in occipital area. No lacerations or other cranial defects were noted. Tympanic membranes intact bilaterally with significant bilateral hemotympanum. No "battle signs" were noted. Oropharynx was clear. Bilateral periorbital ecchymoses with minimal edema were present.

Chest, Abdomen, and Extremities: Unremarkable.

Neuro: A lethargic, easily aroused woman who spoke but was very confused. She followed commands appropriately but her attention span was very short. PERRL. Fundi within normal limits. EOMs intact. Facial expression symmetrical. Uvula elevated in the midline and tongue protruded in the midline. Motor function equal and symmetrical in upper and lower extremities. Sensory function intact. DTRs were 1+ to 2+ and symmetric. Plantar flexion seemed to be present; however, the patient demonstrated marked withdrawal and it was difficult to be sure.

Laboratory Studies

CBC, serum electrolyte and chemistry levels, and urinalysis: results within normal limits.

ECG and cervical spine x-ray: within normal limits.

Skull x-rays: suggested partial diastasis of the lambdoid sutures bilaterally. No other fractures were apparent.

CT scan: suggested blood in the posterior fossa. No other abnormalities were seen.

Medical Diagnosis

Cerebral contusion and bibasilar skull fracture.

Management

The patient was admitted to the critical care unit (CCU) and begun on a dexamethasone (Decadron) regimen. The physician planned to evaluate the possibility that Ms. Cunningham had fallen down the stairs because of a seizure episode or syncope secondary to a subarachnoid hemorrhage.

Ms. Cunningham did reasonably well for two days and then developed a marked sinus bradycardia (HR, 34–40/min) which continued for the next ten days. She was transferred out of the CCU to the progressive care unit on June 14. During that night she had a focal seizure followed by a grand mal seizure accompanied by hypotension. She was transferred back to the CCU after a CT scan was done in the radiology department.

The CT scan showed a large area of lucency in the right inferior lobe region. During the course of the day, her LOC decreased and her pupils became fixed and dilated. Because blood had been seen in the posterior fossa on the previous CT scan, angiography was done to rule out a posterior fossa subdural hematoma. The bilateral carotid and right vertebral arteriograms illustrated a right frontal mass which was thought to be edema. No hematomas were found.

A therapeutic regimen to reduce Ms. Cunningham's cerebral edema was instituted which consisted of furosemide (Lasix), mannitol (Osmitrol), pentobarbital sodium (Nembutal) infusion, and mechanical hyperventilation. ICP monitoring was done using a subarachnoid screw. ICP measurements as high as 55 mm Hg were noted. Control of the elevated ICP was achieved with difficulty using large doses of pentobarbital sodium. On June 16, Ms. Cunningham's blood level of pentobarbital sodium was 48 μg/dL and her ICP was 10–20 mm Hg.

Ms. Cunningham was hyperventilated with a mechanical ventilator to maintain her Paco$_2$ in the range of 20–25 torr. She became hypertensive and her BP initially responded to furosemide and mannitol; later, however, propranolol (Inderal), hydralazine (Apresoline), and methyldopa (Aldomet) were required. Electrolyte imbalance was noted on June 18 and was thought to be secondary to the furosemide and mannitol therapy. The furosemide dosage was reduced and the mannitol was discontinued.

On June 19, propranolol was required for control of hypertension. Ms. Cunningham's ICP was maintained in the normal range with decreasing infusion rates of pentobarbital sodium. By June 21, spontaneous eye opening and chewing were noted. On June 23, Ms. Cunningham followed commands by opening and closing her eyes for the nurse. On June 25, she moved her eyes well. Her ICP and ABGs were within normal

limits, so the pentobarbital sodium infusion was discontinued. No spontaneous respirations were noted by June 28, so a long weaning period from the ventilator was predicted. Ms. Cunningham had had an endotracheal tube for 14 days, so a tracheostomy was done and a tracheal tube was inserted.

Purulent drainage was noted around the subarachnoid screw on June 29, so it was removed and sent for cultures. Sputum and urine specimens were also sent for cultures. Chest rhonchi were diffuse. A gram stain of the sputum was done that day and revealed *Staphylococcus* and *Klebsiella* organisms present in the specimen. Chloramphenicol (Chloromycetin) was added to the medications for seven days. On June 30, 2+ beta hemolytic group B *Streptococcus* growth was reported from the subarachnoid screw culture and 4+ *Klebsiella* growth was reported from the sputum and urine cultures. Cephalothin sodium (Keflin) was added for ten days. Ms. Cunningham's respiratory effort was noted to improve over the next week.

Progression of improved muscular movement was noted to be similar to that seen in Guillain-Barré syndrome. She was now able to move her left upper extremity a little bit. Ms. Cunningham's nutritional intake was inadequate for her caloric and protein needs. Because she resisted oral intake, enteral feedings were continued via a soft, small lumen, duodenal feeding tube.

On July 10, Ms. Cunningham became very apprehensive, frustrated, and uncooperative. No progress in weaning from the ventilator or promoting oral food intake was possible. A psychiatric consult was obtained on July 13. The psychiatrist's opinion was that the symptoms were those of organic brain syndrome and were a result of the trauma. Haloperidol (Haldol) therapy was begun and subsequently a marked decrease in her agitation was noted.

Ms. Cunningham's respiratory effort slowly improved and by July 17 SIMV had been decreased to 8/min. Slow improvement in muscle function and strength was noted by the physical therapist. On July 20, SIMV was decreased to 6/min and ABG results remained stable. SIMV was subsequently decreased to 4/min and 2/min. On July 25, respiratory distress occurred and ABG results deteriorated so the SIMV was again set for 8/min. When this episode resolved, new attempts at weaning were met with resistance from Ms. Cunningham. The nurses and respiratory therapists persisted and by July 31, SIMV was again down to 2/min and Ms. Cunningham's respiratory effort and cooperation were better. Late in the day, however, her spontaneous respiratory rate increased from 20 to 30/min and she complained of shortness of breath. Specimens for gram stain and culture were obtained from the tracheostomy. Beta hemolytic group B *Streptococcus* was found to be the infecting organism so a ten-day course of penicillin therapy was given. Ms. Cunningham's motivation and cooperation in weaning were poor so the SIMV was juggled between 2 and 8/min until August 11 when she was left at SIMV of 2/min. The bronchial secretions increased and became purulent with the characteristic odor of *Pseudomonas* infection. This was confirmed by culture and a course of gentamicin (Garamycin) therapy was administered.

On August 15, the ventilator was adjusted to provide continuous positive airway pressure (CPAP) without SIMV. Improvement in Ms. Cunningham's respiratory status persisted and the ABG levels remained stable. Muscle activity and strength continued to increase although she was still unable to stand alone. On August 19, Ms. Cunningham was transferred out of the CCU to the progressive care unit. She was receiving supplemental oxygen by mask but did not require any other respiratory support. The indwelling urinary catheter was removed on August 25 and the tracheal tube was removed on August 27. Ms. Cunningham was pleased with her progress and was able to feed herself. She began to take an interest in her diet and in her surroundings. Her psychosocial status was much improved.

On August 31, approximately three months after admission, Ms. Cunningham was transferred to the rehabilitation unit for continued physical therapy and rehabilitation.

Study Questions

1. What clinical factors should be considered in the assessment of the head injured patient?
2. What role does controlled ventilation play in the care of head injured patients? How is it useful in controlling ICP?
3. What is the purpose of inducing coma with barbiturates in head injured patients? How is it thought to control ICP?
4. Discuss the side effects of dexamethasone, furosemide, mannitol, and pentobarbital sodium.
5. Describe the nurses' role and actions in inducing, monitoring, and discontinuing barbiturate coma.
6. Outline a nursing care plan including nursing diagnoses or nursing problems, outcomes, and interventions for one week of Ms. Cunningham's stay in the CCU. Indicate the four problems that are most important for that week.

MENINGITIS

Units III-15 and I-24

Present Illness

Alan Lewis, aged 50 years, was hospitalized in the CCU with a chief complaint of high fever, severe headache, and stiff neck of 24 hours' duration. Two weeks prior to admission, he saw his physician for purulent drainage from his nose. He was diagnosed as having sinusitis and erythromycin (ERYC) was prescribed. Mr. Lewis became extremely nauseated and stopped taking the erythromycin on the third day. However, he did not notify his physician. The purulent drainage was still present.

Past Medical History

He had had a tonsillectomy and adnoidectomy during childhood. When he was 25 years of age, he had had hepatitis.

Physical Exam on Admission to the CCU

General: Black man, adequately nourished, in moderate distress. Ht, 6 ft, 5 in; wt, 220 lb. Vital signs were: BP, 150/90 mm Hg; T, 104 °F (40 °C); HR, 110/min; RR, 24/min.

HEENT: Normocephalic. PERRLA, 3 mm. Photophobia and pain prohibited complete eye exam, EOMs and fundoscopy were omitted. Tympanic membranes intact and clear. Full, painful sinuses with green, purulent drainage. Pharynx injected and full of green, purulent drainage.

Neck: Nuchal rigidity present. Thyroid normal. Cervical lymph nodes tender, enlarged, and firm. No JVD.

Chest: Heart and lungs clear to percussion and auscultation. Cardiac rhythm was sinus tachycardia.

Abdomen: Flat with active bowel sounds in all quadrants. Soft, nontender, and without organomegaly.

Extremities: Peripheral pulses present, equal, moderate.

Neuro: Cranial nerves II–XII grossly intact. Kernig's and Brudzinski's signs present. DTRs symmetrical and 1+ with plantar flexion.

Laboratory Studies

Hematology: Hct, 40%; Hgb, 12 g/dL; RBC, 4.2 × 10^{12}/L; WBC, 12.0 × 10^9/L.

Electrolyte levels: Na, 150 mEq/L; K, 5.5 mEq/L; Cl, 110 mEq/L; CO_2, 26 mmol/L.

Cerebrospinal fluid: cloudy with pressure of 250 mm H_2O; WBC, 1000 × 10^6/L; protein, 100 mg/dL; glucose, 30 mg/dL.

Gram stain of CSF: positive for *Staphylococcus* organisms. Culture and sensitivity were pending.

Medical Diagnosis

Staphylococcal meningitis.

Management

Antibiotic therapy was instituted with methicillin sodium (Staphcillin) 3 g IV q4h. IV fluids of D5/.2NS at 125 mL/hr were also administered.

Study Questions

1. What initial instructions to the patient might have avoided these unfortunate events?
2. Describe Kernig's and Brudzinski's signs as to what they are, how they are elicited, and their significance.
3. What characteristics of an antibiotic are important for success in treating infections of the meninges?
4. What precautions are needed to prevent patients and personnel in the CCU from contracting Mr. Lewis' meningitis?
5. Explain the essential nursing care required by Mr. Lewis, including nursing diagnoses or nursing problems, outcomes, and actions.

MULTIPLE SCLEROSIS

Units III-16 and III-4

Present Illness

Sarah White, aged 30 years, was a housewife who used to teach dancing. She was admitted with a chief complaint of difficulty walking and upper respiratory tract infection. For three weeks prior to admission she had been unable to walk without using a cane or furniture for support.

Ms. White stated that her difficulty began at age 20 shortly after turning her foot while marching in a parade. She experienced intermittent numbness in her feet, which she associated with the mishap in the parade, so she consulted an orthopedic physician. The physician diagnosed her problem as "hysteria." During the rest of that year, Ms. White had several episodes of numbness in her feet which progressed to her upper extremities over a period of several days. She also noted clumsiness, left knee pain, and inability to judge the relationship of objects in her hands. She then began to have rectal urgency and dribbling of urine

along with the other symptoms. She did not seek medical assistance for these episodes.

She then became pregnant with her first child and during the pregnancy had no episodes of sensory or motor dysfunction. Seven years ago, three months after delivering her first child, the symptoms recurred. At that time, she was told she had multiple sclerosis. She could not state what therapy was prescribed. A year later, she delivered her second child and symptoms recurred again three months postpartum. She had been symptom-free during the pregnancy so she conceived a third child in an effort to obtain a remission. She did well during the pregnancy until three months postpartum when she had an exacerbation which required adrenocorticotropic hormone (ACTH) for control. Three years ago, she had a fourth child, and again was in remission during the pregnancy and had an exacerbation three months postpartum. Since that time, she has had no more children.

Six months ago, she had left knee surgery and was walking without crutches until three weeks prior to admission. On the day this acute episode began, she was on her feet all day at a food fair. She became exhausted and could not walk without crutches or using the wall for support. Her walking did not improve and she caught a cold which quickly developed into bronchitis. Since she had not recovered her strength, she saw her private physician who referred her to a neurologist. Because there was evidence of respiratory dysfunction, the neurologist suggested that she be admitted until remission was achieved.

Past Medical History

Ms. White had no known allergies. She had had the usual childhood immunizations and diseases without sequellae. She fractured her left knee cap 20 years ago and had an arthroscopy six months ago on the same knee. She had been hospitalized for childbirth four times and for multiple sclerosis two times. A herpes virus infection of her left eye nine years ago caused a cataract to develop.

Her parents, spouse, and children (three girls and one boy) were alive and well. There was no family history of significant medical illness and no other family members had multiple sclerosis.

Ms. White was a member of the Baptist Church and did not smoke or drink alcohol. She had always lived in a suburb of a large city. She denied foreign travel. She had been married 11 years to the same husband who was an Internal Revenue Service agent and traveled frequently. Ms. White was active in teaching dance and baton twirling although her exercise was limited by her multiple sclerosis. Her hobbies were crotcheting and reading.

Physical Exam on Admission

General: A small cheerful woman who appeared younger than her stated age and was not in acute distress. Ht, 5 ft, 2 in; wt, 99 lb. Vital signs were: BP, 102/70 mm Hg in both arms; T, 98.2 °F (36.8 °C); HR, 92/min; RR, 20/min.

HEENT: Left pupil clouded with cataract. Right pupil round and reactive. Right fundoscopic exam normal. Left tympanic membrane bulging and without visible landmarks; right tympanic membrane clear. Nasal mucosa swollen, left more than right. White exudate present in pharynx.

Neck: Supple. Slightly enlarged thyroid. No JVD.

Chest: Equal, very shallow excursion. Lungs clear to auscultation and percussion but patient unable to deep breathe. Cardiac rhythm was normal sinus rhythm without ectopics. No rubs, murmurs, or gallops were heard.

Abdomen: Flat with active bowel sounds in all quadrants. Soft, nontender, and without organomegaly or masses.

Extremities: Skin pink, warm, and dry. Peripheral pulses present and equal. Moderate muscle atrophy below the knees bilaterally. Pain in lower extremities on passive ROM.

Neuro: Cheerful, almost euphoric, alert, and oriented. Could do multiplication of 5s. Cranial nerves II–XII were grossly intact. Positive Romberg's sign. Unable to walk without assistance. Light touch, pinprick, position, and vibratory senses intact with right better than left. DTRs were 2+ and symmetrical in the upper extremities. DTRs in the lower extremities were: knee, right 4+ and left 3+; ankle, right 2+ and left 1+. Plantar extension was present, bilaterally.

Laboratory Studies

Hematology: Hct, 41%; Hgb, 14 g/dL; RBC, 4.66 × 10^{12}/L; WBC, 12.1 × 10^9/L.

Coagulation: PT, 12.2 sec; PTT, 40 sec.

Serum electrolyte and chemistry levels: Na, 140 mEq/L; K, 3.9 mEq/L; Cl, 109 mEq/L; CO_2, 21 mmol/L; glucose, 182 mg/dL; BUN, 11 mg/dL; creatinine, 0.7 mg/dL.

Medical Diagnosis

Multiple sclerosis in exacerbation.

Management

Ms. White's spontaneous vital capacity and tidal volume were measured and found to be barely adequate. The physicians did not want to subject her to the risks of mechanical ventilation so she was observed in the critical care unit (CCU). ACTH, 80 units IM, was given every day in an effort to achieve remission of the multiple sclerosis. When improvement in Ms. White's muscle strength was noted, cyclophosphamide (Cytoxan) was added according to an investigational protocol and she was transferred out of the CCU. Two weeks after admission, the physicians considered her to be in remission and the ACTH and cyclophosphamide doses were tapered. She was discharged three weeks after admission without medication and able to walk short distances without assistance. Ms. White confided to the nurse that she was very glad to be going home without a wheelchair.

Study Questions

1. Describe the pathophysiology of the nervous system in multiple sclerosis. Explain how dysfunction of the nervous system results in the signs and symptoms of multiple sclerosis.
2. Why are the initial symptoms of multiple sclerosis frequently misdiagnosed or mislabeled?
3. What are the actions of ACTH and cyclophosphamide? How are these actions helpful in achieving remission of multiple sclerosis?
4. What instruction should Ms. White receive in order to avoid pulmonary infections as much as possible?
5. Identify and explain the nursing diagnoses or nursing problems, outcomes, and actions that are essential to the critical care of patients with multiple sclerosis.

MYASTHENIA GRAVIS

Units III-21 and III-4

Present Illness

Mavis Zimmerman, aged 59 years, was admitted to the CCU with a chief complaint of unusual fatigue and weakness as well as diplopia and difficulty talking. She was well until six months prior to admission, when she noticed unusual fatigue which she attributed to working longer hours in the family store. She also noticed diplopia which she associated with her fatigue. Four days prior to admission, she noted nausea, rapid tiring of her voice, and profound fatigue which limited her walking stamina to one turn about the small family store.

Past Medical History

Her past medical history was unremarkable.

Physical Exam on Admission

General: An elderly woman in moderate distress who appeared chronically ill. Ht, 5 ft, 6 in; wt, 125 lb. Vital signs were: BP, 130/80; T, 97.8 °F (36.6 °C); HR, 72/min; RR, 16/min.
HEENT: Exam findings within normal limits except for neurological status.
Chest: Lungs and heart clear to percussion and auscultation.
Abdomen: Flat with very faint bowel sounds in all quadrants. Soft, nontender, and without organomegaly or masses.
Extremities: Skin cool and moist. Peripheral pulses present, equal, and weak.
Neuro: Weakness of extraocular muscles; ptosis and diplopia present. Muscle weakness of fifth cranial nerve distribution. Unable to hold jaw up. Bilateral seventh cranial nerve weakness. Weakness of sternocleidomastoids. DTRs were symmetrically absent in the upper extremities and diminished in the lower extremities. Muscle strength in extremities was diminished bilaterally and rapid tiring occurred with repeated movements.

Laboratory Studies

CBC, leukocyte differential, serum chemistry and urinalysis: findings were normal.
Chest x-ray: showed a patchy infiltrate.

Medical Diagnosis

Probable myasthenia gravis.

Management

An edrophonium chloride (Tensilon) trial briefly improved strength in the patient's neck and arm muscles. Electromyogram, muscle biopsy, gallium scan, and repeat edrophonium chloride trial confirmed a diagnosis of myasthenia gravis. In spite of steroids and increasing dosages of anticholinesterase medication, Ms. Zimmerman's respiratory function deteriorated. Intubation and mechanical ventilation were required.

The physician decided that thymectomy was indicated. All steroid and anticholinesterase medication was discontinued. The patient was supported with mechanical ventilation, enteral nutrition, and IV fluids until the surgery could be done. The endotracheal tube was left in place longer than usual because the surgeon thought a tracheostomy would interfere with thymectomy.

Study Questions

1. What pathophysiological mechanism is thought to explain the muscle weakness of myasthenia gravis?
2. What is an edrophonium chloride trial and how is it carried out? What is the nurse's role in the test?
3. What benefits do myasthenia gravis patients usually derive from thymectomy? Why was it thought that a tracheostomy would interfere with the thymectomy procedure?
4. Mr. Zimmerman seemed very bewildered by his wife's hospitalization and absence from their home and store. What nursing intervention is appropriate in helping him adjust to these circumstances?
5. Identify and explain the nursing diagnoses or nursing problems, outcomes, and actions for Ms. Zimmerman in the period before thymectomy. How might these change after the surgery?

PARKINSON'S DISEASE

Units III-17 and I-4

Present Illness

Leland Brown, aged 60 years, was a retired newspaper editor admitted with chest pain and a previous history of Parkinson's disease. Mr. Brown's Parkinson's disease was diagnosed 10 years prior to this admission. Medical management had consisted of medications and physical therapy. Initially, Mr. Brown received amantadine (Symmetrel) with only moderate improvement in his symptoms. Trihexyphenidyl (Artane) was added to the regimen and Mr. Brown developed distressing side effects. He stopped taking the medication and became very depressed. With encouragement from his wife and son, he returned to the neurologist who changed the anticholinergic agent to benztropine mesylate (Cogentin). He did very well on the combined amantadine and benztropine mesylate for several years. In the past month, Mr. Brown had several episodes of chest pain that occurred with exercise and were relieved by rest. A severe episode of chest pain occurred in the morning of the day of admission and Mr. Brown contacted his physician. He also explained to the physician that he had been having much more difficulty with tremors and jerky movements. He was admitted to the CCU for evaluation of unstable angina pectoris and drug therapy for Parkinson's disease.

Past Medical History

Mr. Brown's additional past medical history was unremarkable.

Physical Exam on Admission to the CCU

General: A pleasant, thin man who appeared chronically ill and had a flat affect. Vital signs were: BP, 110/70 mm Hg; T, 98.8 °F (37.1 °C); HR, 70/min and regular; RR, 14/min and unlabored.

HEENT: Normal exam except for sebhorrheic dermatitis of the scalp, brow, and nasolabial folds. Sialorrhea (drooling) and dysarthria present.

Chest: Lungs clear to percussion and auscultation. Cardiac rhythm normal sinus with occasional PVB. Heart sounds included normal S_1, physiologically split S_2, and an S_3 gallop. No rubs or murmurs heard.

Abdomen: Scaphoid with bowel sounds present in all quadrants. Soft, nontender, and without organomegaly or masses.

Extremities: Bilateral tremor of the upper extremities which prevented legible handwriting and presented difficulties with eating. Slow movement with muscle rigidity was observed. Pulses were equal and moderate with the exception of bilateral absent posterior tibial pulses.

Neuro: Alert and oriented to self, place, and time. Cranial nerves grossly intact. Walked with a stooped posture and shuffling gait.

Laboratory Studies

Results of admission CBC, serum electrolytes, serum cardiac enzymes, and urinalysis were within normal limits. A 12-lead ECG showed nonspecific ST-T wave changes in the inferior leads.

Medical Diagnoses

1. Unstable angina pectoris; rule out MI.
2. Parkinson's disease with poor control of symptoms.

Management

Mr. Brown was kept in the CCU for three days and monitored for further signs and symptoms of MI. There were no further changes in the waveforms of the 12-lead ECG, nor did the serum cardiac enzyme levels show the expected pattern of elevation. The physician concluded that his chest pain had been angina pectoris rather than myocardial infarction. The medications to control the symptoms of his Parkinson's disease were changed to combined carbidopa and levodopa (Sinemet) and amantadine. His tremors decreased and movements became less jerky.

Late in the afternoon of the third hospital day, Mr. Brown was transferred out of the CCU. The carbidopa/levodopa dose was adjusted and he attended a patient education class about "prudent heart living." He also resumed physical therapy sessions. Because Ms. Brown's health was also failing, the couple was referred to a home health care agency.

Study Questions

1. What is the physiological error thought to be responsible for the symptoms of Parkinson's disease?
2. Describe the signs and symptoms that are usually associated with Parkinson's disease.
3. What are the pharmacological actions of: amantadine; trihexyphenidyl; benztropine mesylate; levodopa; and carbidopa/levodopa? How are these actions helpful in altering the signs and symptoms of Parkinson's disease? What are the nursing implications of administering these medications?
4. What activities of daily living is Mr. Brown likely to need assistance with? What is the best way for the nurse to help him?
5. Explain the essential nursing diagnoses or nursing problems, outcomes, and actions pertinent to caring for patients with Parkinson's disease in the critical care setting.

SEIZURES

Unit II-9

Present Illness

Michael Roho, aged 50 years, was admitted in status epilepticus with a previous history of psychomotor seizures.

Eighteen years ago, the patient experienced head trauma to the right temporal area with decreased LOC for half an hour. He was not seen by medical personnel at the time of the accident. Ten years ago he began having episodes of "feeling strange" and loss of awareness with automatic movements such as mumbling the same phrase and fumbling with his clothing. The episodes lasted 30 seconds and were followed by two- to three-minute periods of confusion. Partial control was obtained with primidone (Mysoline). Eight years ago, he was started on carbamazepine (Tegretol) which was effective until two years ago when he began having grand mal seizures. The grand mal seizures were controlled with phenytoin (Dilantin). The frequency and severity of Mr. Roho's seizures had been increasing during the past year and he was having 10 to 17 seizures per month immediately prior to admission. His wife estimated that one in ten was a grand mal seizure and the rest were "spells." Mr. Roho was embarrassed by his seizures and put off seeing his physician despite his wife's urging.

The morning of admission, Ms. Roho found him in the garage having a grand mal seizure that did not stop in the usual length of time. Ms. Roho called the paramedics who arrived quickly and found Mr. Roho still seizing with tonoclonic movements.

The paramedics protected Mr. Roho from injury, inserted an oral airway with difficulty, provided supplemental oxygen, established an IV access route, and administered diazepam (Valium). The seizures continued and Mr. Roho was transported to the ED. Because the ED staff was very busy, Mr. Roho was admitted to the CCU without evaluation in the ED.

Past Medical History

Ms. Roho reported that Mr. Roho had no history of other previous head trauma. He also did not have a history of diabetes, heart disease, lung disease, or cancer. His family history was sketchy but most persons had lived into their 80s unless an accident claimed their life earlier. There was no family history of epilepsy or other seizure disorder.

Physical Exam on Admission

General: Large man, unconscious, in acute distress with tonoclonic seizure movements. Skin color dusky. Vital signs were: BP, 90 mm Hg, palpated; HR, 120/min; RR, agonal.
HEENT: Facial muscles contracted. Teeth clenched on oral airway.
Chest: Breath and heart sounds inaudible due to seizure activity. Cardiac rhythm was supraventricular tachycardia with muscle artifact.
Abdomen: Flat, tense. Further exam not possible.
Extremities: Peripheral pulses present and equally thready. Moved all extremities with equal strength.

Laboratory Studies

EEG: showed epileptogenic foci in the right temporal lobe on the anterior medial and lateral surfaces.
Blood levels of medications: phenytoin; primidone; and carbamazepine were all below therapeutic range.

Medical Diagnosis

Status epilepticus.

Management

Diazepam, phenytoin, and phenobarbital sodium were administered IV to control the seizure activity. The drugs were successful and the tonoclonic movements stopped. Respiratory support was provided with mechanical ventilation. The nurses monitored Mr. Roho during the postictal period for signs and symptoms of cerebral ischemia and infarction as well as other complications of the status epilepticus.

Study Questions

1. Distinguish between psychomotor, grand mal, petit mal, Jacksonian, and febrile seizures in terms of their causes and manifestations.
2. What observations should nurses make during seizure activity?
3. What equipment for airway management should routinely be placed at the bedside of patients with seizures? How is this equipment used during seizure activity?
4. Describe the complications of status epilepticus and preventive measures that should be instituted.
5. Explain the essential nursing diagnoses or nursing problems, outcomes, and actions for Mr. Roho during the postictal period.

SPINAL CORD TRAUMA

Unit III-18

Present Illness

Gary Smith, a 26-year-old, married construction worker was admitted to the ED following a fall from a scaffold. He momentarily lost consciousness after his fall, but then was fully awake, alert, and oriented. Paramedics who transported him noted that he was awake when they arrived at the scene five minutes after being called and he had not lost consciousness while under their care. Pertinent signs and symptoms noted in the ED were:

- small laceration in right parietal area of skull
- neck pain and paravertebral spasms
- weakness in both arms including hand grips, wrist extensors, and triceps
- sensation decreased below T-1 and absent below T-3 level on anterior chest
- slightly decreased sensation in upper extremities
- no voluntary movement in lower extremities and reflexes absent
- no bowel or bladder control

Mr. Smith was moved to the critical care unit (CCU) after being stabilized in the ED with the following procedures:

- x-rays of skull and chest (no fractures, bone displacement, or other abnormalities found)
- x-rays of spine (vertebral displacement at C-6 noted)
- transfer to a Stryker turning frame
- application of Crutchfield tongs with 20 lb traction
- administration of dexamethasone (Decadron) 20 mg IV
- administration of mannitol (Osmitrol) 25 g IV
- administration of 5% dextrose in lactated Ringer's solution (D5LR) at 100 mL/hr IV
- insertion of double lumen nasogastric tube and connection to low, constant suction
- insertion of indwelling urinary catheter connected to gravity drainage

Past Medical History

His past medical history was unremarkable.

Physical Exam on Admission to the CCU

General: Well-developed, tanned man who appeared apprehensive and his stated age, lying on a Stryker frame in no physical distress. Vital signs were: BP, 130/90 mm Hg in both arms; T 97 °F (36.1 °C); HR, 80/min; RR, 16/min.

HEENT: Small laceration right parietal skull. Ecchymosis developing around laceration. No observable "battle signs." PERRL, 3 mm. EOMs and visual fields intact. Fundoscopic exam within normal limits. External auditory canals clear. Tympanic mem-

branes intact and clear. Nasal septum slightly deviated to left. Nasal mucosa pale and boggy. Nasogastric tube protruding from right naris draining clear gastric contents. Teeth in poor repair and gums inflamed. Pharynx clear. Tonsils slightly enlarged.

Neck: ROM not tested. Trachea midline. Thyroid and lymph nodes nonpalpable. Paravertebral muscle spasms present. No JVD in the supine position.

Chest: Normal configuration. Breath sounds very quiet. Vesicular breath sounds over all lung fields. PMI felt at fifth ICS in left MCL. Cardiac rhythm normal sinus with occasional PABs. Heart sounds normal without rub, gallop, or murmur.

Abdomen: Flat with active bowel sounds in all quadrants. No bruits. Soft, nontender and without organomegaly or masses.

Genitalia: Normal male, incontinent of stool.

Extremities: Pulses present and equal. No deformities. Bruising of right arm and leg.

Neuro: Alert and oriented to person, place, and time. Able to follow commands in examination of cranial nerves II–XII which were grossly intact. Upper extremities had some voluntary movement although it was weak. Voluntary movement and DTRs were absent in lower extremities. Skin sensation was decreased in the upper extremities and markedly diminished in the anterior chest below the T-1 level. There was no skin sensation below the T-3 level.

Laboratory Studies

CBC, differential, serum electrolyte and chemistry levels, and urinalysis: results within normal limits.

Medical Diagnosis

Compression fracture of C-6 with associated spinal cord compression and neurological deficit.

Management

Mr. Smith was admitted to the CCU for observation and supportive medical and nursing care. He was kept on the Stryker turning frame. A turning schedule and skin care routine were established. The Crutchfield tongs were maintained in good alignment and regular pin care was done according to the hospital routine. The nurses observed his respiratory and neurological status very frequently at first. As he became more stable the frequency of the observations was reduced. Mr. Smith's medications were dexamethasone, 5 mg, and cimetidine (Tagamet), 300 mg both q6h IV. The

IV fluids administered in the ED were continued as D5LR at 100 mL/hr. The double lumen nasogastric tube was maintained with low constant suction. Antacids were instilled regularly to keep the gastric pH 5 or greater. The indwelling urinary catheter connected to gravity drainage was maintained. Mr. Smith's primary nurse planned a bowel and bladder training program.

One week after admission, a myelogram demonstrated midline herniation of the intervertebral C6-C7 disk. The herniated disk was removed surgically and anterior spinal fusion was done with bone from a left iliac donor site. Postoperative orders included: vital signs and neuro checks every 15 minutes until stable, then every 30 minutes four times, then every hour for 24 hours; cervical collar; no injections in left hip; nothing by mouth; resume preoperative medications.

On the second postoperative day, Mr. Smith had a respiratory arrest. He was successfully resuscitated, intubated, and mechanically ventilated with a volume ventilator.

Study Questions

1. What are the pathophysiological differences between spinal shock and autonomic dysreflexia?
2. Describe a systematic way of doing and recording the neurological assessment of Mr. Smith.
3. What nursing observations should be made in the first 48 hours of hospitalization in view of Mr. Smith's brief loss of consciousness?
4. What is the purpose of spinal fusion after spinal cord injury?
5. Explain the essential nursing diagnoses or nursing problems, outcomes, and actions for preventing complications of spinal cord injury during the acute care period.

SUBARACHNOID HEMORRHAGE

Units II-11 and III-4

Present Illness

Diane Wells, aged 26 years, was an American Indian woman who was admitted to a tertiary care center with a preliminary diagnosis of subarachnoid hemorrhage, manifested by severe headache.

Two days prior to admission, on awakening and while still lying in bed, Ms. Wells suffered sudden onset of severe headache with nausea and vomiting. She described it as the worst headache she had ever had. She and her boyfriend stated that the headache continued the rest of the day and that Ms. Wells was quite sleepy and stayed in bed, mostly sleeping. By evening she was more awake, then suffered sudden increase in the pain to its original severity and accompanied by a tonic staring spell. Nausea and vomiting followed the staring. Ms. Wells' boyfriend called an ambulance and had her transported to the hospital in a neighboring town where she was admitted for evaluation.

Ms. Wells was febrile (101 °F, 38.3 °C) but had no stiff neck. She was frequently found staring and had nystagmus to the left with left upgaze. There were no other focal findings. A lumbar puncture, described as traumatic, was done and grossly bloody spinal fluid was obtained. The lumbar puncture was repeated the next day, described as atraumatic, and grossly bloody spinal fluid was obtained again. An isotope scan was reported as showing normal findings. The patient was placed on a phenytoin (Dilantin) regimen and seemed to be more alert, though she remained sleepy and occasionally was confused. Apparently, there were no more specific neurological findings.

Ms. Wells remained somewhat confused and more drowsy than usual with a persistent headache for the next 24 hours. On the second day, Ms. Wells was referred by her primary physician to a neurosurgeon at the tertiary center for further evaluation of subarachnoid hemorrhage. The plans for evaluation included CT scan and angiography.

Past Medical History

Ms. Wells was 40% overweight for her height; was not aware of any medication allergies; and had been in good health except for a history of systemic lupus erythematosus of eight years' duration. The lupus had manifested itself mostly in joint problems. The symptoms were managed with prednisone and sulindac (Clinoril) which Ms. Wells took intermittently depending on her discomfort. There was no previous history of vasculitis or renal symptoms associated with the lupus, nor was there a previous history of similar episodes in the past or hypertension.

Her family history was unremarkable. Ms. Wells was employed by Head Start. She did not use tobacco or alcohol.

Physical Exam on Admission to the Tertiary CCU

General: Well-developed, obese young Indian woman, somewhat drowsy but easily aroused. Vital signs were: BP, 140/90 mm Hg; T, 101 °F (38.3 °C); HR, 94/min; RR, 16/min.

HEENT: No exterior lesions. PERRL, 3 mm. Questionable bilateral papilledema on fundoscopic exam.

Ears, nose, mouth, and pharynx were unremarkable.

Neck: Moderate nuchal rigidity without bruits.

Chest: Lungs and heart clear to auscultation and percussion. Cardiac rhythm was normal sinus.

Abdomen: Rounded with normal bowel sounds in all quadrants. Soft, nontender, and without masses or organomegaly.

Neuro: Lethargic, easily arousable but with short attention span. Oriented to self, city, month, year. Without good recall of past few days. Possible mild fluent aphasic anomia. Dysarthric at times. No facial asymmetry, gaze paresis, or other cranial nerve deficit. No nystagmus at present. Right hemisensory loss of pain sensation, especially the right leg more than the right arm. Moderately severe right hemiparesis with considerable weakness of grip, arm drift, and poor movement of right lower extremity. DTRs normally active and symmetrical with absent ankle reflexes. Flexor plantar responses present bilaterally.

Laboratory Studies

Urinalysis: results within normal limits.
Hematology: Hct, 43.0%; RBC, 5.06 × 10^{12}/L; WBC, 6.9 × 10^9/L; platelets, adequate.
Serum chemistry levels: Na, 140 mEq/L; K, 3.5 mEq/L; Cl, 109 mEq/L; CO$_2$, 21.9 mmol/L; LDH, 271 IU/L; uric acid, 3.3 mg/dL; albumin, 3.0 mg/dL; Ca, 8.4 mg/dL; and phosphorus, 4.7 mg/dL.

Medical Diagnoses

1. Subarachnoid hemorrhage possibly due to left middle cerebral artery aneurysm.
2. Chronic systemic lupus erythematosus.

Management

A CT scan done on admission to the tertiary facility showed blood present in the subarachnoid space, particularly the left sylvian fissure, and possible left frontal edema with effacement of the left frontal ventricular horn. Medical orders were:

1. fluid restriction to 3000 mL/day
2. bed rest with commode privileges
3. IV fluids D5/.2NS at 75 mL/hr
4. dexamethasone (Decadron) 12 mg IV now, then 4 mg IV q6h
5. aminocaproic acid (Amicar), IV infusion at 1.5 g/hr
6. phenobarbital, 64 mg by mouth or IM q8h

7. psyllium hydrophilic mucilloid (Metamucil), 1 packet (6.4 g) daily
8. acetaminophen (Tylenol), 625 mg q4h as needed for temperature higher than 100 °F (37.8 °C).

The day after admission a consulting physician saw Ms. Wells in regard to her systemic lupus erythematosus. The consultant's note indicated that Ms. Wells had arthritis and arthralgia as the major manifestations of the lupus. These symptoms were present in her wrists and fingers and to a lesser extent the other joints of her upper and lower extremities. The symptoms had been well controlled with intermittent prednisone and sulindac. The consultant noted that Ms. Wells was unaware of renal or central nervous system problems such as vasculitis of the kidney or brain. The consultant examined Ms. Wells and found no joint deformities, no palpable spleen, no pericardial rub, and no pleural rubs.

Later that day, angiography showed a single aneurysm (5–6 mm) of the left posterior communicating artery with spasm of the proximal portion of the left posterior cerebral artery. The neurosurgeon noted that the aneurysm could be managed surgically but elected to postpone surgery until Ms. Wells was more stable. She was returned to the CCU with orders for continuation of the previous orders. Ms. Wells and her boyfriend were informed of the gravity of the situation, the proposed intervention, and possibility of death. Both seemed to understand the explanations made by the physician and reinforced by the nursing staff. Ms. Wells and her boyfriend spoke with Ms. Wells' parents by telephone. The neurosurgeon spoke with them later in the evening.

A week later, a second CT scan showed less subarachnoid blood, with some blood still in the left sylvian fissure. The ventricles remained small without evidence of dilation or other obvious change since the previous scan. No new areas of blood, no shift of midline, and no obvious parenchymal hematoma were noted. Surgical removal of the aneurysm was scheduled for the following week.

Study Questions

1. What functions do the structures adjacent to Ms. Wells' aneurysm serve? What signs and symptoms would indicate enlargement or rupture of the aneurysm?
2. What is the purpose of the aminocaproic acid infusion? What are the nursing implications of administering this drug?
3. What are the actions of: dexamethasone; phenobarbital; psyllium hydrophilic mucilloid; and

acetaminophen? How would these actions be beneficial in managing Ms. Wells' subarachnoid hemorrhage?

4. What independent nursing measures should augment the medical approach to reducing the risk of new bleeding from the aneurysm?

5. If Ms. Wells has an exacerbation of her arthritis and arthalgia, what effect might her usual regimen of prednisone and sulindac have on her current acute problem of subarachnoid bleeding?

6. Outline the essential nursing diagnoses or nursing problems and outcomes for patients with subarachnoid bleeding? How would this plan be altered postoperatively?

TRICYCLIC ANTIDEPRESSANT INGESTION

Units II-12 and I-23, II-2, II-13, III-5, III-10

Present Illness

John Bradford, aged 20 years, was found semicomatose in his dormitory room by friends. The paramedics were called and responded promptly. At the site, they established an IV access route, administered supplemental oxygen, and attempted to obtain information about the patient. They then transported him to the ED and reported to the staff that the patient had three short generalized seizures and became comatose enroute to the hospital. He was quickly evaluated in the ED and then admitted to the CCU. The police cooperated with the hospital personnel in locating Mr. Bradford's parents and requesting permission to treat him.

Past Medical History

His past medical history was not available.

Physical Exam on Admission to the CCU

General: Deeply comatose, young man who was unresponsive to painful stimuli. There were no signs of trauma. Vital signs were: BP, 145/95 mm Hg; rectal T, 101.4 °F (38.5 °C); HR, 180/min and irregular; RR, 13/min.
HEENT: Pupils equal and dilated (7 mm) with minimal response to light. Fundoscopic exam was unremarkable. The mucous membranes of the mouth were dry and no unusual odors could be detected on the breath.

Chest: Lungs and heart were clear to auscultation and percussion. The cardiac rhythm was atrial fibrillation with a rapid ventricular response.
Abdomen: Flat with markedly diminished bowel sounds. No masses or organomegaly found.
Extremities: Warm, dry, and normal in appearance. No evidence of past parenteral drug abuse. DTRs symmetrical and hyperactive. Plantar response was extension bilaterally.
Neuro: Deep coma. No response to pain or other stimuli. Spontaneous respirations appeared adequate.

Laboratory Studies

Blood, gastric, and urine samples: obtained and sent to the laboratory for drug screens.
ECG: atrial fibrillation with very rapid ventricular response. Prolonged QT interval. ST-T wave abnormalities consistent with subendocardial injury present in the anterior leads. (See Figure 9–2.)

Medical Diagnosis

Coma of unknown origin. Possible drug ingestion.

Management

Several minutes after very slow IV administration of 2 mg physostigmine salicylate (Antilirium) the patient became alert and oriented. His cardiac rhythm dramatically reverted to a normal sinus rhythm. On questioning, the patient stated that he had ingested 50 tablets (25 mg each) of amitriptyline (Elavil) in an attempt to commit suicide. He said he had not taken any other medications nor had he drunk any alcoholic beverages. Later, the preliminary results from the drug screens indicated high levels of amitriptyline and no other toxic substances.

Over the next six hours, the patient gradually became less oriented and more agitated. His cardiac rhythm showed increasing irritability with ectopic activity and then ventricular tachycardia suddenly developed. His BP dropped to 100/60 mm Hg. The usual lidocaine (Xylocaine) bolus of 1 mg/kg was given. The slow IV administration of another 2 mg physostigmine salicylate produced immediate return to normal sinus rhythm and once again the patient became alert and oriented.

Study Questions

1. What are the manifestations and mechanisms of amitriptyline toxicity?

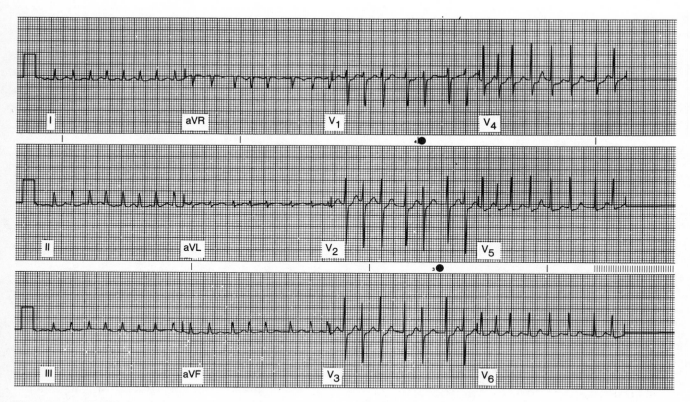

Figure 9–2 Atrial Fibrillation with Very Rapid Ventricular Response and Anterior Subendocardial Injury. *Source:* Cardiology Department of St. Mark's Hospital, Salt Lake City, Utah.

2. How can the potential severity of amitriptyline toxicity be assessed and complications be avoided?

3. What drugs or other treatment methods can be used to alter the toxicity of amitriptyline?

4. What constitutes appropriate management of amitriptyline toxicity?

5. Outline a nursing care plan for Mr. Bradford; include aspects that are specific to the medication he ingested as well as psychosocial considerations.

Chapter 10

Gastrointestinal Case Studies

ACUTE PANCREATITIS

Units II-19 and II-2, III-10

Present Illness

Joseph Martinez, a 68-year-old Hispanic man with a previous history of cholecystitis, experienced sudden agonizing knifelike pain in the epigastrum that radiated through to his back. The pain began while he was golfing on the ninth hole with friends. He decided to finish the hole and cut his game short. His golfing partners, concerned that he was suffering a heart attack, drove him to the ED. Enroute he became nauseated and vomited several times.

Mr. Martinez was evaluated in the ED. Supplemental oxygen was administered, an IV access route was established, and pain medication was given. Blood was drawn for laboratory tests and an ECG and a chest x-ray were done. He was admitted to the critical care unit (CCU).

Past Medical History

The patient had no history of heart disease, vascular disease, diabetes, or renal disease. He had had two episodes of cholecystitis in the past two years which were managed medically.

Mr. Martinez stated that he was a nonsmoker and a social drinker. He lived with his wife in a retirement community. Prior to his retirement, he had been a professional house painter.

Physical Exam on Admission to the CCU

General: A large, burly man in acute distress from pain. Ht, 6 ft; wt, 245 lb. Vital signs were: BP, 100/60 mm Hg; T, 100 °F (37.8 °C); HR, 120/min and regular; RR, 24/min.
Head, Eyes, Ears, Nose, and Throat (HEENT): Normal findings on examination.

Neck: Supple, without palpable lymph nodes or thyroid.
Chest: Symmetrical with equal excursion. Lungs clear to percussion and auscultation. Cardiac rhythm was sinus tachycardia without ectopy. Heart sounds were normal S_1 and S_2 without rubs, murmurs, or gallops.
Abdomen: Large, rounded with minimal bowel sounds in all quadrants. No bruits heard. Soft, extremely tender, especially in the epigastric region. Limited palpation discovered no organomegaly or masses.
Rectal: No masses. Soft brown stool with negative guaiac test.
Extremities: Pulses present, equal, and faint. ROM limited at hips. Otherwise moved extremities well with equal strength. IV infusing into left forearm. IV site patent, without signs or symptoms of infiltration or phlebitis.
Neurological status (Neuro): Patient alert and oriented to person, place, and time. Cranial nerves grossly intact. DTRs 1–2+ and symmetrical. Bilateral flexor plantar responses present.

Laboratory Studies

Serum chemistry levels: Na, 135 mEq/L; K, 3.9 mEq/L; Cl, 95 mEq/L; CO_2, 27 mmol/L; BUN, 31 mg/dL; creatinine, 1.4 mg/dL; uric acid, 8.1 mg/dL; LDH, 227 IU/L; SGOT, 18 IU/L; total CK, 73 IU/L; total bilirubin, 1.6 mg/dL; direct bilirubin, 0.4 mg/dL; alkaline phosphatase, 206 IU/L; serum glutamic pyruvic transaminase (SGPT), 129 IU/L; total protein, 8 mg/dL; albumin, 4.9 mg/dL; Ca, 10.8 mg/dL; phosphorus, 3.9 mg/dL; cholesterol, 209 mg/dL; amylase, 3500 IU/L; and gamma glutamyl transferase (GGT), 61 IU/L.
CBC: RBC, 5.74×10^{12}/L; Hgb, 17.3 g/dL; Hct, 53.5%; mean corpuscular volume (MCV), 93.2 cubic microns; mean corpuscular hemoglobin (MCH), 30.2 pg; mean corpuscular hemoglobin concentra-

tion (MCHC), 32.4%; and WBC, 9.3 × 10⁹/L; with bands, 2%; segs, 79%; lymphs, 11%; monos, 5%; eos, 3%; and platelets, adequate.

Urinalysis: results within normal limits.

Chest x-ray: within normal limits.

ECG: Sinus tachycardia. Normal axis. Nonspecific ST-T wave changes. (See Figure 10–1.)

Medical Diagnoses

1. Probable acute pancreatitis of edematous or hemorrhagic origin.
2. Previous history of cholecystitis.

Management

The physician planned to eliminate MI, ulcer disease, and abdominal aortic aneurysm as other possible causes of Mr. Martinez' acute pain. The medical orders were:

1. bed rest with commode privileges

2. IV fluids of D5/.45NS with KCl, 20 mEq/L at 80 mL/hr
3. meperidine (Demerol) 75–100 mg IM q4h as needed for pain
4. nothing by mouth (NPO) with double lumen nasogastric tube connected to low constant suction
5. ECG and cardiac enzymes every 8 hours for three times
6. flat plate x-ray of the abdomen
7. serum chemistries and serum amylase in the morning
8. obtain blood and urine cultures if temperature is greater than 102 °F (38.9 °C). Then begin administering, ampicillin (Omnipen), 1 g IV q6h, and gentamicin (Garamycin), 70 mg IV q6h.

The nurse made Mr. Martinez comfortable in bed and then administered 100 mg of meperidine IM. The nurse explained the routines of the CCU while carrying out the medical and nursing orders. When Mr. Martinez stated the meperidine was relieving his pain the nurse inserted the double lumen nasogastric tube

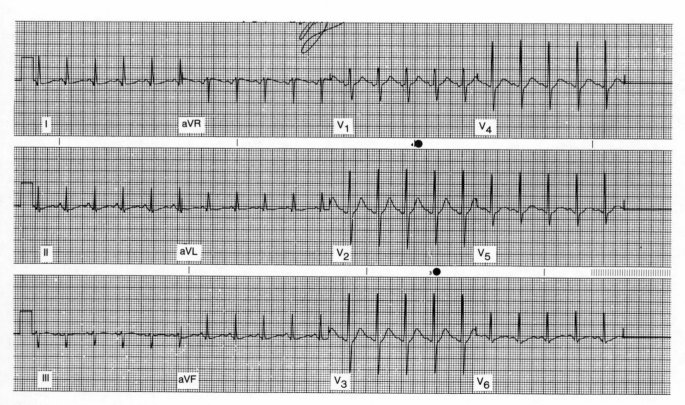

Figure 10–1 Sinus Tachycardia. Nonspecific ST-T Wave Changes. *Source:* Cardiology Department of St. Mark's Hospital, Salt Lake City, Utah.

and connected it to low constant suction. The x-ray technician brought the portable machine to the CCU. The nurse assisted in positioning Mr. Martinez for the flat plate x-ray of his abdomen. Following the x-ray, the nurse arranged a period of uninterrupted rest for Mr. Martinez. At the end of the rest period, Mr. Martinez' temperature was 103 °F (39.4 °C) so the nurse obtained samples for blood and urine cultures. The ampicillin and gentamicin were added to the regimen.

Subsequent laboratory results and ECGs confirmed the diagnosis of acute pancreatitis.

Study Questions

1. Explain the pathophysiology pertinent to acute pancreatitis.
2. How does Mr. Martinez' history of cholecystitis relate to his current acute pancreatitis?
3. Why are infection and fluid volume deficit anticipated as complications of acute pancreatitis?
4. What clues in the history, physical exam, and admission laboratory results would lead the health care team to conclude that Mr. Martinez did not have an MI? An abdominal aortic aneurysm? Ulcer disease?
5. What nursing outcomes to the following nursing diagnoses would be desirable?

   Anxiety

   Comfort, alterations in: Pain

   Fluid volume deficit: Potential

   Nutrition, alterations in: Less than body requirements
6. Complete the nursing care plan by indicating appropriate nursing actions required to achieve each outcome.

ESOPHAGEAL PERFORATION

Units II-17 and I-23, I-24, III-5

Present Illness

Thomas Black, aged 75 years, was admitted to the hospital the morning of June 7. The previous evening, he had swallowed a piece of meat that lodged in his esophagus. He was not having difficulty breathing on admission, but he had vomited all his gastric contents without sensing dislodgment of the meat.

He had a history of peptic ulcer disease since age 50. Dysphagia had developed a few years ago and worsened considerably over the past nine months. An episode in September was especially difficult, with food

being lodged for six hours prior to passing into his stomach.

Rigid esophagoscopy was done the afternoon of admission under general anesthesia. Erythematous, inflamed mucosa and a hiatal hernia were viewed but no foreign body was located. Later in the evening of June 7, he complained of pleuritic-type chest pain. Results of cardiac and pulmonary exams were negative. An upper GI series the next morning showed extravasation of contrast media posterior to the esophagus at the T1 level and extending into the lower mediastinum. A chest x-ray demonstrated bilateral accumulation of pleural fluid. His temperature was elevated with heart rate and blood pressure normal. Inadvertent esophageal perforation was diagnosed.

On the morning of June 9, coarse rales were heard in both lung fields posteriorly from the midchest to the bases with dullness to percussion to the right side from midchest to the base. It was decided to manage the perforation conservatively, as cervical esophageal perforations normally respond well to such treatment. Antibiotics, cimetidine (Tagamet), and nasogastric suction were initiated and continued for five days.

Mr. Black continued to accumulate fluid in his chest and developed lung consolidation, shortness of breath, fevers ranging between 101 and 102 °F (38.3–38.9 °C), and an elevated WBC count. An exploratory thoracotomy was done with drainage and debridement of an empyema and chest tube insertion five days after the incident. The drainage was cultured and antibiotics were prescribed as indicated by the culture sensitivities. After surgery, his fever, elevated WBC count, pleural effusion, and lung consolidation all continued. Six days later, he was draining frank pus around the chest tube and his temperature rose to 102 to 104 °F (38.9–40 °C). His right flank was reddened and pitting edema was present over most of his back. The pus was again cultured and the antibiotic therapy was adjusted.

Surgical procedures for open drainage of the cervical area from the pharyngoesophageal junction, gastrostomy, and gastrojejunostomy were performed on June 30, approximately three weeks after the original incident. Four chest tubes were placed to drain the copious amounts of pus. Cultures were done, the antibiotic sensitivities were reviewed, and appropriate antibiotics were administered.

On July 7, a massive clot was removed from the abdominal wound and a bleeding vessel was ligated. His soft tissue infection was noted to have extended. Nutritional status and pulmonary function were now very poor despite attention to pulmonary toilet and enteral nutrition. The patient was confused, combative, and restless. He was obviously critically ill and septic. The cellulitis continued and debridement was again performed on July 14. Cultures were done and the antibiotic regimen was reviewed. By this time, almost all of his right lateral chest was an open, gaping wound with purulent drainage. Layering of the fluid was demonstrated on chest x-ray with numerous adhesions formed around the chest tube. His right flank and back were grossly cellulitic, with extensive superficial and soft tissue infection involving the posterior mediastinum, parenchymal lung, and pleural space.

For seven days, following the July 14 debridement, he remained relatively stable, with temperatures to 101 °F (38.3 °C), and WBCs 26.0 × 10⁹/L. The morning of July 22, a large hematoma, 15 × 23 cm was noted in the wound and surgical removal was scheduled. His prognosis was very guarded. Admission to the critical care unit (CCU) was planned following the surgery.

Past Medical History

Mr. Black was allergic to penicillin. He could not remember which childhood illnesses he had had. He had a history of peptic ulcer disease and hypertension in adulthood. Surgeries in the past were appendectomy and tonsillectomy.

Mr. Black's family history was unremarkable. His religious preference was Roman Catholic. He used alcohol occasionally and had a 15 pack per year history of cigarette usage. The patient was a retired construction worker.

Physical Exam Prior to Surgery (July 22)

General: Obviously short of breath and uncomfortable, with moderate diaphoresis. Vital signs were: BP, 130/90 mm Hg; T, 101.2 °F (38.4 °C); HR, 104/min; RR, 28/min with supplemental oxygen at 10 L/min by mask.
HEENT: Sparse hair of normal texture. PERRLA. EOMs full. Nasal septum midline. Full dentures. No oral lesions or cyanosis.
Skin: Diaphoretic. No areas of breakdown except chest and back described in "Present Illness."
Neck: Supple. Carotid pulses full and without bruits. Thyroid smooth and not enlarged.
Chest: Bilateral coarse rales heard posteriorly from midchest to diaphragm. Dullness to percussion over right base. Copious amounts of yellow sputum suctioned from oropharynx. Apical pulse regular and tachycardic. Grade 2/6 systolic murmur heard at the apex; physiological split S₂ heard at the base. No rub or murmur appreciated.
Abdomen: Protruberant with active bowel sounds in all quadrants. Appendectomy scar in lower right

quadrant. Soft, mildly tender along the costal border. No masses or organomegaly.
GU: Normal genitalia of uncircumcised male.
Extremities: No cyanosis. No clubbing or edema. Peripheral pulses equally palpable and of moderate intensity.
Neuro: Alternating periods of lucidness and confusion.

Laboratory Studies

The culture results of the purulent drainage indicated various organisms such as *Bacteroides, Enterococcus, Staphylococcus,* and hemolytic *Streptococcus.* His sputum contained *Klebsiella* organisms and *Staphylococcus aureus.* The culture sensitivities were used to guide the antibiotic therapy. He received varied appropriate antibiotics, including gentamicin (Garamycin), clindamycin (Cleocin), cephalothin sodium (Keflin), chloramphenicol (Chloromycetin), and vancomycin (Vancocin).

Medical Diagnoses

1. Esophagitis secondary to foreign body.
2. Esophageal perforation with mediastinal cellulitis and infection.
3. Sepsis secondary to mediastinal infection.
4. Pulmonary infection and lung consolidation secondary to mediastinal infection.

Management

Mr. Black's wound was debrided, cleansed, and irrigated in the operating room on July 22. The hematoma was removed and the bleeding vessel was ligated. He was in poor condition when he returned to the CCU postoperatively for monitoring and dressing changes.

Study Questions

1. What infection control measures are need in the CCU?
2. What is the likely final outcome of Mr. Black's illness?
3. What emotional supports could be provided to Mr. Black and his family?
4. Identify appropriate nursing diagnoses or nursing problems and outcomes for Mr. Black's nursing care plan.
5. Explain appropriate nursing intervention that will aid in achieving the expected outcomes.

FULMINATING HEPATITIS

Units II-18 and I-23, I-24

Present Illness

Bonnie Watkins, a 37-year-old white, married, hospital laboratory technician, was diagnosed as having hepatitis B in early June. She remained at home but experienced increasing nausea, vomiting, and anorexia. On June 29, her husband brought her to the ED in moderate distress. She was admitted to an isolation room on a medical nursing unit for management of dehydration and malnutrition.

Past Medical History

Her past medical history was unremarkable. Ms. Watkins and her husband were parents of four children aged 2, 5, 8, and 11 years.

Physical Exam on Admission

General: Pleasant, jaundiced, and fatigued woman. Ht, 5 ft, 8 in; wt, 145 lb. Vital signs were: BP, 130/80 mm Hg; T, 98 °F (36.7 °C); HR, 100/min and regular; RR, 24/min.

HEENT: Normocephalic. Icteric scleras and conjunctivas. Normal fundoscopic exam. EOMs full. External ear canals clear. Tympanic membranes intact and icteric. Nasal septum midline. Pharynx clear.

Neck: Supple. Thyroid not enlarged. Cervical lymph nodes not palpable. No JVD.

Chest: Symmetrical excursion. Breasts were without masses. Lungs were clear to percussion and auscultation. Heart sounds were normal S_1 and S_2 with a soft systolic murmur at Erb's point. No rubs or gallops.

Abdomen: Rounded with faint bowel sounds in all quadrants. Soft with right upper quadrant tenderness. Lower liver border at umbilicus. Spleen not palpable.

Extremities: Peripheral pulses all present, strong, and equal. No asterixis.

Neuro: Oriented to person, place, and time. Cranial nerves II–XII intact. Very fatigued and slow in movements. Gait slow and unsteady. DTRs 2+ and symmetrical with plantar flexor responses present.

Laboratory Studies

Serum chemistry levels: Na, 138 mEq/L; K, 3.9 mEq/L; Cl, 105 mEq/L, CO_2, 28 mmol/L; glucose, 100 mg/dL; BUN, 4 mg/dL; creatinine, 0.8 mg/dL; uric acid, 3.9 mg/dL; LDH, 577 IU/L; SGOT, 2640 IU/L; total bilirubin, 18 mg/dL; direct bilirubin, 14.5 mg/dL; alkaline phosphatase, 262 IU/L; SGPT, 2955 IU/L; total protein, 5.7 mg/dL; albumin, 2.6 mg/dL; Ca, 8.0 mg/dL; phosphorus, 3.5 mg/dL; cholesterol, 146 mg/dL; and GGT, 110 IU/L.

Hematology: RBC, $4.25 \times 10^{12}/L$; Hgb, 10.9 g/dL; Hct 32.6%; WBC, $6.0 \times 10^9/L$; with bands, 19%; segs, 57%; lymphs, 12%; monos, 16%; eos, 2%; and platelets, adequate.

Coagulation: PT, 17.0 sec; PTT, 46.9 sec.

Urinalysis: amber; specific gravity, 1.007; pH, 6.0; and Ictotest, positive for bile.

Medical Diagnosis

Active hepatitis B.

Management

The patient experienced increasing difficulty and her status deteriorated. Her SGOT level was in the normal range two weeks after admission and SGPT level was in the normal range three weeks after admission.

Three weeks after admission she was critically ill and was transferred to the critical care unit (CCU). At the time of transfer, she was thought to be septic secondary to a urinary tract infection. Her mental status had declined and she was confused most of the time. She was alert and oriented occasionally and did not exhibit asterixis. She was hemodynamically unstable so invasive monitoring and cardiovascular support were instituted.

During the fourth week after admission the SGPT level was below the normal range and her downhill course accelerated. On the 28th hospital day the CCU nurse's physical assessment indicated:

General: Comatose with minimal response to deep pain; very jaundiced; critically ill. Wt, 187 lb. Vital signs were: BP, 120/60 mm Hg; T, 98 °F (36.7 °C); HR, 120/min and regular; RR, 20/min and deep; RAP, 5 mm Hg; PAP, 24/12 mm Hg, mean 16 mm Hg; PCWP, 10 mm Hg.

HEENT: Normocephalic, PERRL, 5 mm. Icteric scleras. Thin, soft, 8F duodenal feeding tube in place through right nostril. Clamped at present. Supplemental oxygen at 40% per face mask. Coarse, loud expiratory sound as patient exhaled through closed lips.

Chest: Triple lumen IV catheter in place at right subclavian site. Rhonchi scattered through lungs. Diminished breath sounds in the bases. Cardiac rhythm sinus tachycardia. Heart sounds normal S_1

with physiological split S_2 and S_3 gallop. Soft systolic murmur heard at Erb's point. No pericardial rubs heard.

Abdomen: Slightly distended with no bowel sounds in any quadrant. Soft with lower liver border at umbilicus.

GU: Normal female genitalia. Indwelling urinary catheter draining cloudy urine. Rectal tube draining liquid maroon stool.

Extremities: Pulses present, equal, and bounding. No spontaneous movement. 2+ pitting edema. Arterial line in right femoral artery. Pulmonary artery thermodilution catheter in right femoral vein. Site oozing blood and requiring dressing changes q4h.

Serum chemistry results: Na, 133 mEq/L; K, 4.2 mEq/L; Cl, 96 mEq/L; CO_2, 30 mmol/L; glucose, 594 mg/dL; BUN, 0 mg/dL; and magnesium (Mg), 1.6 mg/dL.

Blood gas results (F_{IO_2} 0.40): Sa_{CO}, 2.8%; Sa_{O_2}, 91.8%; Pa_{O_2}, 69 torr; Pa_{CO_2}, 38 torr; pH 7.47; base excess, +4.4; actual HCO_3, 27.5 mEq/L; Hgb, 9.2 g/dL; Ca_{O_2}, 11.6%; Sv_{CO}, 2.2%; Sv_{O_2}, 76.8%; Pv_{O_2}, 44 torr; Pv_{CO_2}, 39 torr; pH 7.45; base excess, +3.9; actual Hco_3, 27.1 mEq/L; Hgb, 9.1 g/dL; Cv_{O_2}, 9.7%.

The nurse regulated the ordered IV fluid of 50% dextrose in 0.45% normal saline with potassium chloride, 20 mEq/L at 100 mL/hr, and administered the medications that were ordered:

1. gentamicin (Garamycin), 130 mg IV q8h
2. cefoxitin (Mefoxin), 2 g IV q6h
3. nafcillin (Unipen), 2 g IV q6h
4. dexamethasone (Decadron), 4 mg IV q6h
5. fresh frozen plasma, 1 unit q8h
6. regular insulin sliding scale for the following blood glucose levels q4h
   100–200 mg/dL, no insulin
   200–300 mg/dL, 10 units IV
   300–400 mg/dL, 15 units IV
   400–500 mg/dL, 20 units IV
   >500 mg/dL; call physician for orders.

Ms. Watkins died of fulminating hepatitis B and overwhelming hepatic failure on July 30, one month after admission and seven weeks after diagnosis.

Study Questions

1. Why did the hepatic enzyme levels become normal or below normal prior to the patient's death?
2. Why was the BUN level 0 mg/dL 36 hours prior to death?
3. What is asterixis? How is it assessed? What is its importance?
4. What infection control measures were needed in the CCU to protect Ms. Watkins, her visitors, CCU personnel, and other patients?
5. Which of the following were the four most important patient care problems in the nursing diagnoses during Ms. Watkins' stay in the CCU?
   Airway clearance, ineffective
   Bowel elimination, alterations in: Diarrhea
   Breathing patterns, ineffective
   Cardiac output, alterations in: Decreased
   Communication, impaired verbal
   Fluid volume, alterations in: Excess
   Gas exchange, impaired
   Mobility, impaired physical
   Nutrition, alterations in: Less than body requirements
   Sensory perceptual alterations
   Skin integrity, impairment of: Potential
   Urinary elimination, impairment of: Alterations in patterns
6. Plan appropriate nursing outcomes for the four diagnoses identified in question 5.

GASTROINTESTINAL BLEEDING

Units II-16 and II-13

Present Illness

Gertie Illingham, aged 50 years, was a black woman with a previous history of peptic ulcer disease. Ms. Illingham was home alone when she felt faint and dizzy while vacuuming. She sat down to rest and noticed that she was perspiring profusely although it was mid-December and the room was cool. Because of abdominal cramping, she went to the bathroom and passed a large, loose, tarry stool. She became nauseated and vomited a large amount with the appearance of coffee grounds. She called her physician who recommended that she meet him in the ED. A neighbor drove Ms. Illingham to the hospital.

On arrival in the ED, Ms. Illingham fainted at the clerk's desk. She was placed on a stretcher where she quickly regained consciousness. Her vital signs were: BP, 90/50 mm Hg; HR, 150/min; and RR, 24/min. A 16 gauge IV catheter was inserted into her left antecubital vein with difficulty and rapid infusion of normal saline was begun. A double lumen nasogastric tube was inserted through her left naris and connected to low constant suction with immediate return of gastric contents. The nasogastric drainage had a coffee-grounds appearance and a positive guaiac test. A second 16 gauge IV catheter was inserted into her right forearm and 5% dextrose in 0.45% normal saline solution was rapidly infused. A 16F indwelling urinary catheter was inserted and connected to a urinemeter. There was immediate return of 50 mL clear, dark amber urine which was sent to the laboratory for analysis. Blood was drawn and sent to the laboratory for CBC with differential, PT, PTT, and blood typing and crossmatching. The blood bank was asked to crossmatch four units of blood and to continue to crossmatch as the blood was used so that three units were always in reserve.

The critical care unit (CCU) staff were notified to expect Ms. Illingham. The admitting medical diagnosis was "active gastrointestinal (GI) bleeding." After stabilization in the ED, Ms. Illingham was transferred to the CCU. The neighbor called Mr. Illingham and told him that his wife had been admitted to the hospital.

Past Medical History

Ms. Illingham's past medical history included peptic ulcer disease diagnosed when she was 28 years old. She had been hospitalized twice in the past for GI bleeding, when she was 30 and when she was 45 years old. Both episodes required two transfusions and were controlled with medical management. Current medications consisted of multivitamins, 1 daily; cimetidine (Tagamet), 300 mg four times daily; and simethicone magnesium aluminum hydroxide (Mylanta), 30 mL before meals and at bedtime.

Ms. Illingham smoked one pack of cigarettes per day and consumed one or two alcohol drinks (highballs) per day with dinner. She generally ate a light, bland breakfast and lunch and then joined her family in eating heavy, spicy foods at dinner. She also usually ate a late night snack which was rich with dairy products and carbohydrates. Ms. Illingham had received instruction about a bland ulcer diet, but did not follow it very well. Her family did not like the foods she was allowed and she did not like to cook two diets. Mr. Illingham particularly enjoyed hot spicy foods such as chile and curry. He expected his wife to prepare, eat, and enjoy these meals with him.

Mr. and Ms. Illingham lived in their own home in a lower class neighborhood in the inner city. Their six children attended middle school and high school while living at home.

Physical Exam on Admission to the CCU

General: A very diaphoretic, black woman in moderate distress with pale mucous membranes. Com-

plaining of nausea and weakness. Concerned about her husband and youngest child. Ht, 5 ft 4 in; wt, 150 lb. Vital signs were: BP, lying, 100/60 mm Hg, sitting, 85/50 mm Hg; T, 96.6 °F (35.9 °C); HR, lying, 90/min, sitting 120/min; RR, 24/min.

HEENT: Normocephalic. PERRLA, 5 mm. EOMs intact. Normal fundoscopic exam. External ear canals impacted with cerumen and tympanic membranes not visualized. Double lumen nasogastric tube in left naris connected to low constant suction and draining dark red gastric contents with the appearance of coffee-grounds. Pharynx reddened. Teeth in poor repair. Gums reddened and bleeding.

Neck: Supple. No palpable cervical lymph nodes or thyroid enlargement. No JVD while supine.

Chest: Symmetrical with equal excursion. Lungs clear to percussion and auscultation. Cardiac rhythm sinus tachycardia with rare PVBs. Heart sounds normal S_1 and S_2 without rubs, gallops, or murmurs.

Abdomen: Rounded with bowel sounds present in all quadrants. Soft, very tender right upper quadrant. Lower liver border 2 cm below the costal margin. Spleen not palpated.

GU: Normal adult female external genitalia. Indwelling urinary catheter draining scant amounts of dark amber urine. Frequent, maroon-colored liquid stools.

Extremities: No deformities noted. Peripheral pulses present, equal, and weak. Movement and strength equally good in all extremities. IV infusion of normal saline at 30 mL/hr in left antecubital vein. IV infusion of D5/.45NS at 150 mL/hr in right forearm. IV sites patent without signs or symptoms of infiltration or phlebitis.

Neurological: Alert and oriented to person, place, and time. Cranial nerves II–XII grossly intact.

Laboratory Studies

Serum electrolytes, CBC, urinalysis, PT and PTT: results were within normal limits.

Medical Diagnosis

Active GI bleed secondary to peptic ulcer disease.

Management

While receiving report from the ED, the nurse reviewed the medical orders which were:

1. CCU routine for vital signs, intake and output, cardiac monitor

2. NPO
3. bed rest with commode privileges
4. double lumen nasogastric tube connected to low constant suction
5. iced saline lavage per nasogastric tube until clear as needed for active bleeding
6. simethicone magnesium aluminum hydroxide every hour per nasogastric tube to keep gastric pH greater than 5 when no active bleeding
7. transfuse one unit of crossmatched packed RBCs now over two hours
8. transfuse crossmatched packed RBCs as needed to maintain Hct 33–37% and arterial systolic pressure 90–100 mm Hg
9. hematocrit after each unit of packed RBCs has infused
10. IV fluids D5/.45NS at 150 mL/hr for four hours then at 125 mL/hr
11. replace nasogastric drainage milliliter for milliliter with IV normal saline
12. cimetadine, 300 mg IV q6h

In the process of doing the initial assessment and making observations, the nurse explained to Ms. Illingham the purpose and function of the nasogastric tube as well as the IVs and indwelling urinary catheter. The nurse also told Ms. Illingham that for the time being she would not be able to eat or drink anything by mouth. The nurse showed Ms. Illingham the commode at the bedside. During the assessment, the nurse established a calm, reassuring rapport with Ms. Illingham. The nurse raised the head of Ms. Illingham's bed to 30 degrees so that significant blood loss would be readily apparent.

The nurse had anticipated the need for iced saline lavage and had assembled the required equipment before Ms. Illingham arrived in the CCU. As soon as the initial assessment of Ms. Illingham's condition was completed, the nurse began the iced saline lavage through the nasogastric tube. The nurse instilled about 250 mL at a time before withdrawing the fluid, repeating this procedure until the aspirate was clear and no longer blood-tinged. During the lavage, the nurse prevented Ms. Illingham from chilling by keeping warm blankets over her and being careful not to drip the iced solution on her. The nurse used 4 L of normal saline mixed with ice and spent 20 minutes lavaging Ms. Illingham's stomach. When the lavage was completed, the nurse instilled 30 mL of simethicone magnesium

aluminum hydroxide down the nasogastric tube to keep the gastric pH greater than 5. The nurse checked the gastric pH 30 min later.

While the first nurse was doing the gastric lavage, another nurse obtained a unit of crossmatched packed RBCs. The two nurses followed the hospital procedure for beginning the transfusion through the IV in the left antecubital vein. The nurse monitored Ms. Illingham's vital signs carefully during the transfusion making certain that her arterial systolic pressure was in the desired range. The first dose of cimetadine was obtained and infused through the IV in Ms. Illingham's right forearm.

Study Questions

1. Describe the pathophysiology responsible for Ms. Illingham's presenting signs and symptoms.
2. Why were Ms. Illingham's admission hematocrit and hemoglobin with normal limits? Would you expect them to be low in view of her recent hemorrhage?
3. What nursing interventions could be instituted to assist Ms. Illingham in complying with the bland diet at home? When would it be appropriate to initiate these interventions?
4. Identify realistic nursing outcomes for each of Ms. Illingham's nursing diagnoses:
   Anxiety
   Bowel elimination, alterations in: Diarrhea
   Comfort, alterations in: Pain
   Coping, ineffective: Family and individual
   Fluid volume deficit: Actual
   Noncompliance with diet
   Nutrition, alterations in: Less than body requirements
   Tissue perfusion, alterations in: Duodenal
5. Identify the two nursing diagnoses listed in question 4 that are most important during Ms. Illingham's first eight hours in the CCU. Explain the appropriate nursing actions required to achieve the desired outcomes.
6. Someone from the blood bank calls and says they are having difficulty locating and crossmatching enough blood for Ms. Illingham. They would like you (the nurse) to tell the physician to take Ms. Illingham to surgery. What is the most appropriate course of action?

Chapter 11

Endocrine Case Studies

ACUTE ADRENAL INSUFFICIENCY

Unit II-23

Present Illness

James Verne, aged 50 years, was admitted for diagnosis and initial management of suspected adrenal hypofunction with acute adrenal insufficiency. For the past five years, Mr. Verne had been under considerable stress in managing his failing contracting business. Initially, he dismissed his complaints of fatigue and weakness as job-related. Lately, the symptoms had been difficult to ignore and were associated with anorexia, nausea, and vomiting. He had lost 30 lb over the past three months without dieting. He complained frequently of feeling cold and had two syncopal attacks in the month prior to admission. He found that although he spent essentially all his time indoors at the office, his skin had become as dark as his employees who worked out-of-doors.

This morning he did not get up at his usual early hour and told his wife that he felt gravely ill. Ms. Verne telephoned the family physician who instructed her to take Mr. Verne to the ED. After evaluation in the ED, Mr. Verne was admitted to the critical care unit (CCU).

Past Medical History

The past medical history was obtained from Ms. Verne. She stated that Mr. Verne had no allergies to medications. He had been very allergic to ragweed when they were first married. During the first ten years of their marriage, Mr. Verne had frequent asthma attacks which required epinephrine (Adrenalin) injections. The asthma attacks diminished in frequency during his middle years and Ms. Verne could not remember when he last had an attack.

Mr. Verne also had a past history of coccidiomyco-

sis which was active for several years late in adolescence and in early adulthood. No physician had told Mr. or Ms. Verne of changes in the routine chest x-rays for some time. Mr. Verne was diagnosed as hypertensive ten years ago. His blood pressure had been well controlled with daily exercise and dietary salt restriction.

Mr. Verne and his wife had been married 35 years and had three grown children who were married and lived out of state. His contracting business had done very well until five years ago when a decline in housing starts placed him in financial straits.

Physical Exam on Admission to the CCU

General: A thin, well-tanned man who seemed mildly confused. Ht, 6 ft, 2 in; wt, 190 lb. Vital signs were: BP, 100/60 mm Hg; T, 96.5 °F (35.8 °C); HR, 58/min; RR, 12/min.

HEENT: Normocephalic. Numerous gray-brown freckles on forehead. PERRLA, 4 mm. Normal fundoscopic exam. EOMs full. External ear canals clear. Tympanic membranes clear and retracted. Nasal turbinates slightly reddened with clear exudate. Brown freckles on oral mucosa. Pharynx clear.

Neck: Supple. Nonpalpable thyroid and cervical lymph nodes.

Chest: Symmetrical excursion. Areolas darkly pigmented. Lungs clear to percussion and auscultation. Cardiac rhythm sinus bradycardia without ectopy. PMI at sixth ICS in left MCL. Heart sounds quiet with normal S_1 and S_2; without gallops, rubs, or murmurs.

Abdomen: Flat with active bowel sounds in all quadrants. Normally unexposed skin appeared tanned. Soft, nontender, and without organomegaly or masses.

Genitourinary system (GU): Normal adult male external genitalia.

Extremities: Pulses present, equal, and faint. Normal hair distribution.

Neurological status (Neuro): Oriented to person, place, and time but very slow to answer questions. Cranial nerves II–XII grossly intact. DTRs 1+ and symmetrical. Bilateral plantar flexor responses.

Laboratory Studies

Serum chemistry results: Na, 125 mEq/L; K, 6.2 mEq/L, Cl, 89 mEq/L; CO_2, 19 mmol/L; glucose, 45 mg/dL; BUN, 37 mg/dL.
Hematology: Hct, 50%; WBC, 3.5×10^9/L.
Chest x-ray: normal lung fields. Small heart.

Medical Diagnosis

Possible acute adrenal insufficiency. Possible Addison's disease.

Management

Shortly after arriving in the CCU, Mr. Verne vomited a large amount of bile colored gastric contents and then developed coma and shock. His vital signs were: BP 60/10 mm Hg; HR, 50/min; RR, 8/min and gasping. He was quickly resuscitated with rapid IV infusion of a large amount of normal saline; hydrocortisone sodium succinate (Solu-Cortef), 100 mg IV; tracheal intubation; and artificial ventilation. A double lumen nasogastric tube was inserted and connected to low constant suction. An indwelling urinary catheter was inserted and connected to a urinemeter. Mr. Verne's condition stabilized as he became alert and oriented, had adequate spontaneous ventilation, and maintained an adequate cardiac output and blood pressure. Efforts were made to confirm the diagnosis of Addison's disease.

The physician ordered diagnostic tests of adrenal, thyroid, and pituitary function. Results of the 24-hour urine collection for 17-ketosteroids (17-KS) and 17-hydroxycorticosteroids (17-OHCS) indicated that adrenal secretion of cortisol, corticosterone, cortisone, and 11-hydroxycorticosterone was inadequate. Results of the plasma cortisol response to ACTH test confirmed the diagnosis of Addison's disease. Thyroid and pituitary function test results were within normal limits.

Fludrocortisone (Florinef) acetate, 0.1 mg daily, and hydrocortisone (Cortef), 20 mg daily, were prescribed as replacement therapy. Mr. Verne responded well and was transferred out of the CCU four days after admission.

Study Questions

1. What fluid and electrolyte imbalances are usually associated with adrenal insufficiency? How does the pathophysiology of adrenal insufficiency create these imbalances?
2. What are the expected results of the plasma cortisol response to ACTH test and 24-hour urine collection for 17-KS and 17-OHCS in adrenal insufficiency? How are the tests conducted and what are the nursing responsibilities during the tests?
3. What risks will subsequent critical illness pose for Mr. Verne?
4. What nursing observations would be important in a critically ill patient with a history of adrenal insufficiency?
5. How might chronic adrenal insufficiency be managed during a critical illness?
6. Identify the essential nursing diagnoses or nursing problems and desired outcomes for Mr. Verne. Explain the nursing actions required to achieve the outcomes.

ACUTE HYPERTHYROID CRISIS

Unit II-24

Present Illness

Helen Jones, aged 25 years, was at home recovering from "walking pneumonia" when she suddenly became agitated, tremulous, disoriented, diaphoretic, and tachypneic. Her boyfriend brought her to the ED for management of her very sudden critical illness.

In the ED, an IV catheter was inserted and Ms. Jones was given 2 mg propranolol (Inderal) in an effort to control her supraventricular tachycardia. The dose was given as an IV bolus slowly over two minutes with careful monitoring of her cardiac rhythm and vital signs. Her ventricular rate slowed and her blood pressure decreased slightly. A nasogastric tube was inserted and 400 mg propylthiouracil (PTU) was crushed, mixed with water and given through the tube. She was judged reasonably stable and quickly admitted to the critical care unit (CCU).

Past Medical History

Ms. Jones was diagnosed as being hyperthyroid while in her teens and at the age of 20 had a surgical subtotal thyroidectomy. Since the surgery, she had done well and not required medication. She had no other medical problems and her family history was noncontributory. The patient lived alone, was employed as a secretary, did not smoke, and rarely drank alcohol.

Physical Exam on Admission to the CCU

General: An acutely ill woman extremely agitated and delirious. Oriented to name only. Unable to cooperate with examination. Ht, 5 ft, 2 in; wt, 98 lb. Vital signs were: BP, 150/70 mm Hg; T, 104.8 °F (40.4 °C); HR, 180/min; RR, 38/min.
HEENT: All structures appeared normal. PERRL, 6 mm.
Neck: Supple. Old thyroidectomy scar.
Chest: Symmetrical. Lungs had a few scattered rales in the posterior bases. Cardiac exam normal. Cardiac rhythm atrial tachycardia with frequent PVBs.
Abdomen: Flat with very active bowel sounds in all quadrants. Soft and nontender without masses or organomegaly. Incontinent of liquid brown stool.
Extremities: DTRs 4+ and symmetrical with plantar flexion present.

Laboratory Studies

CBC and differential, serum electrolytes and cold agglutinin: results were compatible with recent mycoplasma infection.

Medical Diagnosis

Acute hyperthyroid crisis.

Management

Ms. Jones was admitted to a private room in the CCU. The nursing staff made every effort to provide a quiet, nonstimulating environment by keeping the door closed and the lights turned down. In addition they enlisted the aid of Ms. Jones' family and boyfriend to keep visits quiet and peaceful. The medical orders were:

1. bed rest
2. CCU routine for cardiac monitor and intake and output
3. vital signs every 15 minutes until stable, then q1h for 24 hours
4. administer IV fluid of Isolyte M at 100 mL/hr
5. oxygen at 4 L/min by nasal cannula
6. maintain nasogastric tube for medications if patient cannot take them orally
7. sodium iodide, 1 g in 500 mL D5W infused over

24 hours. Begin 2 hours after propylthiouracil was given in ED.
8. hydrocortisone sodium succinate (Solu-Cortef), 100 mg IV now and 50 mg IV q6h subsequently
9. propranolol, 40 mg orally or nasogastric q6h
10. erythromycin (Erythrocin), 175 mg IV q6h
11. acetaminophen (Tylenol) suppository, 625 mg q4h as needed for temperature greater than 101 °F (38.3 °C)
12. cooling blanket for temperature greater than 102 °F (38.9 °C)

During the first 24 hours of her stay in the CCU, Ms. Jones gradually became less agitated and delirious. Her vital signs decreased into her normal range. She was very embarrassed to learn from her boyfriend that she had been using profane language and physically striking members of the nursing staff.

Study Questions

1. Relate the pathophysiology of hyperthyroid crisis to the presenting signs and symptoms.
2. What independent nursing measures can be used to provide a quiet environment for patients in the critical care unit?
3. Why must propranolol be given slowly and with careful monitoring when it is administered IV?
4. What are the pharmacological actions of the prescribed drugs (propylthiouracil, sodium iodide, propranolol, and hydrocortisone sodium succinate)? How do they alter the effects of acute hyperthyroidism?
5. Describe an appropriate way of talking to Ms. Jones about her aggressive behavior in the CCU.
6. Identify and explain the essential nursing observations, diagnoses or problems, and actions required to prevent death in the life-threatening crisis of acute hyperthyroidism.

DIABETES INSIPIDUS

Unit II-22

Present Illness

Tyler Daniels, aged 26 years, was in the hospital recovering from surgical clipping of an aneurysm on the anterior communicating artery. Three days after surgery he began voiding large quantities of very pale urine. His IV intake at the time was 80 mL/hr and his oral intake was minimal. The nurse found the specific gravity of the urine to be 1.002 and calculated his urine output as more than 200 mL/hr for four consecutive hours. The nurse observed that during the past two hours Mr. Daniels' BP had declined from 120/80 to 110/70 mm Hg and that his heart rate had increased from 68 to 110/min. The nurse notified the neurosurgeon of the large unconcentrated urinary output and the changes in the vital signs.

Past Medical History

Mr. Daniels had suffered severe headaches and the diagnosis of cerebral aneurysm led to the cerebrovascular procedure. The surgical procedure had gone well and Mr. Daniels was recovering as expected.

Physical Exam at the Onset of Diuresis

General: A swarthy young man who appeared his stated age and was alert and oriented. Ht, 5 ft, 11 in; wt, 190 lb. Vital signs were: BP, 110/70 mm Hg; T, 98.4 °F (36.9 °C); HR, 110/min; RR, 12/min.
HEENT: Normocephalic. Dressing dry and intact. No ecchymosis visible. PERRLA, 4 mm. Normal fundoscopic exam. EOMs full. External ear canals clear. Tympanic membranes clear. Nasal turbinates pink and moist. Oral mucosa pink and moist. Pharynx not injected.
Neck: Supple. Nonpalpable thyroid and cervical lymph nodes.
Chest: Symmetrical excursion. Lungs clear to percussion and auscultation. Cardiac rhythm normal sinus without ectopy. PMI at fifth ICS 2 cm left of MCL. Heart sounds normal S_1 and S_2; without gallops, rubs, or murmurs.
Abdomen: Flat with active bowel sounds in all quadrants. Soft, nontender, and without organomegaly or masses.
GU: Normal adult male external genitalia.
Extremities: Pulses present, equal, and moderate.
Neuro: Oriented to person, place, and time. Cranial nerves II–XII grossly intact. DTRs 1 to 2+ and symmetrical. Bilateral plantar flexor responses present.

Laboratory Studies

Osmolality levels: plasma, 289 mosm/L; urine, 108 mosm/L.
Serum Na level: 150 mEq/L.

Medical Diagnoses

1. Post anterior communicating aneurysm clipping.
2. Diabetes insipidus secondary to manipulation of the pituitary.

Management

The neurosurgeon ordered 2.5 units of aqueous vasopressin (Pitressin) to be given immediately IM. The urine output was reduced to 60 mL/hr in 30 minutes and the urine osmolality level two hours later was 760 mosm/L.

Study Questions

1. List the key signs and symptoms of diabetes insipidus and describe the related pathophysiology.
2. What is the action of vasopressin? What are the differences in drug activity and administration between aqueous vasopressin and vasopressin in oil?
3. Persons with chronic diabetes insipidus and normal thirst mechanisms usually maintain normal fluid and electrolyte balance when they are alert and have access to food and water. What nursing observations and actions are required to compensate when patients are not alert and/or do not have unlimited access to food and water?
4. Identify the essential nursing diagnoses or nursing problems and desired outcomes for Mr. Daniels which are related to diabetes insipidus; include the potential side effects of vasopressin therapy. Explain the appropriate nursing actions required to achieve the outcomes.

DIABETES MELLITUS

Unit II-21

Present Illness

Simon Black was a 72-year-old white man who was admitted to the critical care unit (CCU) in diabetic ketoacidosis. On the day of admission, Mr. Black was found at home in a confused and combative state by his daughter. He had apparently been vomiting, forgotten to take his insulin, and also had not eaten for some time. He resisted going to the hospital but his daughter was able to usher him to the car. Enroute to the hospital, he lost consciousness. He was evaluated in the ED and therapy was initiated before he was admitted to the CCU.

Mr. Black's adult onset diabetes mellitus (AODM) was diagnosed 20 years ago. He was first managed with oral hypoglycemic agents. However, five years ago they became inadequate for good control and he was placed on an insulin regimen of isophane (NPH) insulin (NPH Iletin), 70 units subcutaneously every morning, and regular insulin (Regular Iletin), 10 units subcutaneously every evening. Mr. Black was very compliant and kept his diabetes in good control until a year ago. He was hospitalized several times in the past six months for ketoacidosis, due to poor compliance with his regimen and consequent poor control of his diabetes. He was discharged three weeks prior to this admission and did not keep his follow-up clinic appointment.

Past Medical History

Mr. Black had no known medication allergies and had received the influenza and pneumococcal vaccine two years previously. His past hospitalizations were: (1) tonsillectomy in childhood; (2) diagnosis of AODM 20 years ago; and (3) poor diabetic control: 5 years ago, 1 year ago, 6 months ago, 4 months ago, 2 months ago, and 3 weeks ago. Mr. Black smoked two packs of cigarettes a day from age 20 to 55. He rarely drank alcohol.

Mr. Black's mother and father died in their 70s of diabetes and heart disease, respectively. Mr. Black was the youngest of seven children. All of his siblings were dead with the exception of a sister who was living in a nursing home in another city. Mr. Black did not know his siblings' health histories.

Mr. Black's wife died a year ago at age 70 from a stroke. He and his wife had three children. Their son died in early adulthood but their two daughters were alive and well. One daughter lived close to Mr. Black and had been trying to watch out for him. He had retired from his job as a bus driver when he was 65 years old. Mr. Black lived alone and was financially dependent on his social security income.

Mr. Black's daughter stated that she had noticed significant changes in her father's behavior since her mother died one year ago. He no longer showed interest in his hobbies of stamp collecting and gardening. He seemed very forgetful, but when she tried to help him he was offended, angry, and refused her offers of assistance. She thought his diet was inadequate. Before his wife died, he shared in the cooking but now viewed it as an unnecessary chore. When she invited him to her house he rarely came and when she took food to him it often stayed uneaten in the refrigerator.

Physical Exam on Admission to the CCU

General: A thin, wasted man who looked his stated age and was confused. Ht, 5 ft, 10 in; wt, 140 lb. Vital signs were: BP, 100/60 mm Hg; T, 99.2 °F (37.3 °C); HR, 120/min; RR, 12/min, regular and deep.

HEENT: Normocephalic. PERRL, 2 mm. Pale conjunctiva. Lenses and corneas cloudy. EOMs intact and peripheral vision reduced. External ear canals partially occluded with cerumen. Tympanic membranes intact. Normal nasal mucosa. Lips dry and cracked. Teeth and gums in poor repair. Dry buccal mucosa with several healing lesions. White coating on tongue. Fruity odor to breath. Tonsils absent.

Neck: No JVD while sitting up 45-degree elevation. No palpable thyroid or cervical lymph nodes.

Chest: Symmetrical. Spine had slight increase in upper curvature. Lungs were clear to percussion and auscultation. Cardiac rhythm was normal sinus. Heart sounds were normal S_1 and S_2; no gallops, rubs, or murmurs were heard.

Abdomen: Scaphoid, with faint bowel sounds. Very poor skin turgor. Soft and nontender without organomegaly or masses.

Extremities: Limited ROM in all joints. Peripheral pulses present, equal, and weak in carotid, radial, and femoral arteries. Equal and faint in the popliteal arteries. Absent in both posterior tibial arteries and the left dorsalis pedis. Barely palpable in the right dorsalis pedis. Skin dry, pale, and thin with poor turgor. No hair below the knees. Large ulcer on left heel.

Neuro: Awake but somewhat confused. Oriented to person and place. Followed simple commands slowly and with difficulty. Answered appropriately most of the time. Cranial nerves II–XII intact. Unsteady in transfer from bed to chair.

Laboratory Studies

Hematology results: Hgb, 14 g/dL; Hct, 45%; WBC, 15.0×10^9/L.

Serum chemistry levels: Na, 130 mEq/L; K, 5.0 mEq/L; Cl, 95 mEq/L; CO_2, 7 mmol/L; glucose, 640 mg/dL; BUN, 31 mg/dL.

Urinalysis results: specific gravity, 1.020; glucose, 4+; acetone, 4+.

ABG results: pH, 7.01; Pao_2, 75 torr; $Paco_2$, 22 torr; HCO_3, 6.8 mEq/L.

Medical Diagnosis

Diabetic ketoacidosis secondary to uncontrolled diabetes mellitus.

Management

Mr. Black received normal saline by rapid IV infusion and an initial dose of regular insulin as an IV push. Subsequently, the regular insulin was delivered as a continuous IV infusion and titrated to the results of hourly blood glucose measurements. His serum potassium was monitored along with the blood glucose. As his blood glucose declined to the normal range, his serum potassium decreased and supplemental IV potassium chloride was required to maintain the serum potassium in the normal range. His LOC also improved as his blood glucose and serum electrolyte levels became more normal. After several days, he was transferred out of the CCU.

Study Questions

1. Explain the pathophysiology of diabetic ketoacidosis and how the usual signs and symptoms result.
2. Differentiate the pathophysiology of diabetic ketoacidosis from that of hyperosmolar nonketotic acidosis.
3. Compare and contrast the presenting signs and symptoms of diabetic ketoacidosis with those of hypoglycemic reaction (insulin shock).
4. What nursing interventions might help improve Mr. Black's compliance with the diabetic regimen?
5. What nursing care is indicated by the abnormal peripheral pulses?
6. List the nursing diagnoses or nursing problems for the life-threatening complications of diabetic crises. Identify and explain the nursing actions essential to achieving the most desirable and appropriate outcomes.

SYNDROME OF INAPPROPRIATE ANTIDIURETIC HORMONE SECRETION

Unit II-22

Present Illness

Vincent Powell, a 60-year-old coal miner, was brought to the ED by his family because of mental confusion and combativeness.

His wife and son reported that he had been complaining of anorexia, a nonproductive cough, as well as unusual fatigue and weakness for the past seven months. During this time, he had lost 40 lb. During the past two weeks, he was unusually irritable and occasionally irrational. The day before admission, the patient's confusion and disorientation became so severe that he tried to hit his wife. Because she could not manage him alone, she asked her son to come and stay with them.

The next morning, Mr. Powell had a grand mal seizure and was obviously gravely ill so Ms. Powell and her son brought him to the ED for evaluation.

Past Medical History

Ms. Powell reported that her husband drank six 12-oz beers daily and that he had smoked two to three packs of cigarettes per day for the 35 years of their marriage. She had never met any of Mr. Powell's family so could not give a family medical history. In addition, Mr. Powell had rarely seen a physician for illnesses and had never had a routine physical examination.

Physical Exam on Admission to the CCU

General: Thin, disoriented, and irritable man who appeared older than his stated age and coughed frequently. Vital signs were: BP, 140/80 mm Hg, supine and standing; T, 98.8 °F (37.1 °C); HR; 100/min and regular; RR, 18/min.
HEENT: Structures were normal.
Neck: Supple. Firm 2 × 3 cm lymph node in right supraclavicular area. Thyroid not enlarged. JVD to the angle of the jaw while sitting up 45 degrees.
Chest: Increased AP diameter and increased curvature to thoracic spine curvature. Dullness to percussion in right base. Lungs had scattered rhonchi and diminished breath sounds in the right base. Heart sounds were: normal S_1 and S_2 with S_3 and a soft systolic murmur at the base. No pericardial friction rub was heard.
Abdomen: Flat with active bowel sounds in all quadrants. Soft with mild tenderness in right upper quadrant. Liver palpable 5 cm below right costal margin.
GU: Normal genitalia of adult male.
Extremities: Peripheral pulses present, equal, and bounding. No deformities. Normal hair distribution.
Neuro: Confused, oriented to self only. Unable to follow instructions for cranial nerve exam. DTRs symmetrically diminished with bilateral plantar flexion.

Laboratory Studies

Serum chemistry levels: Na, 115 mEq/L; K, 3.8 mEq/L; Cl, 80 mEq/L; CO_2, 25 mmol/L; BUN, 15 mg/dL; glucose, 90 mg/dL; creatinine, 0.9 mg/dL; calcium, 7.2 mg/dL; total protein, 5.8 mg/dL; osmolality, 235 mosm/L.
Urine osmolality: 260 mosm/L.
X-ray results: skull, normal; chest, mass in lower right lobe.

ECG: normal with nonspecific ST-T wave changes.

Medical Diagnosis

Severe hyponatremia secondary to water intoxication.

Management

The physician suspected that Mr. Powell might have syndrome of inappropriate antidiuretic hormone (SIADH) secretion. Further diagnostic studies were planned and carried out. The supraclavicular lymph node was biopsied. The pathology report identified the node as oat cell carcinoma.

Mr. Powell's serum cortisol was 10 μg/dL in the morning. A 24-hour urine collection was done and 17-ketosteroids excretion was found to be 9 mg/day and sodium excretion was 150 mEq/day.

Mr. Powell's fluid intake was restricted, furosemide (Lasix) was administered, and hypertonic saline was carefully infused. As he diuresed, his serum sodium gradually returned to normal levels and his sensorium improved. Ms. Powell was very glad to see her normally gentle husband resume his former behavior.

Study Questions

1. List the key signs and symptoms of SIADH secretion and describe the pathophysiology that produces them.
2. Compare and contrast the pathophysiology of diabetes insipidus with that of SIADH secretion.
3. What diagnostic studies assist in confirming the diagnosis of SIADH secretion? What are the nursing responsibilities in conducting these tests?
4. What safety precautions should be implemented for Mr. Powell because he is confused and oriented to self only?
5. Identify the essential nursing diagnoses or nursing problems for Mr. Powell that are related to SIADH secretion. Explain the appropriate nursing actions required to achieve the desired outcomes.
6. What nursing observations and actions are required to compensate for patients who are not alert and/or do not have access to food and water and therefore cannot use normal physiological mechanisms to achieve fluid and electrolyte balance?

Chapter 12

Perinatal Case Studies

ABRUPTIO PLACENTA

Unit III-22

Present Illness

Caroline Holt, aged 38 years, was admitted to the obstetrical department at 38 weeks' gestation having had no prenatal care. She complained of sharp, burning abdominal pain of two hours' duration accompanied by dark, bloody drainage from her vagina.

Ms. Holt, gravida 5, had no prenatal care for her previous pregnancies. Her four children were delivered at home by her mother and a lay midwife. She had planned the same for this baby but was disconcerted by the presence of pain without labor contractions and the vaginal bleeding. She was accompanied by her husband, mother, and the lay midwife.

Past Medical History

Ms. Holt stated she had been in good health all her life and that she saw physicians only when absolutely necessary. Mr. Holt said that he thought doctors charged too much for too little.

Physical Exam on Admission

General: Pleasant woman, with a concerned manner, not in acute distress. Mild swelling of hands and feet. Vital signs were: BP, 100/70 mm Hg; T, 98.6 °F (37 °C); HR, 90/min; RR, 18/min.
Head, Ears, Eyes, Nose, and Throat (HEENT): Unremarkable.
Chest: Symmetrical. Lungs and heart clear to percussion and auscultation.
Abdomen: Fundus 36 cm above the symphysis pubis. Fetal heart tones, 140/min, in right lower quadrant. Fetus in vertex position. Abdomen tender and rigid.

Genitourinary system (GU): External genitalia of normal adult female. Dark red blood draining from vagina. Vaginal exam by physician with speculum showed dark red blood oozing from cervical os. Cervix 50% effaced with os dilated 2 cm. Presenting part at −1 station.

Laboratory Studies

Hematology results: Hgb, 12.0 g/dL; Hct, 36%.
Urinalysis results: protein, 1+; glucose, 0; acetone, 0.

Medical Diagnosis

Pregnancy of 38-weeks' gestation complicated by abruptio placenta.

Management

An hour after the initial exam, the nurse noted that the fundus had become "woody" and risen to 38 cm above the symphysis. Ms. Holt's BP was 96/64 mm Hg and her heart rate was 100/min. The fetal heart rate was 100/min. An immediate cesarean section was carried out and a stillborn male infant was delivered. Resuscitation of the infant was unsuccessful.

Ten minutes after delivering the baby, Ms. Holt's BP dropped to 80/40 mm Hg and her pulse climbed to 120/min. The placenta was delivered with a large retroplacental blood clot. Blood loss was estimated as 2500 mL. The physician ordered the first of four units of blood to be transfused. Ms. Holt was transferred to the critical care unit (CCU).

Ms. Holt remained in the CCU for 36 hours. By the end of her stay, she had received the four units of blood and her BP and pulse remained stable when she was both supine and upright. Her uterus was firm with moderate to heavy lochia when her bladder was empty. When her bladder was distended her lochia increased quite a bit. She was transferred out of the CCU with cautions to void frequently. The remainder of her physiological postpartum course was uneventful.

Mr. and Ms. Holt received much emotional support from their family and friends. They were able to initiate the grieving process while Ms. Holt was still in the hospital.

Study Questions

1. Discuss the pathophysiology of abruptio placenta.
2. Describe the usual presentation of abruptio placenta.
3. What hospital and community resources are available to support Mr. and Ms. Holt as they grieve for their stillborn infant? How might they gain access to these resources?
4. Describe the usual nursing care required in the immediate postpartum period.
5. Explain the salient points of postpartum assessment for each of the following: uterus, lochia, episiotomy/incision, breasts, bladder, bowel, phlebitis, and emotional state.
6. Outline a nursing care plan for Ms. Holt with emphasis on her postpartum hemorrhage. Include nursing diagnoses or nursing problems, outcomes, and actions.

PLACENTA PREVIA

Unit III-22

Present Illness

Sophia Nelson, aged 26 years, was admitted to the obstetrical department at 34 weeks' gestation having had excellent prenatal care. She was accompanied by her husband and complained of a large amount of bright red bloody drainage from her vagina. She estimated that she had lost three cups of blood at home. She denied pain and labor contractions.

Ms. Nelson, gravida 2, had delivered her first child without difficulty 18 months prior to this admission. She had a brief period of vaginal bleeding one week prior to admission.

Past Medical History

Her past medical history was unremarkable.

Physical Exam on Admission

General: Very pale woman, in moderate distress. Vital signs were: BP, 90/50 mm Hg; T, 97.6 °F (36.4 °C); HR, 120/min; RR, 20/min.
HEENT: Unremarkable.
Chest: Symmetrical. Lungs and heart clear to percussion and auscultation.
Abdomen: Fundus 34 cm above the symphysis pubis. Fetal heart tones, 146/min, in left upper quadrant. Fetus in transverse position. Abdomen soft and nontender.
GU: External genitalia of normal adult female. Bright red blood draining from vagina. Vaginal exam was not done at this time.

Laboratory Studies

Hematology results: Hgb, 12.0 g/dL; Hct, 36%.
Urinalysis results: protein, 0; glucose, 0; acetone, 0.

Medical Diagnosis

Pregnancy of 34-weeks' gestation complicated by placenta previa.

Management

Twenty minutes after admission, Ms. Nelson was taken to the operative delivery room where she was prepared for vaginal examination with a "double setup." A sterile vaginal examination was done by the physician which showed the cervix to be 1 cm dilated and uneffaced. Spongelike tissue was felt covering the os. Following the exam, Ms. Nelson's vaginal bleeding increased slightly.

A cesarean section was done using spinal anesthesia and a live baby girl weighing 2.3 kg (5 lb.) was delivered. The baby had an Apgar score of 6 at one minute and 8 at five minutes. The placenta was completely obstructing the cervical os. Blood loss was estimated as 2000 mL. The first of three units of packed RBCs was transfused and Ms. Nelson was transferred to the critical care unit (CCU).

Ms. Nelson remained in the CCU for 36 hours. By the end of her stay, she had received three units of packed RBCs and her BP and pulse remained stable both supine and upright. Her uterus was firm with moderate lochia when her bladder was empty. She was transferred out of the CCU on the second postoperative day. The remainder of her physiological postpartum course was uneventful.

Study Questions

1. Discuss the pathophysiology of placenta previa.
2. Compare and contrast the usual presentations of placenta previa and abruptio placenta.
3. What hospital and community resources are available to support Mr. and Ms. Nelson as they care for their premature infant? How might they gain access to these resources?
4. Describe ways in which nurses can facilitate mother-infant bonding when the mother is in the CCU and the infant is in the hospital nursery.
5. Outline a nursing care plan for Ms. Nelson with emphasis on monitoring her recovery from the spinal anesthetic. Include nursing diagnoses or nursing problems, outcomes, and actions.

Chapter 13

Multiple System Case Studies

ACQUIRED IMMUNE DEFICIENCY SYNDROME

Units III-4 and I-24

Present Illness

Gerald Brown, a 30-year-old barber, was admitted for evaluation of heat intolerance, tachycardia, and complaints of increasing cough, weakness, and shortness of breath. When he was first hospitalized, Mr. Brown had a low-grade fever without adenopathy and his mucous membranes appeared normal. He subsequently began to have temperature spikes and became gravely ill. Chest x-rays showed bilateral interstitial infiltrates. ABGs demonstrated desaturation with a Pao_2 of 37 torr on room air. He was transferred to the critical care unit (CCU) for respiratory support.

Results from a transbronchial biopsy confirmed a diagnoses of *Pneumocystis carinii* pneumonia. Cultures for *Neisseria gonorrhoeae* were negative. The patient reported homosexual activity and problems with recurrent rectal ulcers, as well as unintentional weight loss of 30 lb over the previous six months. Antibiotic therapy of IV trimethoprim and sulfamethoxazole (Bactrim) was administered. Temperature spikes became less dramatic and his respiratory status improved. The pulmonary infiltrates seen on the chest x-ray persisted with the left side infiltrate more extensive than the right. Subjectively, the patient reported decreased shortness of breath and decreased respiratory effort.

The patient then developed a florid rash which was thought to be due to the trimethoprim/sulfamethoxazole, so the drug was discontinued after a total of eight days of therapy. An infectious desease consult was sought for evaluation of the course of treatment and suggestions for achieving further improvement.

Past Medical History

The patient had been in good health other than intermittent abdominal discomfort and recurring rectal ulcers. Family medical history was not pertinent to the patient's current problems.

Physical Exam on the Tenth Hospital Day

General: Flushed, alert, cooperative, underweight, white man in no acute distress. Vital signs were: BP, 120/80 mm Hg; T, 98.8 °F (37.1 °C); HR, 80/min and regular; RR, 20/min.

Head, Ears, Eyes, Nose, and Throat (HEENT): Structures were normal on exam.

Integumentum: Hair, skin, and nails, as well as tympanic membranes and mucous membranes of mouth and pharynx appeared normal. Decreasing diffuse rash over neck and chest.

Neck: No adenopathy, thyroid enlargement, or venous distention.

Chest: Rales noted in left base. No wheezes noted. Normal cardiac exam.

Abdomen: Scaphoid with bowel sounds present in all quadrants. Soft, generally tender without organomegaly, masses, or point tenderness.

Genitalia: Normal adult male without evidence of herniation or mucosal lesions.

Rectal: Mucosa had no lesions at time of exam.

Extremities: No pedal edema. Normal ROM.

Neurological status (Neuro): Alert and oriented to person, place, and time.

Laboratory Studies

CBC: WBC, 2.2×10^9/L; RBC, 3.91×10^{12}/L; Hgb, 10.9 g/dL; Hct, 34.1%, MCV, 87.7 cubic microns; MCH, 27.7 pg; MCHC, 31.8%; platelets, 0.137×10^{12}/L.

Differential: Meta, 1%; bands, 16%; segs, 43%; lymphs, 27%; and monos, 13%.

Helper Suppressor T C ratio test: 0.2% of control (1.5).

Hepatitis-associated antigen (HAA): positive.

Neisseria gonorrhoeae culture: negative.

Anal virology: positive for *Herpes Simplex II*.

Right lung biopsy: positive for *Pneumocystis carinii*.

Palatal mucosa biopsy: positive for Kaposi's sarcoma.

Medical Diagnoses

1. Acquired Immune Deficiency Syndrome (AIDS). Homosexual risk group.
2. *Pneumocystis carinii* pneumonia.
3. Kaposi's sarcoma.
4. Perirectal herpes.
5. Sulfa allergy with diffuse rash and documented leukopenia.
6. Positive HAA.

Management

Mr. Brown's skin rash continued to fade after discontinuation of the trimethoprim/sulfamethoxazole medication. His pneumonia was treated with pentamidine isethionate (Lomidine), 280 mg (4 mg/kg) IM every morning for 14 days. CBC, platelets, serum chemistries, and urinalysis results were used to monitor for signs of toxicity. His respiratory insufficiency required artificial ventilation until clinical improvement was noted on the sixth day of the pentamidine isethionate regimen.

The nurses recognized Mr. Brown's potential problems and watched for signs and symptoms of their development. They also took preventive measures where possible. He remained in isolation and the nurses made an effort to communicate to him that it was the disease and not he that was being isolated.

Study Questions

1. Describe the theory that currently explains the immunological deficiency of AIDS.
2. Explain the current view of the link between male homosexuals and development of AIDS.
3. What other patient populations are at risk to develop AIDS?
4. What key observations should be made of Mr. Brown's skin and mucous membranes?
5. What side effects might result from Mr. Brown's pentamidine isethionate therapy?

6. Identify and explain the nursing diagnoses or nursing problems, outcomes, and interventions that should be included on Mr. Brown's nursing care plan.

BURN INJURY

Unit III-24

Present Illness

Henry Gregory, aged 40 years, was brought to the ED two hours after receiving an acute burn injury. The patient sustained second and third degree burns when gasoline spilled on his clothing and ignited while he was priming the carburetor of his farm tractor.

Past Medical History

Mr. Gregory reported that bilateral inguinal hernias were repaired in the past. He denied chronic cardiac, pulmonary, renal, or hepatic disease. He stated that he drank alcohol rarely and did not smoke.

Physical Exam on Admission to ED

General: An alert and oriented, large, white man in acute distress. Ht, 6 ft, 1 in; wt, 220 lb. Vital signs were: BP, 120/70 mm Hg; T, 99 °F (37.2 °C); HR, 124/min; RR, 20/min.

Skin: First degree burns of external ears and top of scalp. Second and third degree burns of face, neck, entire right arm and hand, anterior trunk, genitalia, anterior thighs, and right side of posterior trunk. Total burn approximated 50% of his body surface area. The burns of his anterior trunk and right arm and hand, which accounted for approximately half of the burn, were third degree.

HEENT: Burns as above. Fundoscopic exam normal. Tympanic membranes intact. Singed nasal hairs. Coughing up carbonaceous sputum. Oral mucous membranes moist.

Chest: Symmetrical with equal respiratory excursion. Lungs clear to auscultation. Cardiac sounds normal. Cardiac rhythm normal sinus.

Abdomen: Flat with active bowel sounds in all quadrants.

Extremities: Peripheral pulses all present and equal. No edema at present. DTRs in lower extremities 2+ and symmetrical. normal ROM.

Neuro: Alert and oriented to person, place, and time. Able to follow commands.

Laboratory Studies

Admission laboratory data included: Hgb, 17.2 g/dL; Hct, 50%; WBCs 25.0 × 10⁹/L; and serum chemistry levels all at the upper limits of normal ranges.

Medical Diagnoses

1. Second and third degree burns of 50% of body surface area.
2. Inhalation injury assumed because of facial burn, singed nasal hair, and carbonaceous sputum.

Management

In the ED, Mr. Gregory's airway, breathing, and circulation were assessed before the extent of the burn injury was assessed and calculated. The burns were covered with clean sheets when the assessment was complete.

Because the burn covered more than 20% of his body surface area, fluid resuscitation was begun with IV administration of Ringer's lactate solution. The Parkland formula was used to calculate the fluid requirement. The results of the calculation indicated that Mr. Gregory would need 20 L of Ringer's lactate in the first 24 hours. IV catheters were inserted into veins in burned areas and then sutured in place. An endotracheal tube was inserted and supplemental oxygen was provided because of the evidence of inhalation injury despite Mr. Gregory's apparently adequate spontaneous respirations. The regional burn center was contacted and arrangements were made for transport.

When Mr. Gregory arrived at the burn center his airway, breathing, and circulatory status were again assessed before attention was turned to the burn wounds. The fluid resuscitation was evaluated and continued during the admission assessment. The extent of the burns was evaluated by size and depth. A body diagram was colored to depict the location of the burns as well as the depth. Available skin donor sites were also assessed and marked on the body diagram. As soon as Mr. Gregory was considered stable, his burns were given an initial cleansing and debridement with water and surgical soap. The size and depth were assessed again. The assessment was reviewed and compared to the admission assessment to be certain that no large discrepancies existed.

At the burn center, Mr. Gregory's nursing problems were recognized as:

- potential acute respiratory insufficiency
- potential burn shock
- potential fluid and electrolyte imbalance
- potential sepsis
- potential malnutrition
- potential contractures and/or other residual deformities
- patient and family anxiety related to burn injury and therapy
- patient and family anxiety related to altered body image

When Mr. Gregory was hemodynamically stable and recovered from the burn shock, he was taken to the operating room at the burn center where his burns were surgically debrided and skin grafting was begun.

Study Questions

1. Discuss the current theory and practice approach to infection and infection control in burn victims.
2. What information is needed in order to calculate the amount of fluid required for resuscitation by the Parkland formula? Was the initial calculation for Mr. Gregory of 20 L in the first 24 hours correct? How much of the fluid should be administered during the first eight hours?
3. What other fluid resuscitation formulas are currently in use? How are they similar? How are they different?
4. Differentiate between the following wound coverings: physiological dressing; allograft (homograft); xenograft (heterograft); and autograft.
5. Identify and describe the management of burn patients during the acute, intermediate, and recuperative phases of recovery.
6. Identify and plan nursing care for Mr. Gregory's resuscitation, stabilization, and transfer to the burn center. Include actual and potential nursing diagnoses or nursing problems with outcomes and actions appropriate to the first 48 hours after injury.

DISSEMINATED INTRAVASCULAR COAGULOPATHY

Units III-3 and III-23

Present Illness

Delma Vienna, a 29-year-old, white woman, sustained multiple trauma in an automobile accident. Her very dirty wounds were cleansed and sutured in the ED and she was transferred to the CCU in skeletal traction. During the first 48 hours, she was in shock and required dopamine hydrochloride (Intropin) support of her blood pressure as well as several units of packed RBCs. On the fifth hospital day she began to ooze blood from lacerations and venipunctures that had been closed and dry.

Past Medical History

Her past medical history was unremarkable.

Physical Exam on the Fifth Hospital Day

General: Adequately nourished woman in moderate distress. Multiple sutured lacerations and skeletal traction pin sites oozing dark red blood. Ht, 5 ft, 8 in; wt. 140 lb. Vital signs were: BP, 100/60 mm Hg; T, 99 °F (37.2 °C); HR, 98/min; RR, 30/min.
HEENT: All structures normal on exam.
Neck: Supple, no lymph node or thyroid enlargement.
Chest: Symmetrical with normal AP diameter. Scattered rhonchi throughout lung fields. Cardiac rhythm: normal sinus without ectopy. Heart sounds: normal S_1 and split S_2 without rubs, murmurs, or gallops.
Abdomen: Flat with no bowel sounds. Soft, mildly tender, without organomegaly or masses.
Extremities: Skeletal traction for bilateral femoral fractures. Peripheral pulses present and weak. Moved arms with equal strength. Able to wiggle toes.
Neuro: Somnolent but oriented to person, place, and time. Followed commands. Cranial nerves II–XII intact. Upper extremity DTRs 1–2+ and symmetrical.

Laboratory Studies

Platelet count: 0.066×10^{12}/L.
PT and PTT: results were within normal limits.
Serum level of coagulation factors V and VII and fibrinogen: decreased.
Serum level of fibrin split products: increased.

Medical Diagnoses

1. Multiple trauma with bilateral femoral fractures.
2. Shock.
3. Disseminated intravascular coagulopathy (DIC)

Management

A solution of heparin sodium, 20,000 units in 500 mL D5W, was prepared and infusion at 100 units/hr was begun. After the heparin therapy was instituted, replacement of coagulation factors was carried out with administration of platelets, fresh frozen plasma, and cryoprecipitate. The nurses assessed the patient's status frequently, provided comfort measures, and intervened appropriately when problems occurred.

Study Questions

1. What other acquired bleeding disorders are seen in critical care? How does their pathophysiology differ from DIC?
2. What aspects of the history and physical assessment should alert the health care team to the development of an acquired bleeding disorder?
3. Why and when are heparin sodium infusions used in managing DIC?
4. Discuss the coagulation factors contained in each of the blood products used for Ms. Vienna: packed RBCs, platelets, fresh frozen plasma, and cryoprecipitate. What are the essential nursing actions for proper administration of them?
5. Complete a nursing care plan for Ms. Vienna. Include nursing diagnoses or nursing problems, outcomes, and interventions.

MULTIPLE SYSTEMS FAILURE

Unit III-25

Present Illness

Ray Wayne, a 60-year-old pharmacist, was admitted to the hospital for surgical placement of a single coronary artery bypass graft (CABG) to his left coronary artery mainstem. He had a history of severe angina pectoris that was never totally controlled with a medical regimen. This lack of control was partially due to the patient's adjustments of his own medications. The patient had consulted at least two physicians in regard to his angina and had considered and refused surgical intervention. He subsequently consulted a urologist for complaints related to benign prostatic hypertrophy. The urologist recommended transurethral prostatic resection but requested consultation by a cardiologist for evaluation of the patient's cardiovascular status prior to scheduling the surgery. Because he had a high grade left coronary artery mainstem lesion and was a high risk for spinal or general anesthesia, the patient was advised to have CABG surgery before the prostatic resection.

Mr. Wayne was admitted on May 2 and the CABG surgery was performed on May 4. In the early postoperative period, he recovered well from the general anesthesia and was extubated within 24 hours on May 5. Late in the same day that he was extubated, nursing and medical personnel noted that his BP was very labile and that his ABG values indicated that his spontaneous ventilation was becoming inadequate. In the early morning of May 6, two days after surgery, a nurse charted that the labile BP was related to his level of consciousness. Keeping the patient awake was recommended as an intervention to achieve a stable BP. During the day, he developed acute respiratory failure and his ABGs deteriorated. He was reintubated at 1600 hours on May 6 and a pulmonary consult was sought on May 8.

Past Medical History

Mr. Wayne's past medical history was positive for long-standing CAD, hypertension, and benign prostatic hypertrophy. The physician noted that past lung cytology had been positive for cancer. However the patient denied history of lung cancer, diabetes, and kidney disease. Mr. Wayne had been hospitalized twice for angina but no MIs had been documented. His family's medical history was noncontributory.

Physical Exam on the Fourth Postoperative Day

General: Comatose, elderly man who appeared older than his stated age. Ht, 5 ft, 10 in; wt 180 lb. Vital signs were: BP, 105/40 mm Hg; T, 98.6 °F (37 °C); HR, 90/min; RR, 20/min by mechanical ventilator.
HEENT: Normocephalic, atraumatic. PERRL, 3 mm. Eyes open with dry corneas. Mild arteriovenous nicking and no papilledema on fundoscopic exam. Tympanic membranes intact with good light reflexes. Nasal septum midline with slightly reddened mucosa. Endotracheal tube and oral airway taped in place. Edentulous.
Neck: Supple, trachea midline and prominent. Thyroid slightly enlarged. JVD to jaw angle while sitting up 45 degrees.
Chest: Barrel shaped with equal excursion. Breath sounds equal bilaterally with scattered rales and rhonchi. Precordium without heaves or thrills. PMI in sixth ICS midway between left midclavicular and anterior axillary lines. Heart sounds included: S_1 and S_2 as well as a summation gallop and a grade 3/6 systolic ejection murmur heard best in the aortic area.
Abdomen: Scaphoid with faint bowel sounds heard only in the lower quadrants. Soft and without masses or organomegaly.
GU: Normal adult male external genitalia. Indwelling urinary catheter draining clear amber urine.
Rectal exam: Enlarged smooth prostate. Soft brown stool, 1+ positive guaiac test.
Extremities: Pulses present, equal, and strong in arms. Femoral pulses equal and moderate. Right popliteal, posterior tibial, and dorsalis pedis pulses moderate, left weak or faint. Hair more sparse and skin thinner on left leg than right.
Neuro: Comatose, responded to deep pain with generalized movement sometimes and with purposeful withdrawal at other times. DTRs 2+ and symmetrical with bilateral plantar flexion.

Laboratory Studies

Sample laboratory results from admission (on May 2) and from May 8 were:

Test	Admission	May 8
Coagulation time		
PT (sec)	11.5	12.5
PTT (sec)	30.5	38.5
Serum chemistry levels		
Uric acid (mg/dL)	9.2	8.5
Total protein (g/dL)	5.7	5.0
Albumin (g/dL)	3.5	3.0
Total bilirubin (mg/dL)	0.6	1.4
Direct bilirubin (mg/dL)	0.2	0.5
Calcium (mg/dL)	8.7	7.6
Phosphorus (mg/dL)	3.8	1.8
Alkaline phosphatase (IU/L)	56	77
Cholesterol (mg/dL)	228	124
LDH (IU/L)	282	876
SGOT (IU/L)	25	102
SGPT (IU/L)	22	56

Medical Diagnoses

1. Coronary heart disease.
2. Postoperative single coronary artery bypass graft (CABG).
3. Acute respiratory failure secondary to Adult Respiratory Distress Syndrome (ARDS).
4. Episodes of arterial hypotension and hypertension.
5. History of benign prostatic hypertrophy (BPH).
6. History of lung cancer.

Management and Clinical Data

The patient was maintained and treated symptomatically for a week. In that time, he exhibited failure of his cardiac, renal, cerebral, and gastrointestinal systems in addition to his acute respiratory failure. Serum chemistry results of May 2, 8, and 15 were:

Serum chemistry levels	May 2, on admission	May 8, 0600	May 8, 1800	May 15, 0600
Na (mEq/L)	145	128	128	129
K (mEq/L)	3.3	3.2	3.8	4.3
Cl (mEq/L)	105	92	91	98
CO_2 (mmol/L)	29	22	24	21
Glucose (mg/dL)	96	132	147	166
BUN (mg/dL)	29	26	26	51
Creatinine (mg/dL)	1.5	1.5	1.5	2.4

Hematology results on May 2, 8 and 15 were:

Test	May 2	May 8	May 15
RBC ($\times 10^{12}$/L)	4.35	5.14	3.81
Hgb (g/dL)	13.4	15.8	11.3
Hct (%)	41	47.4	34.9
MCV (cubic micrometers)	94.3	92.1	91.6
MCH (pg)	30.8	30.7	29.7
MCHC (%)	32.7	33.3	32.3
Platelets ($\times 10^{12}$/L)	0.300	0.169	0.130
WBC ($\times 10^{9}$/L)	6.3	9.7	13.9

Examples of cardiopulmonary data were:

Test	May 8, 0550	May 8, 1600	May 8, 1710	May 15, 0600
BP (mm Hg)	118/50	130/58	72/50	180/30
MAP (mm Hg)	64	86	50	100
PAP (mm Hg)	61/29	42/22	42/23	37/16
mean PA (mm Hg)	42	31	Not recorded	27
PCWP (mm Hg)	Balloon broken	18	Not measured	15
Qt (L/min)	6.6	5.6	4.3	5.2
Urine output (mL/hr)	50	80	40	60
Temperature (°F)	98.6	99.8	Not measured	100.8
(°C)	37	37.7	Not measured	38.2
Heart rate (beats/min)	90	141	138	118
Respiratory rate (breaths/min)	20	36	36	27
Ventilator settings				
FIO_2 (%)	0.65	0.65	0.65	0.55
VT (cc)	820	870	870	800
SIMV (breaths/min)	14	10	10	6
PEEP (cm H_2O)	7.5	15	15	7.5
Arterial blood gases				
arterial pH	7.49	7.51	7.52	7.43
$PaCO_2$ (torr)	34	32	28	33
PaO_2 (torr)	50	59	70	63
SaO_2 (%)	86.6	89.6	93.7	92.3
HCO_3 (mEq/L)	24.6	25.6	23	22.1
Base excess (arterial)	2.3	4.3	1.8	−0.9
SaCO (%)	1.4	1.8	1.8	1.7
Hgb (g/dL)	15.0	15.7	15.6	11.7
CaO_2 (vol%)	17.6	19.2	19.6	14.5
Venous blood gases				
Venous pH	7.44	7.47	7.49	
$PvCO_2$ (torr)	39	39	30	
PvO_2 (torr)	29	33	32	
SvO_2 (%)	57.4	60.1	55.9	
HCO_3 (mEq/L)	26.6	27.7	23	
Base excess (venous)	2.9	4.7	1.0	
SvCO	1.1	1.5	1.5	
Hgb (g/dL)	15.0	15.7	15.6	
CvO_2 (%)	12.0	13.2	12.1	

On May 15, the following nursing care plan was in use:

Nursing problem	Nursing outcome	Nursing intervention
Ventilator dependency due to ARDS	Extubation	Wean with SIMV and PEEP
Hypotensive episodes with decreased LOC and hypovolemia	Stable arterial BP	Monitor Hct, BP, PCW Monitor blood volume Infuse ordered blood products Titrate ordered vasopressor infusion
Hypertensive episodes	Stable arterial BP	Monitor as above Titrate ordered, vasodilator infusion
Sinus tachycardia with frequent multifocal PVBs	Normal sinus rhythm without ectopy	Monitor cardiac rhythm Titrate ordered, procainamide (Pronestyl) infusion
Malnutrition	Adequate calories Positive nitrogen balance	Enteral feedings Assess for tolerance and advance if possible
Diarrhea due to enteral formula	Formed stool Skin intact	Rectal tube Frequent linen change
Hematuria and oliguria with hypotension	Adequate clear urine	Monitor Hct and coagulation studies Send ordered urine specimen to lab Maintain BP; diuretic if ordered

Study Questions

1. Discuss the probable interrelationships of failed systems in this patient in terms of whether the failure and/or management of one system is contributing to the failure of another system.
2. What further observations should the nurses make of the cause and effect relationship of the patient's labile BP, LOC, and urine output? How should these be carried out and documented?
3. How might the patient's diarrhea be managed?
4. How can skin breakdown be prevented?
5. Review and revise the nursing care plan using appropriate nursing diagnoses or nursing problems, outcomes, and interventions.

MULTIPLE TRAUMA WITH SHOCK

Units III-23 and II-25, III-25

Present Illness

Martha Miller, a 26-year-old nurse, was involved in an automobile accident on her way to work. Approximately 20 minutes elapsed between the time of the accident and the arrival of paramedics. She sustained abdominal injuries as well as multiple fractures. The fractured bones included: four ribs of the left chest; left humerus; right femur, tibia, and fibula. Rapid IV infusion of normal saline was started at the scene by the paramedics. The paramedics judged her spontaneous ventilation to be adequate so they administered oxygen by mask and stabilized her chest with external sand bags. They splinted her fractured extremities and transported her to the ED. When she arrived in the ED, her vital signs were: BP, 80/50 mm Hg; HR, 118/min; and RR, 30/min.

Resuscitation and evaluation was continued in the ED. Ms. Miller's spontaneous respirations were evaluated and thought to be adequate, so administration of oxygen by mask was continued. Her abdomen was irrigated and bright red blood returned. A second IV catheter was inserted and type-specific whole-blood infusion was started. An arterial line was inserted in the left femoral artery. Her vital signs were relatively stable so she was taken to the Operating Room for an exploratory laparotomy. The general surgeon found that her spleen had ruptured and her liver was lacerated. The spleen was removed and the liver was repaired. While the general surgeon was operating on her abdomen, the orthopedic surgeon placed her left arm and right leg in skeletal traction. The patient was transferred to the critical care unit (CCU) at the end of the procedures.

Past Medical History

Her past medical history was not available.

Physical Exam on Admission to the CCU

General: Pale, adequately nourished woman with dry, cool skin, lying quietly in bed. Vital signs were: BP, 90/60 mm Hg; T, 100.4 °F (38 °C); HR, 110/min; RR, 24/min while receiving oxygen by mask at 15 L/min.
HEENT: Normocephalic. No external signs of trauma. PERRL, 3 mm. Tympanic membranes intact with good light reflex. Nasal septum midline. Double lumen nasogastric tube inserted in right naris and connected to low constant suction. Oral mucous membranes moist. Cough reflex intact.
Neck: Carotid pulses full without bruits. No JVD while sitting up 30 degrees. Thyroid and cervical lymph nodes not enlarged.
Chest: Symmetrical with ecchymosis over left anterior ribs (3–7). Scattered rhonchi change with coughing. Breath sounds diminished in the posterior bases. Cardiac rhythm: sinus tachycardia without ectopics. PMI in fifth ICS and left MCL. Normal heart sounds of S_1 and S_2 without rubs, murmurs, or gallops.

Abdomen: Distended. Large midline dressing intact and dry. No bowel sounds heard. Nasogastric tube position correct, connected to low constant suction. Soft and tender to palpation.
GU: Normal female external genitalia. Indwelling urinary catheter draining pink tinged urine at 30 mL/hr.
Extremities: Left and right leg in skeletal traction which was in good alignment. Skin discoloration over fractures. Lump of muscle spasm apparent in right thigh. Moved all four extremities with equal strength within limits of traction. Arterial line in left femoral artery functioning well. IV infusions were D5NS at 125 mL/hr infusing in left arm and packed RBCs at 75 mL/hr infusing in right arm. IV and arterial sites were patent and without signs or symptoms of infiltration or phlebitis.
Neuro: Sleepy, responded slowly but appropriately to questions. Oriented to person and place but not time. Followed commands well. Cranial nerves II–XII grossly intact. Accessible and testable DTRs were 2+.

Laboratory Studies

Hematology: RBC, 3.52×10^{12}/L; Hgb, 12.1 g/dL; Hct, 34.7%; WBC, 12.3×10^9/L.
Differential: polys, 77%; bands, 18%; lymphs, 5%; and platelets, 0.069×10^{12}/L.
Serum chemistry levels: Na, 134 mEq/L; K, 5.1 mEq/L; Cl, 100 mEq/L; CO_2, 28.5 mmol/L; glucose, 117, mg/dL; and BUN, 78 mg/dL.
ABGs: pH 7.23; $Paco_2$, 50 torr; Pao_2, 85 torr; Sao_2, 95%; HCO_3, 25 mEq/L.

Medical Diagnoses

1. Multiple trauma sustained in motor vehicle accident.
2. Hypovolemic shock.

Management

Initially, the patient's hypovolemic shock was treated with IV infusion of D5NS and packed RBCs. Two units of fresh frozen plasma and four packs of platelets were also infused. On the second day at 1400 hours, she deteriorated and had an arterial pressure of 80/40 mm Hg with a 20 mm Hg paradoxical pulse. A pulmonary artery thermodilution catheter was inserted. Her cardiac pressures were: RAP, 20 mm Hg; RVP, 35/15 mm Hg; PAP, 35/20 mm Hg; and PCWP, 20 mm Hg. Cardiac output (Qt) was 2 L/min and systemic vascular resistance (SVR) was 23 RU. She was assumed to have a pericardial tamponade secondary to a steering wheel injury. Pericardiocentesis was done with removal of 100 mL blood from the pericardial sac. The patient's cardiac pressures and clinical status subsequently improved.

Six hours later, at 2000 hours, the patient's vital signs were: BP, 100/70 mm Hg; T, 102 °F (38.9 °C); HR, 120/min; RR, 24/min. In addition, her thermodilution catheter provided the following: RAP, 10 mm Hg; PAP, 20/5 mm Hg; PCWP, 12 mm Hg; Qt, 5 L/min. At this time she was receiving 50% oxygen by mask.

Over the next two hours, her status declined. Her vital signs at 2200 hours were: BP, 90/60 mm Hg; T, 97.8 °F (36.6 °C); HR, 130/min; RR, 32/min. Hemodynamic data were: RAP, 5 mm Hg; PAP, 20/5 mm Hg; PCWP, 4 mm Hg; Qt, 13 L/min. ABGs were obtained while the patient was still breathing 50% oxygen by mask. The ABG results were: pH 7.49; $Paco_2$, 30 torr; Pao_2, 84 torr; Sao_2, 96%; HCO_3, 22.5 mEq/L.

She was assumed to be septic and was given methylprednisolone sodium succinate (Solu Medrol), 2 g IV. Broad-spectrum antibiotic therapy was started and a fluid challenge of 500 mL normal saline was infused over one hour. Her skin color assumed a gray cast while her BP was less than 90/60 mm Hg and her urine output was less than 20 mL/h. A dopamine hydrochloride (Intropin) infusion of 5 μg/kg/min was begun at midnight. Over the next 30 minutes, her vital signs became: BP, 80/40 mm Hg; HR, 140/min; RR, 40/min and labored. Hemodynamic data was: RAP, 10 mm Hg; PCWP, 18 mm Hg; and Qt, 10 L/min. She continued to breath 50% oxygen through a mask and ABG results were: pH 7.20; $Paco_2$, 32 torr; Pao_2, 50 torr; Sao_2, 78%; HCO_3, 15 mEq/L. The dopamine infusion was increased to 10 μg/kg/min.

Because she seemed on the verge of respiratory arrest, the patient was intubated and artificial ventilation was begun at 0100 hours.

Study Questions

1. What could be responsible for Ms. Miller's shock state?
2. What are the goals of medical management in shock?
3. Since Ms. Miller's PCWP was last measured at 18 mm Hg, what precautions and observations should be taken in continuing to administer IV fluids?
4. What priority does fracture management assume within the context of multiple trauma?
5. Identify Ms. Miller's two most pressing actual nursing diagnoses or nursing problems and two most probable complications. Establish appropriate nursing outcomes for the next 12 hours.

6. Explain the nursing actions needed to accomplish the outcomes set forth in answering question 5.

MUSCULOSKELETAL TRAUMA

Unit III-23

Present Illness

Michael Roberts, an 18-year-old white man, was injured when he lost control of the motorcycle he was driving and crashed into a tree. He was thrown from the motorcycle and sustained musculoskeletal injuries. He was wearing a helmet at the time of the accident.

The accident was discovered by some passersby about an hour after it happened. The people who found him splinted his obvious fractures and took him to a small, nearby hospital in their car. At the hospital, his injuries were evaluated and management was begun. An IV access route was established and D5LR was infused at a slow rate. Tetanus toxoid was administered IM. X-rays of his skull, cervical spine, chest, and extremities were done. No abnormalities were found on the x-rays of Mr. Roberts' skull and cervical spine. A right lateral chest tube was inserted because the chest x-ray indicated a small right pneumothorax. The x-rays of his extremities showed fractures of the right femur, right radius, and right ulna.

Mr. Roberts was taken for a CT scan to evaluate the extent of his head injury. No specific structural changes were seen so his altered level of consciousness was attributed to cerebral contusion. He was then returned to the ED for further definitive treatment of his fractures. The fractures in his arm were reduced under local anesthesia and his right arm was placed in a cast which extended from the bases of his fingers to mid-upper arm. Skeletal traction pins were inserted in his right femur with aseptic technique. He was then transferred to the critical care unit (CCU) where the skeletal traction apparatus was arranged by the physician.

Past Medical History

Mr. Roberts had been in excellent health all his life although he had acquired a reputation for being "accident prone." He lived in a small resort town with his parents, brothers, and sisters. He worked as an auto mechanic and was well-liked in the community.

Physical Exam on Admission to the CCU

General: Semiconscious and restless young man. Vital signs were: BP, 130/90 mm Hg; T, 100 °F (37.8 °C); HR, 100/min; RR, 20/min.

HEENT: Ecchymosis developing over right eye. PERRL, 4 mm. Ear canals clear. Tympanic membranes intact with slight retraction. Nasal septum deviated to right with inflamed mucosa. No evidence of oral trauma.

Chest: Symmetrical excursion. Breath sounds clear bilaterally but diminished in right upper lobe. Chest tube protruding from right upper thorax connected to waterseal drainage unit. Small air leak detected. Cardiac rhythm normal sinus rhythm without ectopy. Heart sounds included S_1, S_2, and S_4. No rubs or murmurs heard.

Abdomen: Rounded, slightly distended. Faint bowel sounds in all quadrants. Soft, nontender and without masses or organomegaly.

Extremities: Symmetrical upper arms without deformity. No deformity of left lower arm or left leg. Cast on right lower arm still damp. Right-hand color and warmth equal to left. Right fingertips had good capillary refill. Patient able to move fingers easily. Right leg had skeletal traction pins in place. Pin sites fresh, clean, and still oozing small amount of blood. Obvious deformity of muscle spasm present in right quadriceps. Pulses, skin color, sensation, and capillary refill equal in lower extremities. D5LR infusing at a slow rate through left arm. IV site patent and without signs or symptoms of phlebitis.

Neuro: Aroused easily. Oriented to self. Slow response to questions. Repeatedly asked for information about what had happened to him. Unable to give details of accident.

Laboratory Studies

Urinalysis: results were within normal limits.
Hematology results: Hgb, 14.3 g/dL; Hct, 41.7%; WBC, 7.5 × 10^9/L; platelets, adequate.
ABG results on room air: Pao$_2$, 57 torr; Paco$_2$, 34 torr; pH 7.46.
Electrolyte levels: Na, 144 mEq/L; K, 3.6 mEq/L; Cl, 102 mEq/L; CO$_2$, 24 mmol/L.

Medical Diagnoses

1. Cerebral contusion.
2. Right pneumothorax.
3. Fractures: right femur and right radius and ulna.

Management

In the CCU, Mr. Roberts was placed in balanced skeletal traction for conservative management of his fractured femur. Restraints were used on his arms and unfractured leg to prevent him from injuring himself or altering the traction with his restless movements. The fractured leg was not restrained because the nurses thought restraint would interfere with the directional forces of the traction.

His level of conciousness improved with supplemental oxygen of 4 L/min by nasal prongs and he became rational and cooperative. ABGs showed adequate oxygenation and normal acid-base balance. During the night of the second hospital day, Mr. Roberts had a sudden episode of dyspnea, coughing, and pain in his chest. He also became restless and his behavior was similar to when he was admitted. ABG results indicated mild respiratory alkalosis and hypoxemia. His symptoms of coughing, dyspnea, pain, and restlessness gradually diminished, so that by morning he stated that he "felt fine." While the nurses were helping him with his bath, they noticed a rash of petechiae on his upper chest.

The health care team suspected that a fat embolism had caused Mr. Roberts dyspnea and pain so they monitored him closely. However, Mr. Roberts continued to recover and had no further episodes. His right lung re-expanded satisfactorily and the oxygen was discontinued on the fourth hospital day. He was transferred out of the CCU at the end of the week. The skeletal traction was continued on the orthopedic nursing unit until the bone ends were positioned well enough for open surgical reduction of the fracture.

Study Questions

1. What are the cardinal signs and symptoms of fractures?
2. Why were the fractures not reduced until after the CT scan?
3. Mr. Roberts' mother asked the nursing staff to allow her to do some of Mr. Roberts' care. Identify the advantages and disadvantages of including family members in patient care and describe approaches that maximize the advantages and minimize the disadvantages.
4. How does care of patients in skeletal traction differ from those in skin traction? Discuss the correct nursing management of skeletal traction pin sites.
5. Identify and explain the essential points of the nursing care Mr. Roberts received during the week he was in the CCU. Address the nursing diagnoses or nursing problems, outcomes, and actions that are appropriate, including complications such as fat embolism.

ACID-BASE IMBALANCE

For each of the critical care patients depicted in the following vignettes, determine the acid-base balance abnormalities, their probable causes, and suggest appropriate interventions.

1. Mr. N.S., aged 60 years, had sepsis of undetermined origin. His abdomen was the suspected source of infection. Results of ABGs obtained nine hours apart while he was receiving supplemental oxygen by nasal cannula at 4 L/min were:

Component	0600	1500
SaO_2 (%)	90.5	85.2
PaO_2 (torr)	64	52
$PaCO_2$ (torr)	19	21
HCO_3 (mEq/L)	12.9	14.8
pH	7.45	7.46
Base excess	−8.2	−6.5
Hgb (g/dL)	10.7	10.0
CaO_2 (%)	13.3	11.7

Abnormalities:

Probable causes:

Interventions:

2. Mr. T.S., aged 58 years, had chronic obstructive lung disease. Results of ABGs obtained while he was receiving supplemental oxygen by nasal cannula were:

Component	0800	1100	2300
Oxygen flow (L/min)	1	5	3
Arterial blood gases			
$SaCO$ (%)	3.6	3.4	2.7
SaO_2 (%)	80.1	92.8	90.1
PaO_2 (torr)	50	84	67
$PaCO_2$ (torr)	63	62	52
HCO_3 (mEq/L)	33.7	33.6	28.8
pH	7.34	7.35	7.35
Base excess	+5.8	+6.2	+2.6
Hgb (g/dL)	16.1	15.9	15.3
CaO_2 (%)	17.9	20.6	19.2

Abnormalities:

Probable causes:

Interventions:

3. Ms. M.W., aged 68 years, was being resuscitated. Results of ABGs obtained while she was being ventilated with a resuscitation bag and 100% oxygen were:

SaO_2 (%)	97.8
PaO_2 (torr)	86
$PaCO_2$ (torr)	19.7
HCO_3 (mEq/L)	23.7
pH	7.61
Base excess	0.3

Abnormalities:

Probable causes:

Interventions:

4. Ms. P.W., aged 62 years, was being treated for diabetic crisis. Results of ABGs and electrolytes obtained while she was spontaneously breathing room air were:

Blood gases		Electrolytes and chemistry	
Sao$_2$ (%)	<30	Na (mEq/L)	134
Pao$_2$ (torr)	28	K (mEq/L)	3.1
Paco$_2$ (torr)	71.5	Cl (mEq/L)	93
HCO$_3$ (mEq/L)	15	CO$_2$ (mmol/L)	16
pH	7.08	Glucose (mg/dL)	610
Base excess	−13.0	BUN (mg/dL)	48

Abnormalities:

Probable causes:

Interventions:

5. Mr. W.R., aged 58 years, had a history of aortic valve disease and aortic valve replacement with a Starr-Edwards valve prosthesis. He collapsed while he was preparing for discharge and developed fulminating pulmonary edema within two minutes. Results of ABGs obtained while he was being resuscitated and ventilated with a resuscitation bag and 100% oxygen were:

Sao$_2$ (%)	<30
Pao$_2$ (torr)	12
Paco$_2$ (torr)	97.3
HCO$_3$ (mEq/L)	18.2
pH	7.05
Base excess	−7.1

Abnormalities:

Probable causes:

Interventions:

6. Mr. W.Q., aged 48 years, had a cardiac arrest. Results of ABGs obtained during the resuscitation and while he was receiving supplemental oxygen by mask at 15 L/min were:

Saco (%)	2.9
Sao$_2$ (%)	96.1
Pao$_2$ (torr)	140
Paco$_2$ (torr)	18.6
HCO$_3$ (mEq/L)	9.9
pH	7.35
Base excess	−13.1
Cao$_2$ (%)	17.5

Abnormalities:

Probable causes:

Interventions:

7. Rev. I.R., aged 78 years, had complications of brittle diabetes mellitus. Results of ABGs obtained five hours apart while he was receiving supplemental oxygen by nasal cannula at 4 L/min were:

Component	0600	1100
Sao$_2$ (%)	95	97.2
Pao$_2$ (torr)	95	100
Paco$_2$ (torr)	25	29.9
HCO$_3$ (mEq/L)	12.2	19.5
pH	7.23	7.39
Base excess	−13.6	−5.4

Abnormalities:

Probable causes:

Interventions:

8. Mr. L.L., aged 30 years, was in acute distress. Results of ABGs obtained while he was spontaneously breathing room air were:

Saco (%)	0.9
Sao$_2$ (%)	93.9
Pao$_2$ (torr)	101
Paco$_2$ (torr)	16.4
HCO$_3$ (mEq/L)	<6.1
pH	6.94
Base excess	<−22
Hgb (g/dL)	11.8

Abnormalities:

Probable causes:

Interventions:

9. Mr. C.F., aged 50 years, was in acute distress. Results of ABGs obtained while he was spontaneously breathing supplemental oxygen at 10 L/min by mask were:

Sao$_2$ (%)	98
Pao$_2$ (torr)	220
Paco$_2$ (torr)	22
HCO$_3$ (mEq/L)	39.5
pH	7.80
Base excess	+15.3

Abnormalities:

Probable causes:

Interventions:

10. Ms. W.K., aged 19 years, had acute respiratory failure and chronic cystic fibrosis. Results of ABGs obtained while she was artificially ventilated were:

Component	1600	1700	1800	2000
Ventilator settings				
V_T (mL)	500	500	600	600
FIO_2 (%)	1.00	.50	.50	.40
SIMV (breaths/min)	12	16	20	18
Arterial blood gases				
SaO_2 (%)	98	91	98	95.3
PaO_2 (torr)	310	79	130	76
$PaCO_2$ (torr)	113	99.5	58.3	54.7
HCO_3 (mEq/L)	39.8	36.7	29.7	36.7
pH	7.17	7.19	7.33	7.45
Base excess	+7.0	+6.1	+3.2	+11.1

Abnormalities:

Probable Causes:

Interventions:

11. Ms. C.H., aged 79 years, had a flail chest and respiratory insufficiency following multiple trauma. Results of ABGs obtained while she was artificially ventilated with V_T, 600 mL; FIO_2, 0.40; and SIMV, 12/min were:

Component	2000	2100
SaO_2 (%)	80	77.5
PaO_2 (torr)	58	57
$PaCO_2$ (torr)	42.8	53.3
HCO_3 (mEq/L)	14.2	14.7
pH	7.16	7.13
Base excess	−14.5	−13.5

Abnormalities:

Probable causes:

Interventions:

12. Mr. L.D., aged 59 years, had acute respiratory failure and chronic obstructive lung disease. Results of

ABGs obtained while he was artificially ventilated were:

Component	0600	1800
Ventilator settings		
V_T (mL)	900	900
FIO_2 (%)	0.35	0.35
SIMV (no./min)	4	6
Arterial blood gases		
SaO_2 (%)	94.2	95
PaO_2 (torr)	79	91
$PaCO_2$ (torr)	69.7	95
HCO_3 (mEq/L)	32.0	32.3
pH	7.35	7.28
Base excess	+9.2	+9.0

Abnormalities:

Probable causes:

Interventions:

13. Mr. C.C., aged 75 years, had left ventricular pump failure after quadruple coronary artery bypass graft surgery. He was supported with the IABP and artificial ventilation until he had cardiopulmonary arrest at 1500 hours. Results of ABGs obtained were:

Component	1300	1400	1500
Ventilator settings			
V_T (mL)	800	800	Bagging
FIO_2 (%)	0.80	0.60	1.00
SIMV (no./min)	15	15	1:5 with compressions
PEEP (cm H_2O)	10	10	0
Arterial blood gases			
SaO_2 (%)	98	92.2	82.1
PaO_2 (torr)	124	75	33
$PaCO_2$ (torr)	33.1	31.5	43.0
HCO_3 (mEq/L)	16.2	16.4	55.6
pH	7.28	7.29	7.72
Base excess	−9.4	−10.2	+18.9

Abnormalities:

Probable causes:

Interventions:

CARDIOPULMONARY INTERRELATIONSHIPS

For each of the critical care patients depicted in the following vignettes, determine the cardiopulmonary abnormalities, their probable causes, and suggest appropriate interventions.

1. Mr. A.B., aged 60 years, was recovering from abdominal surgery. Selected cardiopulmonary data were:

BP (mm Hg)	100/70	RR (breaths/min)	18
HR (beats/min)	120	PaO_2 (torr)	41
Qt (L/min)	6.8	PvO_2 (torr)	21
MPAP (mm Hg)	38	Hgb (g/dL)	7.5
PCWP (mm Hg)	25	$C(a\text{-}v)O_2$ (%)	3.6

Abnormalities:

Probable causes:

Interventions:

2. Ms. C.D., aged 40 years, had a severe urinary tract infection. Selected cardiopulmonary data were:

BP (mm Hg)	120/80	RR (breaths/min)	16
HR (beats/min)	90	PaO_2 (torr)	89
Qt (L/min)	10.0	PvO_2 (torr)	26
MPAP (mm Hg)	15	Hgb (g/dL)	12.0
PCWP (mm Hg)	12	$C(a\text{-}v)O_2$ (%)	8.0

Abnormalities:

Probable causes:

Interventions:

3. Mr. E.F., aged 18 years, had ARDS following multiple trauma. Selected cardiopulmonary data were:

BP (mm Hg)	80/40	RR (breaths/min)	40
HR (beats/min)	120	PaO_2 (torr)	28
Qt (L/min)	8.8	PvO_2 (torr)	18
MPAP (mm Hg)	20	Hgb (g/dL)	5.3
PCWP (mm Hg)	15	$C(a\text{-}v)O_2$ (%)	2.0

Abnormalities:

Probable causes:

Interventions:

4. Mr. G. H., aged 45 years, was recovering from multiple trauma. Selected cardiopulmonary data were:

BP (mm Hg)	100/60	PVR (RU)	7
HR (beats/min)	110	RR (breaths/min)	16
Qt (L/min)	2.1	PaO_2 (torr)	70
MPAP (mm Hg)	18	PvO_2 (torr)	20
PCWP (mm Hg)	3	Hgb (g/dL)	10.0
SVR (RU)	35	$C(a\text{-}v)O_2$ (%)	9.5

Abnormalities:

Probable causes:

Interventions:

5. Mrs. I.J., aged 28 years, was recovering from thoracic surgery. Selected cardiopulmonary data were:

BP (mm Hg)	90/60	PVR (RU)	5.2
HR (beats/min)	120	RR (breaths/min)	14
Qt (L/min)	2.3	PaO_2 (torr)	75
MPAP (mm Hg)	35	PvO_2 (torr)	26
PCWP (mm Hg)	23	Hgb (g/dL)	14.0
SVR (RU)	30	$C(a\text{-}v)O_2$ (%)	10.0

Abnormalities:

Probable causes:

Interventions:

6. Mr. K.L., aged 60 years, had an acute MI. Selected cardiopulmonary data were:

BP (mm Hg)	100/60	RR (breaths/min)	12
HR (beats/min)	120	PaO_2 (torr)	55
Qt (L/min)	4.3	PvO_2 (torr)	29
MPAP (mm Hg)	25	Hgb (g/dL)	14.0
PCWP (mm Hg)	18	$C(a\text{-}v)O_2$ (%)	7.0

Abnormalities:

Probable causes:

Interventions:

7. Ms. M.N., aged 49 years, was recovering from a cholecystectomy. Selected cardiopulmonary data were:

BP (mm Hg)	90/60	PVR (RU)	1.5
HR (beats/min)	100	RR (breaths/min)	12
Qt (L/min)	6.8	PaO_2 (torr)	90
MPAP (mm Hg)	18	PvO_2 (torr)	45
PCWP (mm Hg)	8	Hgb (g/dL)	14.1
SVR (RU)	10	$C(a\text{-}v)O_2$ (%)	3.4

Abnormalities:

Probable causes:

Interventions:

8. Mr. O.P., aged 39 years, was recovering from thoracic trauma. Selected cardiopulmonary data were:

Component	0600	2400	1800
Ventilator settings			
VT (mL)	790	Extubated	Spontaneous
FIO$_2$ (%)	0.70		0.55 per mask
SIMV (no./min)	12		Actual 18
Arterial blood gases			
SaO$_2$ (%)	94.4		92.0
PaO$_2$ (torr)	68		60
PaCO$_2$ (torr)	35		38
HCO$_3$ (mEq/L)	21.5		24.5
pH	7.40		7.42
Base excess	−2.5		0.5
Hgb (g/dL)	15.6		9.7
CaO$_2$ (%)	18.4		6.7
Venous blood gases			
SvO$_2$ (%)	44.5		50.1
PvO$_2$ (torr)	24		22
PvCO$_2$ (torr)	46		44
HCO$_3$ (mEq/L)	26.6		26.5
pH	7.38		7.3
Base excess	−1.5		1.5

Abnormalities:

Probable causes:

Interventions:

9. Ms. R.S., aged 56 years, was recovering from mitral valve replacement. Selected cardiopulmonary data were:

Component	1200	1400	1500	1700	2100
Ventilator settings					
VT (mL)	500	500	500	500	500
FIO$_2$ (%)	0.50	0.50	0.50	0.50	0.50
SIMV (no./min)	12	12	12	12	12
Blood gases					
SaO$_2$ (%)	88	90	91	92	97
PaO$_2$ (torr)	55	57	62	62	88
PaCO$_2$ (torr)	45	42	42	34	33
HCO$_3$ (mEq/L)	27	24	25	27	17
pH	7.40	7.38	7.40	7.48	7.34
PvO$_2$ (torr)	33	31	29	25	23
Hgb (g/dL)	12.9	15.6	13.6	13.0	10.8
C(a-v)O$_2$ (%)	6.5	7.9	7.7	9.3	10.2
Qs/Qt (%)	35	31	29	23	15

Abnormalities:

Probable causes:

Interventions:

ELECTRICAL MISHAPS

For each of the electrical mishaps depicted in the following vignettes, determine the electrical mishap and the existing electrical hazards and suggest appropriate actions for the personnel involved.

1. The nurse was taking vital signs when the x-ray technician arrived with a portable x-ray machine to take a chest x-ray of the patient. When the technician plugged the x-ray machine into the wall opposite the beds, there was a flash of bright, white light. The technician shrieked and jumped. The room lights dimmed. The bedside cardiac monitors ceased to display the patient's ECG and pressure waveform. The technician assured the nurse that no damage had occurred and that this had happened before with this machine. The technician pushed the plug in the rest of the way and prepared to proceed with the x-ray.

Electrical mishap:

Existing electrical hazards:

Actions:

2. The nurses were receiving a patient from the OR who had just had surgical replacement of the mitral valve. The patient had two peripheral IV infusions, a pulmonary artery catheter, an arterial line, and a direct left atrial line. The bedside monitor was turned on and a nurse was in the process of plugging the pressure transducers into the modules of the monitor. The grounding plug on the stretcher bed had not been plugged in. Suddenly, someone noticed ventricular fibrillation on the bedside monitor. The patient was immediately and successfully defibrillated. Later examination of the rhythm strip showed that the ventricular fibrillation began on a T wave without a preceding PVB.

Electrical mishap:

Existing electrical hazards:

Actions:

3. During assessment of a cardiac patient, the nurse found the temporary pacemaker control box lying in the bed without any cover. The patient was very restless and had disconnected the urinary catheter from the downdrain tubing. The bed was wet with urine and the pacemaker control box was lying on the wet sheets.

Electrical mishap:

Existing electrical hazards:

Actions:

4. After connecting a new patient to the bedside monitor, the nurse noticed 60 cycle interference in the ECG waveform on the monitor screen. The nurse applied new electrodes with careful attention to skin preparation and found no change in the interference. Then the nurse began to unplug the pieces of electrical equipment at the bedside. When the electric patient bed was unplugged, the 60 cycle interference vanished from the monitor.

Electrical mishap:

Existing electrical hazards:

Actions:

FLUID AND ELECTROLYTE IMBALANCE

For each of the critical care patients depicted in the following vignettes, determine the fluid and/or electrolyte abnormalities, their probable causes, and suggest appropriate interventions.

1. **Mr. C.S., aged 50 years, was admitted with hematemesis of one day's duration.** He was found in his boarding house, unconscious and lying in a pool of bloody emesis. He had a history of chronic alcoholism.

Initial Examination:

Vital signs: BP, 80/60 mm Hg; T, 99 °F (37.2 °C); HR, 100/min; RR, 12/min.
Neurological status (Neuro): Lethargic, weak. Positive Chvostek's and Trousseau signs.
Head, Eyes, Ears, Nose, and Throat (HEENT): Soft eyeballs, furrowed tongue. Dry mucous membranes.

Neck: Veins flat in recumbent position.
Chest: Lungs and heart clear to percussion and auscultation.
Abdomen: Very poor skin turgor with tenting. Liver palpable 6 cm below costal margin. Midepigastric tenderness.
Extremities: Cool. Cordlike veins.

Laboratory Results:

Serum chemistry levels: Na, 165 mEq/L; K, 2.3 mEq/L; Cl, 60 mEq/L; CO_2, 61 mEq/L; glucose, 111 mg/dL; BUN, 46 mg/dL; creatinine, 4.6 mg/dL; Ca, 8.4 mg/dL; phosphorus, 8.8 mg/dL.
Hematology: Hct, 60%.
ABGs: pH, 7.58; $Paco_2$, 67 torr.

Abnormalities:

Probable causes:

Interventions:

2. **Ms. T.C., aged 48 years, was admitted with seizures and confusion of unknown origin.** She was found at home, confused and very spastic, with generalized shaking of the upper and lower extremities and frothy saliva in her mouth. Her past medical history included: mental retardation, adult onset diabetes mellitus, hypertension, obesity, and several episodes of syncope of unknown etiology, but no history of epilepsy or head injury. Several combinations of oral hypoglycemic agents and antihypertensive drugs had been used to treat her diabetes and hypertension. At the time of admission her medications were chlorpropamide (Diabinese), 500 mg/day; acetohexamide (Dymelor), 250 mg/day; and polythiazide (Renese), 4 mg/day.

Initial Examination:

Vital signs: BP, 150/95 mm Hg; T, 98.6 °F (37 °C); HR, 110/min; RR, 22/min.
Neuro: oriented to person and place but not to time. Able to follow very simple commands. Cranial nerves II–XII, motor, sensory, and cerebellar functions intact. DTRs 1+ in all four extremities, and plantar flexor responses present. Romberg's sign present. Heel and toe walking required assistance. Patient was unable to perform tandem gait without assistance.
HEENT, neck, chest, and abdomen: normal on physical exam.

Laboratory Results:

Hematology: Hgb, 12.1 g/dL, Hct, 36.5%; WBC, 14.4 × 10⁹/L; polys, 84%; lymphs, 16%.

Serum chemistry levels: glucose, 211 mg/dL; BUN, 20 mg/dL; total protein, 7.5 mg/dL; albumin, 5.2 mg/dL; Ca, 9.3 mg/dL; phosphorus, 2.5 mg/dL; cholesterol, 175 mg/dL; uric acid, 6.7 mg/dL; creatinine, 0.5 mg/dL; total bilirubin, 0.4 mg/dL; alkaline phosphatase, 77 IU/L; LDH, 205 IU/L; SGOT, 85 IU/L; creatinine, 1.2 mg/dL.

Serum osmolality: 242 mosm/kg water. Serum electrolytes: Na, 116 mEq/L; K, 2.7 mEq/L.

Urine osmolality: 440 mosm/kg water. Urine electrolytes: Na, 42 mEq/L; K, 48 mEq/L.

ECG: normal sinus rhythm with PVBs. Abnormal left axis deviation and left bundle branch block. (See Figure 14–1.)

Therapy of 300 mL of 3% saline infused over four hours followed by normal saline with KCl; 60 mEq/L infused at 70 mL/hr resulted in these electrolyte levels:

Electrolyte	Admission, p.m.	Day 1 a.m.	Day 1 p.m.	Day 2 a.m.	Day 2 p.m.	Day 3, a.m.	Day 4, a.m.
Na (mEq/L)	119	112	117	123	130	137	141
K (mEq/L)	3.4	2.8	2.5	3.1	3.3	3.1	3.7
Cl (mEq/L)	81	80	83	88	95	105	105
CO_2 (mmol/L)	27	19	22	22	23	23	24

A water load test done on day 8 produced these results after initial consumption of 1.6 liters in 30 minutes:

Time	Urine volume (mL)	Osmolality (mosm/kg)
0800–0900	80	660
0900–1000	190	196
1000–1100	230	128
1100–1200	140	200

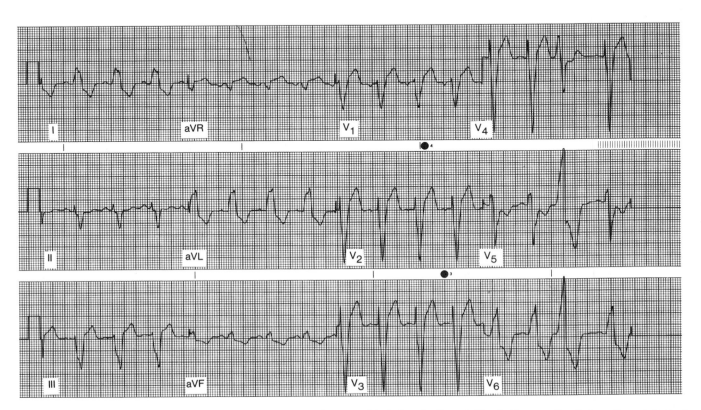

Figure 14–1 Normal Sinus Rhythm with Ventricular Ectopic Beats and Left Bundle Branch Block. *Source:* Cardiology Department of St. Mark's Hospital, Salt Lake City, Utah.

Abnormalities:

Probable causes:

Interventions:

3. Mr. A.R., aged 55 years, was admitted with weakness and lethargy of one month's duration. The patient had a 13-year history of adult onset diabetes mellitus treated with acetohexamide (Dymelor), 250 mg bid, and tolazamide (Tolinase), 250 mg bid. He also had hypertension for several years which was treated with hydrochlorothiazide (Hydro-Diuril), 50 mg bid. He had a history of bilateral calf claudication for two years. A left hemiparesis which developed acutely three years ago had improved.

Initial Examination:

Vital signs: BP, 140/90 mm Hg; T, 98 °F (36.7 °C); HR, 76/min; RR, 20/min.
HEENT: Fundoscopic exam showed venous-arterial ratio of 3:1 with arterial narrowing and tortuosity. No hemorrhages.
Extremities: No pulses palpable in lower extremities below popliteals. No edema. Left leg cooler than right.
Neuro: Oriented to person, place, and time. Able to follow commands. Cranial nerves II–XII intact. Bilateral motor weakness in lower extremities. Sensory, and cerebellar functions intact. DTRs 1+ in all four extremities. Plantar flexor responses present.
Neck, chest, and abdomen: normal on physical exam.

Laboratory Results:

CBC: Hgb, 10.3 g/dL; WBC, 6.8×10^9/L.
Serum chemistry levels: Na, 137 mEq/L; K, 6.6 mEq/L; Cl, 108 mEq/L; CO_2, 15 mmol/L; glucose, 215 mg/dL; BUN, 69 mg/dL; creatinine, 3.6 mg/dL; Ca, 8.8 mg/dL; phosphorus, 2.9 mg/dL.
Urine: specific gravity, 1.015; pH, 5; albumin, trace; sugar, trace. No acetone or abnormal sediment. Na, 91 mEq/L; K, 24 mEq/L; creatinine 78 mg/dL.
Chest x-ray: within normal limits.
Intravenous pyelogram (IVP): poor function and bilaterally mildly contracted kidneys.
ECG: sinus bradycardia with left ventricular hypertrophy (LVH). (See Figure 14–2).

Abnormalities:

Probable causes:

Interventions:

4. Ms. J.Y., aged 56 years, was admitted with progressive weakness and paresthesias of the hands and feet of four days' duration. Hypertension was diagnosed 15 years ago in the Philippines and was initially treated with a combination drug containing thiazides. Six years ago, hypokalemia was diagnosed when she presented with weakness. The thiazide medication was discontinued and she was treated with only methyldopa (Aldomet), 125 mg bid; additionally her diet was supplemented with four to eight bananas per day. For six years she had had nocturia three to four times per night. She denied headaches, licorice ingestion, diarrhea, vomiting, excessive laxative use, oral contraceptive use, or recent use of diuretics.

Initial Examination:

Vital signs: BP, 200/110 mm Hg; T, 98 °F (36.7 °C); HR, 84/min; RR, 14/min.
HEENT: Fundoscopic exam showed mild arteriolar narrowing.
Cardiac: Systolic ejection murmur grade 2/6 heard at the base.
Neuro: Oriented to person, place, and time. Able to follow commands. Cranial nerves II–XII intact. Proximal muscle weakness and paresthesias in lower extremities. Sensory and cerebellar functions intact. DTRs 1+ in all four extremities. Plantar flexor responses.
Neck, lungs, and abdomen: normal on physical exam.

Laboratory Results:

CBC: Hct, 37.6%; WBC, 7.1×10^9/L.
Serum chemistry levels: Na, 150 mEq/L; K, 1.6 mEq/L; Cl, 86 mEq/L; CO_2, 42 mmol/L; glucose, 115 mg/dL; BUN, 15 mg/dL; creatinine, 1.0 mg/dL; Ca, 10.1 mg/dL; phosphorus, 2.5 mg/dL; albumin, 3.9 mg/dL; globulin, 3.6 mg/dL; bilirubin, 0.1 mg/dL; alkaline phosphatase; 2.0 IU/L; CK, 7700 IU/L; SGPT, 35 IU/L; SGOT, 160 IU/L; LDH, 780 IU/L; Mg, 2.5 mEq/L.
Urine electrolyte levels: Na, 149 mEq/L; K, 30 mEq/L.
Chest x-ray: old granulomatous disease.
ECG: classic hypokalemia on admission. Left ven-

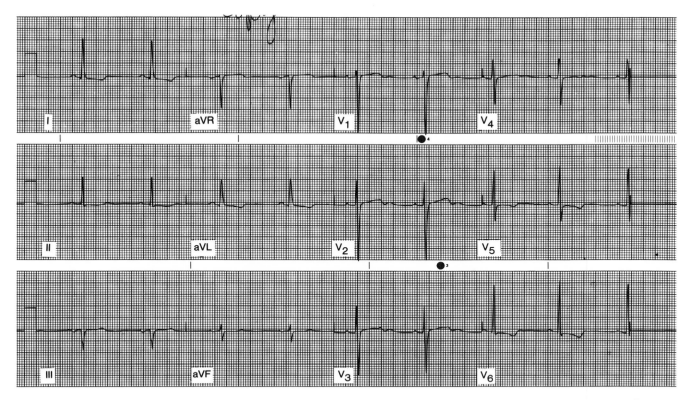

Figure 14–2 Sinus Bradycardia with Left Ventricular Hypertrophy. *Source:* Cardiology Department of St. Mark's Hospital, Salt Lake City, Utah.

tricular hypertrophy when potassium normal. (See Figure 14–3.)

Abnormalities:

Probable causes:

Interventions:

5. Ms. K.M., aged 31 years, was admitted with abdominal pain and vomiting on September 25. She was diagnosed two years ago as having chronic renal failure secondary to chronic glomerulonephritis. One year ago, she had a successful cadaveric renal transplant and had been maintained on immunosuppression of prednisone (Deltasone), 15 mg/day, and azathioprine (Imuran), 100 mg/day since that time. She had a subtotal parathyroidectomy performed 18 months ago for severe renal osteodystrophy. Six months ago hyperglycemia and glycosuria were noted.

At the time of this admission, her serum amylase was 300 IU/L and urine amylase was 54 IU/hr. Ab-

dominal x-ray showed pancreatic calcifications. She was treated with IV fluids, mainly D5/.45NS; nasogastric suction, gentamicin (Garamycin); cephalothin sodium (Keflin); and clindamycin (Cleocin). On October 19, she had a grand mal seizure. She was given 40 mL of 10% calcium gluconate IV and 120 mL of 10% magnesium sulfate IV over four hours. Her seizures stopped and she became somnolent.

Initial Examination:

Vital signs: BP, 110/84 mm Hg; T, 99 °F (37.2 °C); HR, 110/min; RR, 20/min.
Neck: Veins full when supine.
Chest: Bilateral basilar rales.
Heart: Sinus rhythm. Apical systolic murmur and diastolic gallop present.
Abdomen: Distended. Multiple scars, diffusely tender with absent bowel sounds.
Extremities: 1+ pitting edema in lower legs.
Neuro: Somnolent, breathing shallowly, muscles flaccid. Absent DTRs, negative Chvostek's and Trousseau's signs.

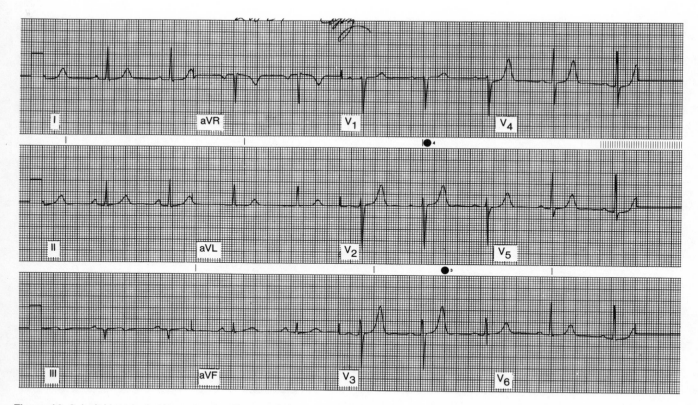

Figure 14–3 Left Ventricular Hypertrophy. *Source:* Cardiology Department of St. Mark's Hospital, Salt Lake City, Utah.

Laboratory Results:

Serum chemistry levels: Na, 134 mEq/L; K, 4.3 mEq/L; Cl, 88 mEq/L; CO_2, 31 mmol/L; glucose, 291 mg/dL; BUN, 14 mg/dL; creatinine, 1.3 mg/dL; Ca, 6.1 mg/dL; phosphorus, 4.4 mg/dL; Mg, 0.7 mEq/L.

Abnormalities:

Probable causes:

Interventions:

NUTRITIONAL SUPPORT

This vignette focuses on aspects of nutritional support. At the end of the vignette, determine the metabolic abnormalities as well as their probable causes and identify appropriate nutritional interventions.

1. J.Z., aged 26 years, sustained multiple trauma in a motorcycle accident. His injuries included:

cerebral contusions
fractures (right upper humerus; left and right pelvic rami; right symphysis pubis; and left acromion and clavicle)
third degree burn of chest wall equal to 10% of body surface area (BSA)
ruptured bladder

During surgical repair of the ruptured bladder, the right iliac artery was found to be lacerated. The accompanying hemorrhage required transfusion of 25 units of blood. Over the next five days, the patient gained 37 lbs and developed classical symptoms of ARDS. He was mechanically ventilated for three days and then extubated. During his occasional lucid intervals, the patient responded appropriately, but refused to give any personal history. His sister said he had a history of heroin addiction but she knew no other details. He was receiving 3600 Kcal per day by parenteral nutrition. A duodenal feeding tube was inserted and enteral feedings were to begin.

Laboratory Results:

Hematology: RBC, 4.93 × 10^{12}/L; Hgb, 15.0 g/dL; Hct, 46.7%; WBC, 21.3 × 10^9/L; lymphs, 9%, segs, 70%.

Serum chemistry levels: Na, 134 mEq/L; K, 3.8 mEq/L; Cl, 103 mEq/L; CO_2, 24 mmol/L; glucose, 94 mg/dL; BUN, 32 mg/dL; Ca, 9.4 mEq/L; phosphorus, 4.9 mg/dL; uric acid, 4 mg/dL; cholesterol, 80 mg/dL; protein, 7.8 mg/dL; albumin, 3.0 mg/dL; bilirubin, 8.6 mg/dL; alkaline phosphatase, 161 IU/L; LDH, 817 IU/L; SGOT, 126 IU/L; osmolality, 290 mosm/kg water.

Urine urea nitrogen: 27 mg/dL.
Calculated oxygen consumption: 717 mL/min.
Calculated required calories: 3477 Kcal/day.

Abnormalities:

Probable causes:

Interventions:

Summary of Cardiac Dysrhythmia Patterns

Exhibit A-1 Normal Sinus Rhythm

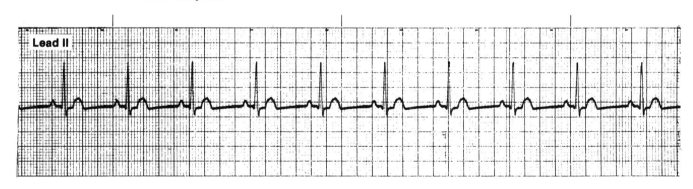

REGULARITY AND RATE
    Ventricular: Regular, 60–100 beats/min.
    Atrial: Regular 60–100 beats/min.
AV CONDUCTION
    P Waves: Sinus in origin. Symmetrical, rounded, upright in
    Leads I, II, aV$_F$.
    P : QRS Ratio: 1 : 1
    PR Interval: 0.12–0.20 sec
IV CONDUCTION
    QRS Duration: 0.04–0.12 sec
DESCRIPTION/COMMENTS
    Regular discharge of sinus node

CAUSES
    Normal heart
SIGNIFICANCE
    Normal rhythm
ACUTE THERAPY
    Initial Choice: n/a
    Alternatives: n/a
CHRONIC THERAPY
    Initial Choice: n/a
    Alternatives: n/a

Source: ECG from Holy Cross Hospital, Salt Lake City, Utah.

Exhibit A-2 Sinus Tachycardia

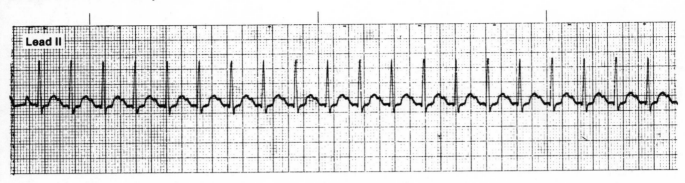

REGULARITY AND RATE

Ventricular: Regular, above 100 beats/min

Atrial: Regular, above 100 beats/min (usually 100–180 beats/min)

AV CONDUCTION

P Waves: Sinus in origin. Symmetrical, rounded, upright in Leads I, II, aV$_F$

P:QRS Ratio: 1:1

PR Interval: 0.12–0.20 sec

IV CONDUCTION

QRS Duration: 0.04–0.12 sec

DESCRIPTION/COMMENTS

Increased rate of sinus node discharge; physiological response to demand for increased cardiac output

CAUSES

Normal heart; tea, coffee, tobacco, alcohol; physical or emotional stress; inflammatory heart disease; coronary artery disease (CAD)

SIGNIFICANCE

Usually not significant except in patient with heart disease; then may cause angina, infarction, congestive heart failure, shock

ACUTE THERAPY

Initial Choice: Usually none. Treatment of cause if symptomatic

Alternatives: n/a

CHRONIC THERAPY

Initial Choice: n/a

Alternatives: n/a

Source: ECG from Holy Cross Hospital, Salt Lake City, Utah.

Exhibit A–3 Sinus Bradycardia

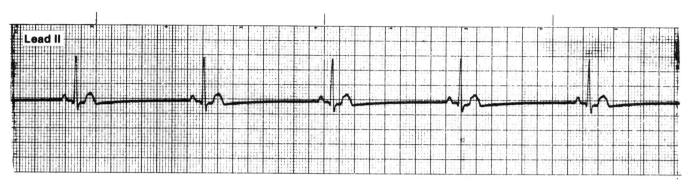

REGULARITY AND RATE
    Ventricular: Regular, below 60 beats/min
    Atrial: Regular, below 60 beats/min
AV CONDUCTION
    P Waves: Sinus in origin, symmetrical, rounded, upright in
    leads I, II, aV$_l$
    P : QRS Ratio: 1 : 1
    PR Interval: 0.12–0.20 sec
IV CONDUCTION
    QRS Duration: 0.04–0.12 sec
DESCRIPTION/COMMENTS
    Decreased rate of sinus node discharge

CAUSES
    Normal heart; athletic variant, sleep; increased parasympa-
    thetic tone or vagal stimulation; intrinsic sinus node disease;
    myocardial infarction (MI); increased intracranial pressure
    (ICP)
SIGNIFICANCE
    Significance depends on rate; if moderate, allows for in-
    creased ventricular filling and decreased myocardial oxygen
    demand; if too slow, inadequate cardiac output results
ACUTE THERAPY
    Initial Choice: Usually none. If symptomatic, atropine, iso-
    proterenol, temporary pacemaker
    Alternatives: n/a
CHRONIC THERAPY
    Initial Choice: Permanent pacemaker
    Alternatives: n/a

Source: ECG from Holy Cross Hospital, Salt Lake City, Utah.

Exhibit A–4 Sinus Arrhythmia

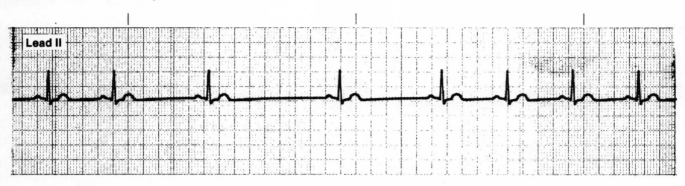

REGULARITY AND RATE

Ventricular: Irregular, 60–100 beats/min. Variation of at least 0.12 sec between longest and shortest cycle or R-R interval

Atrial: Irregular 60–100 beats/min

AV CONDUCTION

P Waves: Sinus in origin, symmetrical, rounded, upright in leads I, II, aV$_F$

P : QRS Ratio: 1 : 1

PR Interval: 0.12–0.20 sec

IV CONDUCTION

QRS Duration: 0.04–0.12 sec

DESCRIPTION/COMMENTS

Rate increases with inspiration, decreases with expiration, in cyclical fashion

CAUSES

Normal heart variation due to sympathetic and parasympathetic stimulation during respiratory cycle

SIGNIFICANCE

Normal variant

ACUTE THERAPY

Initial Choice: n/a

Alternatives: n/a

CHRONIC THERAPY

Initial Choice: n/a

Alternatives: n/a

Source: ECG from Holy Cross Hospital, Salt Lake City, Utah.

Exhibit A–5 Wandering Pacemaker

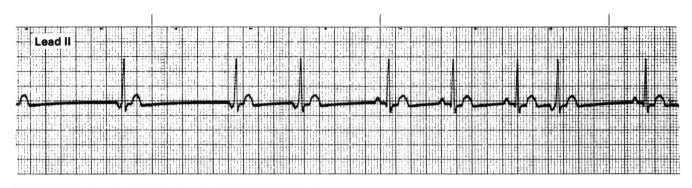

REGULARITY AND RATE

Ventricular: Irregular, RR intervals vary as pacemaker site shifts; cyclic irregularity at any rate (usually 60–100 or slower rate due to parasympathetic dominance)

Atrial: Irregular, P-P intervals vary as pacemaker site shifts; cyclic irregularity at any rate (usually 60–100 or slower rate due to parasympathetic dominance)

AV CONDUCTION

P Waves: Variable; shape, position or direction of P waves change, reflecting different sites of origin of the impulse in sinus, atrial, or junctional tissues

P:QRS Ratio: 1:1

PR Interval: Variable. Length of PR interval varies with different sites of impulse origin

IV CONDUCTION

QRS Duration: 0.04–0.12 sec

DESCRIPTION/COMMENTS

Several pacemakers tending to fire at similar rates, so pacemaker site "wanders" from SA node to atria and/or AV junction; only one site is dominant at a given moment

CAUSES

Normal heart; athletic heart; heart disease. Usually caused by varying parasympathetic tone. When the parasympathetic tone increases, the SA node slows, allowing a pacemaker in atria or junctional area to briefly take over. As parasympathetic tone decreases the SA node rate increases and regains pacemaker control of heart

SIGNIFICANCE

Variant of sinus arrhythmia

ACUTE THERAPY

Usually unnecessary. For bradycardia:

Initial Choice: atropine

Alternatives: isoproterenol

CHRONIC THERAPY

Initial Choice: n/a

Alternatives: n/a

Source: ECG from Holy Cross Hospital, Salt Lake City, Utah.

Exhibit A–6 Premature Atrial Beats or Premature Atrial Contractions or Atrial Premature Beats

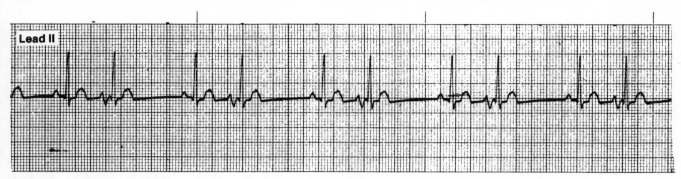

Normal Sinus Rhythm with Premature Atrial Beats

REGULARITY AND RATE
   Ventricular: Regular except for premature beats and pause. Rate is normal
   Atrial: Regular except for premature beats. Rate is normal
AV CONDUCTION
   P Waves: Atrial in origin. Abnormally shaped when compared to dominant sinus P waves, often hidden in preceding T wave
   P : QRS Ratio: 1 : 1 unless blocked
   PR Interval: 0.12–0.20 sec unless blocked; may vary from P-R intervals of impulses originating in SA node
IV CONDUCTION
   QRS Duration: 0.04–0.12 sec duration is the same as dominant QRS unless PAB is aberrantly conducted
DESCRIPTION/COMMENTS
   Impulse arising prematurely in atria, outside sinus node. Coupling interval is variable and pause is usually noncompensatory

CAUSES
   Normal heart; excess coffee, tobacco, alcohol; stress or sympathomimetic drugs; hypoxia; myocarditis, myocardial ischemia, or congestive heart failure; digitalis intoxication. Often the cause is not known
SIGNIFICANCE
   Ectopic atrial focus; usually benign but may precede atrial tachycardia, flutter or fibrillation
ACUTE THERAPY
   Usually none if infrequent. If very frequent, treat underlying cause
   Initial Choice: Sedation or class I agents such as quinidine or procainamide
   Alternatives: Beta blockers; digitalis
CHRONIC THERAPY
   Initial Choice: Quinidine
   Alternatives: Disopyramide, procainamide, amiodarone

Source: ECG from Holy Cross Hospital, Salt Lake City, Utah.

Exhibit A–7 Paroxysmal Atrial Tachycardia

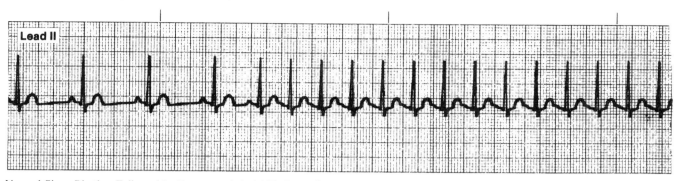

Normal Sinus Rhythm Followed by Paroxysmal Atrial Tachycardia

REGULARITY AND RATE
   Ventricular: Regular, 150–250 beats/min
   Atrial: Regular, 150–250 beats/min
AV CONDUCTION
   P Waves: Atrial in origin; contour slightly different from sinus P waves
   P:QRS Ratio: 1:1 when atrial rate < 200 beats/min. When atrial rate > 200 beats/min, AV block and variable conduction may occur
   PR Interval: 0.12–0.20 sec. May be prolonged
IV CONDUCTION
   QRS Duration: 0.04–0.12 sec, unless aberrant conduction or rate dependent bundle branch block is present
DESCRIPTION/COMMENTS
   Rapidly discharging ectopic focus in atrium, characterized by abrupt onset and termination. Mechanism: reentry at AV node

CAUSES
   Normal heart; stimulation from coffee, tea, tobacco; CAD; hyperthyroidism; rheumatic heart disease; distension of atrial walls seen in congestive heart failure (CHF) of valvular insufficiency
SIGNIFICANCE
   Often well tolerated in young person, but may produce heart failure, shock, angina, or dizziness if cardiac output is inadequate
ACUTE THERAPY
   Depends on patient's tolerance and history of previous attacks
   Initial Choice: Parasympathetic maneuvers, synchronized DC countershock, verapamil
   Alternatives: Procainamide, digitalis, beta blockers, quinidine
CHRONIC THERAPY
   Initial Choice: Digitalis. Drugs listed as alternative may be more effective
   Alternatives: Quinidine, disopyramide, procainamide, beta blockers, verapamil, aprindine, amiodarone, encainide, flecainide

Source: ECG from Holy Cross Hospital, Salt Lake City, Utah.

Exhibit A–8 Nonparoxysmal Atrial Tachycardia

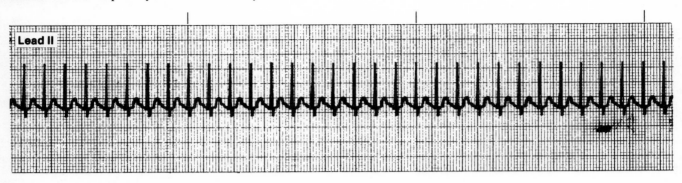

REGULARITY AND RATE

Ventricular: Regular, 160–220 beats/min; may have constant or variable AV block which produces irregular rhythm

Atrial: Regular, 160–220 beats/min

AV CONDUCTION

P Waves: Atrial in origin. Contour slightly different from sinus P waves; may be hidden in T wave of the preceding beat

P : QRS Ratio: 1 : 1 unless physiologic or pathologic block present. If atrial rate above 200 beats/min, block usually is physiological owing to arrival of some atrial impulses at AV node during its refractory period. If atrial rate below 200 beats/min, nonparoxysmal tachycardia, or block greater than 2 : 1, block usually due to pathology

PR Interval: 0.12–0.20 sec; conducted beats may be prolonged

IV CONDUCTION

QRS Duration: 0.04–0.12 sec

DESCRIPTION/COMMENTS

Rapid discharge of ectopic focus in atrium

CAUSES

Secondary to some other event such as digitalis intoxication or CAD

SIGNIFICANCE

Symptoms depend upon ventricular rate and adequacy of cardiac output

ACUTE THERAPY

Initial Choice: If asymptomatic, observation. If digitalis is cause, discontinuation of drug and administration of potassium chloride. If digitalis not cause, digitalis to slow ventricular rate

Alternatives: n/a

CHRONIC THERAPY

Initial Choice: n/a

Alternatives: n/a

Source: ECG from Holy Cross Hospital, Salt Lake City, Utah.

Exhibit A–9 Atrial Flutter

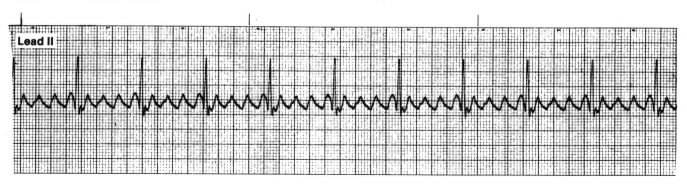

REGULARITY AND RATE

Ventricular: Regular or irregular depending upon constancy of block. Rate depends on degree of block

Atrial: Regular 250–350 beats/min. If AV block is constant, atrial rate is multiple of ventricular rate

AV CONDUCTION

P Waves: Atrial in origin. Flutter (F) waves in sawtooth or picket fence pattern

P : QRS Ratio: Actual ratio usually more than 1 : 1, depending on physiological block

PR Interval: Actually F-R interval. Usually not measured. Not significant

IV CONDUCTION

QRS Duration: 0.04–0.12 sec unless aberrantly conducted

DESCRIPTION/COMMENTS

Rapid discharge of ectopic focus in atrium

CAUSES

Organic heart disease with CHF is usually present. May be due to increased catecholamine secretion or injury to SA node

SIGNIFICANCE

If the ventricular rate is rapid, the cardiac output may decrease and myocardial oxygen consumption increase which predisposes patient to left ventricular failure or myocardial ischemia

ACUTE THERAPY

Carotid sinus massage increases degree of block temporarily but does not terminate dysrhythmia. Drug therapy is seldom successful in restoring normal sinus rhythm, but may control ventricular rate.

Initial Choice: Synchronized DC counter shock, verapamil

Alternatives: Digitalis, beta blockers, overdrive pacing

CHRONIC THERAPY

Initial Choice: Digitalis, quinidine

Alternatives: Disopyramide, procainamide, amiodarone

Source: ECG from Holy Cross Hospital, Salt Lake City, Utah.

Exhibit A-10 Atrial Fibrillation

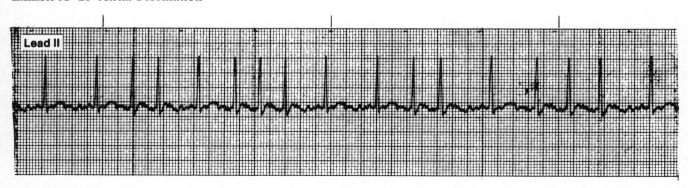

REGULARITY AND RATE
    Ventricular: Irregular, rate varies
    Atrial: Unmeasureable, defined as greater than 350 beats/min
AV CONDUCTION
    P Waves: Atrial in origin. Chaotic fibrillatory (f) waves appear as fine or coarse wavy line
    P : QRS Ratio: n/a
    PR Interval: n/a
IV CONDUCTION
    QRS Duration: 0.04–0.12 sec unless aberrantly conducted, Ashman's phenomenon of long/short cycle lengths predisposes to aberrant conduction
DESCRIPTION/COMMENTS
    Multiple areas of ectopic depolarization in atria with no uniform atrial depolarization

CAUSES
    Normal heart; mitral stenosis; thyrotoxicosis; pericarditis; CAD, hypertensive heart disease
SIGNIFICANCE
    No effective atrial contraction; predisposes to pulmonary or systemic thromboemboli; loss of atrial kick may compromise cardiac output
ACUTE THERAPY
    Initial Choice: DC cardioversion, verapamil
    Alternatives: Digitalis, beta blockers.
    Regular ventricular rhythm in patient on digitalis may indicate digitalis intoxication
CHRONIC THERAPY
    Initial Choice: Digitalis
    Alternatives: Verapamil, quinidine, disopyramide, beta blockers, amiodarone

Source: ECG from Holy Cross Hospital, Salt Lake City, Utah.

Exhibit A–11 Premature Junctional Beats or Premature Junctional Contractions or Junctional Premature Beats

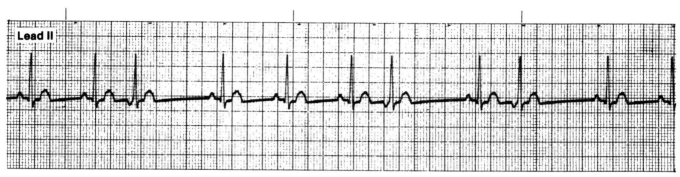

Normal Sinus Rhythm with Premature Junctional Beats

REGULARITY AND RATE
   Ventricular: Regular except for premature beats and pause. Rate is normal
   Atrial: Regular except for premature beats. Rate is normal
AV CONDUCTION
   P Waves: P waves are inverted in Leads II, III, aV$_F$ due to retrograde atrial depolarization and occur before, during, or after QRS
   P : QRS Ratio: Usually 1 : 1 unless blocked
   PR Interval: Less than 0.12 sec or absent
IV CONDUCTION
   QRS Duration: 0.04–0.12 sec; duration is the same as dominant QRS unless PJB is aberrantly conducted
DESCRIPTION/COMMENTS
   Impulse arises prematurely in AV junctional tissue. Early texts may refer to premature "nodal" contractions; however, the impulses do not originate in AV node itself. Coupling interval is variable and pause is usually noncompensatory

CAUSES
   Normal heart; excess tobacco, alcohol; stress; myocarditis; myocardial ischemia in nodal and His bundle area; digitalis intoxication
SIGNIFICANCE
   Ectopic junctional focus; usually insignificant but may precede junctional tachycardia
ACUTE THERAPY
   Usually none if infrequent, if very frequent, treat underlying cause
   Initial Choice: If digitalis is cause, discontinue drug. Sedation or class I agents such as lidocaine, quinidine, or procainamide
   Alternatives: Beta blockers; digitalis
CHRONIC THERAPY
   Initial Choice: Quinidine
   Alternatives: Disopyramide, procainamide, amiodarone

Source: ECG from Holy Cross Hospital, Salt Lake City, Utah.

Exhibit A-12 Paroxysmal Junctional Tachycardia

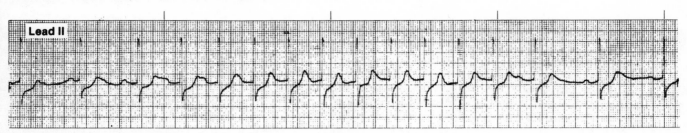

Normal Sinus Rhythm Interrupted by Paroxysmal Junctional Tachycardia

REGULARITY AND RATE
   Ventricular: Regular, 140–250 beats/min
   Atrial: 0 or same as ventricular
AV CONDUCTION
   P Waves: P waves are inverted in Leads II, III, aV_F due to retrograde atrial depolarization and occur before, during, or after QRS
   P:QRS Ratio: 1:1 unless hidden in QRS
   PR Interval: Less than 0.12 sec or absent
IV CONDUCTION
   QRS Duration: 0.04–0.12 sec unless aberrantly conducted
DESCRIPTION/COMMENTS
   Rapidly discharging ectopic focus in junctional area; characterized by abrupt onset and termination. Mechanism is reentry at AV node. May be difficult to distinguish from PAT when P wave obscured or ventricular tachycardia (VT) if aberrancy is present

CAUSES
   Increased catecholamine stimulation; metabolic disturbances; ischemia of AV junctional tissue; MI; digitalis intoxication; myocarditis; postcardiotomy
SIGNIFICANCE
   Rapid rate may produce heart failure, shock, angina or dizziness if there is inadequate cardiac output
ACUTE THERAPY
   Initial Choice: If symptomatic, carotid massage or DC cardioversion. If not symptomatic, digitalis or beta blockers. If digitalis toxicity is cause, discontinue drug
   Alternatives: n/a
CHRONIC THERAPY
   Initial Choice: Prophylactic drugs include beta blockers, quinidine, digitalis, and verapamil
   Alternatives: n/a

Source: ECG from Holy Cross Hospital, Salt Lake City, Utah.

Exhibit A–13 Nonparoxysmal Junctional Tachycardia or Accelerated Junctional Rhythm

Lead II

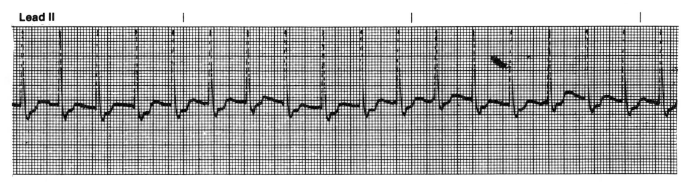

REGULARITY AND RATE
 Ventricular: Regular, 60–100 beats/min; may reach 130 beats/min
 Atrial: 0 or same as ventricular
AV CONDUCTION
 P Waves: P waves are inverted in Leads II, III, aV$_F$ due to retrograde atrial depolarization and occur before, during, or after QRS
 P : QRS Ratio: 1 : 1 unless hidden in QRS
 PR Interval: Less than 0.12 sec or absent
IV CONDUCTION
 QRS Duration: 0.04–0.12 sec unless aberrantly conducted
DESCRIPTION/COMMENTS
 Rapid discharge of ectopic focus in junctional tissue

CAUSES
 Increased catecholamine stimulation; metabolic disturbances; ischemia of AV junctional tissue; MI; digitalis intoxication; myocarditis; postcardiotomy; advanced heart failure; and shock
SIGNIFICANCE
 Symptoms depend on adequacy of cardiac output. Serious dysrhythmia in acute MI associated with high mortality
ACUTE THERAPY
 Treatment of underlying cause
 Initial Choice: DC cardioversion if symptomatic; digitalis, unless cause, then discontinue drug
 Alternatives: Class I agents such as procainamide, quinidine
CHRONIC THERAPY
 Initial Choice: Beta blockers (may be tried), quinidine
 Alternatives: Other class I agents such as disopryramide, procainamide, aprindine, encainide, flecainide, and verapamil

Source: ECG from Holy Cross Hospital, Salt Lake City, Utah.

Exhibit A–14 Junctional Rhythm or Junctional Escape Rhythm

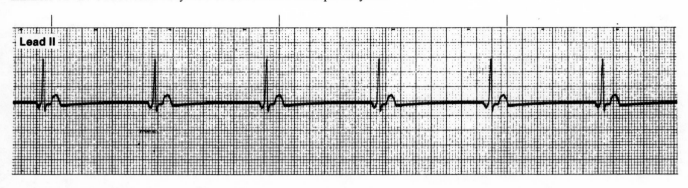

REGULARITY AND RATE
 Ventricular: Regular 40–60 beats/min
 Atrial: 0 or same as ventricular; when AV dissociation occurs, the atrial rate is slower than junctional rate

AV CONDUCTION
 P Waves: P waves are inverted in Leads II, III, aV_F due to retrograde atrial depolarization and occur before, during or after QRS
 P:QRS Ratio: 1:1 unless hidden in QRS
 PR Interval: Less than 0.12 sec or absent

IV CONDUCTION
 QRS Duration: 0.04–0.12 sec unless aberrantly conducted

DESCRIPTION/COMMENTS
 AV junction is potential pacemaker if SA node fails to initiate impulses or discharges too slowly

CAUSES
 Normal heart with suppression of SA node secondary to excessive parasympathetic activity, failure of sinus node due to ischemic damage or drug toxicity due to digitalis or quinidine

SIGNIFICANCE
 Protects patient from asystole. Escape junctional pacemaker is not dependable pacemaker: increased risk of downward displacement of pacemaker; may allow ectopic ventricular foci with rapid rates to take over pacemaker function; slow rate may decrease cardiac output significantly leading to myocardial ischemia or heart failure

ACUTE THERAPY
 Discontinue digitalis or quinidine if toxic
 Initial Choice: Atropine
 Alternatives: Isoproterenol, temporary pacemaker

CHRONIC THERAPY
 Initial Choice: Permanent pacemaker
 Alternatives: n/a

Source: ECG from Holy Cross Hospital, Salt Lake City, Utah.

Exhibit A–15 Premature Ventricular Beats or Premature Ventricular Contractions or Ventricular Premature Beats

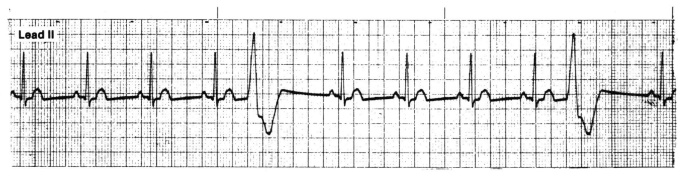

Normal Sinus Rhythm with Unifocal Premature Ventricular Beats

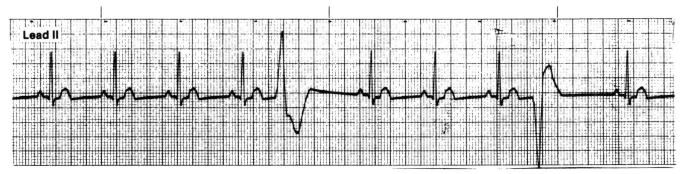

Normal Sinus Rhythm with Multifocal Premature Ventricular Beats

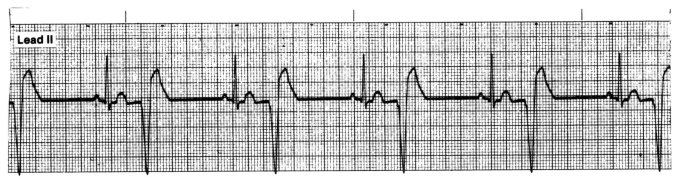

Normal Sinus Rhythm with Ventricular Bigeminy

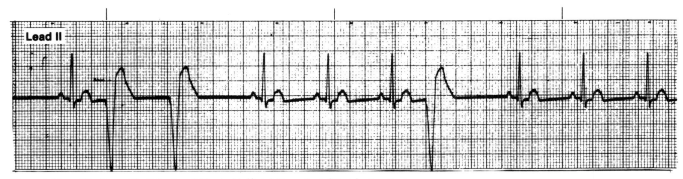

Normal Sinus Rhythm with Paired and Single Unifocal Premature Ventricular Beats

(continues)

Exhibit A–15 (*continued*)

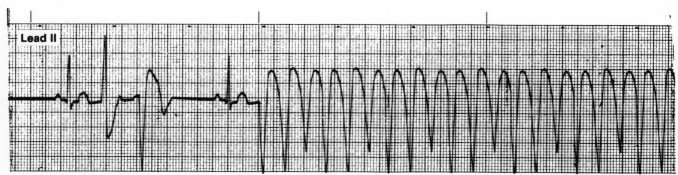

Normal Sinus Rhythm with Paired Multifocal Premature Ventricular Beats and Ventricular Tachycardia Initiated by a Premature Ventricular Beat

REGULARITY AND RATE
Ventricular: Regular except for premature beats and pause. Rate usually normal but PVBs can occur at any rate
Atrial: Regular except for premature beats. Rate usually normal

AV CONDUCTION
P Waves: Usually absent because P wave is obscured by QRS complex although atria do fire independently
P:QRS Ratio: Not considered because atrial and ventricular activity is independent.
PR Interval: None because ventricle is stimulated directly

IV CONDUCTION
QRS Duration: Greater than 0.12 sec, QRS always wide and distorted in shape. Particular shape depends on site of origin, ST-T wave and initial QRS deflection usually opposite normal or dominant QRS complex

DESCRIPTION/COMMENTS
Impulse arrises prematurely in either ventricle. Coupling interval usually constant and pause is usually compensatory

CAUSES
Normal heart; myocardial ischemia or infarction; electrolyte imbalances, especially hypokalemia; excess coffee, tobacco, alcohol; stress or sympathomimetic drugs; hypoxia; myocarditis; CHF; digitalis intoxication

SIGNIFICANCE
Ectopic ventricular focus; may progress to ventricular tachycardia or fibrillation. The sequence of PVB → VT → VF is more likely if:
1. PVCs are frequent, greater than 6 beats/min
2. ventricular bigeminy occurs
3. "R on T" pattern occurs
4. PVCs are multifocal
5. PVCs occur in pairs or couplets
6. more than 3 PVCs occur consecutively

ACUTE THERAPY
None if infrequent. Treat underlying cause, if frequent
Initial Choice: Lidocaine
Alternatives: Procainamide, quinidine, disopyramide

CHRONIC THERAPY
Initial Choice: Quinidine
Alternatives: Disopyramide, procainamide, phenytoin, flecainide, encainide, mexiletine, amiodarone

Source: ECG from Holy Cross Hospital, Salt Lake City, Utah.

Exhibit A–16 Ventricular Tachycardia

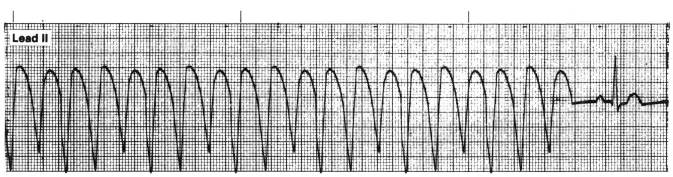

Ventricular Tachycardia followed by Sinus Rhythm

REGULARITY AND RATE
  Ventricular: Regular, 100–220 beats/min
  Atrial: Regular, normal rate
AV CONDUCTION
  P Waves: Symmetrical, rounded as SA node continues to discharge independently during VT but are usually obscured by QRS complexes
  P:QRS Ratio: No relationship between atrial and ventricular activity
  PR Interval: n/a
IV CONDUCTION
  QRS Duration: Greater than 0.12 sec
DESCRIPTION/COMMENTS
  Impulse arises from ectopic focus in either ventricle. Three or more ventricular complexes in succession at a rate greater than 100 beats/min as it usurps pacemaker function

CAUSES
  Coronary heart disease; acute MI; CAD; premature ventricular beat (R on T phenomenon); exercise or emotion induced; IHSS; QT interval prolongation; prolapsed mitral valve; cardiomyopathy; drugs: digitalis, psychotrophic, class I agents; idiopathic ventricular tachycardia
SIGNIFICANCE
  Ominous as may progress to ventricular fibrillation; symptoms depend on underlying heart disease, rate, and duration of VT; may cause angina, cardiac failure, shock
ACUTE THERAPY
  If hemodynamic decompensation, immediate DC countershock, overdrive pacing; if no decompensation, drug therapy depends on etiology
  Initial Choice: Lidocaine, beta blockers
  Alternatives: Procainamide, bretylium tosylate, beta blockers, phenytoin, quinidine, pacing, quinidine-like drugs
CHRONIC THERAPY
  Initial Choice: Quinidine, beta blockers, verapamil, pacing; eliminate drug or reduce drug; quinidine-like drugs
  Alternatives: Disopyramide, procainamide, flecainide, encainide, mexiletine, amiodarone, quinidine-like drugs, phenytoin, stellate blockade, aprindine

Source: ECG from Holy Cross Hospital, Salt Lake City, Utah.

Exhibit A–17 Ventricular Fibrillation

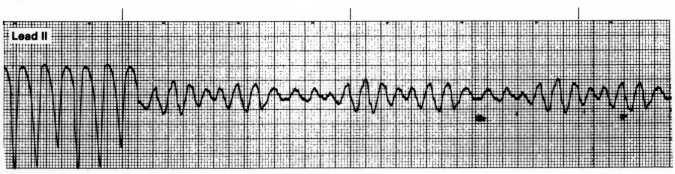

Ventricular Tachycardia Disintegrating into Ventricular Fibrillation

REGULARITY AND RATE
   Ventricular: Chaotic ventricular waves with bizarre configuration and no uniformity, 400–600 beats/min
   Atrial: Usually absent; when present, unrelated to ventricular activity
AV CONDUCTION
   P Waves: Usually not visible when present
   P : QRS Ratio: n/a
   PR Interval: n/a
IV CONDUCTION
   QRS Duration: n/a
DESCRIPTION/COMMENTS
   Chaotic ventricular rhythm without organized ventricular depolarization which produces grossly irregular bizarre EKG deflections

CAUSES
   Acute MI; CAD; electrical shock; premature ventricular beat (R on T phenomenon); dying heart
SIGNIFICANCE
   No cardiac output. Lethal within 4–6 min; symptoms include loss of consciousness; absent blood pressure, pulse, heart sounds, and respirations
ACUTE THERAPY
   Initial Choice: Precordial thump; immediate defibrillation
   Alternatives: Cardiopulmonary resuscitation; lidocaine, procainamide, bretylium, epinephrine, sodium bicarbonate
CHRONIC THERAPY
   Initial Choice: Quinidine
   Alternatives: Disopyramide, procainamide, other new drugs, implantable defibrillator

Source: ECG from Holy Cross Hospital, Salt Lake City, Utah.

Exhibit A-18 Accelerated Ventricular Rhythm

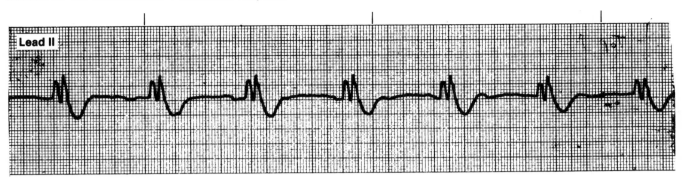

REGULARITY AND RATE
   Ventricular: Regular, usually normal rate 40–100 beats/min
   Atrial: Absent or when present it is unrelated to ventricular activity
AV CONDUCTION
   P Waves: Usually none
   P : QRS Ratio: Atrial activity unrelated to ventricular activity when complete AV block present
   PR Interval: n/a
IV CONDUCTION
   QRS Duration: Greater than 0.12 sec
DESCRIPTION/COMMENTS
   Ventricle becomes pacemaker for heart beating at rate faster than inherent

CAUSES
   Acute MI, SA node ischemia; digitalis intoxication
SIGNIFICANCE
   Benign, usually transient, ventricular rhythm at normal heart rate
ACUTE THERAPY
   Usually no treatment; treatment of cause
   Initial Choice: Discontinue digitalis; atropine
   Alternatives: n/a
CHRONIC THERAPY
   Initial Choice: n/a
   Alternatives: n/a

Source: ECG from Holy Cross Hospital, Salt Lake City, Utah.

Exhibit A–19 Ventricular Escape Rhythm

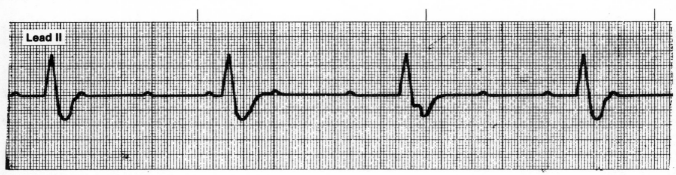

Ventricular Escape Rhythm with Nonconducted P Waves.

REGULARITY AND RATE
Ventricular: Regular, 20–40 beats/min
Atrial: Absent or when present it is unrelated to ventricular activity
AV CONDUCTION
P Waves: Usually none
P : QRS Ratio: Atrial activity unrelated to ventricular activity when complete AV block present
PR Interval: n/a
IV CONDUCTION
QRS Duration: Greater than 0.12 sec
DESCRIPTION/COMMENTS
Ventricle becomes pacemaker for heart, beating at its inherent rate

CAUSES
Failure of higher pacemakers; complete AV block; dying heart
SIGNIFICANCE
Slow escape rhythm which usually severely compromises cardiac output resulting in heart failure, shock, and decreased level of consciousness
ACUTE THERAPY
Initial Choice: Atropine, isoproterenol, temporary pacemaker
Alternatives: n/a
CHRONIC THERAPY
Initial Choice: Permanent pacemaker
Alternatives: n/a

Source: ECG from Holy Cross Hospital, Salt Lake City, Utah.

Exhibit A–20 Primary Ventricular Standstill

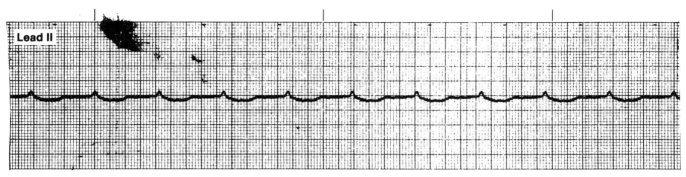

Primary Ventricular Standstill with Nonconducted P waves

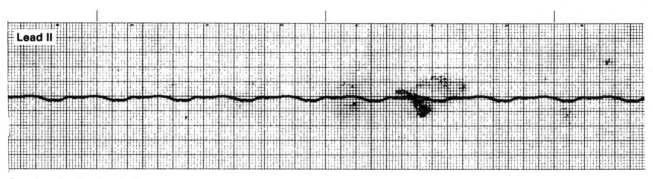

Complete Cardiac Standstill

REGULARITY AND RATE
  Ventricular: None as there is total cessation of ventricular activity
  Atrial: Usually absent but normal when present
AV CONDUCTION
  P Waves: Usually none. Normal sinus when present
  P:QRS Ratio: n/a
  PR Interval: None as atrial activity is not conducted to ventricles
IV CONDUCTION
  QRS Duration: n/a
DESCRIPTION/COMMENTS
  Total absence of ventricular electrical activity. Conduction disorder involving 2 or 3 fascicles of the bundle branches where impulses from the SA node or atria fail to stimulate the ventricles and an inherent ventricular focus does not take over as escape pacemaker

CAUSES
  Subjunctional heart block secondary to MI with necrosis of conduction pathway or fibrosis of the ventricular conduction pathway
SIGNIFICANCE
  Sudden death as absence of heart beat with cessation of circulation results in cardiac arrest
ACUTE THERAPY
  Initial Choice: Precordial thump; CPR; drug support with epinephrine, sodium bicarbonate, calcium chloride, atropine, isoproterenol; temporary pacemaker
  Alternatives: n/a
CHRONIC THERAPY
  Initial Choice: Permanent pacemaker
  Alternatives: n/a

Source: ECG from Holy Cross Hospital, Salt Lake City, Utah.

Exhibit A–21 Secondary Ventricular Standstill

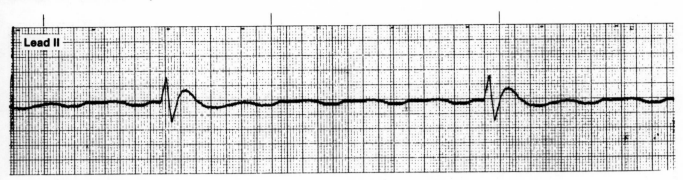

REGULARITY AND RATE
  Ventricular: Infrequent QRS complexes at 10–30 beats/min
  Atrial: Absent
AV CONDUCTION
  P Waves: Absent as atrial death has already occurred
  P:QRS Ratio: n/a
  PR Interval: n/a
IV CONDUCTION
  QRS Duration: Greater than 0.12 sec wide and slurred
DESCRIPTION/COMMENTS
  Terminal event in patients dying of cardiogenic shock or advanced left ventricular failure

CAUSES
  Hypoxia secondary to circulatory failure depresses impulse formation, conductivity, and myocardial responsiveness to stimulation. Mechanical or power failure of myocardium results
SIGNIFICANCE
  Gradual myocardial failure as inadequate tissue perfusion results in hypoxia, metabolic acidosis, and electrolyte imbalance which depress myocardial conductivity. Eventually the electrical activity is inadequate to stimulate myocardium and ventricular standstill develops
ACUTE THERAPY
  Terminal event as the oxygen-deprived myocardium is unable to respond to stimulation and underlying disease is still present
  Initial Choice: n/a
  Alternatives: n/a
CHRONIC THERAPY
  Initial Choice: n/a
  Alternatives: n/a

Source: ECG from Holy Cross Hospital, Salt Lake City, Utah.

Exhibit A–22 Sinoatrial Block or Sinoatrial Exit Block

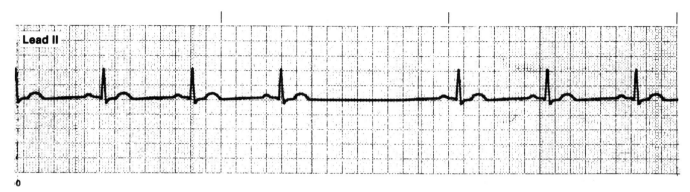

Normal Sinus Rhythm Interrupted by Sinoatrial Block

REGULARITY AND RATE
 Ventricular: Regular except for absence of PQRST complex(s); usually slow rate 40–70 beats/min but may be normal
 Atrial: Regular except for absent P waves with the missed beat(s); usually slow rate 40–70 beats/min but may be normal
AV CONDUCTION
 P Waves: Sinus in origin; symmetrical, rounded, upright in Leads I, II, aV$_F$ except for absent P wave(s)
 P:QRS Ratio: 1:1
 PR Interval: 0.12–0.20 sec
IV CONDUCTION
 QRS Duration: 0.04–0.12 sec
DESCRIPTION/COMMENTS
 Duration of pause is a multiple of normal R-R cycle length suggesting that the SA node continued to discharge normally but impulse was blocked in the SA node and not conducted to the atria

CAUSES
 Failure of sinus node due to ischemia or infarction; increased parasympathetic tone; fibrosis; digitalis or quinidine toxicity
SIGNIFICANCE
 May be transient or prolonged. If transient, no significance. If prolonged, patient develops asystole unless escape rhythm occurs. If the pauses occur frequently or consecutively, cerebral insufficiency manifested as vertigo or syncope may develop
ACUTE THERAPY
 Initial Choice: Atropine
 Alternatives: Isoproterenol, temporary pacemaker
CHRONIC THERAPY
 Initial Choice: Permanent pacemaker
 Alternatives: n/a

Source: ECG from Holy Cross Hospital, Salt Lake City, Utah.

Exhibit A–23 Sinoatrial Arrest

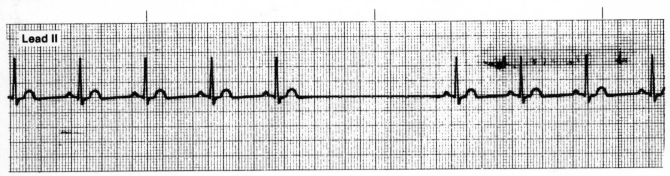

Normal Sinus Rhythm Interrupted by Sinoatrial Arrest

REGULARITY AND RATE
    Ventricular: Regular except for absence of PQRST complex(s); usually slow rate 40–70 beats/min but may be normal
    Atrial: Regular except for absent P waves with the missed beat(s); usually slow rate 40–70 beats/min but may be normal
AV CONDUCTION
    P Waves: Sinus in origin; symmetrical, rounded, upright in I, II, aV$_F$ except for absent P wave(s)
    P : QRS Ratio: 1 : 1
    PR Interval: 0.12–0.20 sec
IV CONDUCTION
    QRS Duration: 0.04–0.12 sec
DESCRIPTION/COMMENTS
    Duration of the pause is not a multiple of normal R-R cycle length, suggesting a failure of the SA node to discharge

CAUSES
    Failure of sinus node due to ischemia or infarction; increased parasympathetic tone; fibrosis; digitalis or quinidine toxicity
SIGNIFICANCE
    May be transient or prolonged. If transient, no significance. If prolonged, patient develops asystole unless escape rhythm occurs. If the pauses occur frequently or consecutively, cerebral insufficiency manifested as vertigo or syncope may develop
ACUTE THERAPY
    Initial Choice: Atropine
    Alternatives: Isoproterenol, temporary pacemaker
CHRONIC THERAPY
    Initial Choice: Permanent pacemaker
    Alternatives: n/a

Source: ECG from Holy Cross Hospital, Salt Lake City, Utah.

Exhibit A–24 First Degree Atrioventricular Block

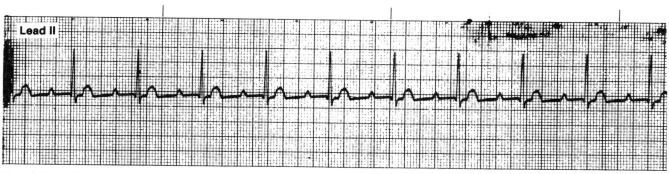

Normal Sinus Rhythm with First Degree Atrioventricular Block

REGULARITY AND RATE
  Ventricular: Regular, can occur at any rate
  Atrial: Regular, any rate
AV CONDUCTION
  P Waves: Sinus or atrial in origin
  P : QRS Ratio: 1 : 1
  PR Interval: Constant and greater than 0.20 sec
IV CONDUCTION
  QRS Duration: Normal 0.04–0.12 sec
DESCRIPTION/COMMENTS
  All impulses are conducted through AV node, but at a slower rate than usual resulting in prolonged P-R interval

CAUSES
  Normal heart with increased parasympathetic tone; ischemia secondary to CAD; digitalis or antidysrhythmic drug intoxication; conduction system fibrosis; myocarditis; cardiac surgery
SIGNIFICANCE
  Relatively benign; may progress to second or third degree blocks
ACUTE THERAPY
  Initial Choice: P-R interval of 0.21–0.28 sec usually require no treatment. P-R interval greater than 0.28 sec or progressive lengthening can be treated with atropine. If P-R interval greater than 0.50 sec, temporary pacemaker indicated
  Alternatives: n/a
CHRONIC THERAPY
  Initial Choice: Permanent pacemaker
  Alternatives: n/a

Source: ECG from Holy Cross Hospital, Salt Lake City, Utah.

Exhibit A–25 Second Degree Atrioventricular Block: Mobitz Type I or Wenckebach

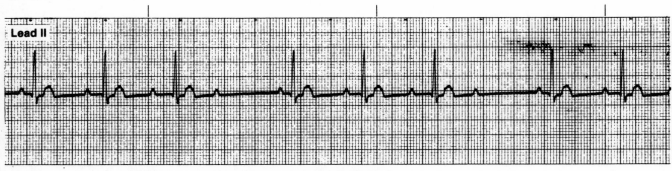

Normal Sinus Rhythm with Mobitz Type I Second Degree Atrioventricular Block

REGULARITY AND RATE

Ventricular: Irregular, but having consistent group beating pattern as progressive shortening of RR intervals before pause occurs. Can occur at any rate

Atrial: Regular, unaffected. Faster rate than ventricle

AV CONDUCTION

P Waves: Sinus or atrial

P:QRS Ratio: 1:1 except for nonconducted P wave(s)

PR Interval: Progressive prolongation until blocked P wave; then repetition of cycle occurs

IV CONDUCTION

QRS Duration: Normal, 0.04–0.12 sec

DESCRIPTION/COMMENTS

Some nonconducted impulses because the impulses are progressively delayed until one reaches the AV node when it is totally refractory. Block usually at level of AV node

CAUSES

Increased parasympathetic tone; digitalis intoxication; acute (inferior) MI

SIGNIFICANCE

Relatively benign; does not usually diminish cardiac output; usually transient; does not usually progress to greater degree of block

ACUTE THERAPY

Usually none necessary

Initial Choice: If symptomatic, atropine, isoproterenol, temporary pacemaker. Discontinue digitalis or quinidine if toxicity is present

Alternatives: n/a

CHRONIC THERAPY

Initial Choice: n/a

Alternatives: n/a

Source: ECG from Holy Cross Hospital, Salt Lake City, Utah.

Exhibit A–26 Second Degree Atrioventricular Block: Mobitz Type II

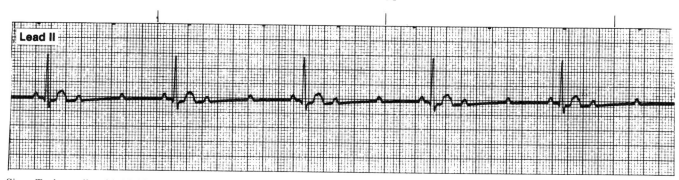

Sinus Tachycardia with Mobitz Type II Second Degree Atrioventricular Block

REGULARITY AND RATE
Ventricular: Irregular, unless blocked beats are occurring at regular intervals. Can occur at any rate
Atrial: Regular, unaffected. Faster rate than ventricle

AV CONDUCTION
P Waves: Sinus or atrial origin
P : QRS Ratio: 1 : 1 except for nonconducted P waves
PR Interval: Constant on conducted beats; normal or prolonged

IV CONDUCTION
QRS Duration: 0.04–0.12 sec

DESCRIPTION/COMMENTS
Some sinus impulses are conducted normally until one is suddenly blocked, block may be varied or occur at 2 : 1, 3 : 1, 4 : 1 intervals. Block usually infranodal (below AV node), commonly at bundle branch level or uncommonly at bundle of His. Wenckebach 2 : 1 conduction is indistinguishable from Mobitz Type II 2 : 1 by ECG alone

CAUSES
Necrosis or fibrosis of conduction pathway; acute (anterior) MI

SIGNIFICANCE
More ominous than Mobitz I: often precedes sudden complete heart block or ventricular standstill because the block is below the AV junction and only the inherent ventricular pacemaker can sustain the heart rate if a long series of blocked sinus impulses occurs

ACUTE THERAPY
Initial Choice: Isoproterenol; temporary pacemaker. Atropine may be helpful but does not decrease degree of block despite increasing the atrial rate and may result in further reduction of the ventricular rate
Alternatives: n/a

CHRONIC THERAPY
Initial Choice: Permanent pacemaker
Alternatives: n/a

Source: ECG from Holy Cross Hospital, Salt Lake City, Utah.

Exhibit A–27 Third Degree Atrioventricular Block

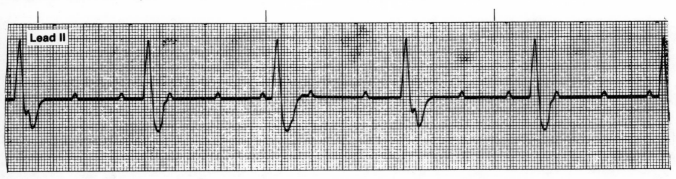

Sinus Rhythm with Third Degree Atrioventricular Block

REGULARITY AND RATE
Ventricular: Regular at 40–60 beats/min when escape pacemaker controlling the ventricles is at the junctional area or 30–40 beats/min when escape pacemaker is at the subjunctional area

Atrial: Regular, unaffected. Faster rate than ventricle

AV CONDUCTION
P Waves: Sinus or atrial origin

P : QRS Ratio: No relationship because atria and ventricles are independent

PR Interval: No P-R interval because of two separate pacemakers

IV CONDUCTION
QRS Duration: 0.04–0.12 sec if escape pacemaker is in the junctional area

Greater than 0.12 sec if escape pacemaker controlling the ventricles is in the subjunctional area

DESCRIPTION/COMMENTS
Absence of conduction between atria and ventricles. AV dissociation occurs with sinus pacemaker initiating atrial rhythm and junctional or subjunctional pacemaker initiating ventricular rhythm

CAUSES
Increased parasympathetic tone; drug effect; AV node damage; acute MI, inferior with junctional escape rhythm, anterior with subjunctional escape rhythm

SIGNIFICANCE
Extremely dangerous dysrhythmia that can suddenly progress to ventricular standstill or fibrillation, particularly when subjunctional escape rhythm is present

ACUTE THERAPY
Initial Choice: Temporary pacemaker for both subjunctional or junctional pacemaker. Atropine may be effective in increasing rate of junctional pacemaker. Isoproterenol may be effective in increasing rate of subjunctional pacemaker

Alternatives: n/a

CHRONIC THERAPY
Initial Choice: Permanent pacemaker

Alternatives: n/a

Source: ECG from Holy Cross Hospital, Salt Lake City, Utah.

Exhibit A-28 Normal Intraventricular Conduction

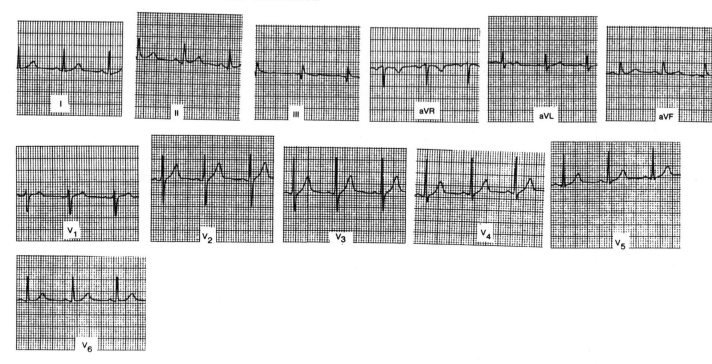

REGULARITY AND RATE
    Ventricular: Regular, 60–100 beats/min
    Atrial: Regular, 60–100 beats/min
AV CONDUCTION
    P Waves: Sinus in origin. Symmetrical, rounded, upright in
    leads I, II, aV_F
    P : QRS Ratio: 1 : 1
    PR Interval: 0.12–0.20 sec
IV CONDUCTION
    QRS Duration: 0.04–0.12 sec
    Lead I : qRS complex
    Lead V_1 : rS complex
    Lead V_6 : qR complex
DESCRIPTION/COMMENTS
    Normal pattern of depolarization in ventricles
    ● left to right through septum
    ● both ventricular free walls simultaneously
    ● reaches right ventricular epicardium sooner than left due to
      larger muscle mass of left ventricle

CAUSES
    Normal heart
SIGNIFICANCE
    Normal rhythm and conduction
ACUTE THERAPY
    Initial Choice: n/a
    Alternatives: n/a
CHRONIC THERAPY
    Initial Choice: n/a
    Alternatives: n/a

Source: ECG is reprinted from *Clinical Electrocardiography for Nurses* by H. Sweetwood, Aspen Systems Corporation. © 1983.

Exhibit A–29 Right Bundle Branch Block

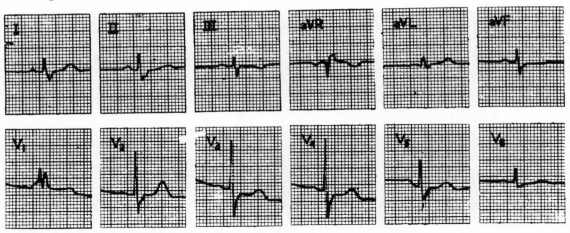

Normal Sinus Rhythm with Right Bundle Branch Block.

REGULARITY AND RATE

Ventricular: Regular or irregular at any rate depending on basic cardiac rhythm

Atrial: Regular or irregular at any rate depending on basic cardiac rhythm

AV CONDUCTION

P Waves: Sinus or atrial in origin

P:QRS Ratio: 1:1 if normal AV conduction. Abnormal AV conduction may be present

PR Interval: 0.12–0.20 sec if AV conduction normal. Less than 0.12 sec if junctional rhythm or accessory pathway present. Greater than 0.20 sec if AV block exists

IV CONDUCTION

QRS Duration: Abnormal with:

- QRS greater than 0.12 sec
- an intrinsicoid deflection greater than 0.07 sec in Leads V_1 or V_2
- triphasic rSR′ in Lead V_1 or V_2
- triphasic qRs with wide late S wave in Leads I, II, aV_L, V_5 or V_6
- secondary ST segment and T-wave changes in Leads V_{1-3}

DESCRIPTION/COMMENTS

Conduction block in right bundle branch resulting in an abnormal activation sequence

CAUSES

Normal heart; CAD; right ventricular hypertrophy; myocarditis; congenital defect; valvular heart disease; premature supraventricular beats (aberration)

SIGNIFICANCE

Isolated right bundle branch block (RBBB) may not be associated with heart disease. RBBB alone is not a good measure of prognosis

ACUTE THERAPY

Initial Choice: None necessary, unless accompanied by block of one division of left bundle branch; prophylactic temporary pacemaker may be required

Alternatives: n/a

CHRONIC THERAPY

Initial Choice: n/a

Alternatives: n/a

Source: ECG is reprinted from *Cardiac Arrhythmias, Practical ECG Interpretation* by S. Mangiola and M. C. Ritota, p. 90, with permission of J. B. Lippincott Company, © 1974.

Exhibit A–30 Left Bundle Branch Block

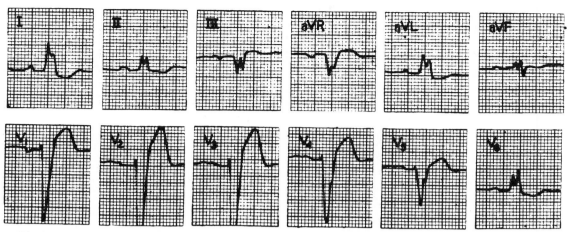

Normal Sinus Rhythm with First Degree Atrioventricular Block and Left Bundle Branch Block.

REGULARITY AND RATE

Ventricular: Regular or irregular at any rate depending on basic cardiac rhythm

Atrial: Regular or irregular at any rate depending on basic cardiac rhythm

AV CONDUCTION

P Waves: Sinus or atrial in origin

P : QRS Ratio: 1 : 1 if normal AV conduction. Abnormal AV conduction may be present

PR Interval: 0.12–0.20 sec if normal AV conduction. Less than 0.12 sec if junctional rhythm or accessory pathway present. Greater than 0.20 sec if AV block exists

IV CONDUCTION

QRS Duration: Abnormal with:
- QRS greater than 0.12 sec
- an intrinsicoid deflection greater than 0.07 sec in leads V_5 or V_6
- monophasic qS complex in leads V_1 or V_2
- monophasic wide R or triphasic RSR′ complex in leads I, aV_L, V_5 or V_6
- secondary ST segment and T-wave changes in leads I, aV_L, V_5 or V_6

DESCRIPTION/COMMENTS

Block in left bundle branch resulting in an abnormal activation sequence

CAUSES

Normal heart; CAD; left ventricular hypertrophy; myocarditis; congenital defect; valvular heart disease; hypertension

SIGNIFICANCE

More serious than right bundle branch block because usually results from more serious disorders. It is often accompanied by cardiomegaly. LBBB may be present in the absence of abnormal cardiac function, and LBBB alone is not a good measure of prognosis

ACUTE THERAPY

Initial Choice: Usually none necessary but may require temporary or permanent pacemaker

Alternatives: n/a

CHRONIC THERAPY

Initial Choice: n/a

Alternatives: n/a

Source: ECG is reprinted from *Cardiac Arrhythmias, Practical ECG Interpretation* by S. Mangiola and M. C. Ritota, p. 91, with permission of J. B. Lippincott Company, © 1974.

Exhibit A–31 Left Anterior Hemiblock

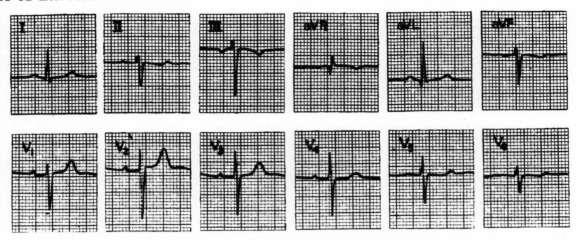

Normal Sinus Rhythm with Left Anterior Hemiblock.

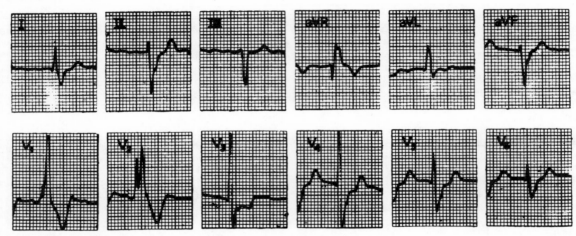

Atrial Fibrillation with Left Anterior Hemiblock and Right Bundle Branch Block.

REGULARITY AND RATE

Ventricular: Regular or irregular at any rate depending on basic cardiac rhythm

Atrial: Regular or irregular at any rate depending on basic cardiac rhythm

AV CONDUCTION

P Waves: Sinus or atrial in origin

P : QRS Ratio: 1 : 1 if normal AV conduction. Abnormal AV conduction may be present

PR Interval: 0.12–0.20 sec if AV conduction normal. Less than 0.12 sec if junctional rhythm or accessory pathway present. Greater than 0.20 sec if AV block exists

IV CONDUCTION

QRS Duration: QRS width: usually normal. QRS axis shifted markedly to the left. Lead I: QRS predominantly positive with small q and tall R waves. Leads II and III: QRS predominantly negative with small r and deep S waves. Lead V_1: QRS predominantly negative with no r wave or with small r and deep S waves

DESCRIPTION/COMMENTS

Conduction delay or block in anterior fascicle of left bundle branch resulting in an abnormal activation sequence

CAUSES

Normal heart; CAD; MI; fibrosis or calcium deposit in conduction pathway; cardiomyopathies; hypertension; aortic valve disease

SIGNIFICANCE

Usually not significant. This fascicle is easily damaged due to its single blood supply, thin structure, and location in high turbulence area of left ventricle. Can mimic an anterior or lateral MI, or left ventricular hypertrophy. Can mask anterior or inferior MI, left ventricular enlargement or RBBB

ACUTE THERAPY

Initial Choice: Usually none. When combined with RBBB or left posterior hemiblock (LPH), prophylactic pacemaker indicated; 33% of patients with RBBB plus left posterior hemiblock (LAH) develop complete heart block

Alternatives: n/a

CHRONIC THERAPY

Initial Choice: Permanent pacemaker

Alternatives: n/a

Source: ECGs are reprinted from *Cardiac Arrhythmias, Practical ECG Interpretation* by S. Mangiola and M. C. Ritota, pp. 89–90, with permission of J. B. Lippincott Company, © 1974.

Exhibit A–32 Left Posterior Hemiblock

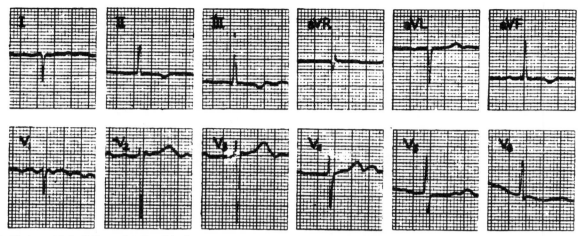

Atrial Fibrillation with Left Posterior Hemiblock.

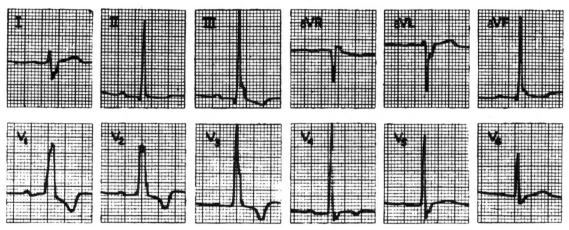

Normal Sinus Rhythm with First Degree Atrioventricular Block, Left Posterior Hemiblock, and Right Bundle Branch Block.

REGULARITY AND RATE
Ventricular: Regular or irregular at any rate depending on basic cardiac rhythm

Atrial: Regular or irregular at any rate depending on basic cardiac rhythm

AV CONDUCTION
P Waves: Sinus or atrial in origin

P : QRS Ratio: 1 : 1 if normal AV conduction. Abnormal AV conduction may be present

PR Interval: 0.12–0.20 sec if normal AV conduction. Less than 0.12 sec if junctional rhythm or accessory pathway present. Greater than 0.20 sec if AV block exists

IV CONDUCTION
QRS Duration: QRS width: usually normal with axis shifted to the right. Lead I: QRS predominantly negative with small r and deep S waves. Leads II and III: QRS predominantly positive with small q and tall R waves. Lead V_1: QRS predominantly negative with no r wave or with small r and deep S waves

DESCRIPTION/COMMENTS
Conduction delay or block in posterior fascicle of left bundle branch resulting in an abnormal activation sequence

CAUSES
Normal heart; CAD; MI; fibrosis or calcium deposit in conduction pathway; cardiomyopathies; hypertension; aortic valve disease

SIGNIFICANCE
Suggests extensive myocardial damage. Fascicle is not easily damaged due to its double blood supply, thick structure, and location in low turbulence area of left ventricle. When LPH combined with RBBB, 70% of patients develop complete heart block

ACUTE THERAPY
Initial Choice: Pacemaker

Alternatives: n/a

CHRONIC THERAPY
Initial Choice: Pacemaker

Alternatives: n/a

Source: ECGs are reprinted from *Cardiac Arrhythmias, Practical ECG Interpretation* by S. Mangiola and M. C. Ritota, pp. 89 and 91, with permission of J. B. Lippincott Company, © 1974.

Exhibit A–33 Ventricular Preexcitation Syndrome: Wolff-Parkinson-White (WPW) Syndrome

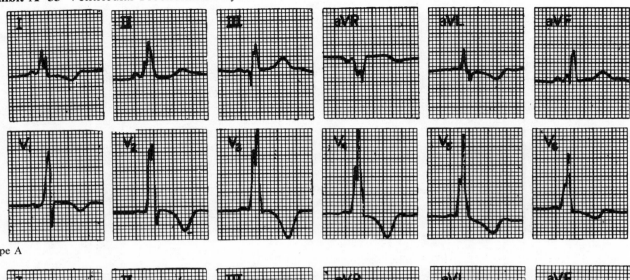

Type A

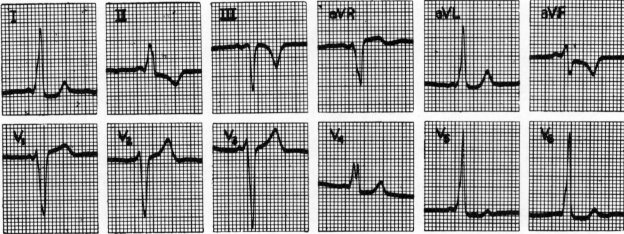

Type B

REGULARITY AND RATE
Ventricular: Regular, can occur at any rate, often associated with paroxysmal tachycardias at rates of 180–200 beats/min
Atrial: Regular, can occur at any rate

AV CONDUCTION
P Waves: Usually normal
P:QRS Ratio: 1:1
PR Interval: Less than 0.12 sec

IV CONDUCTION
QRS Duration: 0.04–0.12 sec when conducted through normal ventricular conduction system. Greater than 0.12 sec when conduction through an accessory pathway produces a delta wave which gives an initial slurring to the QRS. The second portion of the QRS has a normal morphology because the impulse is conducted normally through the ventricular conduction system. In type A, with posterior bypass of the AV node, the QRS complex is predominantly positive in V_1 and V_2 appearing similar to RBBB. In type B with anterior bypass of AV node, the QRS complex is predominantly negative in V_1 and V_2 appearing similar to LBBB

DESCRIPTION/COMMENTS
Ventricular pre-excitation associated with paroxysmal tachycardias

CAUSES
Ventricular pre-excitation occurs when sinus impulses activate a part of the ventricles through an accessory pathway earlier than through the normal conduction pathway. Accessory pathways may be the Kent, Mahaim or James pathways. Usually a congenital anomaly associated with Ebstein anomaly of tricuspid valve or with acquired heart disease

SIGNIFICANCE
Depends on presence and tolerance of paroxysmal atrial and junctional tachycardias, atrial flutter or fibrillation rates. Mimics ventricular extrasystoles and ventricular tachycardia

ACUTE THERAPY
Initial Choice: For re-entry paroxysmal supraventricular tachycardia (PSVT): vagal maneuvers, verapamil.
For atrial flutter and atrial fibrillation: DC cardioversion, procainamide
Alternatives: For PSVT: beta blockade, DC cardioversion, atrial pacing. For atrial flutter and fibrillation: disopyramide, quinidine

CHRONIC THERAPY
Surgical interruption of the accessory pathway
Initial Choice: For PSVT: beta blockade, verapamil
For atrial flutter and fibrillation: quinidine
Alternatives: For PSVT: quinidine, disopyramide, flecainide, amiodarone, encainide. For atrial flutter and fibrillation: disopyramide, procainamide, flecainide, amiodarone

Source: ECGs are reprinted from *Cardiac Arrhythmias, Practical ECG Interpretation* by S. Mangiola and M. C. Ritota, pp. 113–114, with permission of J. B. Lippincott Company, © 1974.

Exhibit A–34 Ventricular Preexcitation Syndrome: Lown-Ganong-Levine (LGL) Syndrome

REGULARITY AND RATE
   Ventricular: Regular; can occur at any rate; often associated with paroxysmal tachycardias at rates of 180–200 beats/min
   Atrial: Regular, can occur at any rate
AV CONDUCTION
   P Waves: Usually normal
   P : QRS Ratio: 1 : 1
   PR Interval: Less than 0.12 sec
IV CONDUCTION
   QRS Duration: 0.04–0.12 sec
DESCRIPTION/COMMENTS
   Variation of WPW syndrome

CAUSES
   Premature activation of ventricles by accessory pathway which bypasses AV node and allows sinus or supraventricular impulse to reach the ventricles earlier causing a short P-R interval. Unlike W-P-W syndrome, the activation of the ventricles occurs entirely through the bundle of His and the bundle branches so that the QRS complex remains normal in configuration
SIGNIFICANCE
   Depends on presence and tolerance of paroxysmal atrial and junctional tachycardias, atrial fibrillation or flutter rates
ACUTE THERAPY
   Initial Choice: For re-entry paroxysmal supraventricular tachycardia (PSVT): vagal maneuvers, verapamil.
   For atrial flutter and atrial fibrillation: DC cardioversion, procainamide
   Alternatives: For PSVT: beta blockade, DC cardioversion, atrial pacing. For atrial flutter and fibrillation: disopyramide, quinidine
CHRONIC THERAPY
   Surgical interruption of the accessory pathway
   Initial Choice: For PSVT: beta blockade, verapamil. For atrial flutter and fibrillation: quinidine
   Alternatives: For PSVT: quinidine, disopyramide, flecainide, amiodarone, encainide. For atrial flutter and fibrillation: disopyramide, procainamide, flecainide, amiodarone

Source: ECG is reprinted from *Cardiac Arrhythmias, Practical ECG Interpretation* by S. Mangiola and M. C. Ritota, p. 114, with permission of J. B. Lippincott Company, © 1974.

Exhibit A-35 Atrial Demand Pacemaker

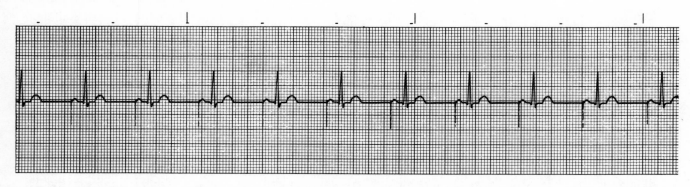

REGULARITY AND RATE

Ventricular: Regular, greater than 60 beats/min depends on set rate of pacemaker

Atrial: Regular, greater than 60 beats/min depends on set rate of pacemaker

AV CONDUCTION

P Waves: Normal or preceded by atrial pacemaker spike

P : QRS Ratio: 1 : 1

PR Interval: Normal or prolonged

IV CONDUCTION

QRS Duration: Normal

DESCRIPTION/COMMENTS

Normal S-A node fails or slows to less than preset atrial rate on pacemaker, an electrical impulse is generated by atrial pacemaker, and initiates atrial depolarization

CAUSES

Failure of S-A node due to ischemia, infarction, parasympathetic tone, fibrosis, infiltrative cardiomyopathies, drug toxicity, or congenital defect

SIGNIFICANCE

Impaired S-A node function

ACUTE THERAPY

Initial Choice: None unless malfunction occurs

Alternatives: n/a

CHRONIC THERAPY

Initial Choice: None unless malfunction occurs

Alternatives: n/a

Source: ECG from Holy Cross Hospital, Salt Lake City, Utah.

Exhibit A-36 Ventricular Demand Pacemaker

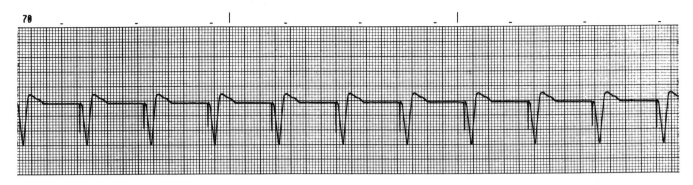

REGULARITY AND RATE

Ventricular: Usually regular, greater than 60 beats/min depends on set rate

Atrial: Usually regular, greater than 60 beats/min

AV CONDUCTION

P Waves: Normal or atrial origin when present, may or may not be followed by QRS complex

P:QRS Ratio: Depends on reason for insertion of pacemaker. Atria and ventricles may be independent.

PR Interval: Normal or prolonged when present

IV CONDUCTION

QRS Duration: Those caused by ventricular pacemaker stimulation are greater than 0.12 sec; wide and bizarre and preceded by spike

DESCRIPTION/COMMENTS

When ventricular rate falls below preset ventricular rate on pacemaker an electrical impulse is generated by pacemaker, and initiates ventricular depolarization

CAUSES

Failure of ventricular conduction in second or third degree heart block

SIGNIFICANCE

Impaired AV node function with or without adequate secondary pacemaker

ACUTE THERAPY

Initial Choice: None unless malfunction occurs

Alternatives: n/a

CHRONIC THERAPY

Initial Choice: None unless malfunction occurs

Alternatives: n/a

Source: ECG from Holy Cross Hospital, Salt Lake City, Utah.

Exhibit A–37 Atrial/Ventricular Demand Pacemaker

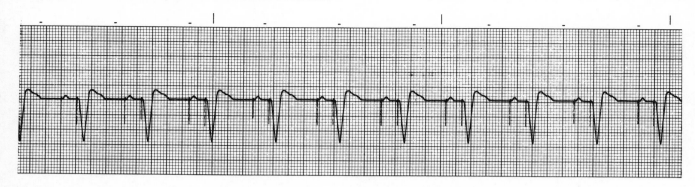

REGULARITY AND RATE

    Ventricular: Regular, greater than 60 beats/min depends on set rate of pacemaker

    Atrial: Regular, greater than 60 beats/min depends on set rate of pacemaker

AV CONDUCTION

    P Waves: Normal or preceded by atrial pacemaker spike

    P : QRS Ratio: 1 : 1

    PR Interval: Normal, determined by set timing interval

IV CONDUCTION

    QRS Duration: Normal or greater than 0.12 sec and preceded by ventricular pacemaker spike causing wide bizarre complex

DESCRIPTION/COMMENTS

    When inherent atrial or ventricular rates fall below preset pacemaker rates the pacemaker stimulus initiates chamber depolarization

CAUSES

    Failure of the S-A node, AV node, or ventricular conduction system due to ischemia, infarction, parasympathetic tone, fibrosis, infiltrative cardiomyopathy, drug toxicity, or congenital defect

SIGNIFICANCE

    Impaired SA and AV node function may be sign of extensive advanced cardiac disease

ACUTE THERAPY

    Initial Choice: None unless malfunction occurs

    Alternatives: n/a

CHRONIC THERAPY

    Initial Choice: None unless malfunction occurs

    Alternatives: n/a

Source: ECG from Holy Cross Hospital, Salt Lake City, Utah.

Clinical Calculations

Some of the calculations and formulas presented in this appendix may seem esoteric. They are provided because critical care units use them to various degrees. In some units a computerized monitoring system calculates and displays the values; in other units staff members calculate them. We believe that the use of derived parameters in nursing practice will increase and nurses should be familiar with the formulas. Derived parameters are only as accurate as the data the computer or calculator receives. Inaccurate raw data yield inaccurate derived parameters. Crucial medical and nursing decisions are made on the basis of this information.

Because nurses are responsible for the quality of raw physiological data sent to computers or used in calculations, they directly affect the accuracy of derived parameters. Nurses who are familiar with formulas are aware of the data used to derive calculated parameters and can judge the credibility of the results. Interpretive information is included to aid development of clinical judgment and decision making. *The normals given apply to adults only.*

CARDIOVASCULAR PARAMETERS

1.1 Cardiac Output (Qt or C.O.)

Cardiac output is measured as liters of blood pumped by the heart in one minute (L/min). It can be measured by thermal or dye dilution techniques or calculated by the Fick equation. Fundamentally, cardiac output is directly proportional to heart rate and stroke volume. (Stroke volume is discussed in Section 1.2 and heart rate is discussed in 1.3.) Cardiac output is increased by larger stroke volume and/or faster heart rate.

$$Qt = stroke\ volume \times heart\ rate$$

Normal Value: 4–8 L/min. A level greater than 8

L/min indicates a hyperdynamic state; less than 4 L/min indicates a hypodynamic state.

Note: an isolated cardiac output measurement is difficult to interpret as to its "normalcy." Decisions should be based on the trend of the cardiac output measurements and the accompanying hemodynamic and physiological data.

Fick Equation

The Fick equation is used to compute cardiac output from oxygenation data and requires that oxygen consumption be measured, which is difficult in the clinical setting. (See Section 1.4.) Dye dilution techniques of cardiac output measurement risk anaphylaxis and are also fairly cumbersome. For these reasons cardiac output is usually measured by the thermodilution technique in CCUs.

$$QT = \frac{oxygen\ consumption\ (mL/min \times 10)}{arterial\ oxygen\ content - venous\ oxygen\ content}$$

1.2 Stroke Volume (SV)

The stroke volume is the number of milliliters of blood pumped by the heart with each heart beat. It cannot be directly measured but is derived by manipulating the cardiac output equation shown in Section 1.1. Physiological demand for increased cardiac output can be met by larger stroke volume independent of the heart rate. However, in persons who are not well-trained athletes, stroke volume and therefore cardiac output cannot usually be increased at rates above 180 beats/min or at rates below 50 beats/min. This is due to physiological limits on cardiac filling related to diastolic filling time.

$$SV = \frac{cardiac\ output \times 1000\ mL/L}{heart\ rate}$$

Normal Value: 60–100 mL/beat.

1.3 Heart Rate (HR)

HR is the number of heart beats per minute. Normal is usually considered to be 60–100 beats/min. Well-trained athletes often have lower resting heart rates and are considered normal variants.

1.4 Oxygen Consumption (Q_{O_2} or V_{O_2})

Q_{O_2} is measured as milliliters of oxygen consumed by the body in one minute. It is measured in the cardiac catheterization laboratory by collecting inspired and expired air, as well as arterial and venous blood, and analyzing the oxygen content of each sample. An accurate, measured oxygen consumption is then calculated:

$$Q_{O_2} = (F_{IO_2} - F_{EO_2}) \times \text{minute ventilation}$$

where F_{IO_2} = fraction of inspired oxygen as a decimal
    F_{EO_2} = fraction of expired oxygen as a decimal
Minute ventilation = volume of gas breathed in and out of the lungs in one minute (see Section 2.2)

An alternate equation is

$$Q_{O_2} = Q_t(Hgb)(1.39)(S_{aO_2} - S_{vO_2}) \times 10$$

where Q_t = cardiac output in L/min
    Hgb = hemoglobin in g/dL
    1.39 = a constant (explained in Section 2.5)
    S_{aO_2} = oxygen saturation of arterial blood
    S_{vO_2} = oxygen saturation of venous blood

Normal Value: approximately 250–300 mL/min.
In the clinical setting it is cumbersome and impractical to collect expired air. Equipment to measure the oxygen level in expired air at the bedside is not yet perfected. Sometimes it is useful to estimate the oxygen consumption by the equation:

$$Q_{O_2} = 3.5 \text{ mL } O_2 \times \text{kg normal body weight}$$

Note: This is reasonably accurate for patients with normal metabolic demand, i.e., adequate perfusion, normothermic, not shivering, or seizing. *It is only an estimate.*

1.5 Body Surface Area (BSA)

BSA is derived from a nomogram such as the Dubois Body Surface Chart by finding the height on the height scale and the weight on the weight scale. A line is drawn between these two points and the surface area in square meters is read from the point on the surface area scale that the line intersects. (A Dubois Body Surface Chart can be found in many critical care and respiratory care texts.)

1.6 Cardiac Index (CI)

CI measures cardiac output in liters per minute indexed to body surface area. It tells how many liters of blood are pumped by the heart each minute to each square meter of body surface area. It is an indicator of tissue perfusion which allows comparison of persons of different sizes.

$$CI = \frac{\text{cardiac output (L/min)}}{\text{body surface area (m}^2)}$$

Normal Value: 2.8–4.2 L/min/m^2 at rest. A level of 2.0–2.2 L/min/m^2 indicates forward failure; 1.5–2.0 L/min/m^2 indicates shock; and less than 1.5 L/min/m^2 indicates severe shock, survival doubtful.

CI can be estimated at the bedside from a modified Fick equation:

$$\text{Estimated CI} = \frac{Q_{O_2} \text{ index} \times 10}{(S_{aO_2} - S_{vO_2}) \times Hgb \times 1.39}$$

1.7 Oxygen Consumption Index (Q_{O_2} Index, V_{O_2} Index)

Q_{O_2} is milliliters of oxygen consumed by the body in one minute indexed to the body surface area.

$$Q_{O_2} \text{ index} = \frac{Q_{O_2}}{BSA}$$

Normal Value: 115–155 mL/min/m^2. Less than 80 mL/min/m^2 indicates severe shock with poor prognosis.

Q_{O_2} index can also be estimated from the equation:

$$\text{Estimated } Q_{O_2} \text{ index} = CI \times C_{(a-v)O_2} \times 10$$

where CI = cardiac index in L/min/m^2
    $C_{(a-v)O_2}$ = the difference in oxygen content between arterial and venous blood (see Section 2.13)

1.8 Stroke Volume Index (SVI)

SVI is the number of milliliters of blood pumped by each heart beat indexed to the body surface area.

$$SVI = \frac{SV}{BSA}$$

Normal Value: 33–47 mL/beat/m^2.

1.9 Stroke Work (SW)

SW is a measure of the amount of work that the ventricle does during a beat and is an indicator of the pumping function of the ventricle. Reported in gram-meters per beat, it is usually calculated and used as the Stroke Work Index described in Section 1.10; therefore, no normals or clinical parameters are given here.

$$SW = (\overline{BP} - VEDP) \times SV \times 0.0144$$

where $\overline{BP}$ = mean blood pressure of the artery receiving the ventricular output, in mm Hg
VEDP = ventricular end diastolic pressure, in mm Hg. In clinical practice the mean atrial pressure is used as the VEDP value.
0.0144 = a conversion factor

1.10 Stroke Work Index (SWI)

SWI measures the amount of work that the ventricle does during a beat indexed to the BSA. It is a more refined evaluation than SW of the pumping function of the ventricles because the calculation includes the major determinants of the mechanical function of the ventricle and is most likely to reflect alterations in cardiac performance. It is reported in gram-meters per square meter per beat (gm-m/m^2/beat).

$$SWI = \frac{Qt \times (\overline{BP} - VEDP) \times 13.6}{HR \times BSA}$$

where Qt = cardiac output
$\overline{BP}$ = mean pressure of the artery receiving the ventricular output, in mm Hg
VEDP = ventricular end diastolic pressure, in mm Hg. In clinical practice the mean atrial pressure is used as the VEDP value.
13.6 = a conversion factor

SWI can also be calculated by using the following equation:

$$SWI = SVI \times (\overline{BP} - VEDP) \times 0.0136$$

Left ventricular stroke work index (LVSWI) is calculated at the bedside by the equation:

$$LVSWI = SVI \times (MAP - PCWP) \times 0.0136$$

Normal LVSWI: 35–50 gm-m/m^2/beat. A value less than 20 gm-m/m^2/beat indicates shock.

If LVSWI is less than 20 gm-m/m^2/beat and PCWP is greater than 15 mm Hg, the shock is probably cardiogenic. If LVSWI is less than 20 gm-m/m^2/beat and PCWP is less than 10 mm Hg, the shock state is probably hypovolemic. However, the most valuable measure of left ventricular function is a plot of LVSWI against PCWP.

Right ventricular stroke work index (RVSWI) is calculated at the bedside using the equation:

$$RVSWI = SVI \times (MPAP - RAP) \times 0.0136$$

where MPAP = mean pulmonary artery pressure
RAP = right atrial pressure

1.11 Systemic Mean Arterial Pressure (MAP)

The arterial pressure mean can be read from a digital pressure monitor or derived by a formula. It is important to understand that it is not a simple arithmetic average but involves calculating the area under the pressure/time curve. The value calculated by the formula will be similar to the digital monitor readout but not exactly the same. The mean pressure value is useful in monitoring arterial pressure and titrating infusions of vasoactive medications. It is also used in other vascular calculations such as the systemic and pulmonary vascular resistances.

$$MAP = \frac{systolic\ pressure + 2(diastolic\ pressure)}{3}$$

or $MAP =$
$$diastolic\ pressure + \frac{(systolic - diastolic\ pressure)}{3}$$

Normal Value: 70–105 mm Hg. When the systemic arterial mean is below 60 mm Hg, coronary, cerebral, and renal arteries are poorly perfused.

1.12 Systemic Vascular Resistance (SVR) or Total Peripheral Resistance (TPR)

SVR or TPR measures the left ventricular afterload. It indicates the energy that the left ventricle must overcome in order to push blood into the aorta and out of the left ventricle. The same basic formula is used by all critical care centers. However, some have simplified it by rounding off or deleting the constant. The first formula presented is the most mathematically correct and calculates the SVR in dynes per second per centimeter to the minus fifth power (dynes/sec/cm^{-5}) as units of work. In the second formula the constant has been rounded off; however, the units remain the same. The third formula drops the constant and calculates the SVR in resistance units (RU).

$$SVR = \frac{(MAP - RAP) \times 79.9}{Qt}$$

or with the constant rounded off:

$$SVR = \frac{(MAP - RAP) \times 80}{Qt}$$

Normal Value (using either formula): 770–1500 dynes/sec/cm^{-5}.

The equation with the constant deleted is:

$$SVR = \frac{MAP - RAP}{Qt}$$

Normal Value: 12–18 resistance units (RU) or total peripheral resistance (TPR) units.

Patients with poor cardiac function may be unable to generate an adequate cardiac output (Qt) in the face of a high systemic vascular resistance (SVR). Such patients may benefit from use of a vasodilator such as sodium nitroprusside (Nipride) which can reduce the SVR. In a patient in shock, an SVR greater than 1500 dynes/sec/cm^{-5} or 20 RU and a PCWP greater than 15 mm Hg is an indication for vasodilator therapy. However, vasodilators are usually not used when the systemic arterial systolic pressure is less than 90 mm Hg. In other words, vasodilating drugs are usually not used when the systemic BP is below normal. In septic shock, SVR decreases are due to vasodilation stimulated by bacterial endotoxins.

1.13 Pulmonary Vascular Resistance (PVR)

A measure of right ventricular afterload, PVR indicates the energy that the right ventricle must overcome in order to push blood out of the right ventricle and into the pulmonary artery. The formulas are similar to SVR described in Section 1.12. PVR is reported as dynes per second per centimeter to the minus fifth power (dynes/sec/cm^{-5}) or as Wood units. It is very useful in following patients with pulmonary embolus, pulmonary hypertension, and other pulmonary vascular disease.

$$PVR = \frac{(MPAP - PCWP) \times 79.9}{Qt}$$

or with the constant rounded off:

$$PVR = \frac{(MPAP - PCWP) \times 80}{Qt}$$

where MPAP = mean pulmonary artery pressure
PCWP = pulmonary capillary wedge pressure

Normal Value (using either formula): <250 dynes/sec/cm^{-5}

The formula can be expressed in Wood units by deleting the constant:

$$PVR = \frac{MPAP - PCWP}{Qt}$$

Normal Value: <1–2 Wood units

A PVR greater than 5 Wood units in early shock, carries an extremely poor prognosis for the patient.

PULMONARY PARAMETERS

2.1 Tidal Volume (V$_T$)

V$_T$ is the volume of air moved in one breath measured in milliliters (mL).

Normal Value for Spontaneous Breathing: 5 mL/kg body weight. Artificially ventilated patients are often ventilated with V$_T$'s of 10–15 mL/kg in order to prevent atelectasis.

2.2 Minute Ventilation (V$_E$)

V$_E$ is the total volume of air moved during a minute measured in liters per minute (L/min). It is usually measured directly but can be calculated:

$$V_E = V_T \times RR$$

where V$_T$ = tidal volume in liters
RR = respiratory rate in breaths per minute

Normal Value: 5–10 L/min.

2.3 Dead Space (V_D)

V_D is the calculated volume of the passageways in the lung that conduct air but in which no gas exchange with the blood occurs. It is reported in milliliters (mL).

$$V_D = \frac{P_{aCO_2} - P_{ECO_2} \times V_T}{P_{aCO_2}}$$

where P_{aCO_2} = pressure of carbon dioxide gas in arterial blood

P_{ECO_2} = pressure of carbon dioxide gas in expired air. It is measured using a Douglas bag or an online CO_2 analyzer.

2.4 Alveolar Ventilation per Minute (V_A)

V_A is the volume of gas exchanged in the alveoli each minute.

$$V_A = (V_T - V_D) \times RR$$

or $\quad V_A = \left[V_T - \frac{(P_{aCO_2} - P_{ECO_2}) \times V_T}{P_{aCO_2}} \right] \times RR$

2.5 Dead Space/Tidal Volume Ratio (V_D/V_T)

Ratio of dead space volume to tidal volume.

$$V_D/V_T = \frac{P_{aCO_2} - P_{ECO_2}}{P_{aCO_2}}$$

Normal Value: 0.3–0.35

2.6 Pulmonary Compliance

Pulmonary compliance measures the capacity of the lungs to accept air; it is measured in centimeters of water pressure (cm H_2O). The fundamental calculation is:

$$\text{Compliance} = \frac{\text{change in volume}}{\text{change in pressure}} = \frac{V_T}{P_I - P_E}$$

thus,

Pulmonary compliance =

$$\frac{\text{tidal volume}}{\text{inspiratory pressure} - \text{expiratory pressure}}$$

In a patient on a ventilator, compliance may be calculated as static compliance or dynamic compliance

depending on whether the *plateau* or the *peak* airway pressure is used.

$$\text{Static compliance} = \frac{V_T}{\text{plateau pressure} - PEEP}$$

$$\text{Dynamic compliance} = \frac{V_T}{\text{peak pressure} - PEEP}$$

2.7 Pressure of Oxygen in Alveolar Air (P_{AO_2})

P_{AO_2} is calculated by the alveolar air equation:

$$P_{AO_2} = P_{IO_2} - P_{aCO_2} \left(F_{IO_2} + \frac{1 - F_{IO_2}}{RQ} \right)$$

where RQ = respiratory quotient = 0.8

$P_{IO_2} = (P_B - P_{H_2O}) \times F_{IO_2}$

P_B = pressure barometric changes with altitude and weather. It is usually measured daily by the hospital pulmonary laboratory. Sea level standard value = 760 mm Hg

P_{H_2O} = pressure of water vapor = 47 mm Hg

2.8 Alveolar-Arterial Oxygen Gradient [$P_{(A-a)O_2}$]

This measurement reflects the efficiency of oxygen exchange across the alveolar capillary membrane. With alveolar hypoventilation, the P_{aO_2} decreases in proportion to the drop in P_{AO_2} and the gradient remains normal. Therefore, hypoxemia due solely to hypoventilation should exhibit a normal $P_{(A-a)O_2}$ despite a P_{aO_2} that is below normal. If the gradient is larger (wider) than normal with a low P_{aO_2}, hypoventilation is not the only cause of the hypoxemia. Additional causes of hypoxia and hypoxemia should be sought.

$$P_{(A-a)O_2} = P_{AO_2} - P_{aO_2}$$

The complete calculation as a one-step equation is:

$$P_{(A-a)O_2} = (P_B - P_{H_2O}) \times F_{IO_2}$$
$$- P_{aCO_2} \left(F_{IO_2} + \frac{1 - F_{IO_2}}{RQ} \right) - P_{aO_2}$$

Normal Value: varies with altitude. At sea level, normal for F_{IO_2} 0.21 (room air) is 8–10 mm Hg; normal for F_{IO_2} 1.00 (100% O_2) is <100 mm Hg.

A gradient greater than 400 mm Hg when F_{IO_2} is 1.00 indicates that the patient probably needs ventilatory support and intubation should be considered if it has not already been done. Normal values for breathing supplemental oxygen where F_{IO_2} is greater than 0.21 but less than 1.00 are not known, although many clinicians have developed rules of thumb.

2.9 Partial Pressure of Oxygen in Arterial Blood (Pa_{O_2})

Pa_{O_2} can be predicted when the fraction of inspired oxygen (F_{IO_2}) is changed by manipulating the previous equation to:

$$\text{Predicted } Pa_{O_2} = (P_B - P_{H_2O}) \times F_{IO_2}$$
$$- Pa_{CO_2}\left(F_{IO_2} + \frac{1 - F_{IO_2}}{RQ}\right) - P_{(A-a)O_2}$$

The Pa_{O_2} can be expected to change about 6 mm Hg for every 1% change in F_{IO_2} when the shunt fraction is less than 7%. (Shunt fraction is presented in Section 2.15.)

2.10 Partial Pressure of Oxygen in Mixed Venous Blood (Pv_{O_2})

Pv_{O_2} is an indicator of tissue oxygenation.

Normal Value: 33–36 torr. A value less than 25 torr indicates severe cardiovascular compromise; less than 20 torr indicates severe shock.

Note that the pH will vary 0.01–0.04 units and the partial pressure of carbon dioxide (Pv_{CO_2}) will vary 1–3 torr higher in mixed venous blood than the pH and Pa_{CO_2} of a simultaneous arterial sample.

2.11 Oxygen Capacity (o_2 capacity)

Oxygen capacity refers to the amount of oxygen that could be carried by the patient's hemoglobin if it were fully saturated. The numbers 1.34 and 1.39 are theoretical values for the number of milliliters of oxygen carried by a gram of saturated hemoglobin. The values are used interchangeably by clinicians in calculations.

$$\text{Oxygen capacity} = 1.34 \times Hgb$$

or, $$\text{Oxygen capacity} = 1.39 \times Hgb$$

Normal Value for Hgb: 12.2–16.2 g/dL

Normal Value for Oxygen Capacity: 16.4–21.7 mL o_2/g or 17.0–22.6 mL o_2/g

2.12 Oxygen Content (o_2 content)

Oxygen content refers to the amount of oxygen carried in the blood and is reported as volumes percent (vol%). The portion attached to hemoglobin is calculated by: $1.39 \times Hgb \times o_2$ saturation, and the portion dissolved in plasma is calculated by $Po_2 \times 0.0031$. Because the portion in plasma is fairly small, some clinicians simplify the equation and calculate only the portion carried by the hemoglobin. The full equations are given here.

Arterial oxygen content (Ca_{O_2}) is calculated by:

$$Ca_{O_2} = 1.39 \times Hgb \times Sa_{O_2} + Pa_{O_2} \times 0.0031$$

Normal Value for Arterial Blood: 16–21 vol%.

Venous oxygen content (Cv_{O_2}) is calculated by:

$$Cv_{O_2} = 1.39 \times Hgb \times Sv_{O_2} + Pv_{O_2} \times 0.0031$$

Normal Value for Venous Blood: 11–16 vol%

2.13 Arterial-Venous Oxygen Content Difference [$C(a-v)o_2$]

The $C(a-v)o_2$ is the difference in oxygen content between arterial and mixed venous blood in milliliters of oxygen per deciliter of blood (mL/dL). In essence, $C(a-v)o_2$ measures the amount of oxygen that is being extracted. When cell oxygen consumption is normal, more oxygen is extracted when blood flow is slow and the difference between arterial and venous oxygen content is greater. Thus, $C(a-v)o_2$ can be viewed as an indicator of the rate of forward blood flow or the adequacy of the cardiac output. The formula is:

$$C(a-v)o_2 = Ca_{O_2} - Cv_{O_2}$$

When combined into one equation this becomes:

$$C(a-v)o_2 = 1.39 \times Hgb \times (Sa_{O_2} - Sv_{O_2})$$
$$+ 0.0031(Pa_{O_2} - Pv_{O_2})$$

Normal Value: 4–6 mL O_2/dL. A value less than 4 mL O_2/dL reflects an increased cardiac output or decreased extraction; a value higher than 6 mL O_2/dL reflects a decreased cardiac output; greater than 8 mL O_2/dL reflects severe cardiovascular failure; greater than 10 mL O_2/dL reflects profound shock.

The tissues cannot extract oxygen when Sa_{O_2} is less than 30% and/or Pa_{O_2} is less than 20 mm Hg.

2.14 Oxygen Transport

The amount of oxygen transported in one minute is measured in liters per minute (L/min).

$$O_2 \text{ transport} = Ca_{O_2} \times Qt$$

2.15 Shunt Fraction (Qs/Qt)

The shunt fraction is that portion of the cardiac output that passes through the lungs without having been oxygenated; it is expressed as a percent. Incomplete oxygenation can occur as a result of anatomical defects or physiological dysfunction. Anatomical shunting involves circulation of blood via abnormal pathways that bypass the alveoli. Physiological shunting involves circulation of blood to alveoli that are not fully ventilated. A certain amount of physiological shunting is always present and varies with activity and body position. Abnormal anatomical shunting occurs in Tetralogy of Fallot, atrial and ventricular septal defects. Pathophysiological shunting occurs in pulmonary atelectasis, pulmonary emboli, and ARDS. The calculated shunt fraction is most accurate when the blood gas samples are drawn while the patient is breathing 100% O_2 so the F_{IO_2} is 1.00. The equation is then:

$$Qs/Qt = \frac{1.39 \times \text{Hgb} \times (1 - Sa_{O_2}) + 0.0031(Pa_{O_2} - Pa_{O_2})}{1.39 \times \text{Hgb} \times (1 - Sv_{O_2}) + 0.0031(Pa_{O_2} - Pv_{O_2})}$$

Normal Value with F_{IO_2} 1.0: 3–5% or <7%. A level of 10–20% indicates a mild abnormal shunt; 20–30% indicates a moderate abnormal shunt; more than 35% indicates a severe abnormal shunt.

When the arteriovenous oxygen content difference is normal and Pa_{O_2} is more than 150 mm Hg with F_{IO_2} 1.0, the shunt can be quickly calculated by:

$$Qs/Qt = \frac{0.0031(Pa_{O_2} - Pa_{O_2})}{0.0031(Pa_{O_2} - Pa_{O_2}) + C(a-v)_{O_2}}$$

RENAL AND METABOLIC PARAMETERS

3.1 Renal Clearance

The renal clearance tests are all tests of renal efficiency in clearing substances from the blood. The basic equation is:

$$C = \frac{U \times V}{P}$$

where C = clearance of substance
U = concentration of substance in urine
V = volume of urine per minute
P = concentration of substance in plasma

Normal Value for Creatinine Clearance: 95–135 mL/min.

3.2 Urine Osmolality

Urine osmolality yields similar information to the urine specific gravity. Osmolality is defined as a property of a solution that depends on the concentration of the solute per unit of solvent. It is distinct from osmolarity which is a property of a solution that depends on the concentration of the solute per unit of total volume of solution. Thus, in order to measure osmolarity one must have the total volume of solution for testing while osmolality can be measured in a sample portion of the total volume.

Normal Value: 50–1400 mosm/L (1 L = 1 kg of water).

Normal Value for a Random Sample: 500–800 mosm/L.

3.3 Serum Osmolality

Serum osmolality can be calculated from the serum sodium, glucose, and BUN values by the equation:

$$\text{Serum osmolality} = 2\,\text{Na} + \frac{\text{glucose}}{18} + \frac{\text{BUN}}{3}$$

Normal Value: 280–295 mosm/L.

3.4 Anion Gap

This measures the balance of cations (Na^+ and K^+) and anions (Cl^- and CO_2^-) in the serum. Anion gap is calculated from serum electrolyte values and is useable only in metabolic acidosis when the serum CO_2 is less than 18 mmol/L.

$$\text{Anion gap} = [\text{Na} - (\text{Cl} + CO_2)]$$

or $$\text{Anion gap} = [(\text{Na} + \text{K}) - (\text{Cl} + CO_2)]$$

Normal Value: <12–15 unmeasured anions (mmol/L). A value of more than 15 in metabolic acidosis indicates accumulation of unmeasured anions, usually lactic acid.

Increase in measured anions is seen in patients with renal tubular acidosis, acetazolamide (Diamox) therapy, ammonium chloride therapy, ureterosigmoidostomy, diarrhea, and external drainage of pancreatic juice. Increase in unmeasured anions is seen in patients with lactic acidosis, renal failure, diabetic ketoacidosis, as well as salicylate, ethylene glycol, methyl alcohol, and paraldehyde poisoning.

3.5 Serum Lactate

Serum lactate is an anion and an indicator of the rate or amount of anaerobic metabolism. It is not measured in the serum electrolytes.

Normal Value: <2.3 mmol/L. A level higher than 3 mmol/L indicates that the patient is probably in shock; more than 15 mmol/L indicates an extremely poor prognosis for the patient.

NEUROLOGICAL PARAMETERS

4.1 Cerebral Perfusion Pressure (CPP)

Useful in monitoring patients with hypotension and/or increased intracranial pressure.

$$\text{Cerebral perfusion pressure} = \text{MAP} - \text{ICP}$$

where MAP = mean arterial pressure, in mm Hg
      ICP = intracranial pressure, in mm Hg

Normal Value: 80–90 mm Hg.
The therapeutic goal is to maintain a cerebral perfusion pressure higher than 50 mm Hg because if it drops below 40 mm Hg, cerebral blood flow is not adequate for normal cerebral function. If the central venous pressure (CVP) is higher than the ICP, CVP is substituted for ICP in the equation. Related cerebrovascular equations are:

cerebral blood flow (CBF)

$$= \frac{\text{cerebral perfusion pressure}}{\text{cerebral vascular resistance}}$$

$$\text{Cerebral vascular resistance (CVR)} = \frac{\text{MAP} - \text{CVP}}{\text{CBF}}$$

4.2 Predicting Outcome for Patients with Coma

In determining apnea the patient should be taken off the ventilator and 100% oxygen delivered through a catheter in the endotracheal tube. The patient should be observed for respiratory activity for at least 10 minutes. There should be a rise in $PaCO_2$ to 60 torr without respirations before the patient is pronounced apneic.

- Twelve hours after coma onset, one may begin to predict survival vs. nonsurvival on the basis of the Glasgow Coma Score. Patients with scores lower than 5 are unlikely to survive as are patients whose scores have decreased since the first examination.
- Twenty-four hours after coma onset, patients with Glasgow Coma Scores of 5 or less are unlikely to survive. Patients with higher scores are likely to survive although their disability may range from a vegetative state to good recovery.
- Three days after coma onset, one can predict:
  - Good recovery or moderate disability if patient is alert and oriented.
  - Severe disability if the only response to stimuli is eye opening.
  - Apallic (vegetative) state if the best response is eye opening to pain and posturing is still present.
  - Brain death if coma, apnea, no cephalic reflexes, no eye movements, and isoelectric electroencephalogram (EEG) are present.

4.3 Predicting Restitution Time Following Coma

The time needed for restitution following coma is related to patient age and coma duration. The end of coma is defined as regaining consciousness such that verbal communication is re-established. Restitution is defined as being complete when the patient returns to work or school. The time needed for restitution can be predicted from the formula:

Restitution time in days
    = coma duration in days [(1.5 × patient age in years) + 15]

MEDICATION INFUSION CALCULATIONS

Note: All of these calculations assume a microdrip administration set is being used and 60 drops (gtts) equals 1 milliliter (mL). The best value for the patient's weight is a "dry" weight, e.g. preoperative weight. This weight is used for drug calculations regardless of those variations in daily weights that reflect changes in fluid status but not lean body mass.

5.1 Rate in Drops per Minute or Milliliters per Hour

This formula is used to determine the infusion rate in drops per minute (qtts/min) or milliliters per hour (mL/hr) for a specified dose in micrograms per kilogram per minute when the desired dose (μg/kg/min), solution concentration, and patient's weight are known.

$$\begin{matrix} \text{gtts/min} \\ \text{OR} \\ \text{mL/hr} \end{matrix} = \frac{\begin{array}{c}(\mu\text{g/kg/min} \times 60 \text{ min/hr} \times \text{patient kg}) \\ \times (\text{mg drug} \times 1000 \ \mu\text{g/mg})\end{array}}{(\text{mL solution})}$$

5.2 Dose in Milligrams per Minute

This formula is used to determine the dose in milligrams per minute (mg/min) when the infusion rate and solution concentration are known.

$$\text{mg/min} = \frac{\text{mg drug} \times \text{gtts/min}}{\text{mL solution} \times 60 \text{ min/hr}}$$

5.3 Dose in Micrograms per Minute

This equation is used to determine the dose in micrograms per minute (μg/min) when the infusion rate and solution concentration are known.

$$\mu\text{g/min} = \frac{\text{mg drug} \times 1000 \ \mu\text{g/mg} \times \text{gtts/min}}{\text{mL solution} \times 60 \text{ min/hr}}$$

5.4 Dose in Micrograms per Kilogram per Minute

This formula is used to determine the dose in micrograms per kilogram per minute (μg/kg/min) when the infusion rate, solution concentration, and patient's weight are known.

$$\mu\text{g/kg/min} = \frac{\text{mg drug} \times 1000 \ \mu\text{g/mg} \times \text{gtts/min}}{(\text{mL solution} \times 60 \text{ min/hr})/\text{patient kg}}$$

$$\text{also:} \quad \mu\text{g/kg/min} = \frac{\mu\text{g/min}}{\text{patient kg}}$$

BIBLIOGRAPHY

Allen, N. "Prognostic Indicators in Coma." *Heart and Lung* 8 (No. 6) November 1979: 1075–1083.

Carlsson, C.A., vonEssen, C., and Lofgren, J. "Factors Affecting the Clinical Course of Patients with Severe Head Injuries. *Journal of Neurosurgery* 29 (September 1968): 242–251.

Clemmer, T. "Practical Aspects in Monitoring the Critically Ill." Paper presented to nursing and medical staff of the Shock and Trauma Intensive Care Unit, LDS Hospital, Salt Lake City, Utah, 1979.

Krasner, J. and Marino, P.L. The Use of a Pocket Computer for Hemodynamic Profiles. *Critical Care Medicine* 11 (No. 10, 1983): 826–827.

Sampliner, J.E. and Pitluk, H.C. "Hemodynamic and Respiratory Monitoring." *in* J.K. Berk and J.E. Sampliner (eds.), *Handbook of Critical Care, 2nd ed.* (Boston: Little, Brown, 1982).

Tilkian, S.M., Conover, M.B., and Tilkian, A.G. *Clinical Implications of Laboratory Tests, 2nd ed.* (St. Louis: Mosby, 1979).

Vij, D., Babcock, R., and Magilligan, D.J. "A Simplified Concept of Complete Physiological Monitoring of the Critically Ill Patient." *Heart and Lung* 10 (No. 1, January 1981): 75–82.

Laboratory Reference Values

Blood Gases

Component	Values			
	Arterial			*Venous*
	Sea level	*4500 ft*		*Venous*
Carbon monoxide (CO) saturation (%)	2.5–5	<2.5		–
Oxygen (O_2)				
saturation (%)	>95	92–94		70–75
pressure (torr)	80–100	68–85		35–40
Carbon dioxide (CO_2)				
pressure (torr)	35–45	34–40		41–51
Bicarbonate (HCO_3)				
content (mmol/L)	19–24	19–24		22–26
pH	7.40 ± 0.05	7.40 ± 0.05		7.36 ± 0.05
Base excess	0 ± 2	0 ± 2		0 ± 2

Cerebrospinal Fluid

Component	Values
Cell count	$0–5 \times 10^6$/L
Glucose	50–80 mg/dL
Protein, total	15–45 mg/dL

Chemistry of Whole Blood, Serum, and Plasma

Component	Values
Electrolytes	
* Calcium (Ca), total	9.2–11.0 mg/dL
Carbon dioxide (CO_2)	24–30 mmol/L
Chloride (Cl)	95–103 mEq/L
* Magnesium (Mg)	1.3–2.1 mEq/L
Potassium (K)	3.8–5.0 mEq/L
Sodium (Na)	136–142 mEq/L
Enzymes	
Amylase	111–296 U/L
Creatine kinase, total	
male	55–170 U/L at 37°C
female	30–135 U/L at 37°C
Creatine kinase, MB fraction	<6.0% of total CK

Component	Values
Enzymes	
Glutamic oxaloacetic transferase (SGOT) also known as aspartate amino transferase (AST)	8–33 U/L at 37°C
Glutamic pyruvic transferase (SGPT) also known as alanine amino transferase (ALT)	4–36 U/L at 37°C
gamma-Glutamyl transferase (GGT)	5–40 U/L at 37°C
alpha-Hydroxybutyrate dehydrogenase (HBD)	140–350 U/mL
Lactate dehydrogenase (LDH)	100–190 U/L at 37°C
Phosphatase, alkaline	20–90 U/L at 30°C
Metabolites	
Bilirubin	
direct (conjugated)	0.0–0.3 mg/dL
indirect (unconjugated)	0.1–1.0 mg/dL
total	0.1–1.2 mg/dL
Cholesterol, total	150–250 mg/dL
Cortisol	
0800–1000 (hours of day)	5–23 μg/dL
1600–1800 (hours of day)	3–13 μg/dL
Creatinine	0.6–1.2 mg/dL
Glucose, fasting	70–110 mg/dL serum
	60–100 mg/dL blood
17–Hydroxycorticosteroids	
male	7–19 μg/dL
female	9–21 μg/dL
after 24 USP units ACTH	35–55 μg/dL
17–Ketosteroids	25–125 μg/dL
Lactic acid, as lactate in whole blood	
venous	5–20 mg/dL
arterial	3–7 mg/dL
Osmolality	280–295 mosm/kg water
Phosphorus, inorganic	2.3–4.7 mg/dL
Proteins	
albumin	3.2–4.5 g/dL
globulin	2.3–3.5 g/dL
total	6.0–7.8 g/dL
Thyroid hormone (T_4) concentration	5.0–11.0 μg/dL
Triglycerides	10–190 mg/dL
Urea nitrogen (BUN)	8–23 mg/dL
Uric acid	
male	4.0–8.5 mg/dL
female	2.3–7.3 mg/dL

* Not included in usual electrolyte panel.

Hematology

Component	Values
Complete blood count	
Hematocrit (Hct)	
female	38–47%
male	40–54%
Hemoglobin (Hgb)	
female	12.0–16.0 g/dL
male	13.5–18.0 g/dL
Mean corpuscular volume (MCV)	80–96 cubic microns
Mean corpuscular hemoglobin (MCH)	27–31 pg
Mean corpuscular hemoglobin concentration (MCHC)	32–36%
Platelet count	$0.15–0.40 \times 10^{12}/L$
Red blood cell (RBC) count	
female	$4.2–5.4 \times 10^{12}/L$
male	$4.6–6.2 \times 10^{12}/L$
White blood cell (WBC) count	$4.5–11.0 \times 10^{9}/L$

WBC differential:	Mean percent	Range of absolute count
Segmented neutrophils (segs)	56%	$1.8–7.8 \times 10^{9}/L$
Band neutrophils (bands)	3%	$0–0.70 \times 10^{9}/L$
Basophils (basos)	0.3%	$0–0.20 \times 10^{9}/L$
Eosinophils (eos)	2.7%	$0–0.45 \times 10^{9}/L$
Juvenile neutrophils (metas)	0%	$0 \times 10^{9}/L$
Lymphocytes (lymphs)	34%	$1.0–4.8 \times 10^{9}/L$
Monocytes (monos)	4%	$0–0.80 \times 10^{9}/L$

*Coagulation**	
Prothrombin time (PT)	9.5–12.0 sec
Partial thromboplastin time (PTT)	60–85 sec
Activated PTT (APTT)	20–35 sec
Fibrinogen	200–400 mg/dL
Fibrinogen split products	10 µg/mL

Erythrocyte sedimentation rate (ESR): Westergren method	
Men under 50 yrs.	<50 mm/hr
Men over 50 yrs.	<20 mm/hr
Women under 50 yrs.	<20 mm/hr
Women over 50 yrs.	<30 mm/hr

* Times may vary depending on reagents used.

Urine Chemistry

Component	Values
Acetone	Negative
Calcium	100–240 mg/24 hr
Chloride	140–250 mEq/24 hr
Creatinine	0.8–1.8 g/24 hr
Glucose	Negative
Osmolality	500–800 mosm/kg water
pH	4.6–8.0
Potassium	40–80 mEq/24 hr
Sodium	75–200 mEq/24 hr
Specific gravity	1.003–1.030
Urea nitrogen	6–17 g/24 hr

BIBLIOGRAPHY

Harper, R.W. *A Guide to Respiratory Care, Physiology, and Clinical Applications*. Philadelphia, PA: Lippincott, 1981.

Henry, J.B. *Todd—Sanford—Davidsohn, Clinical Diagnosis and Management by Laboratory Methods*, 17th ed. Philadelphia, PA: W.B. Saunders, 1984.

Kinney, M.; Dear, C.; Packa, D; and Voorman, D. *AACNs Clinical Reference for Critical-Care Nursing*. New York: McGraw-Hill, 1981.

Krupp, M.A.; Tierney, L.M., Jr.; Jawetz, E.; Roe, R.L.; and Camargo, C.A. *Physician's Handbook,* 20th ed. Los Altos, CA: Lange Medical Publications, 1982.

Abbreviations

ABGs	arterial blood gases	cm	centimeter
A/C	assist/control	cm^2	square centimeters
a.c.	before meals	cm H$_2$O	centimeters of water
AIDS	acquired immune deficiency syndrome	CN	cranial nerves
		CNS	central nervous system
AODM	adult onset diabetes mellitus	C.O.	cardiac output
AP	anterior-posterior	co	carbon monoxide
ARDS	adult respiratory distress syndrome	co$_2$	carbon dioxide
		co sat	carbon monoxide saturation of hemoglobin
ASCVD	atherosclerotic cardiovascular disease	COPD	chronic obstructive pulmonary disease
AV	arteriovenous *or* atrioventricular		
		CPAP	continuous positive airway pressure
bands	band neutrophils		
basos	basophils	CT	computerized tomography
BBB	bundle branch block	CV	cardiovascular
bid	twice a day	CVA	costovertebral angle in physical examination or cerebrovascular accident in medical diagnosis
BP	blood pressure		
BSA	body surface area		
BUN	blood urea nitrogen	Cvo$_2$	venous blood oxygen content
°C	degrees Celsius	D5W	dextrose 5 percent in water
Ca	calcium	D5LR	dextrose 5 percent in lactated Ringer's solution
CABG	coronary artery bypass graft		
CAD	coronary artery disease	D5NS	dextrose 5 percent in normal saline
Cao$_2$	arterial blood oxygen content		
C(a-v)o$_2$	arterial-venous blood oxygen content difference	DIC	disseminated intravascular coagulopathy
CBC	complete blood cell count	dL	deciliter
cc	cubic centimeter	DTR	deep tendon reflex
CCU	critical care unit		
CHF	congestive heart failure		
CK	creatine kinase	ECG	electrocardiogram
CK-BB	creatine kinase isoenzyme found in brain and kidney	EEG	electroencephalogram
		EKG	*see* ECG
CK-MB	creatine kinase isoenzyme found in cardiac muscle	ENT	ear, nose, throat
		EOM	extraocular movement
CK-MM	creatine kinase isoenzyme found in skeletal and cardiac muscle	eos	eosinophils
		ED	emergency department
CI	cardiac index	ESR	erythrocyte sedimentation rate
Cl	chloride	ET	endotracheal

°F	degrees Fahrenheit	LAP	left atrial pressure
FeF 25–75%	forced expiratory flow between the first 25% and 75% of forced exhalation	lb	pounds
		LBBB	left bundle branch block
		LDH	lactic dehydrogenase
FeO$_2$	fraction of oxygen in expired air	LLQ	left lower quadrant
FeV	forced expiratory volume	LOC	level of consciousness
FeV$_1$	forced expiratory volume in the first second of expiration	LPH	left posterior hemiblock
		LUQ	left upper quadrant
FiO$_2$	fraction of oxygen in inspired air	LV	left ventricle
ft	feet	LVH	left ventricular hypertrophy
FVC	forced vital capacity	LVEDP	left ventricular end diastolic pressure
g or gm	gram	LVP	left ventricular pressure
GGT	gamma glutamyl transferase	lymphs	lymphocytes
GI	gastrointestinal		
gtt	drop	m	meter
GU	genitourinary	m^2	square meters
		MAP	mean arterial pressure
h or hr	hour	mcg	microgram. *See also* μg
HCO$_3$	bicarbonate	MCH	mean corpuscular hemoglobin
Hct	hematocrit	MCHC	mean corpuscular hemoglobin concentration
HEENT	head, eyes, ears, nose, throat		
Hgb	hemoglobin	MCL	midclavicular line
hpf	high power field	MCV	mean corpuscular volume
HR	heart rate	mEq/L	milliequivalent per liter
h.s.	hour of sleep	metas	metamyelocytes, also known as juvenile neutrophils
ht	height		
HTN	hypertension	mg	milligram
		Mg	magnesium
ICP	intracranial pressure	MI	myocardial infarction
ICS	intercostal space	min	minutes
ICU	intensive care unit	mL	milliliter
IHSS	idiopathic hypertrophic subaortic stenosis	mm	millimeter
		mm^3	cubic millimeter
IM	intramuscular	mm H$_2$O	millimeter of water
IMV	intermittent mandatory ventilation	mm Hg	millimeter of mercury
in.	inches	monos	monocytes
IU	International Unit	mosm	milliosmole
IV	intravenous		
IVP	intravenous pyelogram	Na	sodium
		NaHCO$_3$	sodium bicarbonate
JVD	jugular venous distention	neuro	neurological
JVP	jugular venous pulse	NG	nasogastric
		NPO	nothing by mouth
K	potassium	NSR	normal sinus rhythm
Kcal	kilocalorie	NTG	nitroglycerin
KCl	potassium chloride		
kg	kilogram	O$_2$	oxygen
		O$_2$ sat	oxygen saturation of hemoglobin
L	liter	OD	right eye (oculus dexter)
LA	left atrium	OHD	organic heart disease
LAD	left anterior descending coronary artery	OS	left eye (oculus sinter)
		osm	osmole
LAH	left anterior hemiblock	OU	both eyes (oculi unitas)

PA	pulmonary artery		RLQ	right lower quadrant
PAB	premature atrial beat		ROM	range of motion
PAC	premature atrial contraction		RQ	respiratory quotient
$Paco_2$	partial pressure of carbon dioxide in arterial blood		RR	respiratory rate
			RU	resistance units
Pao_2	partial pressure of oxygen in arterial blood		RUQ	right upper quadrant
			RV	right ventricle
PAP	pulmonary artery pressure		RVP	right ventricular pressure
p.c.	after meals			
Pco_2	partial pressure of carbon dioxide gas		Sao_2	oxygen saturation of hemoglobin in arterial blood
PCW	pulmonary capillary wedge		segs	segmented neutrophils
PCWP	pulmonary capillary wedge pressure		SBE	subacute bacterial endocarditis
			SEM	systolic ejection murmur
PEEP	positive end expiratory pressure		SGOT	serum glutamic oxaloacetic transaminase
PERRL	pupils equal, round, reactive to light		SGPT	serum glutamic pyruvic transaminase
PERRLA	pupils equal, round, reactive to light and accommodation		SIADH	syndrome of inappropriate antidiuretic hormone
PJB	premature junctional beat		SIMV	synchronized intermittent mandatory ventilation
PJC	premature junctional contraction			
PMI	point of maximal impulse		SV	stroke volume
PO	by mouth (per os)		SVI	stroke volume index
Po_2	partial pressure of oxygen gas		Svo_2	oxygen saturation of hemoglobin in venous blood
polys or PMNs	polymorphonuclear cells, also called neutrophils		SVR	systemic vascular resistance
% Pred.	percent of predicted		SW	stroke work
prn	as needed		SWI	stroke work index
PT	prothrombin time			
PTT	partial thromboplastin time		T	temperature
PVB	premature ventricular beat		tid	three times per day
PVC	premature ventricular contraction		TPN	total parenteral nutrition
$Pvco_2$	partial pressure of carbon dioxide in venous blood		TPR	total peripheral resistance
Pvo_2	partial pressure of oxygen in venous blood		μ^3	cubic micrometer
			U	unit
PVR	pulmonary vascular resistance		UA	urinalysis
			μg	microgram
q	every		UUN	urinary urea nitrogen
qd	every day			
qid	four times per day		V_A	alveolar minute ventilation
qnh	every nth hour, where n is a number		V_D	volume of dead space
			V_E	minute ventilation
q$n$min	every n minutes, where n is a number		Vo_2	oxygen consumption
			vol%	volume percent
Qo_2	oxygen consumption		V_T	tidal volume
Qs/Qt	pulmonary shunt fraction			
Qt	cardiac output		WBC	white blood cells
			wt	weight
RA	right atrium			
RAP	right atrial pressure		$\times 10^n$	times ten to the nth power, where n is a number
RBBB	right bundle branch block			
RBC	red blood cells			

Index